The Other Bolsheviks

THE OTHER BOLSHEVIKS

Lenin and His Critics, 1904–1914

ROBERT C. WILLIAMS

INDIANA UNIVERSITY PRESS
BLOOMINGTON AND INDIANAPOLIS

Manufactured in the United States of America

Library of Congress Cataloging-in-Publication Data

Williams, Robert Chadwell, 1938–
The other Bolsheviks.

Bibliography: p.
Includes index.
1. Communism—Soviet Union—History 2. Soviet
Union—Politics and government—1904–1914. 3. Lenin,
Vladimir Ilích, 1870–1924. I. Title.
HX313.W54   1986   947.08'3   85-45743
ISBN 0-253-34269-4

1   2   3   4   5   90   89   88   87   86

Communism places man in his proper place.
Man as collectivist is immortal.
Only the individual is mortal.

—A.V. Lunacharsky, 1918

I dreamed I saw Joe Hill last night
Alive as you and me.
Says I, "But, Joe, you're ten years dead."
"I never died," says he.

—IWW Song "Joe Hill," 1915

CONTENTS

ACKNOWLEDGMENTS   vii

    Introduction   1
   I. The Word: Lenin, Bonch-Bruevich, and the Art of
      Secret Writing   5
  II. Matter into Energy: Vanguard Party and Workers'
      Collective   29
 III. Self-Sacrifice: Gorky's New Money and Moscow's
      Old Believers   49
 IV. Experience: Leonid Krasin and the Revolution of
      1905   66
  V. Myth: Lunacharsky, Syndicalism, and Collective
      Immortality   81
 VI. Expropriation: Stalin and the Georgians as Bank
      Robbers   105
 VII. Mind over Matter: Orthodoxy against Science   125
VIII. Bolshevism without Lenin: Collectivism and the
      Capri School   144
 IX. Lenin without Bolshevism: Russian Politics and
      German Money   162
  X. A Childhood Disease: Communism over
      Syndicalism   175
 XI. Conclusion: Lenin over Bolshevism   188

NOTES   192
BIBLIOGRAPHY   222
INDEX   229

ILLUSTRATIONS

Enciphered letter from N. K. Krupskaya to the Kursk
   committee   9
V. I. Lenin and V. D. Bonch-Bruevich, 1918   27
Leonid Krasin, 1903   71
Maxim Gorky and Arturo Labriola, 1906   100
Lenin playing chess with A. A. Bogdanov, 1908   110
Police photograph of Kamo, 1908   115
Mikha Tskhakaya   120
Lenin, 1920   180

ACKNOWLEDGMENTS

This book could not have been written without the helpful comments and criticisms of a number of scholars. I am greatly indebted to the following persons for their assistance: Abraham Ascher, Paul Avrich, Kendall Bailes, John Biggart, Sheila Fitzpatrick, Abbott Gleason, Loren Graham, David Joravsky, Peter Kenez, Sidney Monas, Max Okenfuss, Philip Pomper, Alexander Rabinowitch, Janet Rabinowitch, David Ransel, Nicholas Riasanovsky, William Rosenberg, Bernice Rosenthal, Peter Scheibert, Jutta Scherrer, Charles Schlacks, Alfred Senn, S. Frederick Starr, Richard Stites, Robert Tucker, Nina Tumarkin, Adam Ulam, and Reginald Zelnik. All of them helped in one way or another; none should be held responsible for the results.

I am also grateful to the following institutions and libraries for their assistance: the Kennan Institute for Advanced Russian Studies of the Woodrow Wilson International Center for Scholars in Washington, D.C.; the Hoover Institution, Palo Alto, California; the Library of Congress; the Institute for Social History in Amsterdam; the Russian Archive of the Butler Library, Columbia University, New York; Olin Library of Washington University in St. Louis and its Interlibrary Loan Division.

Venita Lake has been an excellent critic, editor, and source of support. Ann Williams has sustained both the author and the book in many ways. They have made this book better than it might have been.

INTRODUCTION

To a historian who grew up in the 1940s and 1950s it is difficult to realize that the Soviet Union developed from a political movement, Bolshevism, that was not only authoritarian and monolithic but also polycentrist and collectivist. Stalinism suggested a linear succession of individual authority in which the infallible ideas of Marx, Lenin, and Stalin all merged into a single orthodoxy. Hierarchy, command, organization, despotism, autocracy, and totalitarianism all were said to characterize a Russian and Soviet political tradition in which the dominance of the individual leader was matched by the passivity, docility, and self-sacrifice to the collective in an ever-modernizing society.

This study of the early years of Bolshevism suggests a quite different conclusion. Lenin certainly envisioned a revolutionary party in which organizational efficiency would transform class struggle into political and social revolution. But the reality of Bolshevism was quite different—a fractious and divided movement of émigré intellectuals and white-collar professionals who continually disagreed over matters of ideology, organization, and money. That Lenin was able to channel such disparity into revolutionary success was a tribute to his political genius and sagacity in the face of continual conflict and division among the other Bolsheviks. The identity of Bolshevism and Leninism was itself a kind of wishful thinking or retroactive mythology.[1]

For Bolshevism and Leninism were not identical before 1917. Bolshevism was a radical movement of Marxist intellectuals from the Russian Social Democratic Workers' Party (RSDRP) associated with the revolution of 1905 and its aftermath. Whereas Lenin spent all but two years of the period 1900–1917 in exile in Western Europe, other Bolshevik leaders led a mobile underground existence inside Russia. They formed a heterogeneous collective of middle-class intellectuals and professional revolutionaries. They did not recognize Lenin as the undisputed, or even primary, leader of their movement. Their common bond was Marxism, but their interpretation of the meaning of Marx's ideas varied widely.

Leninism developed as a political doctrine and style based on Marxist orthodoxy as Lenin understood it, with the help of such luminaries as G. V. Plekhanov and Karl Kautsky. The other Bolsheviks were drawn to modernist currents in European thought, notably relativism in science and syndicalism in politics. Led by the doctor-philosopher A.A. Bogdanov and the electrical engineer L. B. Krasin, the other Bolsheviks sought to revise Marx's ideas for an age in which myth and hypothesis played as great a role as truth and fact. Bolshevism was therefore in

1

constant tension in its formative years between the authoritarianism of Lenin and the collectivist ideas of the other Bolsheviks. Ultimately, this was a creative tension that enabled Lenin to direct a revolution that only appeared to be spontaneous in its mass appeal in 1917. Lenin in the end dominated Bolshevism, and created a successful revolutionary party that combined Jacobinism and collectivism, conscious party authority and manipulated popular myth.

Bolshevism has traditionally been identified with Lenin because of Lenin's canonization in the Soviet Union at the expense of the reputations (and sometimes the lives) of the other Bolsheviks. The party and its members are measured in virtue according to their supposed Leninist behavior and standards. In addition, much early party history has been written either by old Bolsheviks who sought to play down their disagreements with Lenin or by Menshevik rivals who assumed that Lenin's dominant personality and voluminous writings represented the views of the other Bolsheviks. Such was rarely the case.[2]

Lenin's famous dichotomy between consciousness and spontaneity existed within, as well as outside, Bolshevism. The other Bolsheviks had their own consciousness, and favored the manipulation of ideology rather than obedience to party authority. For them, consciousness was a function of individual human experience and varied accordingly from one individual to another. Like many other words in the Bolshevik vocabulary, the word "experience" was a code word. It alluded to the general strike and the view that workers needed strike experience in order to gain revolutionary consciousness. Lenin saw revolution as a form of war in which a vanguard party of disciplined professional revolutionaries seized power; the other Bolsheviks saw revolution as a cultural transformation of human minds, so that the masses would think in terms of the socialist collective, not the bourgeois individual. In the formative years of Bolshevism Lenin's "I" competed with the collectivist "we."[3]

Put another way, Lenin's authoritarianism belonged to a conspiratorial Jacobin tradition in Europe and Russia that emphasized the seizure of power by an elite in an armed uprising, while the other Bolsheviks were drawn to the syndicalist ideal of worker solidarity through the collective experience of the general strike. In this sense, Bolshevism was a fusion of Jacobinism and syndicalism, Lenin's revolutionary authority and Bogdanov's collectivist myth, which proved to be a volatile combination in 1917 and a source of intraparty tension afterwards.[4]

Reading through Bolshevik texts written before 1917, the historian must appreciate that the written word was doubly Aesopian. That is, ideas were disguised to evade the censor, and also to evade rival socialists' suspicions of anarchism, syndicalism, and other revisions of orthodox

Marxist doctrine. The most famous example of Aesopian writing was the great debate between Bogdanov and Lenin over philosophy after 1905, a debate that was also about party politics and money, neither of which could be discussed openly in print. Behind the philosophy of empiriocriticism lay the politics of syndicalism and the intrafractional struggle for party funds; behind Lenin's self-styled materialist orthodoxy lay the politics of dictatorship.

Lenin in his writings portrayed the other Bolsheviks as idealists, revisionists, and even anarchists. But in contrast to the antistate individualism of the anarchist tradition, the other Bolsheviks shared a common commitment to what they called "collectivism." In regard to party organization, collectivism meant the dominance of the party collective, such as the Central Committee, over the will of any individual, such as Lenin. Ideologically, collectivism meant that some Bolsheviks were inclined toward syndicalism, the belief in the efficacy of the mass strike and direct action guided by useful myth. Philosophically, collectivism entailed what Gorky called "god building," the creation of a new socialist religion of science, a cultural myth capable of making the collective believe in their own "we," rather than in the individualist bourgeois "I." Collectivism was a loosely linked body of ideas that set itself against individualism in the name of an ethic of self-sacrifice.[5]

Combined with Lenin's authoritarianism, Bogdanov's collectivism made up a second ideological thrust of Bolshevism. Organized authority through a revolutionary party depended on a collectivist myth believed by the masses. The Lenin-Bogdanov dispute in 1907–1910 over "Machism" and philosophy thus reflected a deeper division within Bolshevism between Leninism and collectivism, a division that forms the subject of this book.[6] In its political language, Bolshevism was divided between Lenin's esoteric cryptography and V. D. Bonch-Bruevich's quasi-religious mass propaganda. In its theory of party organization, Bolshevism was divided between Lenin's Jacobin vanguard and Bogdanov's ideological collective. In terms of party finances, Lenin's willingness to accept the patronage of Gorky, Old Believer millionaires, and German socialists contrasted with the other Bolsheviks' thrust toward expropriation, by violence if needed, of bourgeois wealth from banks and individuals.[7] Ideologically there was a division between Lenin's view of Marxism as absolute truth and Bogdanov's view of Marxism as effective myth. Finally, the Bolshevik vision of revolution was divided between Lenin's underground conspiracy in preparation for class war and Bogdanov's vision of cultural experience. These divisions, of course, were both destructive and creative, producing frequent tensions and, ultimately, revolutionary success.

At the heart of the division between Lenin and the other Bolsheviks lay the question of the role of the individual. The archetypal professional revolutionary, in Lenin's mind, was Lenin himself, whose full-time occupation was revolution; the consequence of this thinking, as Trotsky and Rosa Luxembourg pointed out in 1904, was a political system dominated by one man ruling with the aid of a cult of personality and an obedient party. For the other Bolsheviks the ultimate political act was self-sacrifice for the good of the collective, an act of transcendence in which the bourgeois individual self vanished in the worship of all. Under Stalin the fusion of two traditions, authoritarian individualism and self-sacrificing collectivism, reached a climax in the terrible purge years, when terror and confession merged into a single world of the Gulag Archipelago. Death became commonplace, suicide the handmaiden of murder, and collective immortality the myth that supported Stalin's cult of personality. Yet the idea that the individual human being could and should be sacrificed to the socialist collective characterized Bolshevism from its inception and formed the necessary complement to Leninist authority.

This book traces the history of Bolshevism from its origins in 1904 until the outbreak of World War I, by which time Lenin had taken over control of what was left of the movement. While Lenin's importance is recognized, I have chosen to focus on the long-neglected ideas and actions of the other Bolsheviks in order to show that Lenin was one revolutionary among many in a fractious, polemical, and divided political movement, not the undisputed leader of an obedient party. Lenin was a Bolshevik, but Bolshevism was more than Leninism and not all Bolsheviks were Leninists.

I have deliberately avoided the story of Lenin's rise to power in 1914–1917, a subject in itself, but have included a final chapter on his 1920 polemic with the other Bolsheviks over the issue of syndicalism. Lenin's *Left-Wing Communism* articulates many of the ideas derived from his prerevolutionary experience, and is an echo of that experience.

I

THE WORD

LENIN, BONCH-BRUEVICH, AND
THE ART OF SECRET WRITING

> Blessed is he who keeps the words of the prophecy in this book.
> — THE REVELATION OF ST. JOHN, 22:6

> Marxism without appropriate words is nothing—only words, words, and more words.
> — V. I. LENIN

In the beginning Bolshevism was largely a matter of words. The movement later known as Bolshevism originated in Geneva in 1904 as a Russian Marxist circle with a journal, a library, and a publishing house, following the famous 1903 split between the Bolshevik (majority) and Menshevik (minority) wings of the Russian Social Democratic Workers' Party (RSDRP). Texts were its artillery and words its ammunition in an unrelenting war on the hated autocracy of Tsar Nicholas II. Since 1900 V. I. Ulianov, better known by his conspiratorial pseudonym of Lenin, had been the dominant member of the editorial board of *Iskra* (The spark), the party newspaper. He had also become a master of the art of secret writing, cryptography.

Already in 1904, with Bolshevism still unnamed, the battle of the books played a crucial role in Lenin's struggle against the Russian autocracy. Conditions of unusual censorship prevailed inside Russia, and Bolshevik literature inherited a Russian radical tradition of expressing ideas on two levels: legal and illegal. Legal literature appeared inside Russia with permission of the censor, but managed to contain hidden meanings conveyed through what the great nineteenth-century writer M. E. Saltykov-Shchedrin called "Aesopian" or "slave" language, an oblique and allegorical jargon that provided the alert reader a meaning not obvious to the uninitiated. Illegal literature was generally printed in the relative safety of European exile and smuggled into Russia for illegal distribution; it was therefore subject to arrest and confiscation once it crossed the border.

5

The distinction between legal and illegal literature was part and parcel of Russian Marxism, and Lenin often utilized the techniques of "legal Marxism" so popular in the 1890s. Russian censors took some time before they discovered that the writer V. Ilin, whose lengthy *Development of Capitalism in Russia* was printed inside Russia in 1899, was identical with the revolutionary N. Lenin, whose brief Stuttgart pamphlet *What Is to Be Done?* circulated illegally in Russia after 1902.

In general, the lines between legal and illegal literature were often blurred, and the texts of Lenin and the other Bolsheviks therefore present a challenge to the historian. These texts are rarely straightforward statements of intent or ideas, but oblique codes, allegories, and fables whose meaning is embedded in the censorship conditions inside Russia at the time and in the internecine quarrels of European socialism. Ideally, the language of any text had to be sufficiently secret to escape the censor's eye yet sufficiently open to reach the alert reader and convey a message.

Russian literary censorship protected an unpopular autocratic government in the throes of modernization. To evade that censorship, the Bolsheviks used a system of simple codes and ciphers in their books and party correspondence resembling that employed by many governments in the twentieth century. Textual flexibility was tempered by Marxism's claim to be authoritative and scientific, at precisely the time when science itself was undergoing a major shift in its view of truth, particularly in physics. Bolshevik texts therefore combined scientific authority and socialist myth, a political language of double meanings that articulated orthodox truth for a narrow party elite, and utilized strategies of censorship evasion to reach a broad and barely literate public.

Bolshevism took shape partly as a rebellion against the Menshevik fraction of the RSDRP. But as a secret Russian underground movement, Bolshevism was also divided within itself between Lenin's authoritarian claims to Marxist orthodoxy and the other Bolsheviks' strategies of collectivist myth. For the other Bolsheviks socialism functioned as surrogate religion, rather than as a social science, subject to the shifting experience of the masses and not to the shifting textual exegesis of party authority and authorship.

Lenin came to Munich in the summer of 1900 as a thirty-year-old Marxist revolutionary whose older brother Alexander had gone to the gallows in 1887 believing in the myth of Russian Populism, that a spark kindled by the Russian intelligentsia would some day ignite a popular uprising that would consume the government of the tsars. Hardened by prison and exile, and disciplined by the rigors of debate with the Populists, Lenin was convinced that the openness and spontaneity of a popular uprising must await the organization of revolutionary authority through a political party. As a junior member of the editorial board of *Iskra*, Lenin planned to use the conspiratorial language of Populism and the authority of Marxism to create an organization of revolutionaries that would overturn Russia.

The European émigré environment that Lenin entered was not as amenable to conspiracy and authority as underground groups in Russia. Russian social democrats claimed as many versions of Marxist authority as their admired German mentors. With the 1899 publication of Eduard Bernstein's articles on the possibilities for an evolutionary reform of bourgeois society, rather than a socialist revolution, the revision of Marx's revolutionary predictions produced doctrinal anarchy in the name of freedom of criticism. Revisionism and economism, the primacy of economic over political action, and of strikes over party politics, were in the air. Strikes and other forms of labor unrest were spreading among thousands of workers in France and Italy after the turn of the century, and Marxist authority had its rival in syndicalist myth and direct action. To convert labor spontaneity into revolutionary organization, felt Lenin, would require the language of Marxist authority and the conspiratorial techniques of Russian Populism.

Bolshevik political language from the outset evolved from two quite distinct sources: the Jacobin authoritarianism of the elite party that permeated the thought of Marx, P. N. Tkachev, and N. G. Chernyshevsky, and the experience of the strike associated with syndicalism and the labor movement in the West. Authority found expression in individual authorship, orthodox doctrine, textual exegesis, and cryptography; myth utilized the metaphors and beliefs of the masses in propaganda written by an elite. Both authority and myth were crucial elements in the emergence of Bolshevism.

The Art of Secret Writing

> "Languages are ciphers, wherein letters are not changed into letters, but words into words, so that an unknown language is decipherable."
>
> —BLAISE PASCAL, *Pensees*, No. 45

On March 1, 1887, a group of six young men were arrested on the fashionable Nevsky Prospekt in St. Petersburg in connection with a plot on the life of Tsar Alexander III. One of them was carrying a thick *Medical Dictionary* inside which was found dynamite and bullets tipped with strychnine. Among the plotters was Lenin's brother, Alexander Ulyanov, whose subsequent arrest and execution helped turn Lenin toward a revolutionary career and a war against the hated autocracy. Symbolically, an apparently harmless book concealed secret weapons in that war.[1]

The art of cryptography, or secret writing, is an ancient technique for protecting secrets from an enemy while communicating information to an ally. Since the Renaissance, communication by code and cipher has become a normal part of diplomatic relations among nations in times of peace and war. In the twentieth century, cryptanalysis has produced great successes, including the breaking of German and Japanese codes during World War II. After World War I, communication by cipher became a highly mechanized and mathematical art, later performed with the aid of computers and satellite communication; before World War I it was still a secret craft conducted by the "black chambers" of the European powers and their police with the aid of only the human brain and occasional chemical and x-ray techniques.[2]

The Bolsheviks in 1904 utilized secret communication techniques common in prisons and revolutionary circles in nineteenth-century Russia. Both ciphers (the substitution of one letter or symbol for another) and codes (the use of words with hidden meanings) disguised messages that could pass the censor while retaining forbidden meanings. A particularly popular method of secret communication was to hide a message within a book, either by steganography (hiding a message by writing in invisible inks or lemon juice), or by reference to a specific page, line, and letter using ciphers, or by oblique and coded word meanings. The Bolsheviks used books both to encipher messages in party correspondence and to conceal political meaning in the guise of philosophy, economics, or statistics. Packages of books frequently carried secret messages; legally published tomes conveyed a second level of revolutionary meaning. Any book might carry a double meaning, overt and covert.

Lenin and his wife, N. K. Krupskaya, were both adept at cryptography and the use of Aesopian language to evade the censorship. Lenin's publications and correspondence generally concealed as much truth as they revealed, in ways that only the initiated could understand. In this sense Lenin was no different than Marx or Engels, who also employed parody, satire, and allusion to evade the Prussian censorship in the 1840s. Marx could not publish some of his economic writings until he emigrated to London in the 1850s. He lengthened works such as *The Holy Family* and *The German Ideology* in order to avoid the more strict censorship applied to shorter texts.[3] The writings of Marx and Engels employed an esoteric language forced upon them by the censor that made their writings ideal for publication in Russia. Marxism was both a revolutionary doctrine and a collection of evasive written texts that could pass the censor while conveying a revolutionary message to the initiated Marxist.

Since the eighteenth century, Russian writers had employed fables, allegories, and double meanings to criticize their government without subjecting themselves to prosecution and arrest. The Aesopian language of oblique criticism is a rich Russian tradition that extends from Krylov

An enciphered letter from N. K. Krupskaya in Geneva to the Kursk committee of the RSDRP, March 1905. From *Perepiska V. I. Lenina i rukovodimykh im uchrezhdenii RSDRP s partiinymi organizatsiiami, 1903–1905 gg.*, volume 3 (Moscow, 1977).

to Solzhenitsyn. In the prerevolutionary period, notes Bertram Wolfe, "men found means of conveying a criticism of the regime through a statistical monograph on German agriculture, through the study of a sovereign four centuries dead, the review of a Norwegian play, the analysis of some evil in the Prussian or some virtue in the British state."[4]

In the 1840s Russian radicals published a *Pocket Dictionary of Foreign Words* that was filled with foreign revolutionary ideas in various guises. Under the entry "naturalism" one could find reference to the writings of Fourier, St. Simon, and Owen; under the entry "ocean" appeared the ideas of James Harrington.[5] Yet, as A. V. Lunacharsky noted in 1902, the *Pocket Dictionary* appeared legally in Russia but allowed for the dissemination of socialist ideas.[6] In 1872 the Russian censorship permitted government publication of Marx's *Capital* as a "strictly scientific work" despite its "clearly socialist direction"; noted the censor: "Few will read it, and still fewer understand it." The censorship omitted Marx's portrait, but published his ideas.[7]

The revolutionary author N. G. Chernyshevsky was a master of the legal publishing of illegal ideas. Chernyshevsky's techniques of Aesopian language were as important to Lenin as the concept of an elite revolutionary party. Throughout Chernyshevsky's Victorian novel *What Is to Be Done* and other writings runs the thread of radical ideas in oblique form. Chernyshevsky was a master of metonymy, speaking of one subject in terms of another. It took an alert reader to know that the "author of an article on Pushkin" was the radical literary critic Vissarion Belinsky, or that by "ancient buildings" Chernyshevsky really meant Fourier's socialist community phalansteries, or that by the "necessities of life" he meant arrest by the police.[8]

"You don't understand it," said Vera Zasulich in 1904, "and it's difficult to understand. Chernyshevsky was hampered by censorship and he had to write in allusions and heiroglyphs. We were able to decipher them, but you, the young people of the 1900s, don't have this knack. You read a passage in Chernyshevsky and you find it dull and empty, but in fact there is a great revolutionary idea concealed in it." In his writings Chernyshevsky generally included a "sort of key" to help the reader decode his message. Among Chernyshevsky's best decoders was Lenin.[9]

In the 1890s, after an early exposure to the Jacobin and terrorist ideas of Russian Populism, Lenin became a Marxist. He also adopted the then popular tactic of revolutionary authors known as "legal Marxism," the publishing of long, obscure, and statistical articles and books capable of legally passing the censor. The September 1894 test case of this tactic was the publication of P. B. Struve's *Critical Notes on the Development of Capitalism in Russia.* Other Marxist tomes followed quickly, including G. V. Plekhanov's *On the Question of the Development of the Monist View of History* (December 1894), where the alert reader immediately recognized that the word "monist" really meant Marxist, and Lenin's own *The*

Development of Capitalism in Russia, published under the pseudonym V. Ilin.[10]

In addition to legal Marxism, Lenin also utilized the conspiratorial Populist tradition of secret communication by code and cipher. The essence of underground communication in revolutionary Russia was the use of relatively common and harmless words to carry a second revolutionary meaning. Thus a "hospital" was really a prison, and any inquiry about one's health was an inquiry about one's incarceration, any "illness" being an arrest. "Warm fur" meant illegal literature; "handkerchiefs" meant passports; a "journal" was a double-bottomed suitcase used to smuggle literature. Towns assumed code names: Moscow was "Grachevka" and Saratov was "Babylon." Finally there were the ubiquitous aliases (Lenin had dozens of them), such as "Friend No. 1" or "Phenomenon" for Maxim Gorky and "Absolute" for Elena Stasova, another Bolshevik.[11] The purpose of this Aesopian vocabulary was simply to enable apparently innocuous books and correspondence to carry a hidden meaning to the knowing reader.

Lenin also inherited from Populism a number of conspiratorial cipher techniques common in Russian jails. Getting letters out of prison in nineteenth-century Russia was often achieved by writing in plaintext in invisible ink or lemon juice between the lines of an ordinary letter or book. Equally common was the use of ciphers such as the "Polybius square":

	1	2	3	4	5
1	a	b	c	d	e
2	f	g	h	ij	k
3	l	m	n	o	p
4	q	r	s	t	u
5	v	w	x	y	z

By utilizing this very simple cipher method, a prisoner could convey a message by tapping on cell walls so that any two numbers indicated a letter by designating a column and row. Thus the word "hello" could be tapped out as: 23 15 31 31 34.[12]

A slightly more complex method involved the use of a keyword, which when enciphered and added to the enciphered plaintext word, would produce a second level of encipherment. Thus, using the Polybius square and the keyword "arise" (11 42 24 43 15), one might encipher the word "bomb" as follows:

plaintext	b	o	m	b
cipher plain	12	34	32	12
+ keyword	11	42	24	43
= cipher	23	76	56	55

Repeating the keyword, one could thus encipher any long message either by tapping or by putting the cipher on paper.[13]

Prison codes and ciphers were in common use among Populist revolutionaries of the 1860s and 1870s, as recalled by Peter Kropotkin:[14]

> From all sides I heard knocks with the foot on the floor: 1,2,3,4 . . . 11 knocks, 24 knocks, 15 knocks; then an interruption, followed by 3 knocks and a long succession of 33 knocks. Over and over again these knocks were repeated in the same succession, until the neighbor would guess at last that they were meant for 'kto vy?' (Who are you?), the letter v being the third letter in our alphabet. Thereupon conversation was soon established, and usually conducted in the abridged alphabet; that is, the alphabet being divided into 6 rows of 5 letters, each letter is marked by its row and its place in the row.

This use of the "quadratic alphabet" also appeared in Arthur Koestler's well-known fictional work on the Stalinist purges, *Darkness at Noon*:[15]

> While Rubashov was memorizing the numbers, he tried, being out of practice, to visualize the square of letters with the 25 compartments—5 horizontal rows with five letters in each. No. 402 first tapped 5 times— accordingly the fifth row: v to z; then twice; so it was the second letter of the row: w. Then a pause; then two taps—the second row, f—j; then 3 taps—the third letter of the row: h. Then 3 times and then 5 times; so fifth letter of the third row: o. He stopped. WHO?

Needless to say, such techniques became well known to jailers and political police, who routinely opened mail, exposed hidden messages, deciphered enciphered ones, and employed their own secret means of communication.[16] That did not stop codes and ciphers from becoming part of the political language of the Russian underground and of Lenin's writings.

Lenin as Cryptographer

> Vulgar revolutionism fails to see that words are action too.
>
> —V. I. LENIN, *Two Tactics of Social Democracy*

In her memoirs Krupskaya continually refers to the great conspiratorial skills of Lenin, beginning in the 1890s in St. Petersburg. "He taught us how to write in books with invisible ink," she recalled, "or by the dot method; how to mark secret signs, and thought out all manner of aliases. In general, one felt the benefit of his good apprenticeship in the ways of the Narodnaya Volya Party." At one point Lenin "showed us how to use cipher and we used up nearly half a book."[17]

In the 1880s, Krupskaya was an ardent Tolstoyan who believed in the virtues of asceticism, worked side by side with peasants in the fields, and helped in "correcting" books such as *The Count of Monte Cristo* for a popular and barely literate readership. Lenin, while in prison or in contact with former prisoners, absorbed the usual tactics of Russian underground conspiracy—pseudonyms, ciphers, codes, dots under letters of books in invisible ink—and through his correspondence he extended them to his entire family. His mother and sisters frequently communicated with him by secret means. "I sent books twice a week, on Wednesdays and Saturdays," recalled his sister Anna after Lenin had returned from exile in 1896: "In each package of books was one with an enciphered letter—with dots or dashes in pencil inside individual letters of the alphabet."[18] In this manner the requests for books in Lenin's correspondence and his effusive thanks after receiving them were all part of a system of secret family communication by book code, courtesy of the Russian postal service.

Anna Elizarova was especially informative about Lenin's use of these techniques of encipherment:

> Chemical letters provided greater freedom; in them, besides purely business matters, one could find stories about the latest party news, congresses, and conferences, brief—2 or 3 words—characterizations by Vladimir Ilich of people and trends within the party, qualities rarely used by him in open conversation, decisive opinions. But these letters were destroyed after reading, and not one, understandably, has come down to us. They were written in letters between the lines or, more often, between the lines of books, journals, and clippings. When Vladimir Ilich, enumerating the books he had received, writes that some *Diary of the Engineers' Congress* or *Archive Clipping* "was very interesting and Aniuta sends her special thanks," then this means that it was, of course, written in chemical letters.[19]

In addition to writing in invisible ink in books, Lenin often would use a book code where a keyword indicated a particular page of a particular book, and each pair of numbers indicated a letter of the alphabet that would be found by a specified line and letter in that line. As Anna Elizarova recalled, Lenin and Krupskaya employed this method from the 1890s down to 1917:

> Usually Ilich, wanting precision and economy of style, would introduce a special sign indicating the page of an enciphered letter so one would not have to burrow and search through the books. One would encounter the first sign, say, on page 7. This was a thin pencil stroke, and by multiplying the number of lines by the number of letters in the next line, one would get the correct page; so, if one noted the 7-th letter in the 7-th line, one would go to page 49, where the letter began. . . . This method, changing the page from time to time, was used by us constantly, and even in the letters written by N. Krupskaya just before the revolution in 1915

and 1916, I could determine from the sign the place of a letter within a book.[20]

These techniques explain Lenin's apparently voracious reading habits exhibited in his correspondence, where he often requested new editions of Turgenev in German translation and other obscure reading matter. For each book contained a message to be deciphered that was quite different than the one contained in the legal published text. The sending of secret letters and the mailing of books became a major activity of Lenin and Krupskaya in their editorial work for the RSDRP.

The northern route for smuggling illegal writings and weapons from Europe to Russia ran through Stockholm and Helsinki to St. Petersburg. A common method for sending secret messages was to establish an ordinary text, such as Edward Bellamy's utopian socialist novel *Looking Backward*, as the codebook, and then to use ciphers to indicate a given alphabetical letter in the text. Having agreed on a common page, sender and receiver could communicate by specifying pairs of numbers, each pair indicating the line on the page and the number of letters from the left. In this way by October 1900 Lenin was able to use the commonplace and apparently innocuous journal *Family Pictures* as a vehicle to send correspondence and articles from *Iskra* to party members inside Russia. Chemical letters (correspondence written in invisible ink between the lines) were also reasonably safe, felt Lenin, as long as they did not reveal a person's identity: "Don't write any initials in your correspondence, please," Lenin warned one RSDRP correspondent in London: "The master [police] knows them, although the mail here is completely reliable."[21]

By 1902 Lenin and Krupskaya were using a number of well-known and readily available books to send enciphered messages to Russia, among them a biography of Spinoza, a volume of Nekrasov's poetry, and a novel by Nadson entitled *Mother*.[22] They were not alone. To assist émigré socialists with their correspondence, another Russian Marxist, Vladimir Akimov (V. P. Makhnovets), published in Geneva in 1902 a book entitled *On Ciphers*. In it he described in detail various methods of enciphering messages. Akimov also warned that improper and careless use of codes and ciphers by a revolutionary conspirator could lead the police to comrades inside Russia and even to "the destruction of an entire organization." Hoping to show his "young comrades" the art of cryptography, Akimov described in detail dot-dash methods of highlighting letters in a book, how to use keywords and cipher systems such as the Polybius square, chemical steganography with invisible ink, and book codes.[23]

Akimov was spelling out in detail what Lenin only hinted at in his well-known pamphlet *What Is to Be Done?* published in Stuttgart by the Dietz Verlag in February 1902. Lenin followed his mentor Chernyshevsky in urging the organization of a conspiratorial elite of professional revolutionaries to overthrow the Russian autocracy; he also advocated a socialist party consciousness that would overcome the revisionist and reformist tendencies associated with a more spontaneous labor movement. Lenin noted that Aesopian language was essential:

> In a country ruled by an autocracy, with a completely enslaved press, in a period of desperate political reaction in which even the tiniest outgrowth of political discontent and protest is persecuted, the theory of revolutionary Marxism suddenly forces its way into the censored literature and, though expounded in Aesopian language, is understood by all the "interested."[24]

In case the alert and interested reader did not get the reference to Chernyshevsky in Lenin's book title, he later appended a brief note on Chernyshevsky at the end of his 1909 book *Materialism and Empiriocriticism*, this time in the philosophical guise of a great Russian materialist thinker.

Secret correspondence had its problems. Krupskaya complained about one correspondent that "his letters are very difficult to understand, since he muddles up the ciphers terribly and shortens words too much."[25] Another correspondent included the entire cipher system in the letter itself, undoubtedly a great help to the police who opened the letter. In 1903 the Tver RSDRP committee wrote to *Iskra* that "the cipher is the new book by Adler, *On Unemployment*. The sum of the numerator and the denominator equals the page number."[26] The Jewish labor organization, the Bund, also employed ciphers in correspondence within Russia at this time. The Bund published a book entitled *The Enciphered Letter* in which the author warned of an army of spies and provocateurs among the socialist exiles, and praised Saltykov-Shchedrin as a master of the "Aesopian letter" with its talk of family trifles and the weather, laden with revolutionary meaning for the initiated.[27]

During the summer of 1904, while Lenin was trying to create his own band of followers within the RSDRP in Geneva, another party member, L. A. Fotieva, began helping Krupskaya with RSDRP correspondence at the rate of some three hundred letters a month. Fotieva's job, she later recalled, was to "decipher the enciphered part of the text and rewrite . . . then one had to write the text of a letter to be sent to Russia, encipher the most secret part of it, write the whole letter chemically between the lines of an ordinary letter written earlier that would not arouse the suspicion of the Okhrana. Often the letters we received had mistakes in their ciphers, and we had to spend a long time deciphering them." Codes and keywords were changed without their knowledge; chemical messages did not emerge from the steam of the samovar. Throughout it all Lenin was an avid cryptographer and observer of Krupskaya's own skills with enciphering and deciphering messages. In addition to messages hidden in books and correspondence, émigré newspapers often carried cryptic messages in their classifieds, with "expressions understood only by the addressee."[28]

Ciphers and codes were a routine part of RSDRP communication with Russia. "The code with Bolshak," wrote Lenin to the Tver committee in November 1904, "is a Gambetta cipher: the South American states, 34.b and in the middle," apparently referring to a map in an atlas. "I am sending on Khariton's keyword," wrote N. E. Burenin to Krupskaya in May 1905: "I shall encipher in a simple way, starting with the first letter." Burenin went on to describe the Swedish-Finnish transport and smuggling route and the latest shipment of bombs and revolvers from Bulgaria. A few years later, in November 1909, Lenin received a letter from a party member in Reval suggesting that the two men correspond by chemical underlining in the books written by Lenin's great rival for control of the Bolshevik fraction, A. A. Bogdanov. "You can encipher in A. Bogdanov's *Empiriomonism*," wrote the correspondent, because "I have the third edition of volume one, the second edition of volume two, and the first edition of volume three." It was agreed that each would underline in invisible ink the appropriate letters beginning on page 100. In this way the most turgid book on philosophy could become a Bolshevik codebook.[29]

Censorship and Authority

> This pamphlet was written with an eye to the tsarist censorship. Hence, I was not only forced to confine myself strictly to an exclusively theoretical, particularly economic analysis of facts, but to formulate the few necessary observations on politics with extreme caution, by hints, in an allegorical language—in that accursed Aesopian language—to which tsarism compelled all revolutionaries to have recourse whenever they took up their pens to write a "legal" work.
>
> —V. I. LENIN, introduction to *Imperialism* Petrograd, April 1917

What was the system of censorship with which Lenin and the Bolsheviks had to cope before 1917? Throughout the nineteenth century the Imperial Russian government had established elaborate censorship controls over all private printing presses in order to ensure that forbidden words concerning religion or politics did not reach the literate public. This goal was accomplished by preventing before publication the appearance of any words unacceptable to the censor in a manuscript. The censor himself was often a writer working for the government. Having discovered forbidden words, the censor might forward them to a superior for possible judgment or prosecution in the courts. Or he might simply issue a warning to the editor or the writer. He might also order a journal closed down. In any event, under preventive censorship the crucial period in a book's publication was the period immediately prior to its printing, when the author sought to evade the censor by providing an acceptable, yet still radical, text for publication.

Until 1905 the relevant censorship guidelines were set down in the Censorship Statute issued by the Minister of the Interior in 1865 during the Great Reforms of Tsar Alexander II. The statute provided two broad categories of censorship: one for religious works, which came under the jurisdiction of the Ecclesiastical Censorship of the Holy Synod of the Russian Orthodox Church, and another for secular writings. If a work was considered religious in content, it underwent stricter surveillance and prepublication review. The Ministry of the Interior kept a general catalogue of "forbidden books," not unlike the Index of the Catholic Church in Western Europe.

Length, rather than brevity, was advisable in any book. The longer the text, the less severe the censorship, on the assumption that the readership was small for a long book and large for a short book. The 1865 statute exempted from preliminary censorship "all original writings consisting of no fewer than ten printed signatures [galley proof pages]" and "all translations consisting of no fewer than twenty printed signatures."[30] As a consequence, Lenin and other Russian Marxists became adept at writing long books of apparently dry and harmless content under a legal pseudonym.

The 1905 revolution in Russia broadened considerably the freedom available to Russian writers, editors, and publishers. At first the Ministry of the Interior, which controlled both the police and the censorship, simply forbade any unauthorized news about the "worker question" in 1905, a year of tumultuous political strikes and labor unrest that began with the Bloody Sunday demonstration of January 22, 1905. Nevertheless, a flood of illegal publications began to inundate Russiaas the year wore on. Although the October Manifesto, which prom-ised representative government and civil rights in Russia, did not alleviate the censorship, printers, publishers, and booksellers lobbied extensively for greater freedom and less censorship. Amid a wave of mass protests and strikes at the end of the year 1905, they boycotted publications approved by the censor and published uncensored books themselves.

After the disturbances of late 1905, the Russian censorship virtually collapsed. Printers in cities had been especially active in strikes and trade unions that year and provided a literate vanguard for labor disorders. As a result, the system of preliminary censorship that had been in effect gave way to a less organized strategy—to prosecute writers, editors, and printers after publication, rather than before. Between October 1905 and December 1906, the Chief Administration of Press Affairs closed down 371 periodicals and 97 printing plants; in the courts prosecution of censorship cases led to 607 fines or jail sentences for publishers, editors, and writers. Thus, the censorship continued to function after 1905, but without stricter prepublication controls.

New censorship conditions demanded a new strategy of censorship evasion. Collections of articles by different authors were easier to publish, and more difficult to prosecute, than books by a single author. When thousands of copies of an undesirable book were published, they were subject to confiscation and destruction. More than 350 new publishing houses sprang up between 1905 and 1909, many of them "flying operations" that printed a few pamphlets before being closed down. The same publishing enterprise often bore several different names, as did radical newspapers, in order to confuse the censor and the police. Texts were printed at one plant and book covers at another; the real printer's name and address were usually falsified or omitted. Literary and philosophical titles were given to political texts. Despite such strategies, the police continued to deal harshly with the outpouring of publications that characterized Russian society after 1905.[31]

The Bolsheviks operated within the legal limits of the censorship, as well as outside them. Censors kept a "systematic index" of all literature confiscated each year, including works by Lenin and other Russian revolutionaries.[32] Bookstores sympathetic to the radical movement were raided by the police; apartments were searched; illegal books and pamphlets were seized and destroyed. The crackdown became particularly intense after the June 1907 establishment of greater restrictions on political activity by Prime Minister P. A. Stolypin. The danger of arrest and heightened censorship drove Lenin back into his Geneva exile after an attempt to publish his collected writings through the Zerno house in November 1907 led to their confiscation by the police.[33]

By 1904 Lenin already had considerable experience dealing with the Russian police and censorship. He was a frequent user of Aesopian language, pseudonyms, allegory, ciphers, and codes in both correspondence and book publishing. Lenin's techniques of writing adapted Marxism to Russian conditions, and placed a peculiar stamp on Bolshevik writing and political language that has persisted into the Soviet period. Given a world of double meanings, legal and illegal, permissible and impermissible, any political text could be understood only by its context known to the alert reader. Bolshevik political language consisted not of statements of truth, but allegories of deception, and Lenin's writings remain enigmatic and cryptographic to the uninitiated.

Yet Lenin was not the only architect of Bolshevik political language, which often carried messages to a much broader and less informed public. Lenin's texts were written for the alert reader, usually a party member. Other Bolsheviks developed a different type of political discourse, the language of useful myth. They sought to convey their own collectivist philosophy, not Lenin's authority, to the urban and rural masses of Russia in order to mobilize them to action. The language was often Marxist, but combined with popular and religious motifs. Myth was a powerful element in Russian folk culture, as well as a tactic of European syndicalism. And in 1904 the Bolsheviks most attentive to the use of myth to mobilize the masses of Russia were V. A. Posse and V. D. Bonch-Bruevich, not Lenin. Through Posse and Bonch-Bruevich the legal Marxist and Aesopian techniques of Russian literature were transformed into the collectivist propaganda of Bolshevism.

V. A. Posse and the Syndicalist Myth

From its inception Marxism was haunted by the specter of anarchism, and then syndicalism. Marxism placed great emphasis on authority, consciousness, and science in its claim to predict the ineluctable process of class struggle and revolution in history. Yet the dream of a world without property and state authority persisted in the ideas of Pierre Proudhon, Michael Bakunin, and Georges Sorel, radical thinkers who stressed not the determinate forces of history and social classes, but the spontaneous revolutionary actions of individuals. What Marx called pejoratively "utopian" socialism, as opposed to "scientific," remained a prominent current of European socialist and radical thought in the late nineteenth and early twentieth centuries. One of its central tenets was that socialism was not a scientific truth contained in books, but a collective myth based on the experience of individuals. Upon this distinction rested a crucial difference between Lenin and the other Bolsheviks in matters of political language. Lenin wished to reach party workers through books and esoteric correspondence; other Bolsheviks hoped to convert the Russian masses to Marxism through a more popular literature of socialist myth.

The distinction was not new. Marxist authority, defined in texts, always had its rivals in anarchist spontaneity, articulated in myth and in deed. But for Marx and Engels, authority was essential to the organization of the class struggle against the powers of capitalism.

"As soon as something displeases the Bakuninists," wrote Friedrich Engels in 1871, "they say it's authoritarian, and thereby imagine they have damned it forever." For Marx and Engels, the making of a revolution demanded authority, precisely the element lacking in the Paris Commune of 1871. As Engels put it in criticizing "Pope" Bakunin in 1872:

> Do what you like with authority, etc., after the victory but for the struggle we must unite all our forces in one fascio and concentrate them

at one point of attack. And when I am told that authority and centralization are two things that should be condemned under all possible circumstances, it seems to me that those who say so either do not know what a
revolution is, or are revolutionaries in name only.

Authority, claimed Engels, was crucial to revolutionary organization,
and those socialists who raised the banner of antiauthoritarianism were
simply confused admirers of the mythical general strike.[34]

Around 1900 the anarchist movement that spawned individual violence against heads of state began to give way in Europe to a new and
more collectivist workers movement known as syndicalism. Based on
the emerging French trade union (syndicat) movement, syndicalism
attacked Marxism for its incessant failure to produce a revolutionary
catastrophe, and for the tendency of many socialists to urge a policy of
gradual parliamentary reform that might win from capitalism through
the legislative assembly what workers failed to win in the streets. The
centerpiece of syndicalism was the general strike, that national refusal of
workers to tolerate evil labor conditions, which would paralyze capitalist
society and lead ultimately to a confederation of labor unions capable of
replacing the state.

One rebel against Marxist orthodoxy and authority was Georges
Sorel. Like Eduard Bernstein, Sorel in 1899 was highly critical of the
Marxist tendency to theory rather than action. "It is one thing," he
wrote, "to make social science and another to inspire men's spirits."
Socialism as a doctrine, felt Sorel, was "finished," unless it could provide
tangible successes in the war on capitalism. Such successes could be
attained, Sorel came to believe, only through a sustained effort by
workers to achieve the general strike, a mythical goal that could inspire
revolutionary action even without concrete and present results.[35]

Sorelian syndicalism as it emerged after 1900 in Europe was more a
doctrine about the proletariat than for it. Much of syndicalism was
confined to the pages of socialist journals, where the violent strikes of the
day were chronicled. Syndicalism, like Marxism, was a doctrine created
by bourgeois intellectuals. But syndicalism differed from Marxism in
two respects: first, it emphasized action by workers, not words by
politicians; second, syndicalism was tolerant of, rather than hostile
toward, the church and religion, including Catholicism. For syndicalists,
the collective belief in revolutionary myth, rather than individual
knowledge of revolutionary doctrine, drove men to action.

Georges Sorel called for a new war against the state led by an elite of
socialist monks providing new moral values for the masses. He opposed
the primacy of politics represented by Jacobin authority, the "Blanquist
conspiracy" led by "red Jesuits." Sorel also opposed the politics of
parliamentary participation, with its endless debates and inaction. The
proper mission of syndicalism, felt Sorel, was to produce a new

proletarian culture with the aid of self-sacrificing heroes in search of surrogate immortality. Their goal was an entirely new set of values that could transcend those of bourgeois society, and their means was the general strike.

We shall have ample opportunity to return to syndicalism in the pages that follow. For the moment, suffice it to say that around 1900 syndicalism began penetrating Russia through the pages of legal Marxist and socialist journals. Among them was the journal *Zhizn'* (Life) edited by V. A. Posse, an important forerunner of Bolshevism and its political language. Posse was a radical journalist who had passed through the usual phases of Populism and Marxism only to end up as a leading propagator of syndicalism. His journal, *Zhizn'*, was originally published legally in St. Petersburg at a time when both Populists and Marxists discovered the potential of the "revolutionary proletariat" of Russia's burgeoning towns and cities.[36]

In the early 1890s Posse studied at the University of Jena, where he imbibed the scientific "monism" of the German Darwinian Ernst Haeckel. Haeckel was a widely read popularizer of the biological sciences who argued that all matter, organic and inorganic, was connected in a single whole that could be defined on an elaborate scale of evolutionary progress. Like Aleksander Bogdanov, Posse came to Marxism from a background in medicine and biology, and his organic metaphors persisted even as his doctrinal enthusiasms changed.

By the late 1890s Posse was making a living as a journalist in St. Petersburg writing for the journal *Nachalo* (Beginning), edited by P. B. Struve and funded by the wealthy patroness of radical causes Aleksandra Mikhailovna Kalmykova. Among his cojournalists were the venerable G. V. Plekhanov and the young Lenin. In 1898 Posse founded *Zhizn'* and was able to attract a number of good writers to it, including Maxim Gorky. Posse's editing policies produced constant brushes with the Russian censorship, and a sharp eye for the useful application of Aesopian language.

In 1901 Posse shifted his published operations abroad to escape the censorship. In search of money and contributors, he operated first from London, then Paris, and finally in 1902, Geneva, where he met Lenin.

Before leaving London, Posse discovered V. D. Bonch-Bruevich and through him Tolstoyanism and the antistate proclivities of the Russian sectarians and Old Believers. Bonch also put Posse in touch with a young and very wealthy Russian couple, Grigorii Arkadevich Kuklin, age 21, and his wife Maria, age 25; Kuklin had recently fled Russia with an enormous library and 100,000 rubles in treasury certificates in order to escape military conscription. After Plekhanov made an unsuccessful attempt to secure the Kuklins' largesse for *Iskra*, Bonch persuaded them to aid Posse and *Zhizn'*. This they did by handing ten thousand rubles to Bonch in a London hotel in order to start a new revolutionary journal directed against the Russian autocracy of Nicholas II, especially by utilizing the dissident religious sects.

Free of censorship and well subsidized, *Zhizn'* then reappeared in Paris in the winter of 1901–1902 as an illegal émigré journal. Within a few months it moved to Geneva, where Posse met Lenin: "a man pushing forward and not knowing how to defend himself except by going on the attack," recalled Posse. To Posse, Lenin seemed like some kind of mystic sectarian, a khlyst perhaps, whose asceticism was exceeded only by his total self-confidence and self-assurance. Both Bonch and Posse were impressed by Lenin, whose Jacobinism and drive for revolutionary organization seemed more fruitful than the sporadic political terror of the peasant-oriented Social Revolutionaries. Not surprisingly, the attraction the *Zhizn'* circle held for Lenin at this time was not its ideas, since he disdained both syndicalism and religion, but Posse's money acquired from the Kuklins. *Zhizn'* claimed to be a "social democratic" journal, but its central mission was to galvanize the "revolutionary proletariat" into action. Its articles were eclectic and included essays by Marx, the French syndicalist Hubert Lagardelle, the socialist Jules Guesde, and Wilhelm Liebknecht. Songs and poems illustrated the appeal of proletarian culture, and the strike movement in Europe, America, and Russia was chronicled in detail.

As an émigré journal, *Zhizn'* operated outside the Russian censorship and carried on a running battle against it. "The censored Russian press," it wrote, "does not reflect, but covers up, real life. It does not enlighten, but deceives, the reader."[37] Aesopian strategies of legal Marxism were no longer necessary; the goal of *Zhizn'* was to reach a broad popular peasant and proletarian audience of readers that would some day constitute a popular front against the hated Russian government. Through its pages ran a spontaneous enthusiasm for the role of strikes in building worker solidarity and pointing the way toward a collectivist society of altruism and self-sacrifice.

In Paris, Posse encountered a number of French syndicalists, including Hubert Lagardelle. Posse promptly commissioned Lagardelle to write an essay for *Zhizn'* on the need for antiwar propaganda among French troops; the army, wrote Lagardelle, was like a vampire, sucking the blood of the very workers who composed it.[38] In addition, Posse was able to use the Paris editorial offices of Lagardelle's journal, *Le Mouvement Socialiste*, to receive letters and manuscripts.

Posse favored the ultimate abolition of all private property and the establishment of some form of workers' control over factories, a view common among European syndicalists of the day. He gradually moved away from socialism and Marxism, to which he had never adhered in any very orthodox fashion, toward what he called communism, a federation of proletarian communes, no conscription, and a general strike in the event of a world war. For Posse, the great enemy was the state, and its overthrow demanded a broad front of social groups acting collectively. After the 1917 Russian Revolution, Posse compared his own views with Lenin's *State and Revolution*; Bonch referred to Posse as "our anarcho-Bolshevik." In fact, Posse's ideas reflected the growing syndicalist movement of Western Europe.

As a syndicalist, Posse emphasized direct action through the general strike. In October 1902, when Geneva streetcar workers began a strike that nearly paralyzed the city, closing factories, transportation, and newspapers, Posse was elated. The idea of an international general strike, he wrote, did not seem so impossible a dream now. The key to success was organization of the workers, wrote Posse, not through a political party, but through the experience of the general strike. "Successful general strikes," he concluded, "need the organization of the working class, but such organization itself develops most rapidly out of 'general strikes.'"[39] Not the imposition of authority, but the experience of action would transform worker energy into solidarity and organization.

However much they wanted his money, the Bolsheviks were generally suspicious of Posse's ideas at first. Gorky felt that Posse was mistaken in thinking that, as émigré writers, "we can successfully play the game of Herzen and Bakunin."[40] An old friend of Posse, Gorky refused to join him in emigration. Plekhanov was equally hostile to Posse's interest in religion. "*Zhizn'*," Plekhanov wrote Lenin, "on almost every page talks about Christ and religion. In public I shall call it an organ of Christian socialism."[41] Politically, Plekhanov felt that Posse had not supported *Iskra* in its battle with the rival social democratic journal *Rabochee Delo* (Workers' cause) and should be punished for such heresy. Yet Lenin did not at the time share Plekhanov's hostility to *Zhizn'*, and remained interested in both its syndicalism and its money.

In late December 1901 the *Zhizn'* publishing operation was liquidated and its assets divided. Kuklin, still in possession of at least twenty-five thousand rubles, agreed to subsidize a project of Posse to publish popular socialist pamphlets as a "library of the Russian proletariat," using the *Zhizn'* printing press; Bonch-Bruevich, on the other hand, had become enthusiastic about the émigré RSDRP circle in Geneva, including Lenin and Krupskaya, and wanted to transfer *Zhizn'* operations over to *Iskra*. Lenin, eager to obtain a printing press and a "slush fund," agreed to print some of Bonch's essays on the Russian sectarians in *Iskra*; he also hoped to obtain access to the *Zhizn'* network of distribution inside Russia.[42]

The split between Posse and Bonch led to the organization in 1903–1904 of the very first Bolshevik publishing operation by Bonch and Lenin. Posse, with the aid of Kuklin's money, printed a monumental book entitled *The Theory and Practice of Proletarian Socialism* (1905), in which he articulated his syndicalist theories of the "expropriation of the expropriators," the general strike, proletarian solidarity, and a Russian "communist party" that would include the Social Revolutionaries.[43]

Rejected by Russian social democrats, Posse continued his publishing operations after 1905 with Kuklin's support but remained an isolated propagator of syndicalist and communist ideas quite removed from the Russian socialist and labor movements. He died in 1940. But his interest in syndicalism was not lost on Lenin and the other Bolsheviks.

V. D. Bonch-Bruevich and the Language of God

"What do you think of Bonch?" Lenin wrote Plekhanov in January 1903. "Our 'net gain' was just the two of them—not very much! There is the liquidator (see *Zhizn'* No. 6) Mr. Kuklin. Make his acquaintance through Bonch—couldn't we squeeze something out of him?" Surely, mused Lenin, Kuklin ought to come up with ten thousand rubles or so just because Lenin had defended *Zhizn'* in the past year from attacks by other social democrats. If *Iskra* needed money, here was a likely source.[44]

Vladimir Dmitrievich Bonch-Bruevich (1873–1955) was a Russian scholar in exile who had spent most of his life studying the writings of Leo Tolstoy and the life of Russian religious sects.[45] A quiet intellectual, Bonch's main occupation was the publication and distribution of books to the peasant masses of Russia. Like Krupskaya, Bonch had been a follower of Tolstoy in the 1890s and had helped in the illegal distribution of works such as *The Kingdom of God Is within You* in Moscow and the provinces. His interest in religious publications had gotten him into trouble with the censorship even as a teenager, and he had already been arrested and exiled as a result. In 1899 Bonch left Russia and traveled to Canada, where he lived among the Dukhobors and other sectarians whose refusal to pay taxes or serve in the army made them anathema to the Imperial Russian government and drove them abroad. In his writings for Posse and *Zhizn'* Bonch continued to focus on those dissident religious groups in Russian society who proved willing atgreat personal risk to put the law of God above the laws of Nicholas II. Like Lenin, Bonch saw in Russian sectarians a valuable revolutionaryally.

Marxism as a doctrine of social revolution placed its hopes on the urban proletariat, not the peasantry. Yet Russian Populists, and Lenin after them, recognized the key role of the peasant in any revolutionary enterprise, in the best tradition of Stenka Razin and Pugachev. They noted the violent alienation of the Old Believers from the official state church, dating from the seventeenth century, and sought to turn it to their own revolutionary purposes. Russian religious dissent appealed to Bolshevism even before that movement had acquired a name.

In 1901 Bonch settled among the Russian socialist émigrés of Geneva and became secretary of a new Russian museum which sought to collect the memoirs, correspondence, and other writings of Russian revolutionaries. He also became involved in the production of *Zhizn'* where he wrote articles on the sectarians. In them Bonch noted the importance of Aesopian language as a means for circumventing the censorship and reaching a broad audience. Russia, he wrote, was in a revolutionary mood, and would soon produce a "street battle of an awakened people."[46] To arouse the masses required a new political language that would appeal to their religious instincts and turn them against the state. Socialists could organize the people by persuading them that the government was "Satan" and that "all men are brothers" in the eyes of God. Social democrats must go to the villages and win over the sectarians to their cause with pamphlets that the people could understand in their own language. Secret and illegal congresses of Old Believers were now being held annually, and sects like the Stundists and Dukhobors were subject to increasing police surveillance and persecution. The result was a unique opportunity for Russian social democrats to spread propaganda in the Russian countryside.[47]

In 1902 Lenin persuaded Bonch that *Iskra* and the RSDRP had a brighter future than did Posse's tiny circle, and Bonch left Posse and the Kuklins for his new friends. Lenin was most interested in inheriting the *Zhizn'* transport group and its smuggling operations, which he hoped to use for getting *Iskra* into Russia. He was less interested in Bonch's plan for a Russian library of revolutionary books and periodicals, but agreed to print Bonch's essays on the sectarians in *Iskra*.[48]

Out of their publishing operation emerged Bolshevism. In August 1903 the famous second congress of the RSDRP assembled in London, and produced the well-known split between the Menshevik supporters of Martov and the Bolshevik supporters of Lenin. One resolution, drafted by Lenin and Plekhanov and approved by the congress, stated that Bonch would edit an RSDRP journal directed toward the sectarians under the control of the *Iskra* editorial board.[49] The resultant journal, *Rassvet* (Dawn), appeared in January 1904 in Geneva.

In his writings Bonch called on his Russian readers to band together with the RSDRP against the autocracy to obtain a "time of freedom" that would cast off the yoke of age-old authority.[50] The outbreak of the Russo-Japanese War in early 1904 presented a new opportunity for struggle. Posse called for general strikes throughout Russia. The crucial point, wrote Bonch, was to exhort the sectarians in a political language that they could comprehend:

> If the proletarian-sectarian in his speech requires the word 'devil', then identify this old concept of an evil principle with capitalism, and identify the word 'Christ', as a concept of eternal good, happiness, and freedom, with socialism.[51]

The masses, Bonch argued, were inherent believers in religious myth; throughout history people had engaged in "god creation" *(bogotvorenie)* to sustain their spiritual life. According to sectarian psychology, Christ was not a single individual but a "collective concept." Socialists should appeal to this religious collectivism in their writings.

In addition to *Rassvet*, Bonch and Lenin established a "Library and Archive of the RSDRP" in Geneva.[52] They quickly set about collecting materials, opening a reading room, and providing a socialist meeting place for exiled Russians. Most European cities had their Russian colony of students and political exiles, where libraries and reading rooms provided a political focus and attracted police attention. In the Geneva library Lenin could immerse himself in the writings of Russian revolutionary and Populist thinkers, among them Tkachev and Sergei Nechaev, Jacobin and terrorist leaders of the previous generation. He could scan the writings of Marx and Engels, Guesde and Lassalle, Kautsky and Plekhanov, along with runs of revolutionary journals, such as *Nabat* and *Obshchina*. With the aid of Kuklin, who donated much of his own library, the collection by 1905 contained 4,760 volumes and 2,000 documents.

In June 1904 the Menshevik-dominated central committee of the RSDRP decided to cease publication of *Rassvet*, but Lenin and Bonch refused. "I consider the closing of *Rassvet* premature," wrote Lenin, "and I propose to continue the experiment."[53] Bonch and Lenin now established their own publishing operation, "Vladimir Bonch Bruevich and N. Lenin, Publishers." Supported by Kuklin's money, they were also able to gain control of the library and archive.

By the autumn of 1904 Lenin had been ousted from the editorial board of *Iskra*. In the name of "the majority," Lenin and Bonch brought out a series of political pamphlets by newly acquired supporters such as A. A. Lunacharsky and A. A. Bogdanov.[54] They also used the library as a base for distributing party literature to be smuggled into Russia, and issued a bulletin to solicit new acquisitions. In the meantime *Iskra* refused to publish Bolshevik resolutions, and Bolshevik publications claimed to represent the RSDRP.

Bolshevism was not yet an organized faction. Rather, it was a loosely associated group of Geneva Russian socialists. Only in the winter of 1904–1905 would the Bolsheviks, with the aid of Gorky's money, acquire their own journal. *Vpered* (Forward). Until then they remained a library, a restaurant, and a small publishing house. In January 1905 Bonch left Geneva and returned to Russia. He traveled from town to town setting up yet another publishing operation for the RSDRP, a series of legal publications also entitled *Zhizn'* printed in Berlin. Income went into the party treasury. Assisted by Gorky and his friends I. P. Ladyzhnikov and K. P. Piatnitsky, Bonch's enterprise became a valuable Bolshevik book outlet and source of funds in the lean years after the 1905 revolution. In 1906 Bonch opened a publishing house in St. Petersburg also named *Vpered* and a bookstore, both linked to the central committee of the RSDRP through the revolutionary engineer Leonid Krasin. In

V. I. Lenin and V. D. Bonch-Bruevich, Moscow, October 1918. From
Vospominaniia V. I. Lenina (Moscow, 1979), supplement.

addition to these publishing operations, Bonch continued to pursue his
scholarly investigation of Russian religious sects, and to note the link
between religious mysticism and communism, the "Christian communism" of the Russian villages and the future world of socialism.[55]

Between 1907 and 1917 Bonch lost contact with Lenin, despite
Bonch's role in Bolshevik publishing operations, such as the journals
Zvezda (Star) and *Prosveshchenia* (Enlightenment) in St. Petersburg. Only
in 1917 did they renew acquaintances when Bonch allowed Lenin to use
his St. Petersburg address for conspiratorial correspondence. After the
revolution Bonch served as administrative secretary of the National

Economic Council (Sovnarkom). Ironically this gentle advocate of religious community and collectivism also became one of the chief architects of the cult of the individual hero Lenin. At Lenin's 1924 funeral Bonch arranged the details, chose the inscription over the mausoleum, and orchestrated the great outpouring of portraits, films, photographs, and sculpture of the dead leader.[56]

As for Bonch's pet project, the Geneva party library, most of it vanished into the hands of Lenin and Krupskaya, despite the fact that it was established under the auspices of the RSDRP central committee. When Lenin left Geneva for St. Petersburg in the autumn of 1905 he was concerned about the fate of this remarkable collection of materials on the Russian revolutionary movement, many of them bibliographical rarities, preserving the Populist and Jacobin world of his brother Alexander. Books and periodicals were packed into 132 boxes in Geneva in the winter of 1905–1906 and shipped off to Stockholm for safekeeping by Swedish socialists sympathetic to the Bolsheviks. A suitcase of rare manuscripts remained in Geneva, and was removed by Lenin to Paris in December 1910. Both ultimately found their way to Russia after 1917.[57] Ironically, this library was the property of the wealthy young patron of Posse and Bonch-Bruevich, Kuklin, who died in May 1907, not realizing that his books and his money had become resources of the Bolsheviks in their war of words on Tsarist autocracy.

Lenin and Bonch represented two forms of political language crucial to Bolshevism in its early years. From Populism Lenin borrowed techniques of Aesopian and cryptographic communication useful for initiates of a revolutionary party where only the alert reader would discern the plaintext meaning of a secret language in code and cipher. Cryptography, the handmaiden of war and diplomacy, became the servant of revolution. From European syndicalism and Russian religious sectarianism Posse and Bonch derived a tradition of mythmaking, of quasi-religious collectivism designed for the masses.

From the beginning Bolshevik political language consisted of both authoritarian orthodoxy and ever-changing myth, different techniques for converting mass spontaneity into party consciousness. Lenin sought an esoteric language for a party elite; Bonch espoused an exoteric language for believers in a common religious culture. Both strategies contained elements of Marxism, Populism, and syndicalism, and their fusion enabled Lenin and the other Bolsheviks to build a new political organization for the new twentieth century. In the beginning was the word, and the word became the party, but in neither case was Lenin the arbiter of his own movement, Bolshevism.

II

MATTER INTO ENERGY
VANGUARD PARTY AND
WORKERS' COLLECTIVE

> There is nothing "holy" about theories or
> hypotheses for us; they serve us as
> instruments.
> —Lenin

Bolshevism as a political movement came into being in the midst of two
revolutions, the Russian Revolution of 1905 and the revolution in
physics. Bolshevik political language reflected this fact. The transformation of mass into energy suggested by the relativity theory of the young
Einstein meant in politics the revolutionary transformation of proletarian
matter into party energy by Lenin and the Bolsheviks. Thus the language
of physics provided a convenient Aesopian disguise for the messages of
politics. Early Bolshevik thought combined the philosophy of the
Austrian physicist Ernst Mach, a major influence on Einstein, and the
ideas of Karl Marx, as revised by Lenin and his rival within the Bolshevik
leadership, Alexander Bogdanov. As Bolshevism moved from words to
action, it used the language of physics and philosophy to debate political
issues that could not be discussed in public under censorship.

Organizationally, Lenin favored the domination of the party by an
individual leader through a series of hierarchically organized committees.
Bogdanov espoused a quite different view of organization based upon
ideology and myth; individual workers through the collective experience
of the general strike could attain a sense of socialist community, rather
than bourgeois individuality. The parallel with science was that, around
1900, the scientific view of the material universe as composed of discrete
individual particles known as atoms was giving way, under the influence
of the x-ray and radioactivity, to the notion that the world was made up
of transmutable energy, a universal collective. The long-standing division between spirit and matter thus gave way to a single "monist"
universe of energy.

Insofar as Marxism was a materialist philosophy, the dematerialization
of the world through scientific discovery was highly disturbing. So was
the new view that science was not the empirical accumulation of truth,

29

but the continuing advance of hypothesis. Modernism in science suggested an entire new framework for looking at the world, which
fascinated Bogdanov and other Russian intellectuals attracted to the
thought of Ernst Mach; it was anathema to Lenin, who sought to defend
a nineteenth-century view of science as the accumulation of truth based
on empirical evidence.

In June 1904, before Bolshevism existed as an organized political
movement, Lenin read through some of the works of Enrst Mach in
Geneva and dismissed his views as "nonsense, long-winded claptrap,
rantings, of no scientific value whatsoever." As to Mach's view that the
known world consists entirely of our sensations, and is not a reality
independent of them, Lenin considered that "no one who is not mentally
ill will ever confuse the sensation which is in him with the cause which
is outside him and which gives rise to it."[1]

Curious as it may seem, one cannot understand the emergence of
Bolshevism without examining both the philosophy of science articulated by Mach and Bogdanov and Lenin's violent reaction to it, long
before that reaction became public in his 1909 book *Materialism and
Empiriocriticism*. For in the Aesopian language of Bolshevism, physics
often meant politics and the relativism of Mach became a challenge to the
orthodoxy of Marx. To transform matter into energy meant to transform proletarian spontaneity into revolutionary consciousness, but Lenin
and the other Bolsheviks did not agree as to how this should be achieved.

What Is to Be Done?

As a political philosophy, Bolshevism combined two quite distinct
theories. Best known was the Jacobin theory of organization by dictatorship, a theory that descended to Lenin through Marx and the Russian
Populists. Less obvious was the collectivist theory of organization
through a community of believers in myth, a tradition embracing both
Russian religious orthodoxy and European syndicalism. The polarity of
Bolshevism resembled that of Russian society itself, in tension between
the autocratic tradition of rule by a single individual, the tsar, and the
self-sacrifice and martyrdom embedded in Russian Christianity and
subsequent revolutionary and rebel movements. For Lenin the dichotomy was between consciousness and spontaneity, the revolutionary
party and the proletariat; for Bogdanov it was between authoritarianism
and collectivism. Whatever the distinction, it would appear that Bolshevism contained two political theories and not one.

For Lenin organization meant an elite party of professional revolutionaries, the vanguard of the proletariat, whose decisions took precedence
over the desires of its individual members. The individual party member
was expected to sacrifice for the good of the cause, and to sublimate or

repress personal desires for collective purposes. As critics pointed out as early as 1904, organization soon came to mean obedience to Lenin's authority. In this sense, few Bolsheviks were properly organized. For Bolshevism from the start was a collection of personalities, in exile and in Russia, whose views were often in conflict with Lenin's and the Marxist orthodoxy he claimed to defend.

Lenin also inhabited a Manichean universe of light and darkness in which those who know, the illuminated, must constantly struggle with the blind. Lenin rarely doubted that he possessed the truth, even when outnumbered by his opponents. Leninist consciousness through the party would overcome mass spontaneity that contained the seeds of error, deviation, and heresy.

Lenin defined organization in his book *One Step Forward, Two Steps Back* (1904) in a comment on paragraph one of the RSDRP rules adopted by the London party congress in 1903: "The word organization is usually employed in two senses, a broad and a narrow one. In the narrow sense it signifies an individual nucleus of a collective of people with at least a minimum degree of form. In the broad sense it signifies the sum of such nuclei welded into a single whole . . . the party."[2] Lenin favored a small organization in which the party member was fully committed, rather than a large organization which allowed for more members with looser affiliation. The second view was common enough among the Mensheviks, but the Bolsheviks themselves were divided between Leninists who accepted party authority and other Bolsheviks who sought to organize proletarian myth.

When Lenin arrived in Switzerland in 1900, the RSDRP was barely two years old and without serious organization. Paul Axelrod in Zurich and George Plekhanov in Geneva had lived in Swiss exile for some twenty years, and were involved in establishing a party newspaper, *Iskra*, and a journal, *Zaria*. After several weeks of intense discussion, Lenin set off in late August for Munich, where he established contact with a German socialist of Russian background, Alexander Helphand, known as Parvus. Through Parvus, Lenin soon met the German socialist publisher Adolf Braun, who gave him technical advice on starting a newspaper in Germany. Using the house of Parvus's wealthy friend Dr. Lehmann as a conspiratorial center, Lenin was able to set up the first printing press for *Iskra*—not in Geneva, as Plekhanov had hoped, but in Parvus's Schwabing apartment. Thus, although the editorial board— Plekhanov, Axelrod, Vera Zasulich, and A. N. Potresov—remained in Geneva, Lenin and Krupskaya established de facto control over Russia's first social democratic newspaper in Germany. And in January 1901 Vladimir Ulianov adopted a new pseudonym to confuse the Russian and German police: Lenin.[3]

In the spring of 1901 Lenin began to work out the theory of political organization that would make him famous. In a series of preliminary articles in *Iskra*, Lenin sketched out his vision of the revolutionary party: a kind of "military activity" in which the newspaper would serve as a "collective agitator" and "collective organizer" through a "net of agents" inside Russia.[4] Throughout the articles ran a central theme that originated not with Lenin, but with the German Marxist theoretician Karl Kautsky in 1901 in the pages of *Neue Zeit*: "Socialist consciousness is therefore an element imported into the class struggle of the proletariat from outside and is not something that takes shape spontaneously."[5] To transform the working class into a revolutionary force would take organization from outside, lest it fall into the morass of trade unionism known in Russian circles of the day as "Economism." In March 1902 *Iskra* announced the appearance of these ideas in book form in Lenin's pamphlet *What Is to Be Done?* (*Chto delat?*).

In his famous book Lenin stressed the need for a revolutionary party based on both theory and practice, fusing the "organizational skill" of professional revolutionaries with the "revolutionary experience" of the masses, peasant and proletarian. He rejected both the trade unionism of the Russian "Economists" and Bernstein and the terrorism of Russian Populism for their "subservience to spontaneity." In his "declaration of war" on the autocracy of Nicholas II, Lenin called for "an organization of revolutionaries capable of lending energy, stability and continuity to the political struggle." This organization would counter the surveillance and censorship of the Okhrana, the Russian political police, by the "centralization of the most secret functions" of the party. Party consciousness would channel worker spontaneity into revolutionary energy, and avoid the dissipation of that energy into childish and fruitless efforts at terror, on the one hand, or modest improvements in workers' conditions, on the other.[6]

What is most striking in Lenin's clarion call for a revolutionary organization is its contrast with the reality of social democratic behavior. In theory Lenin described the vanguard party of well-organized intellectuals that would bring conscious revolutionary goals to the inchoate labor movement from the outside. In practice there was no organized party, only a loose coalition of socialist and Marxist exiles and intellectuals, many of whom were in Russia. It is to the world of these Russian *praktiki*, not the world of émigré theories, that we must now turn.

Moscow and Vologda

Other Bolsheviks organized in Moscow and Vologda province after 1900. Already in the late 1890s Lenin's sister Anna Elizarova and her husband, Mark, together with Lenin's brother Dmitry, had established a Moscow Workers' Union which retained connections through Lenin with the better-known St. Petersburg Union of Struggle. By 1896 the

Moscow group boasted some fifty members, including V. V. Vorovsky and M. N. Liadov, who later became Bolsheviks; in 1898 the group promptly declared itself a committee of the newly formed RSDRP. Another central figure in Moscow was N. E. Bauman, an *Iskra* agent who operated under the code name "Mach". In March 1901, however, the Moscow committee was decimated by police arrests, and among the victims were Lenin's sister and brother-in-law, his other sister, Maria, and two brothers of A. V. Lunacharsky.[7]

In 1902 the Moscow committee was reestablished but with a number of important new members. Among them were I. I. Skvortsov (Stepanov), an economist; V. L. Shantser (Marat); two historians, N. A. Rozhkov and M. N. Pokrovsky; a dentist, P. G. Dauge; a young lawyer and syndicalist, Stanislav Volsky; and a number of other intellectuals and professional people—doctors, lawyers, teachers, writers, and professors. By the autumn of 1902 the committee had found a valuable source of patronage, the writer Maxim Gorky and his mistress, the actress Maria Andreeva.

In contrast to Lenin's theory, the Moscow committee of the RSDRP and its *Iskra* agents were neither professional revolutionaries nor devout Leninists. Most were full-time professionals sympathetic to the revolutionary cause, and readers of socialist and Marxist literature. Consequently, as one of them, G. A. Alexinsky, noted, "for the Moscow Bolsheviks Lenin was one of the leaders, but they reserved complete intellectual independence from him and found any kind of blind subordination quite foreign."[8] In Moscow the terms "Bolshevik" and "Menshevik" carried little meaning until after the 1905 Revolution.

In exile Lenin had little real contact with events inside Russia and held a confusing picture of personalities and organizations. Lenin first encountered the writings of the future Bolshevik leader Alexander Bogdanov in the late 1890s, when he reviewed them favorably, thinking that Bogdanov was a pseudonym for Plekhanov.[9] What Lenin read of Bogdanov he admired; he saw in Bogdanov a staunch critic of Kantian idealism and a good Marxist. In October 1901, Lenin and Krupskaya began to correspond with Bogdanov for *Iskra* and found him to be incautious in his communications and independent in his ideas. "We read your letter without knowing the code," Krupskaya admonished Bogdanov from Geneva; "Don't use the same signs for one letter." She added that, while *Iskra* badly needed money, party workers, correspondence, and literature, Bogdanov should elaborate on his "differences with *Iskra*."[10]

Lenin soon learned that Bogdanov was an influential Marxist exile in Vologda province, where he was defending Marxist philosophy against the Kievan exile, Nikolai Berdyaev; that Bogdanov was not very adept at conspiratorial correspondence; and that Bogdanov wished to reprint some *Iskra* pamphlets with his own editorial revisions. "We are very pleased at your proposal to publish brochures," Lenin wrote Bogdanov in April 1902, "but we ask you not to place conditions on accepting or rejecting such brochures *en bloc* without any partial changes." Lenin found Bogdanov's article on party organization unacceptable for publication in *Iskra* because Bogdanov criticized the dominance of a "single individual" and the "dictatorship of one member of the committee." Nonetheless, Lenin, in need of Russian contributors, agreed to publish whatever Bogdanov submitted "in general."[11]

Bogdanov was thus well known to Lenin as an influential Marxist exile in Russia and an independent thinker. Trotsky, who arrived on Lenin's doorstep in London in October 1902, later recalled that "in philosophy we had been much impressed by Bogdanov's book, which combined Marxism with theory of knowledge put forward by Mach and Avenarius. Lenin also thought at the time that Bogdanov's theories were right."[12] In addition, by November 1903 Lenin had been ousted from his editorial post with *Iskra* by the Mensheviks and was badly in need of supporters.

Lenin became more aware of Bogdanov's views after the arrival in Geneva of N. V. Volsky (Valentinov), a Kievan Marxist very enthusiastic about Lenin's plans for a revolutionary party as laid down in *What Is to Be Done?*[13] Like many young people of his generation, Volsky was drawn to Marxism because it was scientific, optimistic, voluntaristic, and European. In Kiev he had also been involved in workers circles with a strong religious bent, where Christ-like carpenters led Bible discussions and espoused the labor theory of value. In the spring of 1904, Volsky introduced Lenin to the philosophy of Ernst Mach. As a self-styled *starik*, or elder, accustomed to the adulation of younger followers, Lenin was not pleased with the independence of thought exhibited by Volsky and Bogdanov. Exhausted and depressed from his struggle with the Mensheviks after the second RSDRP congress, Lenin now perused the writings of Ernst Mach. In so doing he discovered an entire world view that threatened his own Marxist orthodoxy, but would become an essential ingredient of Bolshevism. Lenin's Jacobinism confronted Bogdanov's collectivism.

The Collectivism of Alexander Bogdanov

Lenin's major rival within the Bolshevik fraction was Alexander Aleksandrovich Malinovsky, who generally wrote under the pseudonym Bogdanov. Together with the engineer Leonid Krasin and Lenin, Bogdanov headed the Bureau of Committees of the Majority in 1905 and was in essence the leader of Bolshevism inside Russia. As the bank robber, bandit, and Bolshevik coconspirator Kamo wrote in 1905, "Leonid Borisovich Krasin introduced me to a great man. Together they run the military-technical center of the Bolsheviks. You must understand that this man knows everything. He writes scholarly books, he makes bombs and dynamite. He also treats patients, you know, as a doctor."[14]

In Leninist hagiography and historiography Bogdanov has come down to us as a left-wing renegade who played dissident to Lenin's correct and orthodox leadership. In the West he has been rediscovered as a kind of father of systems science, precursor of Norbert Wiener and cybernetics, author of endless tomes on empiriomonism, tectology, and other scientistic systems he devised or renamed. He has even been cited as an intellectual relative of the Italian communist Antonio Gramsci. In fact, Bogdanov was the major leader of Bolshevism inside Russia in the period 1905 to 1907 and a significant rival of Lenin in the European emigration afterwards. Bogdanov's thought represented a second strand of Bolshevism, i.e., collectivism, that was as significant in shaping the ethos of Bolshevism as was Lenin's Jacobinism.[15]

Bogdanov was born in 1873 in Tula, the grimy industrial town to the south of Moscow that had been an armaments center since the seventeenth century. He was the second oldest of six children born to a schoolteacher. After graduating from Tula gymnasium, Bogdanov attended Moscow University from 1891 to 1894, where he studied natural sciences and medicine. Because of his involvement with radical student organizations, Bogdanov was expelled from the university in December 1894 and exiled to his hometown of Tula. Here he underwent the shift from Populism to Marxism common among his generation in the 1890s, disseminated socialist literature among workers, and encountered a group of like-minded young radicals with whom he would ultimately enter the ranks of Bolshevism.[16]

Between 1894 and 1896 Bogdanov pursued the study of medicine at Kharkov University while living in Tula and participating in a Marxist discussion group. A central figure in the group was Ivan Ivanovich Savelev, a worker in one of Tula's armament factories. Another was V. A. Rudnev (Bazarov) (1874–1939), a Tula native also exiled from Moscow University to his home province. The circle also included Ivan Ivanovich Skvortsov (Stepanov) (1870–1928). The central idea of the group was that the labor movement should be led by workers, assisted by intellectuals—the same notion introduced, to Lenin's dismay, into St. Petersburg in the mid-1890s by Polish Marxists.

Skvortsov had been trained as an economist, and the Tula group was intrigued by the possibility of developing Marxism in accordance with new economic theories and changing realities. In 1897 Bogdanov published *A Short Course in Economic Science*, a Marxist economic tract favorably reviewed by Lenin. In 1898 he probed more fundamental questions in his *Basic Elements in the Historical View of Nature*. Skvortsov and Bazarov combined to produce their work *Social Movements of the Middle Ages and the Reformation*, following Karl Kautsky in associating economic class struggle with religious millenarian movements. In addition, in 1899 Bogdanov graduated in medicine from Kharkov University, spent the next winter in jail in Tula, and in May 1900 was exiled to Kaluga Province. He was then exiled for a three-year term to Vologda Province. In 1902 Bogdanov was joined in exile in Vologda by the twenty-six-year-old Anatoly Vasilevich Lunacharsky (1875–1933), who soon married Bogdanov's nineteen-year-old sister. By 1902 Vologda had become the center of a remarkable Marxist literary and philosophical circle which found itself embroiled in great debates with another Marxist turning away toward idealism, Nikolai Berdyaev.

Berdyaev was a young philosopher from Kiev, a traditional source for the influx of western ideas and religious beliefs into Russia. Around 1900 he was undergoing a complex conversion from Marxism to idealism not unlike the shift to neo-Kantianism common in Western Europe at the turn of the century. Kant had divided the world into eternal noumena and transient phenomena, spirit and matter, the ideal and the real. At the core of Kant's philosophy lay the importance of the individual acting according to moral and ethical ideals, the categorical imperative. In reaction to nineteenth-century materialism and positivism, with its cult of science, Berdyaev now moved to defend the individual against the tyranny of social progress, and religious and ethical values against scientific knowledge.

In his *Subjectivism and Individualism* of 1901, Berdyaev cited the "strivings of Faust" to achieve knowledge and power over nature and defended the individual's spiritual elevation and "idealistic enthusiasm" in the search for eternal truth. The essence of the world was not matter but spirit, the ideal and not the real. The Russian intelligentsia in its fervor for a radical transformation of society had given up on religion and ethics, but it was precisely these sources of idealism that were now needed to overcome the materialism of the day. A "spiritual rebirth" of the proletariat was more important than material gains, wrote Berdyaev. He attacked Marxist materialists for their "positivist alchemy" in which they claimed to answer religious questions with a system of social science and economic thought. Ideas and ideals, not the material needs of the class struggle, move individuals to action.[17]

Faced with this challenge, Bogdanov and the other Vologda exiles began to develop arguments against Berdyaev's idealism. One of Lunacharsky's first acts upon arriving in Vologda in February 1902 was to dash off (in one hour and ten minutes) an article, "The Tragedy of Life and White Magic," that roundly attacked Berdyaev from a Marxist standpoint. In search of an outlet for their writings, Bogdanov wrote Lenin in Geneva in March 1902 that "there is a group of people ready and able to give you literary cooperation" by writing brochures "for broad layers of the urban population."[18]

Lenin's initial response to Bogdanov's offer did not bode well for their future relationship. Bogdanov had sent on various manuscripts written by members of his circle for publication in *Iskra*. Although Bogdanov agreed with Lenin initially that the "one-person principle" was crucial to effective conspiratorial organization, he objected when Lenin attempted to edit Bogdanov's own manuscript. Unless Lenin printed his essays unaltered, Bogdanov threatened, he would send them to the Socialist Revolutionaries or another socialist group for publication. Bogdanov also complained in the spring and summer of 1902 that Lenin had not sent the essays to the address that Bogdanov had indicated. Although Bogdanov enciphered the key parts of his own letters, many Russian socialists were placed under arrest that summer in Moscow and Vologda, and communication between Vologda and Geneva became increasingly difficult because of police surveillance.[19]

In September 1902 Bogdanov wrote Lenin that the Vologda circle would "try to cooperate with *Iskra*" and asked for a set of new addresses, enciphered in the pages of Heinrich Heine's book *Bimini*. Yet communication remained difficult, and throughout 1903 Bogdanov concentrated on organizing literature for a new legal Marxist journal published in Moscow and entitled *Pravda* (Truth). Bogdanov apparently had only a distant knowledge of the Bolshevik-Menshevik split that summer. In February 1904 he left Russia for Geneva and met Lenin for the first time. Cut off from the RSDRP and its Menshevik majority, Lenin now sought support from Bogdanov and his circle; by early 1904 Bogdanov, Lunacharsky, Skvortsov, and Bazarov had all arrived in Geneva.[20]

In 1904 Lenin needed Bogdanov, a well-known socialist philosopher and journalist with good contacts inside Russia. "Bogdanov promised to attract money to the Bolshevik treasury," recalled Valentinov, "to develop contacts with Gorky, to win over Lunacharsky, a lively writer and good speaker who was making his debut in literature (he married Bogdanov's sister), Bazarov, and some young Moscow professors who were flirting with Marxism."[21] At the time Lenin was a man without a party; Bogdanov offered new followers, new writers, new ideas.

Politically, Bogdanov shared with Lenin a Marxist and socialist view of the world, but one characterized by independence of thought and attention to a wide variety of then popular European thinkers. Like Lenin, he disliked the Menshevik émigrés who claimed to speak for the workers of Russia, and placed greater emphasis on practical revolutionary activity inside Russia. In Geneva in 1904 Bogdanov produced a series of political pamphlets in which he attacked the Russian government and its prosecution of the Russo-Japanese War; criticized the liberals as bourgeois intellectuals who were simply "temporary allies" of the proletariat in the common campaign for a "democratic constitution"; and urged the RSDRP to free itself from liberal slogans and fight for its own party "self-consciousness." The pamphlets appeared under the pseudonym Riadovoi, or "Rank-and-file."[22]

For Bogdanov, socialism meant the ultimate nationalization of the means of production in the hands of the proletariat. But unlike Marx and Lenin, Bogdanov laid great emphasis on technology and industrial machinery in shaping worker consciousness. In addition to allying with peasants and liberals, Bogdanov urged workers to "unite in unions, strikes, and any other means to compel capitalists to improve the workers' wage condition and the government to legislate factory laws beneficial to the workers." Workers must struggle constantly to organize themselves into "syndicates" or trade unions; "thus the workers will unite in larger and larger masses: hundreds, thousands, even tens of thousands" and would take over "a small number of large enterprises, rather than a lot of small ones." In none of his writings did Bogdanov place much emphasis on a revolutionary party or even on politics; instead, he emphasized the consciousness of workers developed through the experience of the general strike. Although Bogdanov's writings showed a certain affinity for European syndicalism, his politics reflected a much broader and more complex philosophical view of the world, an outlook based on collectivism.[23]

Bogdanov's philosophy had begun to emerge in his *Short Course on Economic Science* and was further developed in a series of books and articles written between 1901 and 1906. Like other Marxists of the day, Bogdanov viewed history as class struggle progressing through the phases of feudalism, capitalism, and socialism outlined by Marx and Engels. Yet instead of the labor theory of value Bogdanov placed a new emphasis on energy, technology, and state planning in shaping the economic future. Progress for Bogdanov meant the domination of nature by man, a domination facilitated by the machine. He even predicted a socialist future of "automatic mechanisms in which the worker's role is almost exclusively supervisory and controlling over the machine's actions."[24] The energy multiplied by machines would create a new planned society of harmony, freedom, and progress that would replace the inequities of capitalism. Following the works of Edward Bellamy and H. G. Wells, Bogdanov developed the utopian strands of Marxism into his own philosophy of a socialist future.

Underpinning Bogdanov's notion of socialism was a broader concept of collectivism that emerged first in the critique of Berdyaev's ethical individualism. To Berdyaev's idealism, Bogdanov counterposed the ideas of Marxist realism. Bourgeois society, wrote Bogdanov, had created a kind of individual authoritarianism that justified class oppression. The individual personality had become a fetish of bourgeois society and thought, propped up by the false dichotomy between the ideal and the real. A society of two hostile classes created dualist categories of thinking. Socialism would create a philosophy of "monism" in which the entire world consisted of energy and its transformations, and where individualism and egoism, represented in the thought of Berdyaev and

Kant, would disappear. For Bogdanov all ideas and ideologies were merely forms whereby we organize our experience. Science itself is based on collective experience, the shared data of scientists. Socialism would be not merely a political system, but a new philosophy, whose center was not the bourgeois individual but the socialist collective.

Collectivism would come into being when the consciousness of the masses had moved away from thinking about their own "I" to the common "we." Authority would give way to cooperation and worker solidarity, individualism to collectivism, the "merging of individual lives into one grandiose whole." The authoritarian division between the ideal bourgeoisie and the real proletariat would disappear. The revolution would be an "explosion of ecstasy that seizes society."[25]

In *Pravda* in 1904 Bogdanov wrote of the need for a "collectivizing of man" (*sobiranie cheloveka*). The idea of "Man," he wrote, is a "whole world of experience." "A group lives as a whole; there is no individual personality (*lichnost'*), no idea of 'I', as a special center of interests and goals." The "I" or self is the product of a world of specialization, division of labor, and authoritarian dualism. The true man is not an individual but a collective "comrade" (*tovarishch*). "Man has not yet arrived," concluded Bogdanov, "but he is nearby, and his silhouette shows clearly on the horizon."[26]

For Bogdanov collectivism was a religion, and even promised a triumph over death. The individual was "nothing more than the chaos of experience." Individual immortality was a Christian and bourgeois delusion. But collectivism would provide a kind of surrogate "victory over death" in which the individual would live on through the memory of the collective. It would also be an ideology, an organizing form of experience that would shape the socialist world view of the masses.[27]

Bogdanov's syndicalism, positivist faith in science, and collectivism were also shared to one degree or another by other Marxist writers in Vologda and Moscow. In 1904 they had responded to Berdyaev's collection of essays *Problems of Idealism* with their own *Essays on the Realistic World View*. In contrast to the dualism of the ideal and the real, they substituted the monism of Marxism. S. Suvorov, following Ernst Mach's *Analysis of Sensations*, argued that the world is mere chaos until our mind organizes our experience into useful knowledge and myth. Lunacharsky called for a new positivist "science of values" in aesthetics that would transcend the class-bound religions and art of bourgeois society. Socialism through art should express its "Promethean aspirations" and aspire to a "victory over spontaneity" in which humanity would produce Nietzschean "supermen." Socialism for Lunacharsky would bring about nothing less than a new "religion of humanity."[28]

In another essay Bazarov criticized the Kantian moral absolutes defended in *Problems of Idealism*. Citing Mach and Richard Avenarius, Bazarov argued that the "autonomous personality" of the individual in bourgeois society did not really exist except as a "completely empty, meaningless formula." Idealism was the product of an "authoritarian metaphysics" in a master-slave society dominated by the bourgeoisie. Bogdanov added an essay in which he revised the Marxist labor theory of value and argued that the law of supply and demand in the marketplace, not simply the labor expended in the production of goods, determined economic values. V. Shuliatikov wrote a critique of bourgeois individualism in contemporary Russian literature, and V. A. Friche characterized the art and literature of capitalism as a form of neurosis.[29]

The collectivist critique of individualism persisted in 1903 and 1904 in the pages of various Russian literary journals. Lunacharsky called for a new religion of science, claiming that "the fear of death does not exist for an active positivist." For Lunacharsky, the importance of Mach's thought was not its sensationalist critique of metaphysics, but its portrait of the self or "I" as "something which continues to exist in other persons even after my death." Socialist immortality would consist of eternal life in the memory of the collective.[30]

Writing in *Pravda*, Bazarov also continued to contrast the individualist hedonism and egoism of bourgeois society with the moral altruism of socialism. Even in modern science, he noted, "autocratic" laws of nature were giving way to more "democratic" concepts of the universe. For Lunacharsky the realism of Marxism surpassed the false idealism of bourgeois thought, still dressed, he argued, "in Kant's old frock coat."[31]

The arrival of Bogdanov and members of the *Pravda* circle in Geneva in 1904 presented Lenin with a dilemma. On the one hand, Lenin desperately needed supporters in his war on the Mensheviks, especially writers of the quality of Bogdanov and Lunacharsky. On the other hand, Bogdanov's revisionism threatened to give the Mensheviks an opportunity to attack the Bolsheviks for their philosophical heresies. Neither Lenin nor Bonch-Bruevich wished to be criticized as bad Marxists. Nonetheless, the Lenin-Bonch publishing operations, fortified by Kuklin's money, continued to print not only Marxist writings but Populist and syndicalist ones as well. In addition, they published considerably more copies of pamphlets by Bogdanov and Lunacharsky than by Lenin.[32] The two new Bolshevik writers brought a well-honed literary style and a sharp-edged independence of mind not well suited to Lenin's authoritarianism. For Lenin, Bogdanov and Lunacharsky represented both a political asset and a philosophical danger.

In February and March 1904 Lenin was hard at work in Geneva writing *One Step Forward, Two Steps Back*, his vitriolic attack on the Mensheviks and their behavior during and after the second party congress of 1903. Volsky found Lenin going through a "startling change" in which he became increasingly emaciated, dull-eyed, and depressed. He even gave up his habitual games of chess.[33] It was a moment of choice: conciliation with the Mensheviks, or a new departure with a new group of followers. The Menshevik Paul Axelrod charged that Lenin was in the process of forming a "Jacobin club," an "organizational utopia of a theocratic character." In *One Step Forward*, Lenin accepted the label "Jacobin" and announced his further progress toward a hierarchical and dictatorial model of the revolutionary party.

In May 1904 Volsky persuaded Lenin to examine the writings of Ernst Mach and Richard Avenarius, writings that appeared to provide philosophical underpinnings for much of Bogdanov's thought. After three days of poring through Avenarius's *Critique of Pure Experience*, borrowed from the Social Revolutionary émigré Viktor Chernov, Lenin was furious. Denouncing the ideas of Mach and Avenarius as "worthless, confused, and idealistic theory," Lenin filled eleven small lined notebooks with a handwritten attack on their philosophies. Volsky described Lenin's attitude as "savage intolerance." Lenin concluded only that "a man who builds his philosophy on sensation alone is beyond hope. He should be put away in a lunatic asylum."[34]

Volsky thought that Mach and Avenarius could provide a "better epistemological foundation" for Marxism than materialism. George Plekhanov, the doyen of Russian Marxist theory, disagreed. "Avenarius? Mach?" Plekhanov asked Volsky; "Are you dragging these fellows out of the basement of bourgeois thought in order to 'correct' Marxism with their help?" For Plekhanov, who had not yet read either Mach or Avenarius, it was enough to see the hydra of revisionism. Lenin agreed, noting that "social democracy is not a seminar where different ideas are compared. It is the fighting class organization of the revolutionary proletariat."[35]

At issue was nothing less than the entire philosophical basis of Marxist materialism. Volsky sympathized with the ideas of Mach and Avenarius because, he said, they "utterly demolish all metaphysics in a most revolutionary way." Lenin, on the other hand, agreed with Plekhanov that Marxism was a kind of absolute and orthodox truth that should not be revised, at least by others. "There is only one answer to revisionism," Lenin told Volsky. "Smash its face in."[36]

What were the ideas of Ernst Mach, and how did they come to enter Bolshevism through the writings of Alexander Bogdanov in 1904?

Ernst Mach and the Politics of Empiriocriticism

> I see Mach's greatness in his incorruptible scepticism and independence.
> —Albert Einstein
> Nonsense, long-winded claptrap.
> —V. I. Lenin

What Lenin called "Machism" was a major trend in European philosophy of science in 1904. Ernst Mach (1838–1916) was a well-known Austrian physicist and philosopher whose copious writings argued that all metaphysics should be eliminated from science, that time and space were not absolute entities but categories of the human mind, and that the world is only the sum of our sensations of it. For Mach there was no dualism of mind and matter, but only a monism of sensations. Since sensations and experience vary from one individual to another, Mach articulated a relativistic view of the universe that for a time exerted a powerful influence on the young Albert Einstein. As a radical critique of materialism and atomism, Mach's thought was also anathema to Lenin. Mach represented a transitional philosophy at the turn of the century, a nineteenth-century system builder whose very system contained a relativism and scepticism toward all belief systems that anticipated the new century as well.[37]

Mach's significance lay in his positivist relativism, grounding all science in experiment and hypothesis, in anticipation of the later Vienna Circle; his reduction of science to the symbolism of hypothesis, convention, and form; and his political stance of liberal socialism, which made him attractive to such Austrian socialists as the young Friedrich Adler (1879–1960). Adler fused the ideas of Mach and Marx into a new theory of socialism that proved attractive to Bogdanov and threatening to Lenin.

Mach expressed his ideas in a variety of books that were continuously reprinted in Europe and Russia between 1905 and 1915: *The Conservation of Energy* (1872); *The Science of Mechanics* (1883); *The Contribution to the Analysis of Sensations* (1886); and *Knowledge and Error* (1905). In them Mach developed a theory of the physical universe that was considerably different from the great Newtonian synthesis of mechanics that had dominated physics since the end of the seventeenth century.

Mach lived in an age when the picture of a universe made up of tiny hard objects known as atoms was being demolished by new discoveries. In 1895 Wilhelm Conrad Roentgen discovered the mysterious x-ray whose photographs appeared to demonstrate the penetrability of matter. By discovering the electron in 1897, J. J. Thompson showed that atoms were not hard and irreducible, but composed of still smaller particles. The initial discoveries of radioactivity by Marie Curie and Ernest Rutherford between 1896 and 1905 showed further that certain forms of matter could emit energy as radiation and in the process be transmuted into new forms and elements. Albert Einstein's three famous physics papers of 1905 also argued that matter was merely a convertible and transformable form of energy, which appeared to be the primal substance of the universe.

But if matter was merely a form of energy, was energy a substance or a hypothesis? For the German physicist Wilhelm Ostwald, a follower of Mach, energy was indeed the primal substance in a monist universe. Energy was the potential to do work, and all matter was a form ofenergy. Atoms were only the hypotheses of the scientists. Everything that occurs in the universe is a transformation of energy, which is eternal and immortal, since it can neither be created nor destroyed. For Ostwald all matter was either "form-energy" or "volume-energy," and "the continued use of the word 'matter' has become unsuited to scientific language." Ostwald's energetics, in short, undermined materialism as an unscientific world view in an age of major scientific discovery.[38]

In addition, Ostwald suggested that energetics provided a kind of immortality for the collective, if not the individual. Matter decays and dies; energy is immortal. "Energy will outlive everything else in the universe," proclaimed Ostwald. Individual atoms die; the collective of mankind in all its generations lives on through "self-sacrifice for the sake of humanity." In this sense Ostwald's critique of atomism was also a collectivist critique of individualism.[39]

Mach, too, characterized himself as a monist who rejected the Cartesian dualism of spirit and matter, as well as the dualism inherent in Bishop Berkeley's notion that *esse est percipi*, to be is to be perceived. Berkeley had argued that the world exists only as perceptions in our mind. Mach argued that "the world is our sensations" and rejected any dualist division between self and other, ego and world, in favor of the new monism. Most attractive for some Russian Marxists and collectivists was Mach's argument that "the ego must be given up" in favor of the collective. What Lenin attacked was Mach's relativism and sensationalism; what Bogdanov borrowed from Mach was his collectivism.

In Geneva in 1904 Mach's ideas were all the rage, as they were in Zurich and other Swiss centers of learning. Young physics students absorbed Mach's criticism of Newtonian space-time absolutes as a "conceptual monstrosity" and welcomed his portrait of science as hypothesis, rather than absolute truth. Objects now became complexes of sensations, and matter a form of experience. Albert Einstein discovered Mach's ideas while a student at Zurich in 1897; by 1904 Mach had a profound effect on Einstein's thought, both by emphasizing the need for science to agree on useful conventions, such as space and time, and by identifying reality with sensations. Yet Einstein never did share Mach's critique of atomism, and later moved away from Mach to the view that science consisted of laws, not hypotheses; that the velocity of light was absolute, not relative; and that reality consists of more than our sensations.[40]

The fullest explanation of Mach's views was his *Analysis of Sensations*, originally published in 1886. In it he argued that material bodies were nothing more than complexes of our sensations situated in space and time. More important for Marxists and socialists, Mach leveled a philosophical broadside at the very notion of an individual: "The ego is as little absolutely permanent as are bodies. That which we so much dread in death, the annihilation of our permanency, actually occurs in life in abundant measure." The self, as a complex of sensations, does not die but simply changes form. The individual and the idea of individual immortality are useful fictions. In general, wrote Mach, "no point of view has absolute, permanent validity. Each has importance only for some given end."[41]

Mach also reiterated the difference between his own monism and Berkeley's dualism of spirit and matter. Under the influence of Buddhism, Mach argued the need to "get rid of the conception of the Ego as a reality which underlies everything." The self, like all matter, was merely a "mental symbol standing for a relatively stable complex of sensational elements." Loss of self in the collective was the answer to individualism, which was merely another useful hypothesis.[42]

Mach therefore stood for a radical critique of materialism, of absolute truth, and of individualism. At least some Marxists felt that his views might well modernize and supplement, rather than threaten, the ideas of Marx and Engels, and among them was Friedrich Adler.

In Zurich in 1904 Friedrich Adler was another rebellious physicist and mathematician in the mold of his great friend, Albert Einstein. Thin, pale, and blond, he was the son of the Austrian socialist leader Victor Adler, and a brilliant and rising physicist in his own right; when Einstein accepted the post of Associate Professor of Theoretical Physics at Zurich University in 1909, it was only because Adler had first turned down the position himself as an act of generosity to his friend. Fanatical, sensitive, and widely read, Friedrich Adler was steeped in the writings of Marx and Mach, Kautsky and Einstein. He bridged the two worlds of physics and politics, and attempted to reconcile them in his own writings.

For Adler, Mach had provided an entire new philosophy of science in which theories were not truths, but tools, useful hypotheses to be tested and refined. Mach read the young Adler's physics papers and offered support and praise. Like other Marxists of the day, Adler felt that Marx's theories were somewhat outmoded. Capitalism had generated as much material progress and social reform as class struggle, and nationalism was as much a force in prewar Europe as socialism. As soon as he began reading Mach and Ostwald in the summer of 1903, Adler realized that Marxist materialism could no longer measure up to the standards of modern physics and its discoveries. To be a scientist and a Marxist was not easy, and Adler hoped to find in Mach a philosophy of reconciliation.[43]

Politically, Mach was a liberal socialist. As a representative to the Austrian parliament, Mach worked for the nine-hour day and electoral reform. He criticized both church and state for their excesses of authority, the "robbery of the many by the few," and hoped for a more equitable socialist and anticolonialist future. Most important was the streak of collectivism that Mach found in Buddhism, an elimination of the ego and the self that argued against the notion of personal immortality. For Mach the existence of the individual was a useful fiction, and individual death a dissolution of the body into nothingness and Nirvana.

Mach's collectivism had a powerful influence on Adler through its relativism, its scepticism toward all dogma, and its critique of mechanical materialism. As a physicist and a socialist, Adler carried Mach's message to many other socialists before 1914. Among them was Alexander Bogdanov. In the end Adler's relativist critique of all authority took a violent and anarchist turn when, in 1916, he assassinated the Austrian prime minister, Count Sturgh. In this instance Lenin was quite correct to see in Mach's thought a threat to his own brand of Marxist orthodoxy, as well as a rival philosophy of political extremism.

Mach was a popular thinker in Geneva in 1904. The sixth edition of his *History of Mechanics* had just appeared, and he offered an up-to-date, scientific philosophy that fit well the needs of young socialists to be both radical and scientific. His relativism and collectivism found a welcome response among many socialists, especially in his radical critique of individualism. "The ego," wrote Mach, "must be given up. It is partly the perception of this fact, partly the fear of it, that has given rise to the many extravagances of pessimism and optimism, and to numerous religious, ascetic, and philosophical absolutes."[44] And it was Mach's monism, collectivism, and relativism that soon divided Lenin and the other Bolsheviks on matters of both philosophy and politics.

The empiriocriticism of Mach and the fusion of Mach and Marx by Friedrich Adler provided considerable reinforcement for Bogdanov's emerging collectivism, but they were neither its first nor its only elements. Bogdanov had already worked out the view that political organization meant the organization of worker experience, just as the human mind organizes experience to undestand the world. Under capitalism, the atomized experience of individuals predominated; under socialism, experience would be organized collectively in a philosophy of altruism, self-sacrifice, and proletarian culture. But how?

Already in 1904 it was clear that Bogdanov sought to organize workers' experience through ideology and myth, not a political party. Like Lenin, he recognized the need to impose consciousness upon the workers from outside through an intellectual elite. But for Bogdanov, ideas, more than power, ruled the world and would galvanize the proletariat to action. Lenin saw himself, with Plekhanov's assistance, as a correct interpreter of Marxist orthodoxy. Bogdanov saw himself as a philosopher reinterpreting Marx in the light of changing historical and social conditions, the creator of a universal organizational science of society. Bogdanov and the *Pravda* circle in Moscow now joined Lenin in Geneva to establish a new political movement: Bolshevism.

The Origins of Leninism

By the summer of 1904 Bolshevism had developed little beyond what it had been a year earlier after the second RSDRP congress, a fractious group of émigré Russian Marxists with a poorly coordinated network of agents and correspondents inside Russia. It was not a "disciplined order of professional committeemen, grouped round a band of conspirators who were all linked by personal allegiance to their chieftain, Lenin," as one historian described it.[45] In fact, even before the term "Bolshevism" came into use, the fraction was divided between Lenin's tiny circle in Geneva and an RSDRP committee dominated by Marxist intellectuals in Moscow.

Lenin had lost control of the *Iskra* editorial board and resigned in disgust. In Geneva the dominant RSDRP leaders were all sympathetic to Martov and the Mensheviks, social democrats with whom Lenin shared an attitude of mutually suspicious peaceful coexistence. Russia was caught up in the throes of an ill-fated war with Japan, and Lenin was unable to acquire any funds from the *Iskra* board, to win over local RSDRP committees inside Russia, or to convene a new party congress. He had been expelled from the party central committee and condemned in print for his independent publishing operation with Bonch-Bruevich and Kuklin. In August 1904 Lenin was a man without a party.

One can hardly argue that in 1904 "while his competitors had merely adherents, Lenin had followers."[46] Lenin's Geneva circle consisted of M. N. Liadov (Mandelshtam), who directed the smuggling operations for *Iskra* into Russia, Krupskaya, Bonch-Bruevich and his wife, and the Lepeshinskys. P. N. Lepeshinsky, characterized as an "Oblomov" by Lenin, ran a Russian restaurant in Geneva together with his wife, Olga, who later achieved a certain notoriety in the 1940s as Stalin's favorite cell biologist. N. V. Volsky (Valentinov) and his wife also worked in the restaurant. Volsky was already suffering private doubts about both Marx's philosophy and Lenin's personality.

The new arrivals from Russia were hardly obsequious followers of Lenin. Bogdanov and Lunacharsky were established Marxist writers of some reputation. They were joined in Geneva by P. G. Dauge from the Moscow RSDRP committee, who spent three days with Lenin bringing him up to date on the Moscow party organization.[47] Bogdanov arrived in Geneva in May 1904, after meeting Trotsky, whom Bogdanov disliked immediately.[48] In Geneva Bogdanov met Lenin for the first time.

When the RSDRP central committee endorsed Menshevik control of the *Iskra* editorial board, it deprived Lenin of the right to represent the central committee abroad and prohibited publication of his writings without permission of the central committee. *Iskra* also refused to publish articles by Bogdanov, although the Mensheviks did not know the true identity behind Bogdanov's pseudonym Riadovoi.[49] While Plekhanov and the Mensheviks attended the Amsterdam meeting of the Second International in August, Lenin and Krupskaya spent several weeks with the Bogdanovs and two other Bolshevik couples in a tiny Swiss village discussing the necessities of organizing a new political party.[50]

Bogdanov proposed coopting Lunacharsky, Skvortsov, and Bazarov for literary work on a new publication to counter the Menshevik-controlled *Iskra*. Yet Lenin wanted nothing to do with Bogdanov and his Machist philosophy, however much he needed his reputation and his pen. After two days of furious discussion and debate, Bogdanov and Lenin declared a truce in matters of philosophy and an alliance in matters of politics. Politically, Bogdanov deferred temporarily to Lenin as the "greatest man in our party." Philosophically, he continued to hold to his collectivist views. The result was the "Declaration of the Twenty-Two," a Bolshevik manifesto read aloud by Lenin at the Lepeshinsky restaurant. In it he attacked the Mensheviks and proclaimed the need for a new organ and a new party.[51]

Lenin and Bogdanov continued to bring out pamphlets critical of the Mensheviks, thanks to Bonch's money and contacts with a French publisher. The Bolsheviks divided themselves into an "editing board" (Lenin, Vorovsky, Olminsky, and Lunacharsky) in Geneva and a "practical center" for operating illegally inside Russia (Bogdanov, Gusev, Zemliachka, Liadov, Litvinov). The first group began working on the creation of an émigré newspaper in Geneva; the second group left for Russia, where it constituted itself as the "Bureau of Committees of the Majority" (BKB). The final meeting of the entire Bolshevik group, complete with German beer and a holiday atmosphere, took place at the Cafe Landolt in Geneva.[52]

As Lenin admitted, the problem now was an acute shortage of funds. On the eve of Bloody Sunday, the Bolsheviks remained a tiny émigré circle of Russian Marxists united by a common penury. The term "Bolsheviks" was not yet in use, but only the terms "majority" (*bolshinstvo*) or "group of the majority" (*gruppa bolshinstva*). In October 1904 Krupskaya wrote Bogdanov, now living in Tver, requesting more action and better communication. Lenin also asked Bogdanov to establish a code name or alias for the writer Maxim Gorky. "In general," wrote Lenin, "the money situation is very desperate, since a lot is needed to send people to Russia (a great demand) and for transport." At the very moment when there was a "complete schism" in the party, complained Lenin, "Russia is organizing and expects decisive steps from us."[53]

On November 21, 1904, Lenin wrote Bogdanov again that "the majority needs to get out its own organ; for this we need money and correspondents. We must work hard to obtain both." Lenin also complained about lack of information about events inside Russia. "Not one letter, not one communication about the writers' group in Moscow," he wrote. "What about Bazarov, Fritsche, and the others?" Bogdanov's "great plans," muttered Lenin, had turned into a "great fiction."[54]

In fact, Bogdanov was not inactive. In December 1904 he assembled in Moscow a group of new members of the majority's bureau. This assemblage made it clear that Bolshevism was now a geographically divided movement consisting of a committee network inside Russia headed by Bogdanov and an émigré circle in Geneva headed by Lenin. This division between Russia and "the other shore" was compounded by the organizational difference between Bogdanov's collectivist myth and Lenin's Jacobin authority. But at the moment each man needed the other; Lenin was especially dependent on Bogdanov's network inside Russia for funding an émigré newspaper in Geneva. This need was soon fulfilled by a most unlikely source of Bolshevik support, the Moscow Old Believer community.

By late 1904 it was evident that Leninism and Bolshevism were not identical. Leninism referred to the plans for party organization of a newspaper laid down in *What Is to Be Done?* But, as was pointed out, in the book "there is no plan of organization, although at the time there was a lot of talk about a 'Leninist' plan. That meant only the creation of a party organ."[55] Inside Russia, however, the young Stalin found Lenin to be a real "mountain eagle" for his stress on consciousness over spontaneity. "This is the significance of Leninist thought," wrote Stalin in October 1904. "I call it Leninist because no one in Russian literature has expressed it so clearly as Lenin."[56]

The term "Leninism" appeared earlier than the term "Bolshevism." The words "Leninist" and "Martovist" emerged in 1904, but the terms "Bolshevik" and "Menshevik" did not become widespread until the end of the year, and the distinction between old and new supporters of *Iskra* was more common. Even in 1905, Bolshevik publications came out under the name of *Vpered*, the Geneva newspaper, or of the "V. Bonch-Bruevich and N. Lenin Publishing House for Social Democratic Party Literature." Lenin himself did not use the term "Bolshevism" until late 1907.[57]

Bolshevism had little organizational or political identity until the revolution of 1905. By the time the term "Bolshevism" came into use, it encompassed both Lenin's exile circle in Geneva and Bogdanov's network inside Russia, and represented an uneasy alliance between Leninists and collectivists in both philosophy and politics. Lenin's Marxist orthodoxy and Bogdanov's Machist collectivism were mutually necessary, and ultimately competitive, doctrines of political organization, often couched in the language of science. Together they formed Bolshevism.

III

SELF-SACRIFICE

GORKY'S NEW MONEY AND MOSCOW'S OLD BELIEVERS

Even though he sacrifices his life, the basis of the sacrifice is personal calculation or an intense burst of egoistic passion. Most cases of so-called self-sacrifice do not deserve that name.

—N. G. CHERNYSHEVSKY

The self-sacrificing man is more blind and cruel than others.

—L. N. TOLSTOY

Among the Russian people there can always be found ten persons who are so dedicated to their ideas and who so warmly feel the misfortunes of their motherland that for them it appears no sacrifice to die for their cause.

—ALEXANDER ULYANOV, 1887

Bolshevism came into existence with considerable support from wealthy Russian sympathizers. Life in European exile was a perpetual hand-to-mouth existence, and by late 1904 Lenin was desperate for funding to create a new organization and a new party journal. Despite his antipathy to religion, Lenin willingly accepted financial support from the wealthy Old Believer community of Moscow, with the aid of Bogdanov. Christian self-sacrifice pervaded the kenoticism and asceticism of the Russian orthodox church. During the 1905 revolution the Bolsheviks appealed to this tradition by funding their operations with the aid of Russian capitalists, notably Gorky's friends among the Morozov family. Financially, Bolshevism originated in the largesse and spirit of self-sacrifice of the very sector of Russian society it hoped to expropriate. And the arbiters of these finances were Bogdanov and Leonid Krasin, not Lenin.

The events of Bloody Sunday in January 1905 caught the Bolsheviks unprepared and divided between Lenin's émigré circle around *Vpered*

49

(Forward) in Geneva and an emerging Russian underground network headed by Bogdanov and Krasin. For Lenin, the major source of funding appeared to be the Socialist Party of Germany (SPD). Since 1903, SPD leaders such as Karl Liebknecht had assisted Russian social democrats in smuggling copies of *Iskra* into Russia, providing legal aid for arrested party members, and establishing safe houses to help them avoid the Okhrana. They also fought the German government's attempts to expel Russian students and socialists as "undesirable aliens." Yet by late 1904 SPD head August Bebel was frustrated by the deepening division between Bolshevik and Menshevik fractions of the RSDRP. Bebel began working toward an SPD policy that would dominate Russian–German relations for the next decade, namely, to make SPD aid to the RSDRP conditional upon the unification of the rival fractions into a single party.[1]

SPD support widened, rather than narrowed, the RSDRP schism. The Menshevik leader Paul Axelrod warned his friend Karl Kautsky that the Bolsheviks were "Bonapartists" and "Jacobins," heirs of the radical tradition of Russian Populism who sought to make party organization into a fetish. For Axelrod, Lenin was a dictator and centralist whose methods mirrored those of the Russian political police.[2] Lenin repaid Menshevik criticism in kind. In January 1905 A. M. Essen wrote that the RSDRP was in a state of crisis, "divided into two parts. On the one side stand all the Russian *praktiki*, and on the other, our foreign émigrés (Plekhanov, Axelrod, and the other editors of *Iskra*)." There were really two parties now, he warned, an émigré center around *Iskra* in Geneva without committees inside Russia and "the literary group of N. Lenin" around *Vpered* which controlled a "majority of committees" inside Russia. He did not use the terms Bolshevik or Menshevik.[3]

About the same time, Leonid Krasin wrote Lenin that he had met with Kautsky in Berlin about RSDRP party finances. Kautsky insisted that the two fractions make peace. Axelrod complained to Kautsky about the "Leninist clique in the party" which had created "demoralization and madness." In Berlin, Bolsheviks and Mensheviks engaged in separate fund-raising activities. More important, by early February 1905 the SPD had raised some ten thousand marks for the Russian Revolution and given it to Axelrod for the RSDRP; Axelrod had retained the money for the Mensheviks, who controlled the party central committee. Despite Lenin's complaint that "we have a right to part of this sum," the Mensheviks appeared to control funds obtained from the SPD. Bebel proposed that both fractions now submit their disputes to a five-man SPD court of arbitration. Axelrod and the Mensheviks at a February 7 meeting agreed to Bebel's offer of mediation, asking that Klara Zetkin and Kautsky be the arbiters of disputed funds.[4] But Lenin declined the offer. Yet the notion that the SPD might be the arbiter of RSDRP funds was to be revived five years later, in 1910, under circumstances even less favorable to Lenin.

Lenin reacted to Bloody Sunday with great excitement. Here was revolutionary opportunity, but opportunity that the Bolsheviks were as yet ill prepared to seize. When Father Gapon arrived in Geneva, Lenin plied him with questions about the mood of the masses in St. Petersburg. Energy, not talk, was needed, felt Lenin, especially the energy of youth. Krupskaya immediately wrote to the party committee in Petersburg asking what Bogdanov was doing and urging them to reprint an article from *Vpered*, to be written in invisible ink in a subsequent letter. Lenin urged the Moscow committee to improve its correspondence with Geneva, using invisible ink between the lines of books. Yet Krupskaya constantly complained that correspondence arrived late, poorly addressed, with the codes and ciphers muddled up. Cryptography often further confused party organization inside Russia.[5]

Ousted from the RSDRP central committee, Lenin began working through Bogdanov and Krasin inside Russia to convene a third party congress, which he hoped would be dominated by Bolsheviks. "We need young forces," he wrote Bogdanov; "I would advise shooting on the spot anyone who says there are no such people. From the dark people of Russia we must recruit the youth more boldly and broadly that ever before, without fearing them. . . . Young people will determine the outcome of the struggle, young students and especially young workers."[6] By March the *Vpered* office in Geneva had a list of some 260 addresses inside Russia for correspondence. Yet Lenin's revolutionary organization remained inchoate and incomplete.

In April 1905 the third RSDRP congress convened in London. Many of the delegates were Bolsheviks recruited inside Russia by Bogdanov, but, as Axelrod pointed out to Kautsky, "many of the so-called 'hards' are definitely opponents of Lenin." The Geneva exiles were increasingly out of touch with events inside Russia. Geneva, Krasin pointed out, was *zagranitsy*, out of the country and out of contact; the émigrés were a "barrier hindering further correct development of the party." Krasin hoped that "as many comrades as possible will rapidly join us in Russia" and concluded that "a united RSDRP can only be created by concentrating our greatest forces inside Russia, around a Russian center. We must expend our energy in this direction, and make the Russian center the real center of our party life, placing at its disposal as much material support and literary talent as necessary."[7]

In late May 1905 Bebel wrote Axelrod that "the German comrades are growing increasingly dissatisfied with the ever widening schism among Russian social democrats."[8] He warned that future financial support was jeopardized by the schism. Yet the Menshevik and Bolshevik fractions were becoming increasingly divided, ideologically and geographically, between émigré Geneva and revolutionary Russia. Until his return to St. Petersburg in November 1905 Lenin, too, would remain an exile, and the main work of securing financial support of the Bolsheviks would be carried on inside Russia, not outside. Bogdanov and Krasin proved masters of the art of fund raising and the politics of self-sacrifice.

Maxim Gorky and the Origins of *Vpered*

In 1902 Lenin discoverd that the Russian writer Maxim Gorky was sympathetic to the radical socialist parties of Russia, including the Social Revolutionaries and the RSDRP. "Everything you wrote about Gorky is very welcome," he wrote an RSDRP agent in Moscow, "especially since money is desperately needed." The agent, code-named Natasha, had been sent to Moscow from Geneva on Lenin's orders to cultivate Gorky, who had donated some money to *Iskra* in 1901. In October 1902 she reported that Gorky wanted "to help us however he can, mainly with money, of course." The result was that Gorky agreed to provide an annual contribution of five thousand rubles to the RSDRP, four thousand to *Iskra* and one thousand to the Moscow party committee.[9]

In breaking with the Mensheviks, Lenin had cut himself off from the major source of RSDRP financial support. His goal immediately became to recruit Gorky as a donor for the emerging Bolshevik fraction and its new journal, *Vpered*. On December 3, 1904, Lenin wrote Bogdanov that "to delay the foreign organ of the majority (for which only the money is needed) is inexcusable; whatever has happened, the amount of money we need, a few thousand, must be obtained to get started, or we shall fail." Ten days later the Geneva Bolsheviks resolved to bring out *Vpered* as the weekly journal of "the majority," and Lenin and Krupskaya fired off a number of letters to sympathetic party members requesting contributions to a *kush* or slush fund.[10]

The main hope for funds from inside Russia was Bogdanov. On December 15 Krupskaya wrote Bogdanov that Gorky wanted to meet him and that Gorky should be given a code name, despite his "lack of a conspiratorial sense." On December 30 she repeated to Bogdanov the complaint about a "terrible lack of money" and the complete schism with the Mensheviks and urged him to make contacts with "the Muscovites." In the meantime Bogdanov had written Lenin that Gorky "will give immediately three thousand rubles for our organ and promises even more in the future. . . . At the congress he will give another five thousand and promises to use all his connections to provide security on the material side." In late December 1904 Gorky sent Bogdanov a check for seven hundred rubles; on January 19, 1905, he followed with another three thousand. The Bolsheviks were solvent.[11]

As a consequence of Gorky's generosity, the Bolsheviks were able to bring out the first and second issues of *Vpered* in January 1905. As Lenin pointed out in a letter to Bogdanov, Russian support greatly helped the Geneva publication:

We have finally started *Vpered*. The day after tomorrow number two comes out. The reception has been favorable and everyone is very efficient here. We think everything will turn out fine as long as we are not bankrupt. (We need 400 francs [150 rubles] for each number but we have only 1200 in all).

In these first months our need is hellish, since if we don't have an accurate output, then the whole position of the majority suffers a great, hardly beneficial, blow. (Don't forget this and drag out a little more, especially from Gorky.)[12]

At the same time Lenin was frustrated by Bogdanov's lack of communication. He wrote Litvinov that Bogdanov should be scolded for only writing twice in the past month "not a line for *Vpered*. Not a word about affairs, plans, connections."[13]

In fact, Bogdanov had been overtaken by the rush of events as the massacre of innocent Russian petitioners by the Tsar's troops on January 22, 1905, ushered in a more radical phase of the revolution. Bloody Sunday marked the end of naive monarchism and faith in tsarist benevolence in the eyes of the Russian peasant and worker. It also provided Lenin and his Geneva circle with a signal for revolutionary action that found them quite unprepared. Events inside Russia outran Marxist theories in exile. Until November 1905 Lenin remained abroad and was therefore often out of touch with the dramatic events now unfolding inside Russia.

The Politics of Self-Sacrifice

Bolshevik collectivism had roots in long-standing Russian values of individual self-sacrifice. The suffering, martyrdom, humility, and sacrifice of Christ was deeply embedded in the texture of Russian religious thought and practice, and the lives of Russian saints were a litany of suffering. The Old Believers, heretics in the eyes of the official church for their adherence to their own version of the truth, suffered persecution for centuries at the hands of the government and sought escape in mass immolation, colonization, and, finally, economic mutual aid.

The Russian intelligentsia also exhibited a persistent delight in sacrificing the interests of the individual for the good of the collective, living and dead, past and future. "Outside our circle," wrote the literary critic Vissarion Belinsky in 1841, "I have met excellent men of greater actuality than ourselves; but nowhere have I come upon men with such an insatiable thirst for life, with such enormous demands on it, and with such capacities for self-sacrifice for the sake of an idea. . . . Social solidarity or death," concluded Belinsky, "that is my motto."[14]

In his *Historical Letters*, written in 1869, Peter Lavrov called for a new generation of revolutionary heroes who would lose their individuality in the collective struggle for justice. "Vigorous, fanatical men are needed, who will risk everything and are prepared to sacrifice everything. Martyrs are needed, whose legend will far outgrow their true worth and their actual service." The anarchist Michael Bakunin also urged "clear thinking and collective action." "A voluntary, absolutely conscious and completely unforced sacrifice of oneself for the sake of all is," wrote Dostoevsky in 1863, "a sign of the highest development of individual personality, its highest power, highest self-possession, and highest freedom of individual will."[15]

In the 1870s Russian Populism produced numerous martyrs for the people, the *narod*, young men and women of high ideals who sacrificed family and career for a life of clandestine revolutionary activity. For them immortality lay in the collective remembrance of great deeds, such as the murder of Tsar Alexander II in 1881. Russian Marxism had articulated the sacrifice of individual happiness for the class struggle. Plekhanov wrote: "Morality is founded on the striving not for personal happiness, but for the happiness of the whole: the clan, the people, the class, humanity. This striving has nothing in common with egoism. On the contrary, it always presupposes a greater or lesser degree of self-sacrifice."[16] Another convert from Populism to Marxism, Vera Zasulich, also urged the development of an ethos of collective "solidarity" of the proletariat through self-sacrifice, as opposed to the more authoritarian and Jacobin tendency embodied in the writings of both Marx and Lenin.[17]

Finally, Father Gapon, the priest who achieved great influence among St. Petersburg workers after 1900, articulated the vision of self-sacrifice as a link between Christianity and the labor movement.

> Is it not my duty to sacrifice myself, my own "I," for the sake and peace of those who brought me up? I also fathomed another truth—self-sacrifice. No wonder the symbol of our life is a cross. Only self-sacrifice of serious and enduring efforts for the welfare and spiritual peace of those closest to you as well as neighbors can bring an individual the so-called relative happiness, i.e., self-satisfaction. If an individual became permeated with this idea, he could be reconciled with the idea of predestination, with the yoke prepared for him by Life.[18]

Gapon's speeches mesmerized thousands of Petersburg workers in the period leading up to Bloody Sunday and moved them in the language of the orthodox church, not Marxism. The Bolsheviks slowly realized that the most effective appeal was one which began, not with a quotation from Marx, but with the phrase "Father Gapon says."

Maxim Gorky also expressed the spirit of self-sacrifice in his plays and novels. At the turn of the century Gorky was one of Russia's best-known writers, a man of impoverished origins from the river trading town of Nizhny Novgorod. His writings evoked the broad soul of peasant Russia and the rapid growth of the new industrial towns with their restive proletariat and rising merchant and business classes. Gorky's realistic and unvarnished portrait of Russian life among the "lower depths" of society, his reputation as a writer, and his financial success all made him a target of emerging radical political parties in Russia, parties that needed support. Both Gorky and Maria Andreeva were sympathetic to the Social Revolutionaries and the RSDRP after 1900, and Gorky soon became a crucial source of support for the Bolsheviks, as he had been for the RSDRP.

In 1902 Maria Andreeva became extremely active collecting funds for arrested students and organizing concerts to raise money for the radical movement, including *Iskra*. She was also a personal friend of several future Bolshevik leaders, notably L. B. Krasin, N. E. Bauman, and Yurii Krzhizhanovsky. In 1903 Gorky put Krasin in touch with the wealthy manager of an estate in Ufimsk, A. D. Tsiurupa, who became an RSDRP contributor. Gorky sent his own donations to Krasin in Baku. By 1904 Gorky and Andreeva were well known to the Okhrana, which described Gorky as a "very unreliable man politically" and searched Andreeva's apartment for evidence that the Moscow Art Theater was a source of funds for *Iskra*.[19]

In early 1904 Andreeva separated from her husband and began living with Gorky in a civil marriage. She also joined the RSDRP and in the autumn of 1904 established contact with Litvinov in Riga, where she was performing in Chekhov's "Uncle Vania" with the Moscow Art Theater. Between October and mid-December 1904, Gorky and Andreeva lived in Litvinov's apartment. Through Litvinov they first heard of Lenin's ouster from the RSDRP and of the emergence of a new Bolshevik fraction. By late December, M. N. Liadov had arrived in Riga from Geneva and persuaded Gorky that he should contribute money to help establish *Vpered*.[20]

Krasin was the conduit for Gorky's contributions to the Bolsheviks. On January 11, 1905, Gorky noted that he had sent Krasin's brother Hermann, in Moscow, a check for two thousand rubles for *Vpered*. Two weeks later the Okhrana dutifully informed its Paris branch that "Gorky gave the central committee of the party a monthly subsidy of two thousand rubles, of which one thousand came from him personally and one thousand was collected by him from his friends." The Okhrana also observed that Bogdanov—"by profession a physician"—was sending Gorky's money to Lenin in Geneva, seven hundred rubles in December and three thousand more in January. The police were thus well informed about Bolshevik finances from the beginning.[21]

Shortly after Bloody Sunday, Gorky was arrested in connection with Gapon's activities and incarcerated in the dread Peter and Paul Fortress in St. Petersburg. The result was an international outcry against the imperial government, which together with the payment of ten thousand rubles bail by Gorky's wealthy friend, Savva Morozov, resulted in the famous writer's release from jail. Exhausted by their ordeal, Gorky and Andreeva left to recuperate in the Crimea.

Throughout 1905 Gorky became more deeply committed to the revolutionary movement growing inside Russia. In June he wrote a long letter to the priest Gapon, leader of the petitioners on Bloody Sunday, arguing that "the worker has no friends except workers, so the whole working class must be organized as a family." The working class must not depend on the intelligentsia for its leadership, argued Gorky, a view that Lenin considered to be "sentimental socialism." "Only socialism renews life in this world," wrote Gorky, "and it must become the religion of the working man." He continued:

> We don't need an independent workers' party separate from the intelligentsia, but we must involve the largest possible number of conscious workers in the party, workers whose minds are unprejudiced and whose class consciousness has developed, become clear, and created a new man.[22]

Gorky's idea of a workers' party transforming society through a socialist religion was not shared by Lenin. But Lenin did share with Gorky an enthusiasm for the peasant as an agent of democratic and revolutionary change, and a desire for an organization that would prevent a repetition of the sacrifices of Bloody Sunday.

Gapon, in his January 1905 petition to the Tsar, had fueled Gorky's fire of enthusiasm with his rhetoric of sacrifice:

> We have reached that frightful moment when death is better than the prolongation of our unbearable sufferings. . . . Would it not be preferable for all of us, the toiling masses of Russia, to die? Let the capitalists and officials, the embezzlers and plunderers of the Russian people, live and enjoy their lives. . . . Do not turn Thy help from Thy people. Lead them out from the grave of lawlessness, poverty, and ignorance. . . . There are two paths before us: one to freedom and happiness, the other into the grave. Sire, show us either of them and we will follow it, even if it leads to death. Let our lives be a sacrifice for suffering Russia. We do not regret this sacrifice, but offer it willingly.[23]

Gapon's call for self-sacrifice also provided an opportunity for Bolshevik self-promotion.

By the end of 1905 Gorky had established a number of publishing operations designed to enrich the Bolshevik treasury. Since 1902, Gorky had allowed his works to be translated by the "Slavic and Northern Literature House" in Munich, operated by two émigré socialists, Julian Marchlewski and Alexander Helphand (Parvus). According to the original agreement, Parvus and Gorky would each keep twenty percent of the income from this operation, and the remaining sixty percent would go to the RSDRP. But Gorky had received neither royalties nor an accounting from Parvus and was taking him to court. In September 1905 Gorky and Bonch-Bruevich seized the initiative and set up another publishing house, Demos, in Geneva; the purpose was to obtain money for the Bolsheviks by publishing Russian works in translation in Europe. In December 1905 Demos was moved to Berlin and reestablished as the publishing house of Gorky's friend I. P. Ladyzhnikov, again to raise money for the RSDRP.[24]

Throughout 1905 Gorky pursued a variety of schemes, including a "cheap library" for workers that would utilize publishing operations to disseminate socialist literature and simultaneously enrich the RSDRP treasury. The legal Bolshevik journal *Novaya Zhizn'* (New Life), published in St. Petersburg in late 1905 was one product of Gorky's efforts. Another was the use of the Znanie publishing house for the RSDRP's Central Committee to publish in large numbers the "cheap library" books for workers. An agreement between Znanie and the Bolsheviks, represented by Krasin, was duly signed in October 1905, and a second legal journal, *Bor'ba* (Struggle), printed in Moscow.[25]

All of this was complicated by the fact that in December 1905 Ladyzhnikov accused Parvus of embezzling 130,000 marks from the RSDRP and violating the 1902 agreement to publish Russian literary translations abroad and provide party funds. Parvus had disappeared to Italy with his mistress and the party's share of the money. Lenin, Gorky, and Krasin demanded a party court of arbitration to bring Parvus to heel, and Gorky promised that Parvus's political career was finished. Instead Parvus joined Trotsky in developing the theory of "permanent revolution," based on the experience of 1905.[26]

Despite these complications, by the spring of 1906 Znanie had succeeded in publishing thirty-six books and brochures with a total circulation of some seven hundred thousand copies. *Novaya Zhizn'* also achieved a substantial circulation (50,000) but was outdone by the far larger circulation of Parvus's and Trotsky's *Russkaya Gazeta* (Russian journal). The literature of the Petersburg soviet, or workers' council, of 1905 thus proved far more popular than the legal Marxism of a divided RSDRP.[27]

Gorky also began to work out his theory of "god building," the notion that socialism could become a surrogate religion for the masses. Life, he wrote, is a "struggle of masters for authority and of slaves for emancipation from the yoke of that authority." In contrast to the soul-destroying culture of the West, Russia was a "god bearer" (*bogonosets*) among all peoples. The world of modern capitalism and the bourgeoisie was a world of individualism in which the "I" is always at the center, whereas socialists should strive to create a world of the collective, mankind, the people. Russian passivity and suffering should give way to a new heroism of the masses, too long deceived and suppressed by the church, the state, and the power of capital. "Only the people," wrote

Gorky, "have the energy of youth and the pathos of heroism, only the people's strength, the eternal source of living energy can resurrect the country for a new life."[28]

Gorky's philosophy of self-sacrifice was most clearly enunciated in 1906 in his novel *Mother*. The hero of the novel, Pavel, carries the invincible faith of both socialism and Christianity in his breast. Using the metaphors of the Christ-like collective, the revolutionaries write pamphlets for the village, "so the people will die for the cause." As Rybin puts it, "let thousands of us die to resurrect millions of people all over the earth! That's what! Dying's easy for the sake of resurrection! If only the people rise!"[29]

Throughout Gorky's novel runs a strong current of religious martyrdom in which a bright socialist future will provide immortality for the individual through the collective memory. The individual revolutionary martyr can never die, because individual deeds live on in memory of others. And the reward of self-sacrifice lies in the future kingdom of justice. More than any other writer of the day, Gorky fused the traditional Russian vision of Christian collectivism with the new vision of industrial socialism appearing in revolutionary Russia. In so doing he became a key link between the manipulators of self-sacrifice, the Bolsheviks, and the Old Believer capitalists of Moscow.

Morozov Money and Bolshevik Finances

A major source of Bolshevik funds in the formative years of the fraction was the wealthy Moscow merchant Savva Timofeevich Morozov.[30] The leader of the Morozov merchant dynasty of wealthy Old Believers, Savva Morozov had contributed hundreds of thousands of rubles to the Moscow Art Theater and numerous other causes. Endowed with flashing eyes, a brusque voice, and an easy laugh, Morozov was an ebullient man of tremendous energy and willpower whose shrewd and calculating mind and enormous fortune enabled him to snub grand dukes and pursue his own interests with impunity. Among these interests were Maxim Gorky and the Bolsheviks.

Savva Morozov was a progressive industrialist. Since 1857, the Morozov textile mills in the town of Orekhovo-Zuevo near Tver had produced everything from army uniforms to calico dresses. After a strike in 1885 and his father's death in 1889, Savva made every effort to insure the well-being of his own workers—new homes, good medical care, safety equipment, shorter working hours, and no punitive fines for misdemeanors on the job. The formation of an RSDRP committee in Tver and another strike in the factory in February 1904 pushed Morozov further in the direction of improving labor conditions and cooperating with the very socialism that sought to overturn his capitalist enterprise.

He instituted a profit-sharing plan for his workers and made friends with Gorky, neither of which appealed to his mother, Maria Fedorovna, the major shareholder in the Morozov family operations.

Gorky first met Morozov in 1904 as a patron of the Moscow Art Theater and was struck by his Tatar face, his doctrine of hard work, and his interest in the organizing power of ideas. An occasional reader of Marx, Morozov was also familiar with chemistry and the new developments in nuclear physics. He viewed revolution as an inevitable part of Russia's westernization and modernization in the industrial age. Only workers organized in a socialist manner, felt Morozov, could effectively oppose the more dangerous and destructive forces of peasant anarchism in Russia. Only western science and technology could harness the tremendous "potential energy" of Russia. Since 1902 Morozov had been donating two thousand rubles a month to the RSDRP and *Iskra*. In 1905 the Bolsheviks were determined to divert this generosity and self-sacrifice through Gorky to their own benefit.

In the winter of 1904–1905 Krasin, the Bolshevik electrical engineer who worked in one of Morozov's factories, asked Gorky to approach Morozov about donating to the Bolshevik cause. Morozov, as a reader of *Iskra*, was already familiar with some of Lenin's ideas and agreed to meet with Gorky and Krasin to discuss the matter. At the meeting Morozov offered to provide twenty thousand rubles a year to the Bolsheviks; Krasin boldly replied that twenty-four thousand rubles was a more appropriate figure. Thus began the monthly two-thousand-ruble donations funneled from Morozov via Gorky to Krasin, Bogdanov, and eventually Lenin.[31]

After the revolution Krasin recalled that "it was considered a sign of status in radical or liberal circles to give money to the revolutionary parties, and among those who made monthly donations of five to twenty-five rubles were not only wealthy lawyers, engineers, and doctors but also directors of banks and government officials."[32] Morozov, Krasin noted, contributed regularly to the party, the last time two days before his suicide on May 13, 1905, in a sanatorium near Cannes, France.

Morozov's ultimate self-sacrifice was probably due to his mother's decision to remove him as director of the Morozov enterprises in April 1905. In mid-April Maria Andreeva wrote that Morozov was in a deep depression, isolated from friends, neglecting his daily affairs, refusing to answer correspondence. In May Morozov sought refuge in the French sanatorium, where Krasin found him to be cheerful but deranged. Morozov told Krasin: "I know that you did not make such a long journey simply to inquire about my health." Krasin admitted that "the party needs money, lots of money," upon which Morozov thrust out a package saying "here is everything I have."[33]

Two days later Morozov shot himself through the heart. His grief-stricken workers believed that Morozov had not died, but had given away his vast wealth and taken up the life of a wandering Christ-like holy man, traveling through Russia and spreading the true word among other factory workers. Gorky and Andreeva felt they had lost a noble friend and a great man, a man of energy and resourcefulness, but also a man easily influenced by others. "Like all very rich men," wrote Andreeva, "he was very distrustful, suspicious, and stingy with people, but, once convinced, gave up his soul and rewarded a relationship for any small favor given to him."[34] In the case of Bolshevism, Morozov in the end sacrificed his money, his soul, and his life.

The suicide of Savva Morozov did not mean the end of Morozov contributions to the Bolshevik treasury. At the third RSDRP congress in April 1905, Krasin pointed out that expenses were now running over six thousand rubles a month; "the committees have not paid the central committee, there are no systematic contributions, and the central committee cannot even establish a budget." Regular contributions were essential, said Krasin, and the party "must live by its own means, and not on bourgeois charity."[35] Yet in the spring of 1905 bourgeois charity was keeping the Bolsheviks going.

The place of Savva Morozov was now taken by N. P. Schmidt, a young nephew of Morozov, who had just come of age to inherit the Morozov furniture factory in Moscow. Both Morozov and Gorky were mentors of Schmidt, who read the works of Marx and Lenin, encouraged the Bolsheviks to send agitators into his factory, and used his wealth to improve working conditions. Schmidt's radical enthusiams were shared by his younger brothers and sisters, Ekaterina, Elizabeth, and Aleksei. Together this family circle of very young and very wealthy Morozovs constituted a veritable treasury on which the Bolsheviks hoped to lay hands as soon as possible. According to Ekaterina, the "revolutionary wave submerging Russia swept over us," and she became active in Marxist women's circles and the RSDRP committee in Moscow.[36]

On May 1, 1905, N. P. Schmidt reduced the work day in his factory from 11 1/2 to 8 hours. He also raised wages, introduced a fund to reimburse workers who were either sick or on strike, and opened a hospital inside the plant. Shortly thereafter Schmidt also became involved with the Moscow Bolsheviks and with Gorky. By October 1905 Gorky persuaded him to contribute fifteen thousand rubles as a loan with which Gorky could publish the legal Bolshevik journal *Novayia zhizn'*.[37]

The revolutionary wave that inundated Russia in early 1905 provided the Bolsheviks with a flood of new sympathizers, especially in the wake of Bloody Sunday. Men like Krasin, Bogdanov, and Gorky moved easily in the well-to-do circles of Moscow and St. Petersburg, and were persuasive in their efforts to find wealthy donors. Morozov and Schmidt did not understand the fine points of socialist ideology or politics, but they did see in the Bolsheviks a party of energy and will capable of organized action against the hated tsarist regime. Bolshevik organization and fund raising thus met with great success because of the propensity for self-sacrifice articulated by Gorky, Morozov, and Schmidt. For all their European and Marxist rhetoric, the Bolsheviks thus laid claim to a rich Russian inheritance.

Engineer of Revolution: Leonid Krasin

Leonid Borisovich Krasin (1870–1926) was one of the most remarkable Bolshevik leaders before and after 1917. As a Russian, his wife Liubov later observed, he exhibited "the preeminent national characteristic— readiness for self-sacrifice."[38] The Bolsheviks were supposed to be full-time professional revolutionaries; Krasin was an electrical engineer by day and a revolutionary in his off-hours. From the time he entered the St. Petersburg Technological Institute in 1887 until his death, Krasin was a major figure in the history of Russian social democracy, a middle-class professional engineer capable of organizing both charity and expropria- tion as mechanisms of self-sacrifice profitable for the Bolshevik treasury.

Krasin, like so many of his generation, became a Marxist in the 1890s, and first met Lenin in the socialist circle of M. I. Brusnev at the St. Petersburg Technical Institute. After a typical period of arrest, exile, and parental rescue, Krasin completed his engineering education at the Kharkov Technical Institute in 1900. He also worked part-time on the Trans-Siberian Railroad, then under construction. In June 1900 Krasin arrived in the sprawling and violent oil town of Baku on the Caspian Sea, where he went to work for another Marxist electrical engineer, R. E. Classon. Here they designed, constructed, and operated an electrical generating station for the oil industry. They also became involved in the Marxist circles of Baku and in smuggling copies of the new RSDRP journal *Iskra* from Europe into the Caucasus.

In 1901 Krasin set up an underground printing press in Baku to print illegal literature in Russian, German, Georgian, and Armenian. This secret printing operation was not known to either the police or the local RSDRP committee, and operated successfully until 1907. Here the technical know-how and financial aid of Krasin in matters of typesetting, paper, matrices, and inks combined with his revolutionary enthusiasms to produce a remarkable underground press. In October 1903 Krasin was coopted into the RSDRP central committee, and took over the key job of fund raising for the party. Even more important, two months later Krasin obtained through Gorky an interview with Savva Morozov, from which came both a two-thousand-ruble monthly contribution to the RSDRP and Krasin's new job as manager of the Morozov factory power station at Orekhovo-Zuevo. In addition, Krasin succeeded in finding another wealthy source of revolutionary donations in the person of the actress Vera Kommissarzhevskaya, whom he met in Baku in 1903 and whose box office receipts helped keep the underground press operating.

By the summer of 1904 Krasin was running the Morozov power plant at Orekhovo-Zuevo. He was also under Okhrana surveillance as a well-known social democrat fund raiser, who received substantial donations from well-to-do lawyers, doctors, bankers, and engineers, as well as from his employer, Savva Morozov. In July 1904 Krasin attended a meeting of RSDRP committeemen in Moscow, where party factionalism was condemned and Lenin was deprived of his position on the central committee for attacking the Mensheviks.

The relationship between Morozov and Krasin was one of mutual admiration. For Krasin, Morozov was a thoroughly westernized Russian with great entrepreneurial drive and spirit, a "new type with a great future." For Morozov, Krasin was an "ideal worker" and leader; "if one had thirty such men, they could create a party stronger than the German one," felt Morozov. Both Krasin and Morozov believed that Russia could only achieve real progress through a combination of revolution and industrialism.[39]

Bloody Sunday produced a sympathy strike at the Morozov plant, but Krasin was not there. Rather, he witnessed the dramatic violence in St. Petersburg, and shortly thereafter attended a meeting of the RSDRP central committee in Moscow at Andreeva's apartment. After Gorky's arrest, Krasin fled to Geneva. He then accompanied Lenin to London in April 1905 for the third party congress. Here he contacted other Bolshevik leaders, including Bogdanov and Lunacharsky, before going on to Cannes to see Savva Morozov. Shortly after Krasin's visit, the wealthy and tormented Morozov committed suicide, leaving some one hundred thousand rubles to Maria Andreeva, who gave it to the Bolsheviks.[40]

Krasin, not Lenin, initiated Bolshevik plans for armed units capable of striking against the Russian government in 1905. In January he set up under the central committee a "Military Technical Group" (*Boevaia tekhnicheskaia gruppa*) to supervise the illegal tasks of the party: gunrunning, explosives purchase and construction, and the arming of workers. Hand grenades, rifles, and dynamite were purchased in Western Europe and smuggled into St. Petersburg by the northern route via Stockholm and Helsinki. At one point Krasin even designed a bomb, although most work was carried out by two chemists code-named Alpha and Omega. A bomb laboratory was set up in Gorky's apartment in Moscow and protected by Georgian bodyguards. Weapons were obtained from France, Bulgaria, and Macedonia.[41]

For Krasin, Bloody Sunday revealed a pressing need for action inside Russia, not émigré arguments in distant Geneva. At a meeting of the Moscow RSDRP committee in early February, Krasin recalled that "we considered it irrelevant to waste money and time, and to risk sending dozens of people abroad, in order to clear up what seemed to us to be inessential petty squabbles in Geneva between Lenin and his friends on one side and Plekhanov and the Menshevik 'Iskraites' on the other."[42]

By the spring of 1905 Krasin had returned to Russia and joined Andreeva in plotting to transfer her funds as beneficiary from Morozov's life insurance policy to the party treasury. By now Krasin's role in the emergence of Bolshevism was taking shape; he would be the central figure inside Russia in procuring funds and weapons. In so doing he would prove to be a master in the art of transforming Russian self-sacrifice into Bolshevik financial solvency.

A. V. Lunacharsky and the Religion of Self-Sacrifice

> Communism places man in his proper place. . . . Man as collectivist is immortal. Only the individual is mortal.
>
> —A. V. LUNACHARSKY, February 1918

A. V. Lunacharsky was another Bolshevik who saw great possibilities in appealing to the Russian penchant for self-sacrifice. Lunacharsky was a Marxist journalist and literary critic who absorbed much of the collectivist philosophy of his brother-in-law, Alexander Bogdanov, along with European positivism and socialism. For Lunacharsky, revolution meant not simply a political insurrection or the triumph of class struggle but the creation of a new proletarian culture, a surrogate religion of science that would some day enable man to conquer even death.[43]

Lunacharsky's religion of humanity flourished in his cultural activities after the revolution, when he became commissar of public enlightenment and an architect of the Lenin cult. Lunacharsky felt that death did not exist for a believing positivist. Death could be vanquished by the collective eternal memory of the transient individual. In 1918 Lunacharsky, mourning the death of another Bolshevik leader, said that "such men do not die; they rise from their graves in full armor, giants. Such victims never stay buried." The Christ-like Bolshevik hero had "acquired life eternal" and "gone into the sleep of the immortals." "Such men are immortal," added Lunacharsky, "they are unkillable. They give their whole heart to a cause which is eternal."[44]

The parallel between European socialism and early Christianity was commonplace after the turn of the century, mainly through the writings of the leading German Marxist theoretician, Karl Kautsky. For Kautsky, early Christianity was a proletarian revolution against the slave economy of the Roman Empire. The widespread belief in the resurrection of the dead and the coming of the kingdom of God was a useful myth employed by both Jews and Christians. Jesus had died, but achieved his immortality through the church; socialist parties would carry on the work of self-sacrificing heroes of the labor movement.[45]

There were other influences as well. From Ernst Renan, Lunacharsky acquired the notion that progress in history meant the scientific organization of humanity. Human knowledge and reason would ultimately "organize God" and provide a new priesthood of scientists reminiscent of St. Simon and Comte. The French writer Jules Romains also wrote about the great force of the collective and the fact that individuals may die but live on in collective memory; his doctrine of "Unanimisme" was popular in France after 1900 and his "Manuel de Déification" of 1910 articulated the same notions of "god construction" expressed by Bogdanov, Gorky, and Lunacharsky.[46]

Contact with Bogdanov and Berdyaev in exile in Vologda made Lunacharsky a much more eclectic and independent thinker and writer than Lenin imagined a Bolshevik should be. In 1905, in fact, Lenin became an editor and censor of Lunacharsky's prose. When Lunacharsky wrote in *Vpered* in January 1905 that he expected a "general strike organized by social democrats," Lenin scratched out the words "general strike" and inserted "general uprising," Nonetheless, Lunacharsky's utopian and apocalyptic prose came through in his promise that "crowds of workers will march through the streets and squares, and students and city poor people will flock to their red banner." In contrast with Lenin's controlled and Aesopian writing style, Lunacharsky was poetic, ebullient, and romantic; syndicalist myth predominated over party authority as a means to encourage individual self-sacrifice.[47]

Bloody Sunday convinced many Bolsheviks that the Russian people had lost their naive monarchist faith in the tsar and would be receptive to the appeals of socialism. M. N. Liadov was struck by Gapon's appeal to the masses as a "revolutionary people." He joined the march on the Winter Palace and reported the massacre to Bogdanov later. Lunacharsky wrote a pamphlet entitled "How the Petersburg Workers Marched to the Tsar" in which he noted that Gapon acted for "all the poor of Russia." Published by Lenin and Bonch-Bruevich in Geneva, the pamphlet was addressed to peasants inside Russia, who presumably could read it. Lunacharsky urged his readers to refuse to pay taxes or serve in the army, to form revolutionary village committees, to demand their rightful land ownership, and to help overthrow the autocracy. Workers and peasants together should work toward a republic and then the "brotherly society" of socialism. Indeed, there was as much attention to Christ as to Marx in Lunacharsky's pamphleteering. "Christianity, in all its forms, even the purest and most progressive," he wrote, "is the ideology of the downtrodden classes, the hopelessly immobile, those who can expect nothing good on earth and cannot believe in their own powers; Christianity is also a weapon of exploitation." But Gapon had shown that the Christian religion could also mobilize the masses to action.[48]

Lenin did not appreciate Lunacharsky's euphoric reaction to Gapon and his religion of labor. Since Lenin was in Geneva and Lunacharsky was not, Lenin remained a severe editor of Lunacharsky's submissions to *Vpered* in early 1905. For example, Lunacharsky included the following passage in a February 1905 article:

> An organization of professional revolutionaries as a closed and autonomous group—this is pernicious Jacobinism, but a solid and centralized party, closely connected with the proletarian masses, aspiring to enlighten and organize it and guide it by revolutionary demonstrations to its true interests—this is a social democratic party.[49]

Lenin left this passage intact, but insisted on adding a subsequent sentence that noted: "Only hopelessly stupid people could conclude that we are becoming bourgeois Jacobins."

Lunacharsky's enthusiasm for Father Gapon and the politics of self-sacrifice articulated the deeper effect that the 1905 revolution had on the formation of Bolshevism. Founded in exile, Bolshevism as a political organization emerged out of the experience of revolutionary Russia, where its supporters included the proletariat, the professional intelligentsia, and even wealthy merchant sympathizers. Until November 1905 Lenin and Krupskaya remained in Geneva, while Bogdanov, Krasin, and the other Bolsheviks dominated fund raising and publishing inside Russia. For them self-sacrifice and collectivism were deeply stamped with the bloody impressions of that Russian winter, when Marxist theory seemed less relevant than Christian martyrdom in mobilizing the masses and obtaining financial support.

IV

EXPERIENCE:
LEONID KRASIN AND THE
REVOLUTION OF 1905

> The Russian Revolution, if you look at it
> even from a distance, is a splendid
> revolution. It has been going on for a long
> time. You and I shall die some time, but it
> will go on living. Fact. You'll see.
>
> —MAXIM GORKY, 1906

The Russian Revolution of 1905 played a crucial role in the formation of Bolshevism, although the Bolsheviks played only a minor role in the revolution. For syndicalism, the central experience of a revolutionary situation was the general strike. The Bolsheviks, too, in later years would speak of the great "experience" of 1905 as a learning experience based on the labor unrest that swept over Russia that year.

Lenin spent most of the year fulminating in Genevan exile. Only in November did he arrive in St. Petersburg, to discover that the real Bolshevik committee work was being done by Bogdanov and Krasin, and that the émigré Bolshevik-Menshevik split did not deter mutual cooperation at the local level inside Russia. Moreover, the Bolsheviks were more attuned to the syndicalist mood of the urban masses, culminating in a national general strike in October, than they were to Lenin's calls for an armed insurrection. In 1905 Lenin was still immersed in exile politics, while Bolshevism was being shaped by revolutionary experience.

Throughout 1905 Lenin theorized about a revolution in Russia led by a peasant majority, rather than an urban proletarian minority. In April 1905 Lenin called for the "energetic support" of "all revolutionary measures taken by the peasantry," including land seizures. The Mensheviks chided Lenin for his un-Marxist approach, but mass violence that summer tended to confirm Lenin's political sense, if not his doctrinal orthodoxy, laid down in his July pamphlet *Two Tactics of Social Democracy in the Democratic Revolution*. The martyrdom of Bloody Sunday and peasant support for the Social Revolutionaries convinced Lenin that an all-Russian revolution must take advantage of the restive and impoverished village as well as the expanding city. How this was to be done was an open question.[1]

The View from Afar

In the early summer of 1905 Lenin and Krupskaya were increasingly confused about developments inside Russia. After the last issue of *Vpered* came out in Geneva on May 18, Lenin began working to take over the central organ of the RSDRP, *Proletarii*, which began publication that same month. By June Lenin was complaining to comrades inside Russia that the party had no money, that Bogdanov was not writing, and that the International Socialist Bureau (ISB) had given nine thousand francs to Plekhanov to distribute among the rival RSDRP fractions.[2]

German social democrats, in the meantime, were attempting to impose unity on their recalcitrant and fissiparous Russian brethren. The doyen of the SPD, August Bebel, requested such authority from the International Socialist Bureau, noting that the RSDRP was now divided into a number of groups engaged in émigré hair-splitting on doctrinal issues, rather than party work inside Russia. Karl Kautsky, on the other hand, urged Bebel not to call openly for RSDRP unification and argued that Bolshevik-Menshevik differences were really insignificant. Behind the scenes, however, Kautsky admitted that the split was a great misfortune and advocated reconciliation. But in July, Lenin rejected Bebel's proposal for an SPD court of arbitration on the Bolshevik-Menshevik split and demanded that he receive half of the money given to Plekhanov by the ISB.[3]

Lenin was equally irritated with the Bolshevik fraction inside Russia. The RSDRP had no good organization, he complained, no leadership, no unity. What was Bogdanov doing? Was he cooperating with the Mensheviks? The syndicalist Stanislav Volsky was added to the central committee—who was he? Why wasn't Lunacharsky sending more articles for *Proletarii*? And so forth and so on.[4]

On August 2, 1905, Bolsheviks and Mensheviks agreed to divide evenly all foreign contributions to the RSDRP, but the SPD refused to allow this. Instead the Germans proposed a complicated division of funds (Bolsheviks and Mensheviks 22.5% each, Poles 20%, Bund 20%, Letts 15%) which only widened political differences. Throughout Europe, Parvus and other German socialists were collecting funds "for the Russian revolution." Yet Lenin complained to the RSDRP central committee in mid-August that "we have no money. The Germans won't give. If you don't come up with three thousand rubles, we have had it."[5]

The Moscow Literary-Lecture Group

In April 1905 the third RSDRP congress resolved to organize a "literary propaganda group" inside Russia that would create "pamphlet literature for use among the peasantry." Aroused by the excitement and violence of Bloody Sunday, the social democrats called for an armed uprising, mass political strikes, and "temporary combat agreements," with the Socialist Revolutionaries.[6] Consistent with these resolutions, the Moscow committee of the RSDRP began producing mass political literature under the leadership of a circle of Moscow intellectuals.

A central figure in Moscow at the time was the syndicalist writer A. V. Sokolov, who wrote under the name of Stanislav Volsky. In December 1904 Volsky had edited a journal *Golos truda* (Voice of labor) in the town of Rzhev near Moscow. In March 1905 the journal was moved to Moscow because of police surveillance, and placed under the editorship of V. L. Shantser (Marat) (1867–1911). The son of an Austrian engineer, Shantser had been active in Marxist study circles in Odessa in the 1890s before coming to Moscow in 1900 and enjoying the usual indignities of arrest and imprisonment. Shantser knew Bogdanov and Skvortsov (Stepanov) from exile days; he also knew Maxim Gorky, N. P. Schmidt, the young historian M. N. Pokrovsky, and other members of the wealthy Morozov family. Shantser became N. P. Schmidt's spiritual father in matters Marxist and utilized the family library for his research. He also became the chairman of the Moscow RSDRP committee and by 1905 was channeling thousands of rubles each month to the party from wealthy sympathizers.[7]

These increasingly ample funds went to finance the new "literary-lecture group" established in the spring of 1905 by the Moscow RSDRP committee to engage in mass propaganda. The group was established on April 9 at the apartment of P. G. Dauge, and included Pokrovsky; Skvortsov (Stepanov); V. Ya. Kanel, a doctor; M. G. Lunts, a writer; V. M. Shuliatikov (Donat), a literary critic; V. M. Friche; N. A. Rozhkov; and numerous other Moscow intellectuals.[8] Friche was a prolific writer expelled from Moscow University for his Marxist politics, a coeditor of the Moscow *Pravda*, and the translator and editor of Sorel's *Reflections on Violence* (1907).[9]

The Moscow literary group was a diverse collection of Marxist intellectuals, not a party cell. V. M. Shuliatikov had developed a Marxist critique of culture, which he portrayed as a reflection of class struggle. Art, literature, and philosophy were merely a "capricious game" played out by the clash of "material aspirations and interests." Shuliatikov called for a new "proletarian world view," rather than an authoritarian political party, to articulate the interests of the working class. Volsky also felt that ideas were the key to maintaining the proletarian revolution. The proletariat was the self-sacrificing vanguard of the Russian people, and the general strike its mobilizing experience. Marxist ideas, not party ideology, united the Moscow literary group, but the varying interpretations of these ideas often fostered individuality and disunity.[10]

During the summer of 1905, the Moscow committee was able to

establish its own publishing house, Kolokol, thanks to the generosity of a millionaire merchant, E. D. Miagkov. Miagkov gave the RSDRP fifty thousand gold rubles and promised one hundred thousand more, on condition that published literature would be equally divided between Marxist and Populist writers. To ensure this, one series of pamphlets was edited by the RSDRP, a second by the Social Revolutionaries. Proceeds were divided equally between the political parties and the publisher. In this manner the Moscow literary circle had access to a well-funded legal publishing operation. Along with N. P. Schmidt, Miagkov became a major contributor to the Bolshevik cause.[11]

While Lenin languished in Geneva, the Moscow RSDRP committee and its literary group printed numerous pamphlets and journals, presided over a network of 123 committees, cells, and circles operating in the Moscow region, and involved thousands of party members in the organizational work of revolution. In early July 1905 the committee delegated Shantser to visit Geneva and bring Lenin up to date on party affairs inside Russia, and to give him samples of RSDRP literature. The Moscow Bolsheviks were an increasingly active group in 1905 and by no means subservient to Lenin's edicts from afar. Until the dissolution of the Moscow literary group in early 1908, it remained an important source of Bolshevik ideas and political literature, drawn more to collectivist theory than to Leninist authority.[12]

Bogdanov against Lenin

By the summer of 1905 it had become apparent that more Bolsheviks were contributing to Bogdanov's publishing operations inside Russia than to Lenin's émigré *Proletarii*. An official Soviet view of 1959 was that Bogdanov "tried to counterpose the popular journal of the RSDRP central committee, *Rabochii*, edited in Russia, to the central organ of the party, *Proletarii*." Bonch-Bruevich had a different interpretation: Bogdanov was "the editor of the first Bolshevik newspaper, *Vpered*," the author of the majority of the pamphlets (*listovki*) printed illegally inside Russia in 1905 by the Bolsheviks, and the major Bolshevik leader in Russia that year. Lenin himself was alarmed by this development.[13]

In June 1905 Bogdanov wrote Lenin that he had set up a number of legal publishing operations in Russia, including Gorky's Znanie and Miagkov's Kolokol, to provide a safe and unofficial voice for party propaganda. Legal editors would run these operations, and income would go to the party. Bogdanov added that the financial affairs of the RSDRP central committee were rapidly improving because of wealthy donors, and that he had been able to establish a new organ of the committee inside Russia, *Rabochii* (*Worker*), which would appear in August. This organ would be manned by the Moscow literary group.

Gorky was still generous, reported Bogdanov, but the Social Revolutionaries were also wooing him.[14]

In addition to Gorky's legal Znanie publishing house and the journal *Rabochii*, Gorky and Bogdanov were also planning a new legal journal for St. Petersburg, *Novaya zhizn'* (New Life). This greatly disturbed Lenin. When *Rabochii* appeared in August, it called for unity among social democrats, a coalition of peasants and the "revolutionary intelligentsia" against the tsar, and a boycott of the experimental parliament, or Bulygin Duma. Most alarming was news from Bogdanov that plans were under way for a Bolshevik-Menshevik unity congress to heal RSDRP wounds. In a letter of August 14 Lenin was furious about negotiations for such a congress, and especially galled because he was now dependent on funds sent to him from Russia by Bogdanov.[15]

Lenin's frequent demands for money irritated Bogdanov and Krasin. In early September they wrote Lenin that they would send him another thousand rubles, but only at the expense of their work in Russia; "if it is unconditionally impossible to edit *Proletarii* with foreign sources of income and we have to support you on a regular basis," they complained, "then we will soon be bankrupt." In addition, what Lenin considered a right, Bogdanov considered a loan. Bogdanov wrote Lenin "we have less and less money, and the thousands of rubles which we have sent you are a loan that we plan to recover." Bogdanov also refused to send Lenin a record of Bolshevik conversations with the Mensheviks on possible unification, or to heed Lenin's strident calls for an "armed insurrection" from the comfortable distance of Geneva.[16]

By October it was apparent that Bogdanov and his central committee journal *Rabochii* had greater funding and political standing among Bolsheviks than Lenin's *Proletarii*, nominally the central organ of the RSDRP. Bogdanov threatened to reestablish *Proletarii* and not to send money to Lenin, but to use it for "other goals." Lenin had been discussing Bolshevik-Menshevik reunification with the International Socialist Bureau in Brussels, proposing a conference in Berlin with the participation of George Plekhanov to settle matters; Bogdanov was sharply opposed. Finally, in late October 1905, Bogdanov wrote Lenin that he should come to Russia to attend a general meeting of the RSDRP soon, recommending Stockholm and Helsinki as the safest route. Unaccustomed as he was to taking orders, Lenin complied.[17]

Krasin and the *John Grafton*

Illegal Bolshevik operations in 1905, such as gunrunning and bomb construction, were directed by Leonid Krasin from a safe house at Kuokkala on the Finnish border, not far from St. Petersburg. Like Bogdanov, Krasin was the beneficiary of numerous fund-raising efforts,

Leonid Krasin, 1903. From B. G.
Kremnev, *Krasin* (Moscow, 1968).

and operated under the cover of his own legal printing company, Delo.
In the late summer of 1905 Krasin resigned his position with the
Morozov Company and went to work as an engineer for the St.
Petersburg Electrical Society, then busy laying cables for electric streetcars in the city. He also managed to get himself elected as the society's
representative to the St. Petersburg soviet, or workers' council, in
October and assisted Gorky in editing *Novaya zhizn'*. But the most
remarkable of Krasin's many activities in the shadowy world of the 1905
revolution was the episode of the *John Grafton*.[18]

During the Russo-Japanese War of 1904–1905 a Finnish socialist named
Konni Zilliacus contrived to organize various Russian revolutionary
factions with Japanese monetary support. A one-time resident of Japan,
Zilliacus met with Japanese agents in Paris and Geneva in the winter of
1904–1905 and arranged to ship a boatload of weapons into Russia by
way of the Gulf of Finland. In the wake of Bloody Sunday, it seemed
appropriate to enlist the services of Father Gapon as well, mainly as a
figurehead for the project. With the aid of Colonel Motojiro Akashi,

Zilliacus settled in London and purchased Browning rifles in America, Mausers in Hamburg, and Wetterli rifles in Switzerland, amounting to some 15,500 weapons, 2.5 million cartridges, and three tons of explosives for good measure. To haul this cargo Akashi purchased a small steamship, the *John Grafton*, and loaded it at sea in August 1905.[19]

Krasin decided that the *John Grafton* could be put to best use by the Bolsheviks, rather than Gapon's disorganized followers. He instructed Gorky to persuade Gapon to aid in this diversion on the grounds that Gapon's followers were already sufficiently armed. Gorky and a friend, the pianist Nikolai Burenin, met with Gapon in Finland to this end, and Burenin contacted Lenin. The plan was to sail the ship to Maxim Litvinov's designated location along the Estonian coast, where storage pits had been excavated to hide the weapons. They would then be moved to an appropriate underground hideaway in St. Petersburg—a cemetery.[20]

In the end, the project was a grand failure of comic opera proportions. On September 7, 1905, the *John Grafton* ran aground on a reef off the Finnish coast and blew up in spectacular fashion. A team of German divers managed to recover some nine thousand rifles from the ocean bottom, and Zilliacus got five hundred more into Russia by way of Stockholm, some of which apparently reached Burenin and the Bolsheviks. But when the Peace of Portsmouth ended the Russo-Japanese conflict, Japanese funds disappeared. Litvinov did engage in similar smuggling operations for a time along the Black Sea coast in 1906. But, in general, the Bolsheviks turned to bank robberies and extortion, rather than smuggling, as a means to obtain money and weapons.[21]

For Krasin the *John Grafton* episode was a fortuitous Bolshevik attempt to cut in on an existing revolutionary smuggling operation. By October he had turned to more pressing matters, including the St. Petersburg soviet, the printing of *Novaya zhizn'*, and the planning of an armed insurrection in Moscow. Once again, Bolshevik schemes were overtaken by revolutionary events, this time a national general strike that attracted the attention of the entire world.

October and *New Life*

The culminating experience of the Russian Revolution of 1905 was a national general strike. During the year, syndicalist theory had become Russian reality. The majority of workers in the industrial towns participated in some form of collective action that year, notably workers in the printing, metallurgical, and textile industries. They handed out leaflets, dropped tools and left their factories, gathered in mass demonstrations, and braved police violence. Very few had distinct loyalties to any political party, and their actions were largely spontaneous.[22]

Initial strikes in the wake of Bloody Sunday early in the year were followed by a lull and then a series of major strikes in the early autumn. On October 20 a railroad strike spread across the country to become the first truly national general strike in history, paralyzing the nation's transport and commerce. On October 26 a citywide representative body of workers from all factories, the soviet, met in St. Petersburg. On October 30 Sergei Witte, prime minister and architect of Russia's industrialization, announced in a manifesto the granting of civil rights and the creation of a new parliament, the Duma.

The social democrats were excited by the strike movement but ambivalent about the Duma. Should they participate in elections to a "bourgeois" parliament or not? Was a revolutionary situation still in existence or not? On October 10 the Moscow city RSDRP conference met to consider Shantser's call for a boycott of any Duma elections; other Bolsheviks, such as Stanislav Volsky and G. A. Alexinsky, plunged into the strike movement, side by side with their Menshevik comrades. Still others marched in protest to free political prisoners. During one of these marches, on October 18, a Moscow Bolshevik leader, N. E. Bauman, was bludgeoned to death with a metal pipe by a member of the right-wing Black Hundreds. His funeral demonstration became yet another example of mass revulsion with the regime of Nicholas II.[23]

The Bolsheviks were beneficiaries of the October events in a number of ways. RSDRP expenditures had multiplied tenfold since the start of the year, thanks to wealthy sympathizers, enabling the party to put out a significant number of brochures and journals. Shortly after arriving in St. Petersburg in late October, Lenin and Krupskaya sent off a letter with Shantser, praising the Moscow committee's work. Together with Krasin, Gorky, and Burenin, Lenin busied himself planning an armed uprising in Moscow, getting Bolsheviks out of jail, and establishing legal and illegal journals. While Andreeva played Liza in Gorky's "Children of the Sun" each night at the Moscow Art Theater, she and Gorky converted their apartment into a secret Bolshevik hideout, meeting place, and distribution point for weapons, including bombs and grenades. They also helped produce two new Bolshevik journals, Bor'ba (Struggle) in Moscow and Novaya zhizn' in St. Petersburg, financed by N. P. Schmidt and the ever-available Morozov largesse.[24]

Moscow, not St. Petersburg, was the center of Bolshevik activity. The Bolsheviks controlled the journal of the Moscow committee of the RSDRP, Bor'ba, and the short-lived Vpered as well. In addition, Shantser became editor of the Izvestiia (News) of the Moscow soviet. The party leaders, Lenin, Krasin, and Bogdanov, were still in St. Petersburg in December. But with the breakup of the St. Petersburg soviet by the police, Bogdanov was arrested and jailed. He whiled away his time writing the third volume of his Empiriomonism, remaining isolated from the major Bolshevik attempt at armed insurrection, the takeover of the Schmidt furniture factory in Moscow.

The "Devil's Nest" and the December Uprising

Moscow reactionaries had called the furniture factory of N. P. Schmidt the "Devil's Nest" for some time. The young Morozov heir had put his workers on the eight-hour day; his 260 employees were said to be the best paid in the furniture business in all of Moscow. Schmidt's plant was also a center of activity for several thousand Moscow woodworkers, who gathered there on a strike September 28 and only returned to work October 4 after significant concessions had been made. The Bolsheviks had organized a joiners' union, established among Moscow carpenters, at the plant. At the age of twenty-three, young Schmidt was widely known as both a Morozov and a friend of the revolution.[25]

In November, production at the Schmidt factory virtually ground to a halt, while political activity greatly increased. The factory had become a Bolshevik headquarters, complete with orators and target practice with Mauser rifles. M. N. Liadov, I. F. Dubrovinsky, and Shantser were all in residence plotting an armed uprising. Lenin, who had bombarded the Bolsheviks with calls for such an uprising from Geneva, was now intrigued. "This is remarkable, simply remarkable," he told Ekaterina Schmidt; "Tell me immediately about this unusual factory."[26]

Shantser and Volsky utilized Schmidt's money and factory to procure a significant number of weapons, collected from a net of secret addresses throughout Moscow. The art nouveau furniture intended to decorate the ornate homes of wealthy Muscovites held racks of rifles and grenades. Schmidt himself, a lover of art, music, and theater, a student of natural history and agronomy, dashed off to St. Petersburg to meet Lenin, and returned to pace back and forth in his apartment muttering "a brilliant man" while crossing himself Old Believer fashion.[27]

On December 5 the RSDRP Moscow committee convened to discuss the matter of a general strike and an armed uprising. Shantser went off to the Schmidt apartment and remained until midnight plotting the course of events. A few days later Shantser was arrested and exiled. The Moscow uprising proceeded without him.[28]

Events reached their denouement on December 16 and 17, 1905, when police and soldiers closed in on the Krasnaia Presnia district of Moscow. Barricades had been thrown up throughout the district, including Nizhnaia Prudovaia Street where the Schmidt factory stood. They did little to stop the crack Semenovsky Guards regiment from St. Petersburg, which moved in with artillery to take the district. Within two days the Schmidt factory and apartment had been largely destroyed, workers' homes burned to the ground, and the rebellion crushed at the cost of one thousand dead or wounded. Schmidt himself was arrested. Police found his basement full of additional rifles and revolvers for the armed uprising. The "Devil's Nest" collapsed, the Bolsheviks experienced their first revolutionary failure, and the young Schmidt passed through prison gates never to return.

But the Moscow uprising was not over for Lenin and the other Bolsheviks. The Schmidt family inheritance became a central factor in Bolshevik émigré politics for the next decade. Schmidt's self-sacrifice would enhance Bolshevik finances.

The Stockholm Congress

The December uprising in Moscow marked the tragic climax of Bolshevik plans for 1905. The dominant experience of that year had been syndicalist, not Jacobin, a general strike, and not a successful armed uprising. Within weeks Lenin retreated to the safety of Kuokkala and a dacha owned by another Bolshevik named Leitesen. Here he set up housekeeping with Krupskaya, her mother, Lenin's sister Maria, all on the ground floor, and the Bogdanovs on the second floor. A Bolshevik headquarters was established, with daily commuting to St. Petersburg, the coming and going of armed messengers, and hopes for increasing revolutionary activity. The urbane bandit Kamo arrived from the Caucasus with revolvers strapped under his topcoat by his mother; Krasin's entire printing plant was moved to St. Petersburg from Baku, and then on to Vyborg when the police closed in. The immediate question was what to do about the new legal organizations established by the October Manifesto, notably the Duma and the trade unions.[29]

In April 1906 a "unification congress" of the RSDRP met in Stockholm to assess the experience of 1905 for the party. Here the division between Lenin and the other Bolsheviks became clearer. Sixteen Bolsheviks voted with Lenin and a Menshevik majority to participate in the upcoming Duma elections; Stalin and fifteen other Bolsheviks abstained, while eleven voted against. When the RSDRP overwhelmingly passed a resolution condemning partisan activities such as seizing money in the name of the party, Lenin was conveniently out of the room. The congress specifically rejected the "expropriation of money from private banks," a favorite activity of both the Social Revolutionaries and, later, the Bolsheviks. As to the newly legalized trade unions, the RSDRP resolved to "give every assistance to the formation of non-party trade unions" and to urge individual party members to join them.[30]

The results of the Stockholm congress were mixed. The RSDRP majority, including Lenin and the Mensheviks, clearly wished to participate in the new legal opportunities made possible by the Duma and the trade unions. On the other hand, the Bolsheviks were not going to let public resolutions limit secret underground activity as long as it seemed efficacious. Krasin felt that Duma activity was insufficient and that "a new revolutionary wave is inevitable"; in private, Lenin agreed. So did Bogdanov after his release from jail in May. But the pursuit of direct action, rather than parliamentary activity, was a syndicalist strategy, and Lenin would soon have to counter the appeal of that strategy within his own fraction.[31]

Lenin and Bogdanov soon found themselves at odds. In August 1906, they cooperated in bringing out the first issue of the new Bolshevik illegal journal, *Proletarii*. But when Lenin read through the third volume of Bogdanov's latest tome, *Empiriomonism*, he became "angry and uncommonly furious." He promptly sat down and penned a long, rambling, and vindictive "declaration of love," a philosophical polemic in three notebooks insulting Bogdanov and attacking his philosophy root and branch. Bogdanov's response was to return it to Lenin with a note saying that he, Bogdanov, would break off personal relations with Lenin unless the document was considered "unwritten, undispatched, and unread."[32]

Then there was the matter of the police. By late 1906 Lenin's inflammatory pamphlets made him a marked man. A Moscow court called one of them "extremely revolutionary" because it "openly calls for an armed uprising." The Moscow police searched E. D. Miagkov's publishing house, a center of Bolshevik operations, and discovered thousands of Lenin's pamphlets, which they confiscated. Finally, the Committee on Press Affairs in St. Petersburg requested the prosecuting attorney to bring Lenin to court for another brochure on the grounds that it "calls for an armed uprising and a dictatorship of the proletariat."[33]

1906 was a year of disarray for the RSDRP and the Bolsheviks. The fissure between Lenin and Bogdanov was widening. In addition to the ongoing disagreement over philosophy and politics, there was the usual question of money. The Russian Revolution of 1905 provided martyrs and victims whose memory could help enrich the Bolshevik treasury. With this in mind, Maxim Gorky was sent to America.

Gorky in America

For a generation of Russians, America had been the promised land. Since the 1880s, Russian Jews in particular had engaged in a massive exodus from tsarist oppression to American liberty. Some thirty-eight thousand Russian Jews entered the United States in the year 1902 alone; in 1905 the figure jumped up to more than ninety thousand. These immigrants often retained their ties to their homeland; many retained political connections. Since the 1880s the Liberation of Labor circle, headed by George Plekhanov, and the Jewish Bund had received donations from immigrant sympathizers in the United States. So did the RSDRP. In 1901 Paul Axelrod complained to Lenin that the Bund was getting more financial aid from America than were the social democrats. In late 1905 the Bolsheviks decided to remedy that situation.[34]

In January 1906 Gorky and Andreeva met with Lenin in Helsinki and agreed to help raise funds for the Bolsheviks on their forthcoming trip to America. In February Gorky left for Berlin, where his public readings raised substantial sums of money for the Russian revolutionary cause. Andreeva was a willing accomplice in these matters, as was Nikolai Burenin. The latter, a concert pianist and son of a wealthy Moscow cotton dealer, helped Krasin set up Bolshevik fighting squads in St. Petersburg in 1905. Burenin would invite notable guests to his mother's estate on the Russo-Finnish border, indulge them in an evening of wine, poetry, music, and magic lantern shows, and send them back to St. Petersburg with illegal literature and weapons hidden in their clothing and carriages. In early 1906 he accompanied Gorky and Andreeva to America.[35]

Sending Gorky abroad to raise money for the Bolsheviks was apparently not Lenin's but Krasin's idea. Andreeva later remembered that Krasin was a shrewd and sympathetic friend who used her as a financial agent; "he told me he needed so much money for this or that, and I tried to carry out his instructions as accurately as possible." Lenin, she recalled, had approved Krasin's idea of sending Gorky to America "to raise funds for the revolution, to agitate on its behalf, and mainly to hinder the grant of credits to the Tsarist government." With this in mind, Gorky, Andreeva, and Burenin set sail on the *Friedrich Wilhelm der Grosse* on April 4, 1906.[36]

For Gorky, America was a vital new nation of smoke, skyscrapers, noise, energy, and capitalist gold—the yellow devil, he called it. Workers toiled for the likes of J. P. Morgan, while eking out a living in East Side slums. New York City was a gigantic machine, human beings its moveable parts. Here Gorky and Andreeva were a scandalous success, the famous writer living in sin with the famous actress, hobnobbing with the rich, the powerful, and socialist intellectuals.[37]

In May 1906 Krasin reminded Gorky in a letter that the revolution was still going on, and that the legal parliamentary struggle advocated by the Mensheviks (and Lenin) was a mistake. What did Gorky think? Money collected in America, warned Krasin, should not go to the Menshevik-controlled RSDRP central committee, but should receive some "special designation." "Otherwise not a kopek will go for weapons and the like." As a solution, Krasin would willingly accept the money and hold it for distribution to ensure that the Mensheviks did not get it.[38]

A further complication was the one hundred thousand rubles left by Savva Morozov for Andreeva. Morozov's mother was suing in court to get the funds, and Andreeva's lawyer, P. N. Maliantovich, was defending her interest. On July 5, 1906, Andreeva wrote Maliantovich that she wished to have the money from the life insurance policy go to Krasin; after some legal complications he received sixty thousand rubles, far more than Gorky could collect in America.[39]

During the summer of 1906, Gorky and Andreeva lived at the Adirondack Mountains summer home of John and Prestonia Martin while Gorky wrote his proletarian novel *Mother*. By then Gorky was disenchanted with this energetic new country, its omnipresent newspaper reporters, wealthy socialists, and bustling cities. The Russian embassy was campaigning to expel him. Meanwhile Krasin wrote that the first Duma had been prorogued by the tsar, and that a "new revolutionary wave" was inundating Russia, leading to a "simultaneous uprising of city, village, and revolutionary elements in the army," an "all-Russian conflagration." Krasin's apocalyptic prognostications and American complications soon convinced Gorky and Andreeva that it was time to embark. On October 26, 1906, they arrived in Naples from New York on the *Princess Irene*, accompanied by the faithful Burenin.[40]

The Morozov inheritance remained a problem. In September 1906, Andreeva wrote her sister, E. F. Krit, that she should take the 89,000 rubles now available from the Morozov life insurance, give 60,000 to Krasin, 15,000 to the Bolshevik K. P. Piatnitsky, 1,000 to Maliantovich for his fee, and keep the remaining 13,000 for herself. (An additional 11,000 rubles went to various Morozov family beneficiaries stipulated in the policy.) The upshot was that Savva Morozov's suicide, his friendship with Andreeva, and Krasin's friendly persuasion had landed Krasin—and not Lenin—a windfall of sixty thousand rubles in the autumn of 1906.[41]

Bolshevik interest in cultivating Gorky therefore did not diminish when he and Andreeva moved to a house on the resort island of Capri off the Italian coast in November 1906. Among their first visitors was Alexander Bogdanov, "an extremely powerful figure from whom we can expect resounding works in philosophy," wrote Gorky. "He will complete in philosophy the same revolution that Marx has produced in political economy. . . . When he succeeds we will see the complete downfall of all remnants of bourgeois metaphysics, the decline of the bourgeois 'soul', and the birth of a socialist soul. Monism has never had such a clear and deep thinking representative as Bogdanov." More prosaically, Bogdanov left Capri with additional funds for the Bolsheviks, participated in a party conference in Berlin, and returned to Moscow—all under the watchful eye of the Okhrana.[42]

In December 1906 Gorky campaigned for the release of Nikolai Schmidt from jail. Schmidt, on trial for his role in the December 1905 uprising, had been charged as a leader in the revolutionary movement and brutally interrogated by the police. By the end of 1906 he was in ill health, desperately unhappy, and mentally disoriented. In an article on the "Schmidt Affair" published in the *London Times*, Gorky argued that Schmidt's fate revealed the "bestial cruelty" of the police state of "Romanov, Stolypin, and Company." Gorky urged Schmidt's prompt release from jail. But this was not to be. In February 1907, Nikolai Schmidt was found dead in his prison cell, either a suicide or a victim of police brutality. Gorky's article—written on the advice of Bogdanov— had been too little and too late.[43]

Morozov money remained an issue for the Bolsheviks. Funds collected by Gorky and Burenin in America were trickling in to the party treasury via the Ladyzhnikov publishing house in Berlin, a convenient cover. They then flowed to Krasin. More important, Savva Morozov's insurance policy had produced tens of thousands of rubles for the Bolsheviks. The Okhrana reported that Krasin ended up with thirty-eight thousand rubles himself. Another twenty-one thousand went to local RSDRP committees; more money was used to pay off old bills for *Vpered* and various smuggling operations. By the spring of 1907 substantial funds had found their way from Gorky and Andreeva to the Bolsheviks via Krasin and Bogdanov, but not necessarily to Lenin.[44]

Maxim Gorky represented both the philosophy and the financial support for Bogdanov's collectivism. Gorky had been a major contributor to the Bolshevik cause, largely because of his admiration for Krasin and Bogdanov. For Gorky, Bolshevism represented a Russian variant of Marxism well attuned to the deepest needs of Russia's dark people, the peasantry, and a socialist philosophy of self-sacrifice.

In February 1906 an anonymous pamphlet on "proletarian ethics" appeared in Moscow under Rozhkov's editorship, probably written by Krasin or Bogdanov, that epitomized the collectivist experience of 1905. The author argued that Marxism had destroyed bourgeois gods but had not replaced them with proletarian gods suitable for the masses. All men and women share an "unconscious longing for immortality" expressed in the will to live and to survive. In a future socialist society the proper instinct would be not egoistic but altruistic. A proletarian ethic would "develop one's 'I' beyond the limits of its individuality, and toward commonality (*obshchnost'*)." In the future socialist society, man would become immortal by his triumph over nature, over death. True immortality would consist only of heroic deeds of self-sacrifice in the interest of the collective, remembered and memorialized by the collective. "The individual," concluded the essay, "is only a bourgeois fetish."[45]

Collectivism represented a survival mechanism after the experience of 1905. Heroes like N. E. Bauman had perished in the bloody streets of Russian cities. Revolutionary parties were in disarray. Only myth, the conscious articulation of revolutionary experience, would keep alive a unity of purpose and a mood of direct action. Lenin and the Mensheviks had chosen the legal tactic of parliamentary participation. Krasin,

Bogdanov, and Gorky wished to keep alive the revolutionary experience of collectivism and self-sacrifice. In so doing, they soon found that collectivism in politics and philosophy had a European name: syndicalism. It is to the relationship of Bolshevism and syndicalism that we now turn.

V

MYTH

LUNACHARSKY, SYNDICALISM, AND COLLECTIVE IMMORTALITY

> Men who are participating in a great social movement always picture their coming action as a battle in which their cause is certain to triumph. These constructions . . . I propose to call myths; the syndicalist "general strike" and Marx's catastrophic revolution are such myths.
>
> —GEORGES SOREL, 1906

In the wake of the 1905 revolution European syndicalism exerted a powerful influence upon Russian Bolshevism. Syndicalism at the time was a worldwide movement whose political roots were nurtured in the soil of Italy and France. Its answer to parliamentary reformism and Marxist politics was economic direct action, the general strike. The strike movement in Russia during 1905 and 1906 seemed to validate this tactic, and Lenin was among those who thought that Marxist ideology might be supplemented by syndicalist experience. But while Lenin was ambivalent about syndicalism, many of the other Bolsheviks were enthusiastic.

As a political party the RSDRP had grown substantially after 1905. By 1907 it claimed some 150,000 members, of whom 46,000 were Bolsheviks, 38,000 Mensheviks, 25,000 members of the Jewish Bund, 25,000 Polish socialists, and 13,000 Latvians. The Mensheviks drew their strength from Georgia and the Caucasus; the Bolsheviks were strongest in the central industrial area around Moscow and in the Urals. Nearly eighty percent of the Bolshevik delegates to the fifth RSDRP congress in London in 1907 turned out to be Russian, as compared with thirty-four percent of the Menshevik delegates. Statistically, at least, Bolshevik appeal lay in the Russian heartland, where the collectivist ethos of self-sacrifice ran deep.[1]

The Russian Revolution of 1905 thus provided fertile soil for planting the seeds of European syndicalism, itself deeply affected by Russian events. Lenin learned much from the spontaneity and mythmaking elements of syndicalism, even as he employed Marxist authority to criticize syndicalism's emphasis on collectivist experience.

81

The London Congress and Parliamentary Politics

In early March 1907 A. V. Lunacharsky arrived at Lenin's safe house in Kuokkala, Finland, and "spoke about his plans to study the latest in West European proletarian life, especially syndicalism." Lenin proceeded to give Lunacharsky advice and to suggest what might be learned from such a study. At the same time Lenin began drafting a resolution for the impending fifth RSDRP congress in which he argued that "a most determined ideological struggle must be waged against the anarcho-syndicalist movement among the proletariat."[2]

Lenin's private interest in and public hostility toward syndicalism reflected his own ambivalence regarding the movement. Within his own circle Lenin now faced a substantial thrust in the direction of revising the teachings of Marx to make them accommodate the recent experience of revolution. Bogdanov had completed the third volume of his monumental book *Empiriomonism* and wished to revise Marxism along the lines of Joseph Dietzgen's "religion of socialism." Lenin was consulting the urbane Armenian adventurer and bank robber Kamo (S. A. Ter-Petrosian), then involved in planning more "expropriations" in Georgia. Lenin's authority was threatened by independent thought and precipitous action inspired by the revolutionary wave which many other Bolsheviks thought had not yet receded.

The choice between parliamentary participation in the new Duma government of Premier P. A. Stolypin and underground revolutionary activity confronted the RSDRP at its fifth party congress held in London in June 1907. Russian socialists assembled here in great number (four hundred or so delegates), but they were a penurious lot. That the congress could afford to meet at all was due to the generosity of Joseph Fels, 54, a Philadelphia millionaire owner of the Fels-Naptha Soap Company and a follower of the single-tax advocate Henry George. Fels loaned the party seventeen hundred pounds to hold its congress, and 240 grateful delegates signed a note agreeing to repay the loan.[3]

The London congress, held from April 30 to May 19, 1907, was originally scheduled for Copenhagen but was cancelled by the Danish police. Instead the delegates ended up in the London Brotherhood Church, a labor church with a mixture of politics and religion that included Ramsay MacDonald among its members. Gorky found the church "unadorned to the point of absurdity," but the RSDRP could not look a gift horse in the mouth. The London congress was the last major party congress before 1917 and included such diverse luminaries as Lenin, Bogdanov, Trotsky, Stalin, Martov and representatives of the Bundist, Latvian, and Polish parties.[4]

The Bolsheviks were a volatile minority at London. Their 89 voting members were outnumbered by a coalition of Mensheviks (88), Bundists (55), Polish-Lithuanians (45), and Latvians (26). But Bolshevism represented the urge to continue the revolutionary activity of 1905 and not to become coopted by the parliamentary opportunities of the Stolypin regime. The Bolsheviks were well known for their revolutionary activity in procuring weapons and money through various expropriations and forced donations; until 1910 the Bolsheviks continued to subsidize the St. Petersburg committee of the RSDRP at a rate of one thousand rubles a month, and the Moscow committee at half that rate. More squeamish comrades succeeded on May 19 in passing a resolution "on partisan activities" which decreed that "party organizations must conduct an energetic struggle against partisan activities and expropriations" and "all specialized fighting squads attached to party organizations are to be disbanded."[5]

In response to this defeat and to the mood of squabbling, debating, and infighting that characterized the congress, Lenin proceeded to create a secret Bolshevik Center to coordinate continuing revolutionary activity advocated by Gorky and the Georgian Bolsheviks, including Kamo, Stalin, and Tskhakaya. The cover for this operation was the editorial board of the new Bolshevik newspaper *Proletarii*. However, the Bolshevik Center would soon have its own disagreements over the question of participation in the upcoming Duma elections.[6]

On June 3, 1907, responding to a two-year wave of violence and political assassination of public officials, Stolypin tightened government control with a coup d'etat that restricted the political activity of Russia's new parliament, the Duma. In one stroke he prorogued the second Duma, arrested sixty-five social democratic delegates and exiled them to Siberia, and promulgated a new electoral law which greatly limited popular representation except for middle-class and gentry property owners. The RSDRP lost support accordingly. Many Bolsheviks now found themselves in jail or exile as the number of political prisoners in Russia increased from 86,000 in 1905 to 170,000 by 1909. The number of strikes declined as well, from 6,114 in 1906 to only 222 in 1910. Everywhere the Stolypin regime repressed revolutionary violence.[7]

Elections for the third Duma in the summer of 1907 deeply divided the RSDRP. A conference of the Moscow RSDRP committee voted fifty-nine to sixteen to boycott the new parliament and to recall delegates if elected. Under the leadership of Stanislav Volsky, a syndicalist, the Moscow RSDRP remained a hotbed of "recallism" and opposition to Lenin until 1909. In St. Petersburg the government continued to arrest party leaders throughout the 1907–1910 period. RSDRP membership declined sharply from 7,300 in June 1907 to 3,000 in early 1908, then to 1,000 in early 1909 and to only 600 by 1910. Similar drops in membership occurred in other Russian cities, and many of the departing members were the most literate and skilled workers. In July 1907 the English journalist William Walling reported that the Bolsheviks were "strongest in the Russian provincial towns" and "nearest the peasants," apparently after a conversation with Lenin. Bolshevism, like the RSDRP in general, was being decapitated by government policies intended to destroy the revolutionary movement. For socialists, the choice between syndicalist direct action and parliamentary participation was a European phenomenon, but especially acute in postrevolutionary Russia.[8]

In mid-June 1907 Lenin left London for Russia and took up his cudgel against those who wished to boycott the Duma. He portrayed boycott-ism as a Social Revolutionary policy of "war on the old regime" which belonged to the "heroic period of the Russian Revolution." Times had changed, argued Lenin, and the RSDRP should participate in parliamen-tary elections along with the bourgeois parties of the day. Yet Lenin stood very nearly alone within the Bolshevik fraction, since the other Bolsheviks were still drawn to syndicalism as a means to perpetuate the revolution.[9]

At the second all-Russian conference of the RSDRP, held in Finland in early August 1907, the Menshevik leader Fedor Dan agreed with Lenin that the party should participate in the Duma. In addition, he noted that the Bolsheviks "have acquired a method for themselves: the *action directe* of the syndicalists.[11] Lenin realized that Bolshevik attraction toward syndicalist direct action could threaten his own authority. He was understandably ambivalent. In November 1907 Lenin wrote an intro-duction to a pamphlet by Lunacharsky in which he noted that syndical-ism was a natural reaction against the opportunistic tactic of parliamen-tary reform. Yet Lenin found Lunacharsky's proposal for a General Labor Council that would include other socialist parties "rather unpracti-cal." Party authority was preferable to labor spontaneity.[10]

Privately, Lenin wrote Lunacharsky that Bolshevism "knows how to take everything living from syndicalism, in order to kill Russian syndicalism and opportunism," adding that "only we can refute syndi-calism with a revolutionary view." By early 1908 Lenin was publicly defending Marxist orthodoxy against syndicalist collectivism. "We have conducted, are conducting, and will conduct," he wrote in *Proletarii*, "a resolute struggle against any attempts to sow the seeds of syndicalism in Russia" at the expense of the "theory of revolutionary Marxism. . . . Those intellectuals who modishly sow the seeds of syndicalism in Russia will never see them brought to fruition." By the autumn of 1908 Lenin was compelled by Menshevik criticism to disavow Lunacharsky's syn-dicalist enthusiasms, responding that "your attempts to connect us with syndicalism will remain unsuccessful, Messrs. Revisionists."[11]

Lenin recognized that syndicalism was now a major influence on Bolshevism which threatened party authority and his own standing as leader. The other Bolsheviks, drawn to the syndicalist movement in Europe and America, were intrigued by a collectivist myth of the general strike and a religion of labor that could keep alive the experience of 1905. For Lenin, labor spontaneity threatened party authority. Indeed, between

1907 and 1910 the other Bolsheviks turned to syndicalism in politics and collectivism in philosophy, and Lenin very nearly found himself a man without a party.

Syndicalism: The French-Italian Connection

In Europe after 1900 syndicalism was an important political and intellectual trend which stressed the role of will, belief, and myth in making workers conscious of their collective desires. Revolutionary syndicalism threatened Marxist socialism by its call to violent action, rather than parliamentary reform, and its treatment of ideas as useful myth, rather than scientific truth. The word *syndicat* meant trade union, and syndicalism placed its hopes in workers, not political parties. Real Marxism meant class struggle between the expropriators and expropriated; strikes created working class solidarity.[12]

Syndicalists consequently placed their hopes in working class experience, not the authority of bourgeois political parties, even socialist ones. The strike was direct class action; the vote was indirect election of party representatives. The syndicalist revolution would not be a sudden seizure of political power, but the gradual expropriation of factories and industries until they were under workers' control.

Syndicalists argued that Marxism had reached a dead end as a materialist social science and rationalist doctrine of revolution. They turned instead to the irrational vitalism of Henri Bergson, with its emphasis on memory, duration, and experience in shaping human activity, and to the sceptical pragmatism of thinkers such as William James and Bertrand Russell. Syndicalism was part of a general reaction against nineteenth-century materialism and positivism, the cult of rational progress and scientific knowledge. In the best tradition of Hume, Berkeley, and Kant the syndicalists stressed the primacy of ideas based on sensations of the world, not on an objective and external reality. Individuals were motivated by intuition, not reason, and therefore subject to the appeal of myth and idea. Syndicalism emerged in a Europe that was rediscovering the irrational.

Syndicalism involved direct action more than coherent ideology. Its leading proponent in France was Georges Sorel, who wrote on a regular basis for Lagardelle's *Movement Socialiste*, a journal expressing the labor militancy of the CGT (Confédération Général du Travail). In early 1906 Sorel published a series of articles later gathered together as his most famous book, *Réflexions sur la violence*. Sorel argued that Marxism had become an "idolatry of words" instead of a revolutionary doctrine, and that only violent conflict would keep alive the catastrophic vision in Marx's thinking, as opposed to its reformist inclinations. For Sorel, the key to worker radicalism was myth, which he defined as "the framing of a future in some indeterminate time," as in the Christian Apocalypse. Myth and ideas, not reality, move the masses to action, and the most important of these is the myth of the general strike. In Sorel's Hobbesian world of brute violence, the key to proletarian action was an "epic state of mind" created by intellectual leaders.[13]

Sorel's doctrine was a doctrine of socialist self-sacrifice to the collective. "The cause for which one sacrificed one's life was less significant than the personality created in the course of battle." True syndicalist direct action would consist of losing oneself through participation in a "heroic movement." "Only heroic movement—with its self-abnegation, its rejection of sensate indulgence, its emotional commitment, its self-sacrifice unto death is singled out from among all other activities as the ideal human condition." Syndicalism as a mood of collectivist self-sacrifice thus had an understandable appeal in post-1905 Russia.[14]

The year 1907 marked the high point of European syndicalism. In April 1907 an international syndicalist congress met in Paris and included Sorel, Arturo Labriola, Robert Michels, and Hubert Lagardelle among its speakers. Lagardelle praised syndicalism as the most effective and cathartic form of socialism, an "outpouring of proletarian energy." Sorel in a speech entitled "The Decomposition of Marxism" portrayed Marx as a maker of myth, not a scientist, and compared the future general strike to the Christian Apocalypse, an "advent of a world to come." Revolutionary syndicalists, he noted, were like medieval monks, members of a holy order to save Marxism and socialism from decay and decomposition.[15]

At an anarchist congress held in Amsterdam in August 1907 Pierre Monatte, a French syndicalist, argued that "syndicalism does not waste time promising the workers a paradise on earth; it calls on them to conquer it and assures them that their action will never be wholly in vain. It is a school of the will, of energy and of fruitful thought. It opens to anarchism, which for too long has been turned in on itself, new perspectives and experiences."[16] But anarchist dreams of total individual freedom from the state and syndicalist myths of a proletarian general strike were also in conflict, and syndicalism in its class orientation was linked more to Marxism than to anarchism. In proletarian syndicalism lay Bolshevik opportunity and Leninist frustration.

During 1907 and 1908, France was wracked by strikes and other labor disorders, usually suppressed in bloody battles with the police. French syndicalism consequently became divided between "ultras" and "politiques," between those advocating continuing strikes and those urging more cautious political reform. The choice between direct action and parliamentary participation created a crisis in French syndicalism. As a result by late 1908 the CGT was in considerable disarray as a radical force in French labor. Some syndicalists even collaborated with the royalist right and its political arm, *Action Française*.[17]

Among those pulled to the right was Sorel. In July 1908 he opposed further collaboration with Jean Jaurès, the socialist leader, and the CGT, as advocated by Lagardelle. Instead he began publishing articles in monarchist reviews and on October 31, 1908, announced his "immediate withdrawal" from *Mouvement Socialiste*. By 1909 Sorel was praising *Action Francaise* despite its obvious anti-Semitic and monarchist direction. In October 1908 Lagardelle wrote that "syndicalism is going through a sad crisis. On the one hand, the infantile stupidities of the 'Guerre Sociale' and noisy Herveism. We must have the courage to oppose those who call for buying revolvers at 50 sou and preparing an 'uprising.' On the other hand, there is pressure by the reformists for an alliance with the socialist party, where both Guesdists and Jaurists are completely against syndicalism." In France, as in Russia, syndicalism was torn between revolution and reform, the strike and the ballot.[18]

In 1907 syndicalism was a worldwide phenomenon. In Great Britain John Turner founded the Industrial Union of Direct Actionists (IUDA), a syndicalist group advocating the formation of "one big union"; a year later the American Industrial Workers of the World (IWW) established a British branch, the Industrial League. In Japan the anarcho-syndicalist wing of the Japanese socialist party, the *Nihon shakai-to*, also was calling for direct action through the general strike, and socialists were deeply divided by the opportunities for parliamentary reform and government repression.[19] But the major European center of syndicalism outside of France was Italy, another source of ideas for the Bolsheviks and Russian syndicalists.

In September 1904 a general strike occurred in Milan, sparked by agrarian disorders in Sicily. The strike leader was the syndicalist Arturo Labriola, who launched thereby a movement that spread throughout Italy. By 1906 an antireformist wing of the Italian Socialist Party had emerged, led by Labriola and Enrico Ferri. Italian syndicalism began in the peasant south of Italy and quickly moved into the cities of the north, encouraged by urban intellectuals steeped in Marxism. It did not approve of the antiauthoritarian individualism of anarchism or the insurrectionary Blanquism of Lenin. Instead, syndicalism in Italy focused on the general strike as a bonding experience for labor unions, a gradual maturation of worker consciousness through education, science, and propaganda. Yet its theories of vanguard leadership often resembled the views of Mussolini and Lenin.[20]

Italian syndicalism emphasized both political organization and collective experience of workers through the labor union. Arturo Labriola saw in the syndicates of labor the nuclei of a future socialist society, and stressed the energy, will, self-reliance, and solidarity of workers. Enrico Leone also urged the proletariat to acquire the virtue of solidarity and self-sacrifice through strike experience, rather than political insurrection. In general, Italian syndicalism placed a greater emphasis on worker consciousness than irrational myth, shared a common distrust of political parties, and by 1906 formed a militant but declining minority within the Italian labor movement.[21]

In June 1907 the Italian syndicalists held a congress in Ferrara and announced that they were abandoning the Italian Socialist Party to form a new Federation of Autonomous Syndicalist Groups. Yet they claimed fewer than five thousand members, as contrasted with the thirty-four thousand members of the Socialist Party. They continued to criticize parliamentary participation and reform, and to advocate strikes, labor unions, and worker initiative as the means toward a socialist order. Enrico Leone argued that strikes, rather than a political party, would "raise the political consciousness of the proletariat" through direct action; he urged a return to the "true Marxist spirit" of class struggle as a way out of the crisis in socialism brought on by parliamentary reform. The politics of self-sacrifice would ultimately lead to an expropriation of the bourgeoisie by the proletarian collective. Through direct action the laboring classes would acquire a "new spirit of solidarity," along with a "new ideology, a new conscience, a new morality."[22]

Italian socialists attracted by syndicalism included the young Benito Mussolini, a Marxist schoolteacher in Oneglia. Like Lenin, Mussolini believed in a vanguard party. Yet he also was greatly attracted by antiparliamentarism and Sorelian heroic self-sacrifice derived from myth. An avid reader of Labriola and Leone, Mussolini in 1908 saw myth as the motivating force for collective self-sacrifice and crowd psychology. By 1910 Mussolini's early Marxism had given way to syndicalism, but with an additional commitment to the revolutionary party.[23]

France and Italy were the major centers of European syndicalism in the years after 1905. But their influence through books and periodicals was widespread and significant, especially in America and Russia.

Solidarity Forever: The IWW

> Our task is to develop the conscious, intelligent minority to the point where they will be capable of carrying out the imperfectly expressed desires of the toiling millions.
> —*Industrial Worker*, November 1910
> We have been naught—we shall be All!
> —IWW version of the *Internationale*
> We are the revolution.
>
> —BILL HAYWOOD, 1912

Syndicalism reached America in the summer of 1905 with the founding congress in Chicago of the Industrial Workers of the World (IWW).

The IWW was a new coalition of left-wing socialists and radical workers, especially miners from the American West, that favored direct action over parliamentary politics. In the IWW, Marxist ideologues like Daniel De Leon mingled with militant labor radicals like Bill Haywood in an uneasy combination of party intellectuals and proletarians. IWW founding principles stressed one big general industrial union, including workers from all industries; a recognition of the primacy of class struggle over political participation; the power of collectivism and solidarity in rallying worker support; and the call for a national labor organization. In its rallying cry of "solidarity forever," its dream of "one big union," and its little red songbook, the IWW represented a syndicalist mood in American labor that gave a permanent legacy to the American left.[24]

The IWW from the outset was enthusiastic about the Russian Revolution of 1905 as an example of militant labor at its collective finest. Haywood dreamed of American labor revolt along Russian lines. The first IWW congress resolved to "urge our Russian fellow workmen on in their struggle" and "pledge our moral support and promise financial assistance as much as lies within our power." Maxim Gorky's arrival in New York in April 1906 to raise money for the Bolsheviks played upon this enthusiasm. Gorky fired off a telegram to Haywood promising that "the day of justice and delivery for the oppressed of all the world is at hand," and Haywood asked Gorky to "convey our best wishes to fellow workers in your native land." "We welcome Maxim Gorky to America," proclaimed the IWW's *Industrial Worker*, "as a representative Industrial Unionist, as a missionary of order throughout the land . . . ; Gorky stands out clearly in the life of the Russian people for exactly what the Industrial Workers advocate in America."[25]

The IWW was divided, however, between socialist party and industrial union partisans. With Haywood in jail, the second (September 1906) and third (September 1907) conventions of the IWW witnessed the rise in influence of Marxist intellectuals led by Daniel De Leon, who saw the party, rather than unions, as the key to organizing the working class. By the time of the fourth IWW convention in September 1908, the IWW was deeply split between Marxist socialists and anarcho-syndicalists. De Leon was denied his seat at the convention, and the clause in proceedings calling for a political party was eliminated. De Leon's ouster from the movement he had organized greatly disturbed Lenin.[26]

Syndicalism in Russia

Syndicalism originated in Russia quite independently of Bolshevism. In 1903 anarchist followers of Michael Bakunin and Peter Kropotkin began to discover French syndicalism and the weapon of the general strike. Their center abroad was Geneva, and their journal was called

Khleb i volia (Bread and freedom). Radical labor unions were romanti-
cized as the keys to a revolutionary future, carrying on the daily struggle
for economic gains and preparing for a future socialist society. Russian
syndicalists called for an all-Russian labor union like the CGT in France.
Fired by the experience of 1905, one syndicalist group, the South Russian
Group of Anarcho-Syndicalists, led by D. I. Novomirsky, claimed some
five thousand members. "God, if he existed," commented one follower,
"must be a syndicalist; otherwise Novomirsky would not have enjoyed
such great success."[27]

Like the Bolsheviks, Russian syndicalists placed great emphasis on
intellectual leadership of the workers. But they also shared an anarchist
distrust of intellectual authority. Novomirsky wrote in 1905 that "socialism is not the expression of the interests of the working class, but of
the so-called *raznochintsy*, or déclassé intelligentsia," which he dubbed
the "new deceivers of the people." They distrusted the state and its
political organ, the parliament, and preferred the general strike to the
ballot box. Workers, not socialist intellectuals, must carry out the central
task of the revolution, namely, the expropriation of the propertied
classes. For Russian syndicalists, revolution was not a sudden seizure of
power but a gradual expropriation of the land, factories, and other means
of production of the capitalist order. Workers should not vote; they
should engage in "gradual mass expropriation" of economic power.[28]

In 1906 syndicalist ideas spread like wildfire across the pages of Russian
radical literature. Translations of the writings of Sorel, Lagardelle, and
Pelloutier, as well as Russian contributions, proliferated. P. Strelsky, in
a book entitled *The Self-Organization of the Working Class*, called upon
workers to organize themselves in labor unions and mutual aid societies,
factory councils and soviets; their guiding principle should be "solidarity
through organization." The Social Revolutionary Victor Chernov noted
that syndicalism had great attraction for those Marxists disappointed
with social democracy and its "primacy of the party" and wishing to
revive the revolutionary elements in Marx's thought.[29]

The most interesting syndicalist writer in Russia was Novomirsky,
who attacked the scientific claims of Marxism and wished to organize the
working class in a national federation of syndicates, or trade unions.
Novomirsky argued that Marxist materialism was "essentially metaphysical," whereas he wished to focus on man's "energy of desire." Like
Bogdanov, Novomirsky sought to replace the authoritarianism of the
bourgeois "I" with the collectivism of society. Harmony, not authority,
was the final goal of society. Social democracy would lead to authority,
centralization, and bureaucracy, a new kind of "collectivism." Communism, on the other hand, would place authority in the hands of the
workers, not the party, in a "free federation of Workers' Associations"
that would make the state, army, and police unnecessary.

Like European syndicalists, Novomirsky praised the virtues of direct action and attacked the constitutional dreams of parliamentary socialism and democracy. Social democracy, he argued, was an ideology of the bourgeois intelligentsia. Instead of party authority, Novomirsky called for a "general, universal expropriation not only of trade but also of industry, finance, and landed capital." He urged a boycott of all state institutions, including the Duma, the army, and even the soviets. In the end Novomirsky was as much an anarchist as a syndicalist, but the mood he articulated left a deep impression upon the Bolsheviks.[30]

Syndicalism was especially influential among Moscow social democrats in 1907. Bazarov, in his book *Anarchist Communism and Marxism*, stressed the importance of the general strike, following the example of industrial sabotage in Italy. "Revolutionary syndicalism," he wrote, "represents a great step forward in comparison with pure doctrinal anarchism" because it utilizes a "systematic struggle" by the proletariat to overthrow capitalism. Yet the state would be a necessary institution under socialism, and syndicalism was "progressive only insofar as it has freed itself from the traditions of anarchism."[31]

Not surprisingly, a Russian edition of Sorel's *Reflections on Violence* appeared in 1907, translated by V. M. Friche, another Moscow social democrat. In a special introduction to the Russian edition, Sorel noted that socialism was in danger of degenerating; but "the same thing can happen to socialism as happened to the church, i.e., it can be resurrected every time that everyone thinks that it is very close to death." For Sorel, the orthodoxy of materialism would have to give way to the myth of direct action if socialism were to survive as a political force.[32]

Syndicalism encouraged Russians to boycott the Duma as a futile parliament. As a variation of socialist thought, syndicalism reached well beyond the anarcho-syndicalists themselves and into the ranks of the social democrats. Syndicalism offered a revolutionary alternative to anarchism; it emphasized the proletarian collective over the party, and expropriation over insurrection. But, as the liberal historian P. B. Struve pointed out, syndicalism also threatened socialism by portraying truth as myth, and Marxism itself as useful strategy, rather than as scientific orthodoxy. Lenin, too, recognized the importance of myth in galvanizing workers to action; the trick lay in portraying myth as truth.[33]

Plekhanov against Syndicalism

The shrewdest observer of the Bolshevik drift toward syndicalism after 1905 was the dean of Russian Marxists, George Plekhanov. Like the Mensheviks, Plekhanov noted the affinity of Leninism for Blanquism and Jacobinism. In addition, he pointed out a much less recognized connection between Machism and syndicalism, a connection essential to understanding the collectivism of Bogdanov and the other Bolsheviks.

In August 1905, Plekhanov attacked the Bolsheviks for trying to revise Marx with the help of Mach. Lenin, Plekhanov charged, had no philosophical understanding of Mach and Avenarius, yet "perhaps even the Marxist Lenin began little by little to come under the influence of the Machists around him." At this time Plekhanov did not use the term "Bolsheviks," but rather "comrades grouped around the journal *Vpered* and now *Proletarii*."[34]

In the wake of 1905, Plekhanov again charged that the Bolsheviks were "Russian Blanquists" under the influence of such thinkers as Nietzsche, Mach, and Avenarius. As for Lenin, "the closer the railroad train carrying Lenin from the station 'Marxism' gets to the station 'Blanquism,' the more often this theoretician, if we can call him that, begins to speak of the peasant in the language of the Social Revolutionaries." Lenin's formula of an alliance between proletariat and peasantry did not sit well with Plekhanov, who charged that the term "Bolsheviks" now meant only "'former Bolsheviks', i.e., people formerly in the majority at the second congress of the RSDRP who are now in the minority."[35]

In 1907 the situation changed dramatically. Lenin and Plekhanov discovered they faced a common danger in syndicalism. For Plekhanov syndicalism was another revision of Marx's teaching, a deviation, an error, a heresy to Marxist orthodoxy; for Lenin syndicalism was a powerful current that threatened to sweep away his own control of the Bolshevik fraction of the RSDRP. Plekhanov, like the Mensheviks, had no trouble attacking syndicalism and Bolshevism directly; for Lenin, the problem was to disentangle himself from a movement appealing to many of his followers.

At the London congress in May 1907 Plekhanov noted in a speech that "in their tactics the Bolsheviks are paving the way for anarcho-socialism, without admitting it themselves. I would not be surprised if there were some syndicalists among them." In an article published that summer Plekhanov argued that Bolshevism combined the dictatorial habits of Blanqui and the philosophical revisionism of Mach. The Bolsheviks, he asserted, "insulted me for pointing out their relationship to syndicalism," although "there is much in common between 'Bolshevism' and syndicalism or anarcho-socialism."[36]

Bogdanov, not Lenin, responded for the Bolsheviks in an open letter to the journal *Vestnik zhizni* in July 1907 attacking Plekhanov's interpretation of Marxism. As a result Plekhanov was asked by "some of my comrades" to reply to Bogdanov:

> But I replied that it would be more useful to deal with Mr. Arturo Labriola, whose views were being peddled in Russia by your fellow thinker, Mr. Anatoly Lunacharsky, under the guise of a weapon "sharpened by the orthodox Marxists." Supplied with an afterword by Mr. Lunacharsky, Labriola's book prepared the way for syndicalism in Russia, and I preferred to work on that and to postpone meanwhile my reply to your open letter.

Lunacharsky's translation of Labriola's *Reformism and Syndicalism* appeared in Russia in 1907, and Lunacharsky considered syndicalism a "healthy reaction"against reformism. Plekhanov, however, charged that syndicalism and reformism were related revisions of Marx, that Labriola was "Bernstein's cousin," and that "this Lunacharsky has a strange 'orthodox' Marxism! Very strange!"[37]

In 1908 Plekhanov precipitated a verbal war on Russian and Italian syndicalists. Labriola published a series of articles responding to Plekhanov's "villainous attack" on him as an idealist, praising the "new revolutionary force of the Syndicate," and distinguishing syndicalism from anarchism. Plekhanov then replied, in a review of a book by Enrico Leone, that syndicalism was basically identical with anarchism. The vanguard of the proletariat was no longer the party, but the syndicate. "Replacing Marxism with syndicalism," concluded Plekhanov, "would be a great step backward for proletarian ideology." Syndicalism was merely another form of revisionism, which was "naive" and had "no clarity of thought." All good socialists and Marxists should oppose "the theory of 'social myth' proposed by Sorel" and the "old anarchist denial of politics" which lived on in syndicalist direct action.[38]

Plekhanov's attack made it difficult for many Bolsheviks drawn to syndicalist tactics to admit their enthusiasms. As Marxists and as social democrats, they shared a commitment to the vanguard party and the need for political participation as well as economic direct action. But they also needed ideological coherence in the wake of revolutionary defeat, and sought within Marxism those ideas that could be applied to a rapidly changing political world. Syndicalism threatened to capture the revolutionary spirit within Marxism. To prevent this, many Russian social democrats in 1907 turned to a little known proletarian philosopher and friend of Marx, Joseph Dietzgen, whose view of socialism as a religion of science promised to provide a useful Marxist myth without admitting any syndicalist associations. In Russian "Dietzgenism" lay the roots of Bolshevik collectivism, god building, and the proletarian culture movement, often Marxist in form but syndicalist in content. And Dietzgenism, like syndicalism, became a powerful element in Bolshevism that Lenin could neither destroy nor ignore.

Joseph Dietzgen and the Religion of Socialism

> Marxism-Leninism has evolved into a secular religion. Unanimity around the Party has taken the place of communism in the Church; the vision of a regenerated humanity on earth, as the outcome of a collective effort to transform the world, has taken the place of the promise of individual immortality.

—Basile Kerblay, *Modern Soviet Society*, 1983
The teachings of socialism contain the
material for a new religion.

—JOSEPH DEITZGEN,
The Religion of Social Democracy, 1875

The idea that socialism was a surrogate religion entered Bolshevism
long before 1917. Bogdanov and Lunacharsky assumed that the masses
would give up their sense of self for the collective only under the
influence of myth, religious or secular. Lenin also stressed the need for
mass manipulation, although he did not admit publicly that it was
essential to Bolshevik strategy. After 1905 Bogdanov, Lunacharsky,
Gorky, and other left Bolsheviks sought Marxist sources to justify the
syndicalist and collectivist thrust of their movement. One major source
was a friend of Marx, Joseph Dietzgen (1828–1888), whose notion that
socialism was a future religion of science became very popular in Russian
and German social democratic circles after the turn of the century.

Dietzgen was the Eric Hoffer of his day, a Rhenish tanner and
self-taught philosopher of the proletariat. After the 1848 revolutions
Dietzgen worked in both the United States (1848–1864) and St.
Petersburg (1865–1869) as a tanner before returning to the Rhineland. In
the 1870s Dietzgen wrote a number of articles for the *Leipziger Volkstaat*
growing out of his 1869 book *The Nature of Human Brain Work*. Praised
by Marx as "our philosopher," Dietzgen enjoyed less popularity in his
own lifetime than after 1900 when his ideas were rediscovered by
European and American socialists.[39]

Dietzgenism formed an essential component in the Bolshevik philosophy of "god building" (*bogostroitel'stvo*). Dietzgen argued that socialist
theory formed the basis for a new religion, the "faith of the proletariat,"
which would "revolutionize everything" and "transform, after the
manner of science, the old faiths." Science would be the new gospel for
the coming revolution of industrial socialism, bringing ultimate salvation
to long suffering humanity. Dietzgen, like Ludwig Feuerbach, argued
that man had created God in his own image, and that Christianity had
become a religion of resignation by the downtrodden to their oppressors.
Bourgeois western civilization had created a dualism of mind and matter,
rulers and ruled, idealism and materialism. This should be replaced by
monism, a "systematic conception of the universe" that would substitute
for religion in a socialist world. The key to monism, argued Dietzgen,
was that "thinking and being, subject and object, exist in the domain of
experience."[40]

Like Mach, Dietzgen argued that we cannot have ideas without first
having sense perceptions of the world around us. All knowledge is
sensation-based. Knowledge is only a "relative truth" and "nature itself,
the absolute truth, cannot be known." Thought and ideas are therefore

as real as matter, and all are part of a monist universe of experience that we know through our sensations. "Socialist materialism," concluded Dietzgen, "is distinguished by the fact that it does not undervalue the human mind as the old materialists did, nor overvalue it as the German idealists did."[41] In Lenin's Manichean universe one was either an idealist or a materialist; for Dietzgen and Mach, one could be a monist in a world of experience that did not distinguish between mind and matter.

Dietzgen's relativism and collectivism were rediscovered by the European left around 1900 as a means of updating Marxism consistent with the radical changes in science and society. Dietzgen's writings appeared in German and Dutch socialist journals, which called him an important proletarian philosopher who had "completed" Marxist thought and provided a useful weapon in the struggle against idealism and neo-Kantianism. Like William James's "will to believe," Dietzgen's innate "religious feeling" suggested that men are generally moved by irrational emotion and a need for faith, and that socialism would have to recognize this side of human nature. The Dutch astronomer Anton Pannekoek was especially enthusiastic about Dietzgen's "proletarian world view" as a weapon to combat the moderate parliamentary reformism of Eduard Bernstein and to provide a socialist religion that would help maintain the faith in the face of revolutionary failure.[42]

Like syndicalism, Dietzgenism had great appeal for the American left before 1914, including the IWW. Dietzgen had lived in Chicago in the 1880s, where his writings were published in the only major socialist journal sympathetic to syndicalism, Charles Kerr's *International Socialist Review*. Kerr published Dietzgen's collected essays in 1906, and together with Ernst Untermann, a founder of the IWW and editor of Dietzgen's writings, helped disseminate his ideas among American syndicalists and left-wing intellectuals.[43]

In 1906 the Dietzgen revival continued with the publication of Dietzgen's correspondence with Marx and Engels. Karl Kautsky, the leading German Marxist of the day, provided an imprimatur by writing that he believed in "the same materialist philosophy that Marx and Engels, on the one hand, and Joseph Dietzgen, in another way, but in the same sense, had founded."[44] By blessing the new trinity of Marx, Engels, and Dietzgen, Kautsky provided Marxist legitimacy for the collectivist and syndicalist enthusiasm of a wide variety of socialists.

In 1907 Dietzgenism spread from Europe to America and Russia. Pannekoek wrote that Dietzgen had shown that "the mind transforms everything that it assimilates," rather than copying reality, so that ideology had a crucial role to play in shaping the "political intelligence" of workers. Schools for workers could help "educate party members, insofar as it can be done, in the theory of socialism." Other writers pointed out that Dietzgenism provided comfort for those coming from a religious background and seeking evidence of a "future life" through collective immortality and remembrance.[45]

In 1907 and 1908 the *International Socialist Review* carried several articles arguing that Marxism and socialism were akin more to religious faith than to scientific truth. Absolute truth was impossible to know; all laws are really tentative hypotheses. Arturo Labriola repeated the point that "parliaments are not and cannot become the organs of a social revolution," and Friedrich Adler enjoined American readers to consider the views of Ernst Mach.[46] This enthusiasm for socialism as religious myth, reflected in syndicalism, Dietzgenism, and Machism, represented an attempt by socialists everywhere to reradicalize Marx in the light of parliamentary politics, social legislation, and intellectual modernism. In Russia the Bolsheviks were especially interested.

The main editor of Dietzgen's writings in Russia was a Bolshevik, Pavl Georgievich Dauge (1869–1946), a Latvian founder of the RSDRP in Riga who later lived in Moscow. Like Krasin, Dauge was a professional by day and a revolutionary by night, pulling Muscovite teeth as a dentist and serving as a liaison between the Moscow committee of the party and the Geneva exiles. Dauge first met Lenin in June 1904 in Lausanne, and again in January 1907 at Kuokkala. At this second meeting Lenin encouraged Dauge to continue his project of editing and translating the writings of Dietzgen for Russian readers. For Lenin, Dietzgenism was desirable as a strategy of legal Marxism, politics in the guise of philosophy, but undesirable as an errant route to the "swamp" of Machism.[47]

In July 1906 Dauge wrote Dietzgen's son, Eugen, that he was planning to translate his father's works into Russian as soon as he had read the writings of Mach and Avenarius. Dauge believed that Dietzgen could serve as a Bolshevik Aesop; "in this way I thought we could use one of the legal possibilities to bring great benefit to the party." Lenin approved Dauge's plans to publish Dietzgen and wrote an introduction to a 1907 edition of Dietzgen's correspondence with Marx and Engels. The project was short lived, however. By autumn 1907 Dauge had stopped publishing Dietzgen and had given all copies of his translations to the Moscow RSDRP committee "for distribution to workers."[48]

Dietzgenism did not escape the watchful eye of Plekhanov, who grumbled that to supplement Marx with Dietzgen's philosophy was "completely impossible." There were many similarities between the ideas of Dietzgen and Bogdanov, who were idealists, not Marxist materialists. "Dietzgen, in fact," wrote Plekhanov, "begins to resemble the very 'original' philosophy of Mr. Bogdanov." One could hardly compare the "code [*kliuch*] of Joseph Dietzgen with the method of Karl Marx."[49]

Both Dietzgen and Mach argued that the world of experience was accessible to all individuals through their sensations. Politically this implied that the proletariat could know as much by its own experience as the party could tell it, since experience and consciousness could not be differentiated. Just as Dauge was drawn to Bogdanov in this respect, Lenin was repelled by the idea and turned for philosophical support to Plekhanov. Bogdanov's *Essays on the Philosophy of Marxism*, published in January 1908, devoted an entire essay to Dietzgen's philosophy, comparing Dietzgenism to ideas of Mach and Avenarius. In the same volume, Lunacharsky called for a new "proletarian monism" and "new religious consciousness" like Dietzgenism, or Sorel's syndicalist philosophy of "social myth."[50]

By 1908 Dietzgenism was a significant influence on those Bolsheviks who sought a new collectivism through useful myth that would mobilize the masses for action. European socialists like Karl Liebknecht, Franz Mehring, and Karl Kautsky were also reading and discussing Dietzgen. Kautsky, puzzled by the internecine quarrel over philosophy in the RSDRP in 1909, wrote that he found "no essential difference between the world views of Dietzgen and Marx. And Mach stands very close to Dietzgen." The Dutch socialist Henriette Roland-Holst also saw in Dietzgenism a "democratic proletarian logic" and "dialectical proletarian materialism" that could guide the proletariat to "social peace" by stressing the "relativity of all things and differences, all opposites and values." Another Dutch socialist, Hermann Gorter, found in Dietzgenism a "new truth" and "philosophy of the proletariat" that would help revolutionize worker consciousness through "intellectual propaganda."[51]

The debate over Dietzgenism continued even after 1910. Ernst Untermann defended Dietzgen's ideas against the "narrow Marxism" of Plekhanov and Mehring, arguing that the monism of Dietzgen anticipated the empiriocriticism of Mach and Avenarius and concluding: "Forward with Marx, Engels, and Dietzgen!" In May 1913 Lenin wrote an article in *Pravda* in which he called Dietzgen "one of the most outstanding social democratic writer-philosophers in Germany," despite the fact that Dietzgen "does not always provide a true exposition of the works of Marx and Engels." For Lenin, Dietzgen was a materialist, but one whose relativism made him "muddled" and led to Machist "mistakes."[52]

Dietzgenism, like syndicalism, led European socialists in the direction of myth rather than truth, relativist hypotheses about social revolution rather than scientific predictions. Marxist predictions of endless class struggle had not materialized, and social reform was undercutting revolutionary warfare. The proletariat needed a religion of socialism and a myth of the general strike more than a social science predicting inevitable but always distant capitalist collapse.

The Russian Apocalypse

Syndicalism and Dietzgenism were only two of many forms of
collectivist and quasi-religious thinking that swept over Russia after
1905. For many, the revolution of 1905 brought dark premonitions of an
end to history, an imminent apocalypse, and a spiritual and cultural
revolution that would transcend all worldly limits, including death itself.
Dietzgen, like Comte and Spencer, anticipated a religion of science that
would undergird socialism. But many other artists, writers, and thinkers
looked to the symbolic and the occult for a deeper vision of reality and
truth. For a time religious revivalism became intellectually respectable,
even on the left.

The end of the nineteenth century produced a deep sense of crisis and
imminent catastrophe for many European thinkers. The speed of modern
life, with its new airplanes, telephones, and wireless communication, led
to the transformative rhetoric of futurism, to new ways of conceptual-
izing space and time, and to a new interest in divine wisdom, the occult,
and religion. In Russia the philosopher Vladimir Soloviev ruminated on
the end of the world, and prophesied the coming of Antichrist in the
form of hordes from the East who would overrun Europe, but would be
followed by a spiritual awakening and resurrection of the dead as proof
of the existence of God in a materialist world.[53]

The symbolist poets and painters of Russia were also preoccupied with
religious motifs, including the riddle of death. In his stories Leonid
Andreev explored themes of immortality and the evolutionary links
between generations of individuals; he prophecied salvation from death
through transcendence of the self in the collective immortality of
remembered achievement and conscious participation in the cosmos. The
philosopher N. F. Fedorov expounded on man's ongoing struggle
against death; science, culture, and collective labor together would
ultimately produce the "death of death" through resurrection of the
dead. The Social Revolutionary writer Boris Savinkov, in his psychological portrait of a terrorist entitled *The Pale Horse* (1913), described
death as a "crown of thorns" toward which the revolutionary felt
"strangely indifferent," with neither joy nor pride at dying for the cause.
Many other Russian intellectuals became obsessed with death, probing
the Bible, local monks, and new occult movements such as theosophy
and anthroposophy for answers. In some cases this led to pessimism and
inaction, in others, to collectivist utopianism.[54]

For A. I. Izgoev, writing in the collection of essays *Signposts* (1909),
Russian youth needed a new ideal of "love for life" to replace the dread
of death—"or that revolutionary work which leads to it." The revolutionary ethos of individual self-sacrifice to the collective, said Izgoev,
amounted to a "love for death." "Death is inevitable, and we need to
teach people to meet it calmly and with dignity. But this is quite different

than teaching people to seek death, to evaluate each thought and action from the point of view of whether or not it threatens one with death."[55]

Yet attitudes toward death were more optimistic on the Russian left than Izgoev made out. Their roots lay in the Enlightenment and in nineteenth-century positivism, with its belief that science could conquer all problems, including death. Darwinism had given socialism an evolutionary explanation for collectivism in which "every living object is an association, a collectivity" and "it is the individual who lives for the species, the only eternal reality of life." New discoveries in cell biology suggested that individuals were all cells of some larger community, that cells are continually being regenerated, and therefore that the cell is "as immortal as man." The biologist Felix Le Dantec wrote that individuals may die but species do not, because "evolution has never been inter-rupted by death." He even predicted the construction of living cells from inorganic matter.[56] A wide variety of European thinkers thus suggested that individuals belonged to a monist universe of eternally existing species and matter which lived on even after its members perished.

The Russian left was influenced both by symbolist preoccupations with "god seeking" (bogoiskatel'stvo), as they called it, and by European positivism and science. Alexandra Kollontai, a leading RSDRP feminist, wrote in 1905 that "we overthrow the former gods in order to set up in their place our deity—society." This urge toward "god building" (bogostroitel'stvo) was less an imitation of symbolism than an answer to it. For Kollontai, socialism provided a new proletarian culture of collectiv-ism which celebrated the virtues of "solidarity, unity, self-sacrifice, subordination of particular interests to the interests of the group." Another socialist, N. A. Rozhkov, felt that in the future the science of medicine would guarantee collective immortality and indefinite prolon-gation of life: "Men who lived many centuries ago will be resurrected in the chemical laboratory. And, of course, they in turn will resurrect those whom they knew and loved. The task of immortality will finally be carried out. We must try to be worthy of future resurrection."[57]

The notion of socialism as a religion of collectivist self-sacrifice was widespread after 1905 and represented a powerful current of thought among the Bolsheviks. For Lenin, such thinking ultimately led to idealism, fideism, and other "swamps" of heretical deviation. But for Lunacharsky they became fused in a new vision of collectivism that combined syndicalist politics with a socialist religion of the future.

Lunacharsky and the Religion of Collectivism

Lunacharsky appears to have discovered syndicalism and the ideas of Joseph Dietzgen in the spring of 1905. Enthusiastic over the appeal of Father Gapon, Lunacharsky placed great hopes in the mass strike and

Maxim Gorky and Arturo Labriola, Italy, 1906. From L. P.
Bykovtseva, *Gor'kii v Italii* (Moscow 1975).

political myth as mechanisms for mobilizing the working classes of
Russia. Between May and September 1905 Lunacharsky wrote a series of
articles on "the mass political strike" in which he cited the works of
Lagardelle and other syndicalists, but found the idea of a general strike as
the means to power to be "naive" and a "pernicious utopia." The mass
strikes in Holland, Italy, and Russia in 1904 were a useful "new method
of struggle" only if properly organized to take advantage of the
"spontaneous solidarity" of workers. After the revolt on the battleship
Potemkin in June 1905, Lunacharsky continued to advocate the mass
political strike as an "opportunity for the proletariat to level a terrible
blow at the power of its enemy," yet dismissed Lagardelle's vision as an
anarchist dream and Henriette Roland Holst's idea of the general strike as
a "foolish utopia." Yet Lunacharsky thought strikes were essential, and
criticized "orthodox" and "narrow" Marxists for ignoring them.[58]

Lunacharsky's ambivalence toward syndicalism—anarchist in tone,
but better than Marxist hair-splitting and inaction—was resolved after he
joined Bogdanov and Gorky in exile. When Gorky settled in Italy, he
discovered syndicalism and immediately set about reading the works of
Lagardelle and Arturo Labriola. In November 1906 Gorky met Labriola
twice, first in Naples and a few days later on Capri, just as Bogdanov
arrived for a visit.[59]

In May 1907 Gorky met Lenin in Berlin in connection with the establishment of a Bolshevik publishing operation. Lenin, in need of money, was effusive in his praise of Gorky's new proletarian novel, *Mother*. After spending three weeks in London in June, Gorky and Andreeva returned to Capri where Gorky, Lenin, Bogdanov, and a number of other Bolsheviks began planning a series of publishing projects designed to fill the Bolshevik treasury. As for Lunacharsky, his Russian edition of Labriola's *Reformism and Syndicalism* had been confiscated by the censor, and he had moved to Florence, where he was "energetically working on syndicalism."[60]

We know from Lunacharsky's letters to his wife, written at the Stuttgart congress of the Second International in August 1907, that he was increasingly interested in syndicalism. Lenin, felt Lunacharsky, was personally very friendly but at the same time "talks viciously about syndicalism." Having been designated the RSDRP representative to a commission on "the syndicalist question," Lunacharsky felt that "Lenin also agrees" that trade unions could "play a decisive role from the angle of the social revolution itself." In the commission Lunacharsky argued that socialist parties and trade unions must work together to draw the "young workers movement" away from "trade unionism and other childhood diseases." With Lenin absent, the commission voted through a resolution "in a truly syndicalist spirit."[61]

Lunacharsky told Lenin that a break between Lenin and the other Bolsheviks over the issue of syndicalism would be a great mistake. Lenin was already preparing to emigrate to Western Europe again, as political persecution worsened inside Russia. Lunacharsky was happy that Lenin agreed to pay him to write articles as his "chief ideological agent abroad," but admitted later that his interest in syndicalism in 1907 alarmed Lenin.[62]

Both Gorky and Lunacharsky were moving toward a new philosophy of collectivism. "I saw Lunacharsky," Gorky wrote a friend in November 1907, "and he is writing a book on religion and working on another. This other one is terribly interesting in its theme and will enjoy great success, I'm convinced of that. Very powerful. It involves the approximation of Bolshevism to syndicalism, i.e., about the possibility of joining socialism with anarcho-socialism." Bogdanov and Lunacharsky in Gorky's view were "the beauty and power of our party, people who give us great hope" in a revolutionary future.[63]

In his writings after the Stuttgart congress, Lunacharsky waxed eloquent about the "heroic strike battle of the Russian proletariat." The Mensheviks were opportunists, the Bolsheviks were monists. Lunacharsky admitted that "Sorel and his cothinkers" could not "embrace Marx's ideas entirely." But syndicalists and Marxists both desired to create a "mass economic organization," despite occasional syndicalist "mistakes." In Moscow everyone was talking about a general strike, and yet the RSDRP had no organization. For Lunacharsky, the best political organization would be a "confederation of syndicates" to encourage "collectivism" among workers. The RSDRP, proposed Lunacharsky, needed a "General Workers' Council" to bring party and trade unions together in a common "class syndicalist organization." Such a syndicalist organization would be a "natural development of Bolshevism."[64]

Lenin was not amused. In November 1907 he wrote that Lunacharsky's views were "infinitely far from the views of Russian syndicalists, Mensheviks, and Social Revolutionaries." But the "inattentive or hostile reader" might easily conclude that Lunacharsky was in league with "Frenchmen or Italians" and some unnamed "Russian muddlers." Lenin admitted that the Bolsheviks should study syndicalism and the "Russian revolutionary experience" of 1905. But Lunacharsky's proposal for a General Workers' Council, said Lenin, was a completely impractical adventure.[65]

In December 1907 Plekhanov attacked Lunacharsky for his interest in syndicalism. Plekhanov opposed any cooperation between a Marxist party and the trade unions. In an Aesopian interpretation, Gorky wrote Lunacharsky that a Plekhanov article attacking syndicalism "is directed not so much against [Arturo] Labriola as against you—although more is said about Labriola." Lunacharsky responded that the Russian Revolution was doomed unless socialists acted to channel the "energy of the rising masses" through the organizational use of "mass psychology." Not the orthodoxy of Marxist dogma, or party organization, but the experience of strike was needed. "The way to do this is through a revised and purified syndicalism," Lunacharsky concluded.[66]

From Stuttgart to Geneva

Lunacharsky was not alone in being deeply affected by the Stuttgart congress of the Second International. For the August 1907 gathering was the high point of organized European socialism in the years before the Great War, a meeting place for left-wing groups from all over the world. It was also an assembly deeply divided regarding opportunities for reform of bourgeois society and the proper ideology for class struggle and revolution. Syndicalism was a major issue at the congress. The general strike appeared deeply threatening to the inactive and the self-satisfied among the delegates. Marxist orthodoxy, defined by German social democracy, encountered French and Italian syndicalism.[67]

The Bolsheviks were well represented at Stuttgart by Lenin, Bogdanov, Lunacharsky, and others. Lenin and Rosa Luxemburg led a movement of the left to proclaim that, in case of a European war, socialists would use all possible means, including the general strike, to guarantee the downfall of capitalism. But aside from proclamations, nothing came of it organizationally. Lenin did, however, make contact with syndicalism and Marxism in America through Daniel De Leon and representatives of the IWW. He even found time to wire a telegram to Bill Haywood, still in jail in America, sending fraternal greetings and expressing solidarity with the American proletariat. Lenin also met the Dutch socialists who would play an important role a decade later in establishing the communist Third International.[68]

Lenin succeeded in becoming the representative of RSDRP on the International Socialist Bureau, the executive body of the Second International, and in keeping involved with the work of other national parties. He also obtained five thousand marks from the SPD for the impending election campaign for the third Duma (as did the Mensheviks and Socialist Revolutionaries). This heightened Lenin's desire not to boycott the Duma elections as suggested by Bogdanov and the other Bolsheviks.[69]

The threat of syndicalism was thus modified by the acquisition of funds. We shall see that Lenin's public acceptance of SPD largesse came at the same time as the successful Bolshevik robbery of the Tiflis State Bank and the hot pursuit of the Schmidt family inheritance, and deepened the division with the Mensheviks over questions of party finances. Plekhanov noted that the Bolsheviks were obviously well off, since they had financed the London congress with the Fels loan and "still have a serious resource in Gorky." Plekhanov also received money from the SPD and duly turned it over to the RSDRP central committee. Lenin did not.[70]

Upon returning to Finland from Stuttgart, Lenin promptly discovered that the new rules of the game established by Prime Minister Stolypin would make effective political activity inside Russia increasingly problematic. During the summer of 1907, the St. Petersburg police were planning to initiate extradition proceedings to get Lenin out of Finland—assuming they could locate him—and requested Lenin's file from the Okhrana. On July 6, 1907, the Department of Police included Lenin on a list of persons subject to search and arrest. A few weeks later they learned from the Moscow Okhrana that Lenin was living in Finland.[71]

By October Lenin was planning to move the Bolshevik journal *Proletarii* abroad. He and Krupskaya were still in their safe house at Kuokkala "in the little company of good friends"—the Bogdanovs, I.F. Dubrovinsky, N.A. Rozhkov, and G.D. Leitesen. Lenin's desire to emigrate increased when the police arrested members of the Moscow Central Bureau of Trade Unions and uncovered stacks of Lenin's pamphlets. In November greater Okhrana surveillance forced Lenin and Krupskaya to move to a new hiding place in a suburb of Helsinki and then on to Stockholm and Geneva. Lenin's "second emigration" had begun.[72]

Emigration did not answer the question of RSDRP policy toward the new Duma. In late October 1907 a conference of fifty-seven party members at Terioki, Finland, resolved to continue to use the RSDRP Duma delegation as a party tribune, and not to boycott the Duma. Lenin, voting with the Mensheviks and the majority, realized this would mean a "war against the boycottists"—including the other Bolsheviks. Lenin, Bogdanov, and Krasin agreed that it was time to move *Proletarii* and other Bolshevik enterprises abroad to escape the police. This included the entire secret Bolshevik Center set up at London six months earlier. But there agreement ended, and in January 1908 Lenin began a period of political struggle in which his greatest rivals and enemies were members of his own Bolshevik fraction.[73]

On November 25, 1907, the Berlin police raided a Bolshevik headquarters at Pankstrasse 52b, the apartment of Osip Piatnitsky. For months they had worked with the Okhrana to identify the perpetrators of the great "Tiflis Ex" bank robbery and the location of the loot. Now they uncovered amidst the piles of illegal literature by Marx, Engels, Lenin, Bebel, and Kautsky a stash of pistols and ammunition sufficient to produce Berlin headlines about a "secret anarchist depot." The Bolsheviks, sniffed Axelrod in a letter to Martov, were obviously anarchists, and not socialists, a criminal element within the RSDRP that could no longer be tolerated.[74]

As Axelrod knew, syndicalism led the Bolsheviks not merely to revisionism and anarchism but to crime. The syndicalists urged direct action through strikes and, finally, the "expropriation" of the capitalist class through workers' control of factories and enterprises. For Lenin and the Bolsheviks, expropriation was not a theory of a revolutionary future or a useful myth, but real direct action: the use of terror and intimidation to expropriate the rich, as individuals and institutions. The syndicalist wave inundated Russia at the same time the Bolsheviks and Lenin embarked upon their most daring expropriation of all: the June 1907 robbery of the Tiflis State Bank.

VI

EXPROPRIATION
STALIN AND THE GEORGIANS
AS BANK ROBBERS

> In the period from 1901 to 1917, hundreds of thousands of rubles passed through my hands for the cause of the Russian Social Democratic Party. Of these sums, my personal contribution can be counted in tens of thousands, but all the rest was scooped out of the pockets of the 'bourgeoisie.'
>
> —MAXIM GORKY, December 1926p

On January 7, 1908, Lenin and Krupskaya arrived once more in what Lenin called "cursed Geneva." The weather was bleak and cold. A stopover in Berlin to see Rosa Luxemburg provided little solace for the defeated revolutionary. The second exile in Geneva had begun. "I have a feeling," Lenin told Krupskaya, "as if I have come here to be buried."[1]

Lenin's immediate concern was to reestablish the Bolshevik house organ *Proletarii*, recently moved from Finland. Gorky wanted Lenin to come to Capri for a visit; Bogdanov wanted the journal printed in a city other than Geneva. Lunacharsky was a necessary contributor; Lenin had given backhanded praise to his latest brochure by proclaiming that "there is no syndicalism in it." Much as he would like to "drink white Capri wine," Lenin wrote Gorky, he now needed to arrange for the printing and weekly transport of *Proletarii* into Russia. Geneva would become his new center of operations.[2]

In early 1908 Geneva was full of exile Russians. The twenty-three hundred Russians studying at Swiss universities were mainly women medical students, by far the largest foreign student contigent. They overlapped with an equally large colony of political refugees. "At that time a huge number of Russian political émigrés had gathered in Geneva," one of them recalled. "Geneva was literally swarming with Russians, and Russian was heard everywhere, in the streetcars, at cafes, in restaurants, and in the streets." Like Lenin and Krupskaya, most of them lived in the Rue Carouge, dubbed *Karushka* by the locals. The Lepeshinsky's restaurant was a virtual Bolshevik club where talk of armed insurrection went on amid the sounds of a piano and tinkling glasses. The Swiss Federal Attorney General complained that "there exists a mass of Russians who are strongly suspected of participating in common crimes," notably, bank robberies inside Russia.[3]

Lenin's arrival exacerbated émigré squabbling between Bolsheviks and Mensheviks. Martov wanted to expel the Bolsheviks from the RSDRP for their illegal expropriations; Plekhanov wrote Axelrod of the need to fight "Bolshevik Bakuninism" within the party. At issue was the entire question of strategy and tactics in a period of diminished revolutionary activity: should the RSDRP concentrate on legal parliamentary tactics and liquidate its underground operations, or should the conspiratorial mechanisms be kept intact? Most Mensheviks favored liquidation, while Lenin and the Bolshevik Center lived in the searchlight of scandal stemming from their latest illegal activity: the Tiflis Ex of June 1907.[4]

Lenin for the moment settled down to his well-accustomed émigré existence. He rejoined old working–class and socialist clubs, began reading the works of Joseph Dietzgen in the local library, and helped set up *Proletarii* using the same typesetting machine and printer that had produced *Vpered* three years before. Lenin, Bogdanov, and I. F. Dubrovinsky made up the editorial board, and Lenin wrote letters to potential contributors. The plan was to ship bundles of the journal into Russia via the southern route, from Capri to Black Sea ports. Thus, Gorky was now important because of his geographic location as well as his money and his political support.

But Gorky was keeping Lenin at arms length. No, he did not want to get involved with the Tiflis Ex robbers who had been jailed. Yes, he would be willing to write for *Proletarii*. The philosophy of Bogdanov appealed to Gorky; Lenin's comments about "stupid syndicalists" irritated him. They could only agree that a conference of the warring Bolshevik leaders was a necessity and should take place on Capri in the spring. Lenin was particularly upset by a recent collection of essays on Marxist philosophy published by Bogdanov. He wrote Gorky that it had "deepened the old differences among the Bolsheviks on philosophical questions." An agreement in the summer of 1904 to maintain neutrality on philosophical matters seemed in danger, for Lenin saw Bogdanov pursuing a "completely false, non-Marxist path." He was "positively furious" at Bogdanov, Lenin wrote Gorky. Mysticism and idealism had even turned up in an article Gorky submitted to *Proletarii*. This was sheer "stupidity," wrote Lenin; a Bolshevik conference was in order. [5]

Lenin's famous February 25, 1908, letter to Gorky detailing Lenin's philosophical disagreements with Bogdanov revealed that political divisions were now apparent within Bolshevism, as well as between Bolsheviks and Mensheviks. The receding of the revolutionary wave, the authoritarian policies of the Stolypin regime, and the socialist interest in syndicalism all contributed to that division. Even more important was the argument among the Bolsheviks concerning the disposition of funds acquired illegally inside Russia. The bank notes from the Tiflis Ex and the money signed over to the RSDRP by Nikolai Schmidt now became central to émigré Bolshevik quarrels. Argued in public on the basis of philosophy or politics, these quarrels often involved money.

Lenin's Geneva

Lenin, upon arriving in Geneva, discovered immediately that the Swiss lakeside city was full of syndicalist, anarchist, and Bolshevik exiles determined to carry on revolutionary activity from abroad. Many were Georgians. In the 1890s Russian anarchists, led by an Armenian doctor, Alexander Atabekian, had established an Anarchist Library in Geneva and published the works of Bakunin and Kropotkin. In August 1903 a group of young followers of Kropotkin established a journal, *Khleb i volia* (Bread and freedom), under the leadership of another refugee from the Caucasus, G. Gogelia (pseudonym K. Orgeiani), his wife, Lydia, and Maria Korn (Goldschmidt). From Geneva they smuggled their literature into Russia, and in 1905 became excited about the possibilities for "revolutionary syndicalism" inside the country.[6]

The leading Georgian Bolshevik was Mikhail Grigor'evich Tskhakaya. Born in 1865, Tskhakaya was the son of a priest, attended the Tiflis Seminary, and passed through the familiar route from Populism to Marxism in the 1890s. In 1891 he had established a commune in Tiflis with Maxim Gorky, before becoming active in the Georgian nationalist party, Mesami Dasi, and the RSDRP. In 1903 Tskhakaya worked closely with Krasin to establish a printing press and distribution network for *Iskra,* having just returned from five years of prison and exile. He attended both the third and fifth RSDRP congresses, and by 1908 was the senior leader of the Georgian Bolsheviks.[7]

Links between the Geneva and Caucasus Bolsheviks emerged in late 1904, as the Georgians felt especially pressed by the more popular Menshevik leadership in Georgia. Among the Georgians with whom Lenin and Krupskaya corresponded that winter was Joseph Stalin (Dzhugashvili), then a young seminarian in the Bolshevik underground cooperating with *Vpered.* Stalin did not attend the third RSDRP congress in London in April 1905, but Tskhakaya did; as the oldest delegate (age 40) he gave the opening speech. The freebooter style of Georgian politics was revealed by his comment: "Whoever heard of anyone voting in the Caucasus! We settle all our business in a comradely way. Five of us have been sent and the number of mandates doesn't matter." Democracy having been thus brushed aside, the Georgian Bolsheviks soon became leaders in the major underground activity of Bolshevism: expropriation.[8]

The Stockholm congress explicitly rejected "the expropriation of money from private banks as well as all forms of compulsory contributions for revolutionary purposes." The London congress also resolved that the party must conduct an "energetic struggle against partisan activities and expropriations," and disband all "fighting squads." These resolutions had little effect on the Bolshevik Center, which continued its underground operations from Geneva.[9]

Even before Lenin arrived in Geneva the other Bolsheviks had established their own journal, *Raduga*, published from June 1907 until February 1908. Financed by a wealthy Armenian sympathizer, the journal had a syndicalist tone and involved most of the other Bolsheviks, including Bogdanov, Lunacharsky, Shantser, and Gorky. Stanislav Volsky drew particular attention to revolutionary syndicalism as an "attack from the left" to which Marxists would have to respond without acquiring syndicalism's "anarchist residue." A substantial collection of stories, essays, and philosophical musings, *Raduga* only caught Lenin's attention in the late summer of 1907; as of October he still had not contributed to the main Bolshevik journal in Geneva.[10]

In the spring of 1908 Lenin was in a difficult position. His writings were being confiscated and destroyed throughout Russia by police. Old philosophical differences with Bogdanov and the other Bolsheviks were reappearing, and the familiar life of a political exile was depressing. Even his own Bolshevik fraction was drifting away toward relativism and syndicalism. Gorky's support for Bogdanov was especially troubling. "I am deeply convinced that you are wrong," Lenin wrote Gorky in late March 1908; Bogdanov's ideas were hostile, philistine, and priestly "from start to finish, from Mach to Avenarius." Philosophical neutrality was no longer possible. A battle among the Bolsheviks was "absolutely inevitable." Lenin wrote that it would be "useless" for him even to visit Gorky on Capri as long as Bogdanov was there; "I cannot and will not confer with people who are allowed to give sermons on the unity of scientific socialism and religion." Party affairs must be kept separate from philosophy. Lenin planned to publish a "formal declaration of war" against the other Bolsheviks. Yet he still held out hope of a conference on Capri, but "only on the condition that I will not speak about philosophy and religion."[11]

Lenin was in a quandary. The twenty-fifth anniversary of Marx's death prompted him to write an essay attacking revisionism in general and Bogdanov in particular as a "neo-mystical and neo-Berkeleyan revisionist," a characterization borrowed from Plekhanov. He also alluded to political "revisionism of the left," the revolutionary syndicalism of Arturo Labriola and Lagardelle, without mentioning Lunacharsky by name. Yet the very people he was attacking were the members of his own fraction, and valuable contributors to *Proletarii*. Without them Lenin was virtually a man without a party, "reading the accursed Machists for days on end" and trying to understand the defection of the other Bolsheviks.[12]

On April 19, 1908, Lenin wrote a final letter to Gorky, his last for eighteen months, and set out to confront his Bolshevik rivals on the island of Capri. Ostensibly the major differences were philosophical and political. But money played a central role in the impending separation of Lenin and the other Bolsheviks.

The Isle of Capri

"You must help me entice Lenin to come to Capri," Gorky wrote Lunacharsky in January 1908. "By the way, do you have his address?" Gorky was currently more fascinated with the syndicalism of Lunacharsky and the imaginative philosophy of Bogdanov, recently expressed in his utopian novel *Red Star*, than he was in Lenin. For Gorky the important Bolsheviks were Bogdanov, the "wonderful thinker," and Lunacharsky, "a living soul." Bogdanov had recently summoned Gorky to Paris for discussions on the future of Bolshevism, and promised to visit him in Capri as well. Perhaps, Gorky suggested, Bogdanov, Lunacharsky, and Lenin could edit a new journal together.[13]

For this a conference was necessary. In February the Lunacharskys arrived on Capri as Gorky's houseguests. Invitations went out to Lenin and Bogdanov to join them. But Lenin was being difficult, as usual. He refused to print Gorky's essay "The Destruction of the Personality" in *Proletarii*, and replied with a long attack on Bogdanov's philosophy. Bogdanov, in contrast, had published has collection of essays on Marxist philosophy, which Gorky found to be "superb." Such Aesopian philosophical works helped fight idealism and mysticism, and could pass the censor without confiscation.[14]

In March, Lenin wrote Gorky that his visit to Capri had been delayed by the International Socialist Bureau investigation of the Tiflis Ex. In addition, an RSDRP "court of justice" had been convened on Capri to discuss disputes between Bogdanov and Lenin, presumably over the same matter; Lenin had sent Kamenev and Zinoviev to testify, rather than come himself. In contrast, Gorky recommended to Burenin that he begin reading all of Bogdanov's works. Both Lunacharsky and Bogdanov were on Capri giving lectures to interested listeners, and Bazarov and Stepanov were on their way. It was time, wrote Gorky, to "summon Il'ich" to Capri.[15]

We know that Lenin spent the last seven days of April 1908 at Gorky's home on Capri, after a train ride from Geneva to Naples and a boat trip to the island, and that the visit was far from idyllic. "I was on the island of Capri in April 1908," Lenin wrote later, "and declared to all three comrades [Bogdanov, Lunacharsky, and Bazarov] my unconditional

Lenin playing chess with A. A. Bogdanov at Maxim Gorky's
house on Capri, 1908. From *Vospominaniia V. I. Lenina*
(Moscow, 1979), supplement.

disagreement with them on philosophy." This disagreement undoubtedly extended to politics and money as well. It was a visit punctuated by
interminable chess games, acrimonious debate, mutual recrimination,
and frequent argument. Finally Lenin told Bogdanov: "I am afraid we
will have to separate for two or three years." For the moment, at least,
Lenin and the other Bolsheviks parted ways.[16]

Money was a major concern. Lunacharsky went on the lecture circuit
to raise funds. Gorky cultivated his musical friends, the conductor Sergei
Koussevitsky and the opera singer Fedor Chaliapin, for generous donations. Chaliapin promised to give twelve thousand roubles for a Bolshevik publishing operation, an encyclopedia; Krasin instructed
Lunacharsky to collect the money if he could. Gorky's own publishing
operations, the Znanie and Ladyzhnikov houses, were in financial
trouble. Ladyzhnikov had to borrow forty thousand marks from a
wealthy sympathizer, M. S. Botkina. Matters of financial concern were
thus primary during Krasin's own visit to Capri in mid-June 1908.[17]

Gorky was engaged in reading Bogdanov's voluminous writings, supplemented by the works of Locke, Hume, and Mach. The Russian intelligentsia, he complained, was now hostile to him, perhaps because they had failed the "test of nerves" in 1905. Gorky even expressed dissatisfaction with his own "god-building" novel *Ispoved* (Confession) when it came out in Berlin in August. Alexinsky was asking for money to help a sick comrade; Gorky too complained that he was now "sick as an old dog." By September 1908 Gorky was proposing that the Bolsheviks establish a "higher party school" on Capri to train Russian party members in philosophy, politics, and underground activity.[18]

Gorky also planned to engage the other Bolsheviks in the "collective initiative" of a great Russian encyclopedia and a series of books on Russian culture (the first, by Bogdanov on the "organization of human experience"). Gorky was particularly anxious to help Bogdanov publish his own works and to subsidize Lunacharsky's new "History of Russian Popular Creativity." A collection of essays on the philosophy of collectivism was also in the planning stage, half of the income to go to Bogdanov and Lunacharsky. Socialism, felt Gorky, must now be turned into a cult, because "its basic core—man's consciousness of his connection with the masses—only grows stronger"; socialism was based on a "joyful, active feeling of kinship of all and each with everyone else," a collective psychology most developed in the proletariat. Individualism, concluded Gorky, must perish.[19]

Lenin's visit to Capri thus marked his isolation from the collectivist endeavors of Gorky and the other Bolsheviks. He was becoming equally isolated from the European socialist community, again over a question of money.

The Fels Loan and the International Socialist Bureau

Upon returning from Capri, Lenin and Krupskaya moved to a new apartment in Geneva on the Rue de Marechet, where they were shortly joined by Krupskaya's mother and Lenin's sister Maria. On May 16, 1908, Lenin left for London, where he spent three weeks at the British Museum reading books useful in his impending attack on Bogdanov and his philosophy. Lenin then wrote down a series of nine questions for Bogdanov: Did he recognize that Marxist philosophy was dialectical materialist? Did he realize that behind that theory lay a recognition that the external world existed and was reflected in the human mind? The entire philosophical inquisition was then read aloud on May 28 by Lenin's proxy, Iosif Dubrovinsky, at a public meeting where Bogdanov and Lunacharsky were speakers. The resultant scandal was duly reported to the Okhrana; Lenin had fired the opening shot in his war on the other Bolsheviks.[20]

Lenin was also being hounded by the International Socialist Bureau in

Brussels to pay off the loan from Joseph Fels that had underwritten the London congress. Completely unexpected expenses and the sad state of party finances made this impossible, replied Lenin. The intelligentsia had deserted the party, and the remaining proletarians could not pay up. Scandal must be avoided at all costs. In addition, Lenin was trying to get funds from Camille Huysmans and the ISB to support Bolshevik delegates in the Duma at home. But Lenin refused even to pay the annual dues to the ISB, so Huysmans understandably withheld ISB support.[21]

By July Huysmans was increasingly perturbed. The Social Revolutionaries had paid their six hundred francs for 1908. Why not the RSDRP? Lenin again demurred. The Fels loan would be discussed at the next central committee plenum in August. In the meantime, payment would have to be delayed. As soon as the central committee met, the dues would be paid immediately. By late September Lenin had managed to send Huysmans six hundred francs (of nine hundred due) so that he was allowed to attend the ISB conference in Brussels in October as the RSDRP representative. Not until January 1909 did Lenin send Huysmans the final three hundred francs.[22]

Things were not much better for the Bolsheviks inside Russia. Lenin himself was wanted by the police. RSDRP committees were losing members and divided on the question of whether or not to recall delegates from the Duma. In Moscow the RSDRP recallists (otzovisty), led by Shantser, were especially strong. Stanislav Volsky and other syndicalists were calling for a Bolshevik congress, a change in the Bolshevik Center, and even the expulsion of Lenin. In the summer of 1908 a St. Petersburg district RSDRP committee also voted to recall the Duma delegates. Numerous party conclaves attacked Lenin and the Mensheviks for their parliamentary participation, whereas Bogdanov and the other Bolsheviks found increasing support for their antiparliamentary rhetoric.[23]

Litvinov, Krasin, and the Politics of Expropriation

Expropriation was the syndicalist and anarchist term for confiscating private property from the rich and giving it to the deserving collective, the workers. "We must have expropriation," wrote Peter Kropotkin in 1891, "prosperity for all as an end, expropriation as a means." For syndicalists and anarchists, expropriation also meant the gradual process of workers' control over factories and labor unions; for the Bolsheviks, expropriation meant armed robbery.[24]

In December 1905, a group of Bolsheviks raided a suburban bank near Tiflis and netted over two hundred thousand rubles for the revolutionary cause. Maxim Litvinov used the proceeds to purchase weapons abroad for Bolshevik fighting squads in the Caucasus. Litvinov's enterprise, directed by Krasin, involved a Georgian connection with Switzerland. Litvinov and "comrades from the Caucasus" operated out of Zurich and Paris, taking orders for rifles from Lenin, getting money from Krasin, and buying weapons in Belgium (with the aid of Huysmans) for dispatch through Bulgaria and Macedonia to Russia. Most shipments followed the southern route to Georgia, from where they were taken to the northern cities as needed.[25]

During 1906, the Bolsheviks and the Social Revolutionaries engaged in hundreds of robberies throughout Russia. The SRs netted nearly one million rubles in a robbery of the Moscow Mercantile Credit Bank in March, and the same from the Mutual Credit Bank of St. Petersburg in October. Krasin organized a number of "exes" (expropriations) in Tiflis and Baku that year, and Bogdanov some others in the Urals. The most successful Bolshevik bandit was Semen Arshakovich Ter-Petrosyan (1882–1922), alias Kamo. In March 1906, for example, Kamo and his group robbed a bank in Kutais using bombs manufactured in Krasin's laboratory, killed a horse, wounded a cashier, and escaped with fifteen thousand rubles to Kamo's apartment. From there the money, hidden in wine bottles, went to St. Petersburg for the Bolsheviks.[26]

During the summer of 1906 Kamo went on a tour of Western Europe inspecting weapons factories with some Georgians. Together Kamo and Litvinov arranged to run guns through Bulgaria to the Caucasus, using money obtained by Krasin from the Ladyzhnikov publishing house in Berlin to buy weapons in Zurich. Litvinov also purchased a ship to transport the weapons. Shortly thereafter, a mail train robbery near Ufa in the Urals netted another 250,000 rubles, some of which went to the RSDRP central committee, the rest to the regional party organizations. In December 1906, the Paris Okhrana reported that Geneva had become the hub city for a network of gunrunning operations by Georgian and Armenian émigrés. Many of them were Bolsheviks.[27]

The Bolshevik underground continued to function throughout 1907, despite Okhrana surveillance in Europe and Krasin's arrest in May on the eve of the Tiflis Ex. But the police were closing in. Krasin's network of fighting squads, established in 1905, was damaged by more arrests in June (including N. E. Burenin). Nevertheless, in July 1907 Litvinov had 910 cases of rifles and machine guns acquired through another Bolshevik, Ludwig Martens, later the first Soviet representative in the United States in 1919. Tskhakaya and the Geneva Georgians were now running an "Ideological Circle of Bolsheviks in Geneva" whose cover was the journal *Raduga*, but whose real purpose was to help Bolshevik illegals and their families escape from Russia.[28]

The final emigration of the Bolshevik underground occurred in the winter of 1907–1908. Russian terror reached into Europe that autumn, when Russian revolutionaries from Geneva tried to rob the bank of Montreux. Anarchists were still sending weapons to Russia via Vienna and Odessa. But these were mere echoes of the violence of 1905. In March 1908 the Okhrana arrested Krasin at his house in Kuokkala, and jailed him in Vyborg; lacking sufficient evidence, the St. Petersburg prosecutor finally released him, and Krasin joined Lenin and the other Bolsheviks in exile. At thirty-eight, he now went to work for the German engineering firm of Siemens and Schukert, without entirely giving up his revolutionary career.[29] But the Bolshevik underground was now in exile, its activities and inheritances a matter of high intrigue. The lack of money had nearly been Bolshevism's undoing in 1904; now the presence of money facilitated its collapse.

Kamo and the Tiflis Ex of 1907

On January 21, 1908, the Swiss Department of Justice reported to the Okhrana that the Geneva police had arrested four young Russian revolutionary exiles with money from a Russian bank holdup. Tipped off by the Munich police, the Swiss picked up Sara Ravich, Tigram Bagdasarian, Migram Khodzhamirian, and Viacheslav Karpinsky—all Bolsheviks associated with "the anarchist journal *Raduga* in Geneva." Other arrests quickly followed in Stockholm, Paris, and other European cities. The architects of the Tiflis Ex had been unmasked.[30]

The robbery of the Tiflis State Bank at 10:30 a.m. on June 12, 1907, caused a sensation in Russia and abroad. The Georgian capital, situated in a narrow valley of the Kura River, was known for its hot sulphur springs, its colorful Armenian and Persian bazaars, and as the headquarters of the first and second Caucasian Army Corps. Its streets were dirty and narrow, even the main Golovinsky Boulevard, which ended abruptly at the city center, Erevan Square.[31]

That morning Phaeton No. 155, an armed stagecoach with two bank officials and a convoy of four Cossacks, was bringing a load of bank notes, coins, and currency to the building on Erevan Square. A second Phaeton followed with three army officers and three additional Cossacks. Crossing Erevan Square they were suddenly assaulted by eight bombs thrown from different positions in the street and on rooftops. Amidst the panic of screaming and bleeding horses and bystanders, the armed robbers drove off with the lead Phaeton and 260,000 rubles in bank notes. The leader of the band, disguised as an observant police officer, quietly left dozens of severely wounded and dead citizens and rejoined his group. A few days later he left for Finland and with the loot stashed in lady's clothing for its final destination—Lenin and the Bolshevik Center.[32]

Since 1905 the mastermind of the Tiflis Expropriation, S. A. Ter-Petrosyan, alias Kamo, had been robbing banks around Tiflis under the direction of Krasin in order to raise money for the Bolsheviks. At first

Police photograph of Kamo,
Berlin, 1908. From L. Shaumian, *Kamo* (Moscow, 1958).

the police suspected the Social Revolutionaries. By July, the Okhrana was systematically watching all Georgians leaving Geneva for the Caucasus in the belief that they were involved. Kamo, having left the money for laundering with Krasin, joined Bogdanov, and Lenin in Kuokkala. He arrived unscathed in Berlin on September 28 under the alias Mirsky. He then moved on to Vienna, Belgrade, Sofia, and Zurich to meet with Maxim Litvinov, continually watched by the police who described him as "an extremely active and bold revolutionary terrorist, highly valued by all the Bolsheviks, even Lenin and 'Nikitich' [Krasin]." On November 9, 1907, Kamo was arrested in Berlin with dynamite hidden under his apartment floorboards, but no money from the Tiflis Ex. Where had it gone?[33]

On November 13, 1907, the Paris Okhrana reported to St. Petersburg that the Tiflis Ex proceeds had all been shipped to "the Bolsheviks, and particularly into the hands of the well-known Krasin and Lenin (Ulianov)." No money had gone to the Mensheviks, who demanded that those involved be expelled from the RSDRP. Krasin, the Okhrana concluded, was "the soul of the whole business," and Kamo was his willing accomplice. The Georgian Bolsheviks in Geneva were clearly involved (Tskhakaya and *Raduga* were mentioned by name), and the money was being laundered through the Ladyzhnikov publishing house in Berlin. The Okhrana predicted that the Bolsheviks would try to cash the Tiflis Ex bank notes in Europe in January 1908, precisely the time of Lenin's arrival in Geneva.[34]

In December 1907, the Bolsheviks shipped the bank notes from the Tiflis Ex into Europe, but were betrayed to the Okhrana by a provocateur, Ya. A. Zhitomirsky. Zhitomirsky, a medical student, was a member of the RSDRP in Berlin. He had also been receiving 250 marks a month since 1902 from the Russian police for his reports on the Bolsheviks. As a Bolshevik, Zhitomirsky was involved in weapons smuggling, the London congress, and several RSDRP central committee meetings; he reported everything—including the activities of Kamo—to the Berlin branch of the Okhrana. In December 1907 Zhitomirsky arrived in Berlin from St. Petersburg with some of the Tiflis Ex notes, and was promptly arrested with Kamo by the Berlin police, who hoped to preserve Zhitomirsky's cover; he was promptly released.[35]

The Okhrana was thus well prepared when the Bolsheviks, having meticulously forged new numbers on all the five-hundred-ruble bank notes, tried to cash in the Tiflis Ex loot at various European banks in January 1908. At one point fifteen Okhrana agents were tailing the organizer of the affair, Litvinov, who was finally arrested with bank notes in his own possession. But Litvinov was quickly freed because no evidence could be found linking him to the robbery. By late January alert bank tellers in Munich, Berlin, Zurich, and Paris had spotted enough notes on a list circulated by the Okhrana so that a number of Bolshevik agents were under arrest and the RSDRP was in turmoil. Kamo feigned insanity in prison so effectively (proclaiming himself Napoleon, singing German songs, and claiming to have consumed ten thousand gallons of vodka), that he escaped trial, was committed to an asylum in June 1908, and only in October 1909 was turned over to the Russian police and jailed in Tiflis.[36]

The Tiflis Ex remained a major embarrassment for Lenin and the Bolsheviks throughout 1908. RSDRP party members were arrested in Tiflis, the Bolsheviks had lost a major source of income, and the Mensheviks were attacking them relentlessly for their criminal activities. In March 1908, the Paris RSDRP group resolved to oppose any further expropriations and disclaimed any party responsibility for the Tiflis Ex; twenty-nine members of the "Paris Bolshevik Ideological Group" promptly opposed the resolution. Lenin was trying to spring arrested Bolsheviks from jail with the help of lawyers and the ISB. Krasin and Litvinov were under Okhrana surveillance. All in all, the Tiflis Ex had not so much enriched the Bolshevik treasury as isolated the Bolsheviks as a criminal element within the RSDRP.[37]

As if the Tiflis Ex affair were not enough, it was quickly followed by another Bolshevik scandal involving substantial sums of money: the Schmidt inheritance.

The Schmidt Inheritance

The Tiflis Ex introduced one discordant note into the relationship between Lenin and the other Bolsheviks; a second financial source of conflict was the Schmidt inheritance. On December 12, 1907, the Okhrana reported from Paris that N. P. Schmidt, having died in his jail cell a few months earlier, had bequeathed nearly a half million rubles to the Bolsheviks via his assistant, M. A. Mikhailov. Schmidt's younger sisters, Elizabeth, 20, and Ekaterina, 24, had reportedly also been persuaded to turn their shares of the inheritance over to the Bolsheviks. But the inheritance was still in probate in Russia, the sisters appeared to be under some coercion, and it was unclear whether Schmidt intended his inheritance to go to the RSDRP or to the Bolshevik fraction. Again, a substantial sum of money further divided Lenin from the other Bolsheviks.[38]

At the center of the Schmidt inheritance stood the shadowy figure of Viktor Konstantinovich Taratuta (1881–1929), known in the underground simply as Comrade Viktor. Taratuta's wife, Olga, was an active anarchist; his nephew Ovsei was involved making bombs in Warsaw and Moscow in 1905. Viktor himself had an apprenticeship in the Jewish Bund, and later in Odessa and Baku branches of the RSDRP. In November 1905 Taratuta escaped from exile and arrived in Moscow, where he met N. P. Schmidt and began courting his sister Elizabeth. By the summer of 1906 Taratuta had become secretary of the RSDRP Moscow committee and was active in the Moscow underground; some socialists suspected that he was actually a police agent. In June 1906 Taratuta went to Odessa to arrange his wife's release from jail, and in the autumn returned to Moscow amidst rumors that he had arranged to embezzle funds acquired by the Social Revolutionaries. Taratuta was forced out of the Moscow committee and became involved with the Bolsheviks.[39]

By the winter of 1906–1907 Taratuta was deeply involved in the shadier side of Bolshevik fund raising, together with Bogdanov and Krasin. Generally this meant handling money from the expropriations. But in February 1907, Nikolai Schmidt was found dead in his Moscow jail cell. Suddenly a substantial part of the Morozov family fortune became of great interest to the Bolsheviks.[40]

In prison Schmidt maintained his loyalty to the RSDRP and asked his lawyer and brother-in-law, N. A. Andrikanis, to make sure that in the event of his death all his property would go to the party. The Bolsheviks were determined to lay claim to it themselves. In June 1907, Taratuta, at Lenin's urging, was elected to the RSDRP central committee. Despite his suspicious background, he spent the summer at Kuokkala with Lenin and Bogdanov while continuing his liaison with Elizabeth Schmidt. He also continued to funnel expropriation money to Bogdanov, while setting his sights on the Schmidt inheritance.[41]

In August 1907 Ekaterina Schmidt met Lenin at the Hotel Imperial in Stuttgart "on questions concerning my brother." Lenin also met with Taratuta in Berlin that month and subsequently in Vyborg at a meeting to discuss the Schmidt inheritance. But in October Andrikanis and Mikhailov visited Gorky at his house on Capri to discuss the Schmidt inheritance, and in December Taratuta emigrated to Paris along with Elizabeth Schmidt. Thus, by the time of the scandal over the Tiflis Ex money in early 1908, it was still unclear who would control the Schmidt inheritance or how it would be exported once probated.[42]

In May 1908, a Moscow court ruled that the Schmidt inheritance of 257,966 rubles was to be divided equally between the two young sisters, Elizabeth and Ekaterina. Presumably Elizabeth's share would then be transmitted to the Bolsheviks via Taratuta; Ekaterina, however, was married to Andrikanis, whose political enthusiasms were not Bolshevik. To mediate the dispute over the inheritance, Krasin arranged a court of arbitration in Paris consisting of Social Revolutionaries representing the Bolshevik Center, on the one hand, and Andrikanis, on the other. To complicate the matter further, much additional property—perhaps two or three million rubles in stock and capital—remained with the Moscow court, which had the only legal document, a notarized letter from Schmidt leaving everything to Ekaterina.[43]

On June 7, 1908, the Paris mediators agreed that Elizabeth's entire share, 128,983 rubles, would go to the Bolsheviks. Only a part (43,983 rubles) of Ekaterina's share would go to them, mainly to pay off old debts and legal fees connected with the December 1905 uprising in Schmidt's factory. But there was another problem. As Krasin wrote Gorky in the autumn of 1908, the Bolsheviks had learned that Elizabeth would not receive any inheritance until and unless she married a "legal" husband, that is, a man not wanted by the Russian police, as Taratuta was. "It would be a real crime for the party," wrote Krasin, "to lose under such exceptional circumstances just because we could not find a bridegroom."[44]

The struggle for party funds between Lenin and Taratuta, on the one hand, and Krasin, Gorky, and Bogdanov, on the other, now focused on the Schmidt inheritance. Taratuta attempted to obtain the inheritance for Lenin; Krasin and Bogdanov suspected Taratuta of being a provocateur. Krasin first proposed that Elizabeth marry N. E. Burenin, but Burenin declined. Krasin then suggested Alexander Mikhailovich Ignatiev (1879–1936), a veteran of Krasin's Bolshevik underground whose father was a general and member of the Imperial State Council. Ignatiev had used his father's estate in Finland as a staging point for smuggling weapons and literature into St. Petersburg. Having been involved in the Tiflis Ex, Ignatiev was now persuaded by Lenin to engage in another adventure: a fictitious marriage to Elizabeth Schmidt.[45]

On October 24, 1908, Ignatiev and Elizabeth Schmidt were joined in holy matrimony at the Russian Embassy Church in Paris for the sole purpose of transferring Elizabeth's inheritance to the Bolsheviks. Following the wedding, a St. Petersburg Bolshevik, S. P. Shesternin, withdrew Elizabeth's inheritance and deposited it in the Credit Lyons Bank, which transferred it to Paris, where Elizabeth withdrew the money and gave it to the Bolsheviks. Taratuta recovered Elizabeth for himself, Ignatiev received funds sufficient to maintain himself in emigration as "Count Ignatiev," and Lenin named Taratuta to the position of business manager of his *Proletarii*. Martov and the Mensheviks, of course, were as unhappy about the disposition of the Schmidt inheritance as they were about the Tiflis Ex.[46]

But which Bolsheviks obtained the Schmidt inheritance? In 1909 Lenin refused to give Krasin money owed him from various Russian underground operations, and Krasin allied himself with Bogdanov against Lenin and his Bolshevik Center. Taratuta, in fact, had replaced Krasin as the comptroller of Bolshevik Center finances, bringing with him Elizabeth's legacy. In addition, Taratuta attempted to recover the second half of the Schmidt inheritance, Ekaterina's, from her husband, N. A. Andrikanis. By a combination of threats and court action, Taratuta managed in fact to obtain some of these funds. The Schmidt inheritance enabled Lenin to continue publishing *Proletarii*. It also further widened the gap between Lenin and the other Bolsheviks.[47]

The Schmidt inheritance continued to plague Bolshevism into World War I. By 1912 Taratuta and Elizabeth Schmidt had retired to a quieter life at a San Remo sanatorium run by Plekhanov's wife, where they raised their two children and gambled at the local casino. Presumably this desertion to the ranks of the bourgeoisie was accompanied by some of the largesse from the Schmidt inheritance. As late as December 1915 the Okhrana reported that the inheritance, by then under the control of three SPD trustees, was known as the "Morozov fund" and was still the object of contention among both Bolsheviks and Mensheviks.[48]

The Schmidt inheritance, like the Tiflis Ex money, was an important factor in Lenin's disputes with the other Bolsheviks in 1908 and 1909. Behind the raging debates on the philosophies of Marxist materialism and empiriocriticism lay the politics of another kind of material: money.

Stalin against Lenin

Both the Tiflis Ex and Schmidt inheritance affairs were echoes of Bolshevik underground operations inside Russia since 1905. As a consequence, Lenin in exile found himself increasingly at odds with those veterans of the underground struggle who were now in prison or exile. One such veteran was Joseph Stalin.

The key link with the Georgian Bolsheviks in Geneva was Tskhakaya.

Mikha Tskhakaya. From A. V.
Maskulia,   *Mikha   Tskhakaia*
(Moscow 1968).

In late July 1908 he received correspondence from jailed comrades in
Baku, including Stalin, noting that they were "firmly convinced of the
correctness of Ilich's position" but were also "strongly interested in
philosophy," including the writings of Dietzgen, Plekhanov, and
Bogdanov. Stalin called the dispute between Lenin and the other
Bolsheviks a "tempest in a teapot," but admitted that the "positive
result" would be a "better acquaintance with the philosophical bases of
Marxism." Stalin also praised Mach's philosophy, described Mach and
Avenarius as "men of science," and urged the Bolsheviks to develop
Marxism "in the spirit of J. Dietzgen, recognizing the good sides of
'Machism.' " Such thoughts could not have pleased Lenin.[49]

After attending the London congress, Stalin returned to Baku as a
labor organizer. Through Krasin, Stalin may well have been involved in
the Tiflis Ex, although there is more speculation and assumption than
evidence on this point. At any rate, Stalin in the summer and autumn of
1907 was closer to Krasin and Bogdanov than to Lenin. Like Bogdanov,
Stalin felt that the "tide of our revolution is rising and not subsiding."
The underground organizations should be perpetuated, not liquidated.
The RSDRP should use the Duma to convince the proletariat of the need
for revolutionary violence, such as the strikes in the oil fields of Baku in

early 1908. On March 25, 1908, Stalin was arrested, jailed, and then exiled to Siberia, but he remained in contact with the Georgian underground network in Geneva.[50]

In May 1908 Tskhakaya wrote a four-page letter to Stepan Shaumian in Baku attacking Lenin and praising Bogdanov. In it he characterized Lenin as a "right Bundist" who wanted to abandon revolutionary tactics for legal operations; Tskhakaya argued that the Bolsheviks should be "hard as stone" and continue their illegal work, guided by the "brilliant philosophical work of Bogdanov, Bazarov, and Lunacharsky." In November Shaumian wrote Tskhakaya that he had convinced the Baku Bolsheviks that Bogdanov was "really correct." He expressed regrets that Bogdanov had left the editorial board of *Proletarii*. Yet Shaumian was "extremely sceptical" about Bogdanov's philosophy, complained about the "hellish conditions" of penury among the Baku Bolsheviks, and in the end supported Lenin. Stalin also decided that "recallism" was a "deviation from strict Bolshevism," but that such "accidental deviations" from "the other ('orthodox') part of our fraction, headed by Ilich," should be tolerated. Reluctantly supporting Lenin, the Georgian Bolsheviks refused to condemn Bogdanov.[51]

In June 1909 Stalin escaped from his place of exile at Solovchegodsk and returned to Baku, where he led an underground existence until he was again arrested in March 1910. During this period, the Baku Bolsheviks remained in close touch with Geneva through Tskhakaya, who continued to support Bogdanov against Lenin. In August 1909 Stalin wrote an article complaining that the RSDRP was now in a "grave crisis," without any "organizational cohesion." The answer, he suggested, was closer party ties with the factories and the recruitment of "experienced and mature leaders from the ranks of the workers." The Baku committee endorsed Lenin's opposition to recallism, god building, and ultimatism, but protested against Lenin's expulsion of Bogdanov and Lunacharsky from the editorial board of *Proletarii*.[52]

Lenin's *Materialism and Empiriocriticism* displeased Stalin when it came out in April 1909. Stalin was more interested in the latest writings of Bogdanov, where "in my view, some individual blunders of Ilich are correctly noted," as were the differences between Lenin and Plekhanov. Stalin was well informed about émigré philosophical disputes, but by no means a supporter of Lenin.[53]

In November 1909, Stalin wrote a letter to *Proletarii* complaining about the "incorrect organizational policy of the editorial board," i. e., Lenin. Stalin admitted that the intra-Bolshevik squabble probably originated with money—"the loot of a large circle of rather insane ultimatist *praktiki*"—but concluded that "joint work is both permissible and necessary." Stalin still valued the underground work of Krasin and Bogdanov and resisted Lenin's schismatic tactics in dealing with them. He remained in this period a Bolshevik, but not always a Leninist.[54]

Krasin against Lenin

Bolshevism began to disintegrate in June 1908 after Lenin's visit to Capri, but Lenin wished to keep that fact a secret. He wrote Taratuta that nothing should be said about Bogdanov's departure from the *Proletarii* editorial board and other intra-Bolshevik disagreements; "unconditional silence" should be maintained about "what has happened to the circle of Bolshevik Center members."[55]

The demise of the RSDRP was not unique in Europe at the time. Socialists everywhere faced the choice between parliamentary participation and more violent strike action. In Germany left-wing social democrats, led by Anton Pannekoek, attacked party opportunism in Bremen during elections for the Prussian Landtag. The Bremen left wing of the SPD was to remain a significant force for syndicalist tactics in Europe into the First World War.[56]

Financial disagreements between Lenin and the Bolshevik underground again surfaced at meetings of the Bolshevik Center and the RSDRP in August 1908. The RSDRP central committee plenum in Geneva established a Foreign Bureau responsible to a Russian Bureau of the central committee inside Russia in an effort to subordinate émigré politics to party policy. The Mensheviks also pointed out again the illegality of Bolshevik expropriations, still under investigation by a party commission. Most important, Bogdanov and Krasin left the Bolshevik Center, whose financial affairs passed into the hands of Lenin, Zinoviev, and Taratuta. Money thus remained a source of conflict between Lenin and the other Bolsheviks.[57]

In October 1908, many Bolsheviks sought to issue an ultimatum to the RSDRP Duma delegation that they subordinate their actions to the party and continue illegal activities outside the Duma. Lenin sharply condemned the ultimatists; Bogdanov, Aleksinsky, Krasin, Lunacharsky, and Shantser supported them. I. F. Dubrovinsky wrote Lenin from St. Petersburg that "Machist-recallist disasters" and "loudmouths" were creating an atmosphere of "disillusionment with Bolshevism" among workers. But there was little Lenin could do except refuse to cooperate with the other Bolsheviks in publishing activity and to continue writing his attack on them, *Materialism and Empiriocriticism*.[58]

Shaumian wrote Tskhakaya from Tiflis in early November asking that Bogdanov be given "heartfelt best wishes" from the Georgian Bolsheviks. They felt that Bogdanov had acted correctly in leaving *Proletarii* and the Bolshevik Center, although they were sad that he had done so. They were also "sceptical or worse" about Bogdanov's philosophy and afraid of a schism within Bolshevism. Bogdanov's theory, they felt, "destroys Marx's system." They advocated fractional unity, but not under the banner of Bogdanovism.[59]

In December 1908, Lenin and Krupskaya moved from Geneva to

Paris, involving themselves in RSDRP and Russian émigré affairs, and distancing themselves from Bogdanov and Switzerland. The party itself, however, continued to disintegrate into rival Bolshevik, Menshevik, Polish, and Latvian fractions.

When Lenin's *Materialism and Empiriocriticism* appeared in April 1909, philosophical disputes with the other Bolsheviks had again become a matter of money. The key figure was Krasin, now an engineer with Siemens and Schukert in Berlin, who imbibed the health regimen of yoga and yoghurt recommended by the Russian biologist Ilya Mechnikov. Krasin remained in touch with Gorky and Bogdanov, but quarreled with Lenin over money.[60]

Krasin actually succeeded in cashing bank notes from the Tiflis Ex after the arrests of Bolshevik agents. At first the Okhrana thought that Krasin in this manner had obtained two hundred thousand rubles; in fact, the amount turned out to be closer to forty thousand. But Krasin had kept the money for his own circle of "recallists" and "ultimatists," as Lenin called them, and was holding out on Lenin. "The right wing of the party," reported the Okhrana, "headed by Lenin, protests against the violation of the party program and Krasin's seizure of party funds." [61]

The Lbov Partisans and the "Sasha Letter"

One other echo of the Bolshevik underground heard in Europe in 1909 also involved money. At about the time of the Tiflis Ex, in July 1907, a group of underground party workers in the Urals gave six thousand rubles to the Bolshevik Center in return for delivery of weapons from abroad. A contract was duly signed between the Perm Partisan Revolutionary Detachment, headed by a man named Lbov, and the Bolshevik Center. Over the next few months this forest brotherhood, an uneasy coalition of Bolsheviks, anarchists, and Social Revolutionaries, went on the warpath, robbing a number of banks, factories, post offices, and wealthy citizens. The central committee of the Perm RSDRP group condemned the Lbov partisan tactics of expropriation, but Lbov had the support of the Bolsheviks, and he had a duly signed contract.[62]

Unfortunately, the Bolsheviks never delivered the promised weapons. On March 18, 1908, the Bolshevik Center promised to pay back the Lbov money, or at least three thousand rubles of it, but did not. While the Okhrana believed that the Bolsheviks were planning more expropriations, including robbing a trainload of gold bullion near Cheliabinsk, anarchist "battle detachments" were still roaming the Russian countryside. In November 1908 anarcho-syndicalists based in Geneva robbed a bank in Bessarabia of eighty thousand rubles, and as late as August 1909 another bank robbery in the Urals town of Miass killed seven people. Thus the violence of expropriation continued in Russia even as the revolutionary wave receded.[63]

The dispute between the Bolshevik Center and the Lbov partisans reached a climax in the spring of 1909. An anonymous article in *Proletarii* noted that worker adventurism in the Urals had played into the hands of the authorities by unnecessary violence and "exomania." Spectacular robberies had been accompanied by a sharp decline in party membership. Lbov himself had finally been arrested, and the article criticized him for playing into police hands, perhaps even as a provocateur.[64]

That summer a two-page "Open Letter to the Bolshevik Center" circulated among Russian socialists in Paris and Geneva, authored by the pseudonymous "Sasha." The letter reviewed the whole sordid matter of the Lbov partisans and reminded the Bolsheviks that they still owed the group their six thousand rubles for undelivered weapons. But which Bolsheviks? Lenin asked for an official investigation of the Sasha letter by a "higher party organ" and linked it with Bogdanov and the recallists; Bogdanov charged that the letter was connected with Taratuta, himself a suspected provocateur. The Okhrana thought the letter provided further evidence of Bolshevik involvement in expropriations inside Russia.[65]

The entire episode of the Sasha letter, like the Tiflis Ex and the Schmidt inheritance, marked the transformation of Bolshevik radicalism into émigré squabbling. But it also illustrated that the divisions between Lenin and the other Bolsheviks, often fought publicly in the realm of philosophy, were also grounded in fierce disputes over the political disposition of Bolshevik funds. Money continued to matter.

VII

MIND OVER MATTER
ORTHODOXY AGAINST SCIENCE

> The next lecture at the club, devoted to
> astronomy, was announced under the
> following title: "The Planet Marx and Its
> Inhabitants."
>
> —EVENII ZAMIATIN, "X," 1926

In the spring of 1908 Lenin launched an attack on the collectivism of his Bolshevik rivals using the Aesopian techniques of Russian literature under the censorship. The vehicle was Lenin's well-known philosophical polemic *Materialism and Empiriocriticism* (1909), now read by millions of devotees and schoolchildren around the world. Lenin's book was a ringing defense of scientific Marxist orthodoxy against the revisionist heresy of idealism, in language borrowed from Plekhanov's earlier attack on Bogdanov. But Lenin also attacked syndicalism in politics and party intrigue in finances. His Manichean world view defended materialism against empiriocriticism, orthodox Marxism against revisionism, and Leninism against collectivism.

A long tome on philosophy, rather than a short pamphlet on politics, the book was thus able to pass the Russian censors and reach into the prison cells and exile colonies of the police. The alert reader, presumably a Bolshevik, could easily recognize that Lenin was attacking Bogdanov's collectivism through Mach's empiriocriticism, a political rival through a European philosopher. Lenin still needed Gorky's money, Lunacharsky's pen, and the revolutionary spirit of syndicalism. But he wished to make a sharp break with the old Bolshevism, that Moscow-centered movement of 1905 led by Krasin and Bogdanov that sought to revise Marxism and persist in direct action. Like the Mensheviks, Lenin wanted doctrinal orthodoxy and parliamentary participation; unlike them, he could not attack directly the syndicalism which attracted members of his own movement. He chose instead to return to the legal Marxist tactics of the 1890s, using philosophical weapons to fight a political war.

When the Tiflis Ex was being organized and many Bolsheviks were inclined toward syndicalism, a wealthy Russian merchant named Blumenberg agreed to finance a new edition of Marx's *Capital*, edited by

125

Lenin and translated by Bazarov and Skvortsov. After editing three galley pages of the volume, however, Lenin gave up the project because of "difficult relations" with the sponsor. He was replaced by Bogdanov. In May 1907 volume two of the classic appeared in an edition of eight thousand copies and promptly sold out. Bogdanov, not Lenin, had become the editor of Marx and the potential source of Bolshevik orthodoxy.[1]

The Return to Legal Marxism

Lenin's writings were being censored or confiscated all over Russia. The Okhrana was well aware that behind the pseudonym "N. Lenin" was hidden "a well-known representative of the RSDRP," Vladimir Ulianov. They knew that Lenin was the author of numerous subversive pamphlets, that he was living in Finland with a German passport, and that he did not own a house. They did not know Krupskaya's name. Tightening police surveillance meant that Lenin would have great difficulty publishing inside Russia, but that the pseudonymous "V. Ilin" would not.[2]

In the summer of 1907 Lenin began editing his collected works under the title *Za 12 let* (After twelve years) in three volumes. Kamenev duly signed a contract with the Zerno publishing house in St. Petersburg to this end. Included in the collection was *What Is to Be Done?* (with some polemical footnotes left out). Volume one contained more than four hundred pages of Lenin's writings from 1895 to 1905. No sooner did it appear than the Committee on Press Affairs condemned it for advocating an armed uprising and ordered the book confiscated from all bookstores. Threatened with arrest, Lenin opted to emigrate.[3]

Lenin also produced a second edition of his legal Marxist study of the 1890s *The Development of Capitalism in Russia*. In this case more lenient censorship conditions enabled him to be less Aesopian than in the first edition; "scholars" now became "Marxists," "supporters of labor" became "socialists," and a "new theory" became "Marxism." In exile, of course, Lenin could be even more explicit; in a March 1908 article on Marx he wrote that the 1905 experience showed the need for a "civil war" in Russia as a means to "expropriate the expropriators." But inside Russia Lenin's works were still being confiscated by the police in their raids on RSDRP bookstores.[4]

In June 1908 Lenin launched his attack on Bogdanov's philosophy, ostensibly because Bogdanov had violated their agreement to remain neutral in philosophical matters. Bogdanov's writings and teaching attracted an increasing number of young Russian Marxists, drawn to the philosophy of Mach and the science fiction of Mars, as well as the writings of Marx. The Bolshevik turn to collectivism demanded an authoritarian response, felt Lenin, but one which could reach readers inside Russia. The answer was to attack Bogdanov's philosophy. But from the point of view of Bogdanov and his supporters, what had begun was a "struggle against Leninism."[5]

Bogdanov and the Philosophy of Collectivism

Bogdanov, like Lenin, had emigrated from Russia and was involved in the political and financial legacies of 1905. Arrested as a member of the St. Petersburg soviet in December 1905, he had spent six months in jail where he completed the writing of the third volume of his magnum opus, *Empiriomonism*. In it Bogdanov completed what he thought to be a synthesis of the ideas of Marx and Mach.[6]

According to Bogdanov, Marx's view that social existence determined man's consciousness was essentially correct. But Bogdanov believed that biological and social necessity drove men toward cooperation and harmony, not class conflict. Like Mach, he argued that knowledge was derived from experience. Each individual had a unique set of experiences which led to knowledge. Society absorbed individual experiences through "collective synchronization" among individuals. More than Marx, Bogdanov recognized that certain elements in the superstructure of society, notably technology and ideology, could have dramatic effects on the economic substructure, the means of production, and even the physical and natural world within which man lived. For Bogdanov, science and tools (in which he included knowledge and language) enabled man to act upon nature.

Bogdanov saw society divided into two main classes, bourgeoisie and proletariat. He also described a technical intelligentsia of scientists, engineers, and managers that could cooperate with the proletariat in using technology, as well as revolution, to create a utopian future society. The telephone, the loudspeaker, the film projector, and the machine shop were as much weapons of revolution as the bayonet and the machine gun. The key to a proletarian future would be the ideology of the technical and scientific intelligentsia, which would use its universal knowledge (tektology, Bogdanov called it) to organize human experience mathematically toward a better future. The world of all men is a product of their experience and therefore subject to manipulation and even control.

In *Empiriomonism*, Bogdanov wrote that all truth was relative, not absolute. Truth was an "organizing form of human experience." In stark contrast to the orthodox scientism of Lenin and Plekhanov, Bogdanov argued that "Marxism denies the unconditional objectivity of any kind of truth, or any eternal truths." Marxism was useful myth, a way of organizing collective experience into socialist ideology, but not the only way, and not the absolutely true way. Experience was the sum of energies of individuals. Progress meant the gradual selection of those classes with the most energy to do useful work, notably the proletariat. Since knowledge was a means of organizing labor, the technical intelligentsia—the Krasins of this world—had a crucial role to play. Like Lenin, Bogdanov held a vanguard theory of political organization of the masses' collective experience, but his vanguard was the technical intelligentsia, not necessarily the party.[7]

Bogdanov was also interested in reaching the masses through imaginative literature that was both Aesopian and utopian, a science fiction that could pass the censor and reach the literate. In November 1907 he published his first such work, the novel *Red Star*. The novel emerged from the European science fiction tradition of Jules Verne and H. G. Wells, the Russian utopianism of Vladimir Odoevsky's *The Year 4338* (1830), and the Aesopian language of Chernyshevsky's *What Is to Be Done?* (1863). In Campanella's *City of the Sun*, the Solarians usually lived at least one hundred years, some to age two hundred, because of a "secret, marvelous art by which they can renew their bodies painlessly every seven years."[8] Bogdanov, too, imagined a future world of scientific triumph which would overcome the limits of aging and death.

Aside from having a linguistic relationship to the name Marx, the planet Mars had long been the object of speculation and imagination. Was there life on the red planet? Percival Lowell's popular *Mars and Its Canals* (1906) suggested the possibility that the markings on the planet's surface visible through telescopes might be of human origin. Bogdanov went further, imagining a socialist society on Mars in which the problems of overpopulation and aging were controlled through euthanasia; clinical death rooms were provided for those tired of life, yet life could be prolonged through blood transfusion. Young blood extended old age through medical science.[9]

Red Star takes the literary form of a manuscript by a Martian named Leonid that has been discovered by a Dr. N. Verner, one of Bogdanov's pseudonyms. Leonid, at 26, is an old party worker who had "joined the revolution under the banner of duty and sacrifice." His girlfriend Anna believes in the sanctity of the "proletarian ethic" and supports the armed uprising planned by a young conspirator code-named Menni. Leonid considers the proletarian ethic a useful aid, but rejects the planned uprising because of insufficient preparation.[10]

Menni and other party comrades have invented a rocket fueled by "minus matter" (electrons?). Menni introduces Leonid to a group of Martians at his apartment, and they travel by rocket to Mars, complete with oxygen supplies, a computer, and zero gravity. The Martians have learned by experience that the collective is more important than the individual. Their science, art, and architecture are all anonymous, created by common labor, so that "names from the past are only the useless ballast of human memory." Martian books articulate a "proletarian philosophy of nature" in which war, slavery, class struggle, and the riddle of death have been surmounted. Giant canals constructed by the previous capitalist society have been taken over by striking workers. Factories are clean and comfortable, vegetables are grown hydroponically underground, muzak fills the air, and time charts indicate the control, distribution, and output of workers. The economy is run by computers and uses no money. Machines have enabled workers to achieve the two-hour day. The idea of individual property no longer exists, and the result is "complete communism."[11]

Most striking is Bogdanov's notion of voluntary death and collective immortality. Hospitals feature rooms for suicides to finish their days in peace and quiet, while the middle-aged are renewed through periodic blood transfusions. Youth is restored to the aging, and "the blood of one man continues to live in the organism of another." In the Martian world, blood transfusion has become a means to collectivism, eliminating the psychology of individualism which persists on earth.[12]

Thus Bogdanov imagined in *Red Star* a brave new world of collectivism that was scientifically advanced, rationally organized and computerized, wise and energetic. It is a world of leisure time, humming machines, and mutual aid and affection. In the end the Martians decide to colonize other planets. On Earth a revolution breaks out but fails for lack of peasant support. The "forces of reaction" organize a "parliamentary comedy" and use violence and terror to suppress the revolution. Despair sets in. Yet the novel ends with the possibility of another revolution. Glorious individual sacrifices are not in vain, and Mars becomes a model future collectivist society.[13]

As an allegory of 1905 and a collectivist utopia, Bogdanov's book greatly upset Lenin. But Krasin and the other Bolsheviks were especially taken by this imaginative vision of a technological and revolutionary future. *Red Star* was an example of a new kind of party literature, science fiction, which could outline socialism in a fictional and Aesopian way, reaching more readers inside Russia. But for Lenin such a medium threatened to revise the teachings of Marx and erode his own authority. This threat became more obvious when the other Bolsheviks rediscovered the teachings of Ernst Mach.[14]

Bogdanov had long been familiar with Mach's empiriocriticism, his relativist and sensationalist approach to science. But in 1906 Mach's writings became even more popular in Russia, and in 1907 Bogdanov edited a new translation of Mach's classic work *The Analysis of Sensations*.[15] Bogdanov's introduction on "What the Russian reader should look for in Mach" also appeared in the widely read German socialist journal *Neue Zeit* and set off a storm of controversy. "It is very definitely to be regretted," wrote a Russian admirer to Mach, "that Mr. Bogdanov has taken so much trouble to write such a completely unsuitable preface to your work. Why this agitation handbill? What has Karl Marx and the 'revolutionary proletariat' to do with your *Analysis?*"[16]

In November 1907 N. V. Volsky (Valentinov) wrote Mach and asked him what he thought of Bogdanov's point that "the principles of Mach's realist philosophy coincide with the basic point of Marx's sociological conception." Was Dietzgen an important influence on Marx and Engels? On Mach himself? Would Mach be willing to help the "Russian empiriocritics" in their struggle against Lenin and other "anti-Machists"?[17]

Mach responded that, yes, he had read Dietzgen on the recommendation of his friend Friedrich Adler, but that the teachings of Marx and Engels were always "completely foreign to my work." Mach portrayed himself as a social democrat, but not a Marxist, "a physicist who seeks a point of view beyond his specialty."[18]

Bogdanov argued that a Russian Marxist could, in fact, learn a great deal from Mach. His positivism provided a useful weapon against idealism and religion, indeed against all metaphysical authority in philosophy and science. His philosophical writings could pass the Russian censorship with little scrutiny. But revising Marxism along Machist lines would also deepen differences within the RSDRP. As the German translator noted, "the very serious tactical differences of 'Bolsheviks' and 'Mensheviks' will be sharpened by the completely independent question, in our eyes, of whether Marxism is in accord with Spinoza and Holbach or Mach and Avenarius as an epistemology."[19]

The German translator was not aware that Ernst Mach's teachings would further widen the gap between Lenin and the other Bolsheviks. No sooner had Lenin arrived in Geneva than he was confronted with an outpouring of party literature reflecting Bogdanov's collectivism. Bogdanov wrote an article for *Raduga* on the philosophy of the proletariat in which he called for an extension of Dietzgen's ideas "to organize humanity for infinite progress and joyous conquest of life." He also alluded to Leninist "orthodoxy" as one of the "opportunist tendencies in philosophy."[20]

Lenin was most disturbed by the appearance in January 1908 of another Bogdanov project, *Essays on the Philosophy of Marxism*. Mach and Avenarius, argued Bazarov, were really more Marxist than Plekhanov in stressing that the very existence of the external world was a materialist hypothesis. Marx and Engels were scientific; Plekhanov was scholastic. Other essays argued against a pessimistic and deterministic interpretation of Marx in favor of optimism and action. Marxism, like modern experimental science, worked with hypotheses and data; ideas shaped all experience, rather than merely reflecting external reality.[21]

Lunacharsky praised Walt Whitman for his "optimistic atheism" and called for a new "proletarian culture." The authoritarian dualism of bourgeoisie and proletariat under capitalism must give way to the collectivist monism of the proletariat. Under a new culture of "religious atheism" the proletariat would say its joyful "Yes!" to life; individual belief in a god would be replaced by collectivist religious myth, following the example of Dietzgen's religion of socialism and Sorel's "social myth" of the general strike. Socialist philosophy would not distinguish between spirit and matter, ideas and experience. "Consciousness does not sit off to one side in a corner, mysteriously reflecting reality," mused Lunacharsky, "but is itself a living reality."[22]

Lunacharsky also indicated the parallel between proletarian culture and syndicalist myth, while criticizing Sorel himself:

> Georges Sorel says: "The general strike may not happen, and even probably will never happen, but one must support its idea in the minds of the proletariat as a social myth, as the leading clarifying idea, so that one constantly tries to attain that degree of violence which our comprehension suggests." A very nasty idea. Since the social revolution is identical with the general strike, both function as myths.[23]

Despite criticizing Sorel, Lunacharsky believed that a "god-building" myth could create a proletarian culture after the revolution. God, after all, was merely "humanity in its highest potential." "We ideologues are raised up by waves from a proletarian sea," and the function of ideology was to provide collectivist myth for the masses.[24]

In the same collection Bogdanov decried the idols and fetishes of bourgeois philosophy, which had found their way into Plekhanov's thinking. Bogdanov's empiriomonism was better suited than Plekhanov's narrow Marxist orthodoxy to harness proletarian energy to the needs of a technical industrial society. Ideas and language are not mere reflections of class interest, but useful tools. Plekhanov made materialism itself into a fetish, an idol, a faith. But matter is not a thing-in-itself distinguished from spirit; it is part of a single monist continuum running from experience to consciousness. Matter is experience, known to us only through our sensations of the world. The world is not external and determined; it can be transformed by consciousness and technology, "the victory of people's social labor over nature by means of machine production."[25]

Bogdanov and his colleagues were calling for nothing less than a major revision of Marxism along the lines suggested by modern science, especially the empiriocriticism of Mach and Avenarius. Bogdanov was more than a Machist. But he shared Mach's view that the world is our sensations and experiences, and that knowledge and hypothesis act upon that world as much as external and material forces. In Aesopian translation, the ideas of the radical, technical intelligentsia can effect a revolution better than either party orthodoxy or proletarian spontaneity. The key to a revolutionary future was collectivist myth, not individual authority—Bolshevik theory, not Leninist dogma.

Bogdanov pointed out that Mach's thought involved both relativist epistemology and a radical destruction of the very notion of self. Indeed, the attack on individualism linked Mach and Marx more than any supposed epistemological agreement or disagreement on how we know the world. In his book *Keys to a School of Philosophy* (1908), Bogdanov attacked Plekhanov's materialism as "childishly naive" and espoused the relativity of truth. Proletarian ideology derived from science and technology through the "labor process," yet truth changes over time, as well as from one individual to another. The trick was to create an ideology for Man, not individual men. "The first and basic characteristic of Mach's analysis of experience," concluded Bogdanov, "is the destructive criticism of the individualist idea that experience belongs to the same subject or 'I.'" For the "I" or self constantly changes, dies, is reborn as a complex of memories, moods, and feelings. Marx and Engels had not created a proletarian philosophy; however, the radical collectivist anti-individualism of Mach and Bogdanov would do so.[26]

Bogdanov's attempt to modernize Marx also threatened Lenin's authority over Bolshevism. Many other Bolsheviks were increasingly attracted to Bogdanov's philosophy. Gorky considered Bogdanov "the most interesting and perhaps the most significant philosopher in Europe"; Shuliatikov called Bogdanov's ideas "epoch making" in their radical critique of the "cult of the autonomous person" and "individualism." Young Bolsheviks in jail inside Russia, such as Nikolai Bukharin and Ya. M. Sverdlov, were also immersed in Mach and Bogdanov as prison reading. "Lunacharsky is right," Gorky wrote Bogdanov in March 1908, "when he says that 'Lenin does not understand Bolshevism.'"[27]

Emigration further widened the gap between Bogdanov and Lenin. For one thing, Friedrich Adler and Ernst Untermann were popularizing the ideas of Mach and Dietzgen to criticze atomism in physics and absolutism in epistemology. They supported a monism linking matter and mind, rejecting the old Kantian dualism. For another, Bogdanov and Lunacharsky in March 1908 brought out a Geneva émigré journal, *Zagranichnaia gazeta* (Foreign gazette), which published Lenin's articles but was not under Lenin's control. In its pages Lunacharsky praised Gorky for avoiding "narrow Marxism" and "crude materialism" in favor of "scientific socialism in its religious significance" and Bogdanov argued that "a theory—any theory, true or false—exists only in the consciousness of people."[28]

The internecine quarrel between Lenin and the other Bolsheviks was not lost on the Mensheviks. Like Plekhanov, they pointed out the connection between Bolshevism and Machism, "a world view without a world." Unnamed Bolshevik philosophers were denying the existence of objective truth in favor of a reactionary world view. "Bolshevik tactics and practices create unconscious Machists and idealists," charged A. M. Deborin.[29]

In 1908 Lenin was the only Bolshevik leader to join Plekhanov and the Mensheviks in condemning Bogdanov's collectivism. Kamenev wrote Bogdanov in May 1908, praising the "revolutionary proletarian character" of his philosophy, even while asking him to join Lenin in condemning "our philosophical opponents." Bogdanov, writing in the name of the Bolshevik Center, noted that Bolshevism as an organization was now almost completely destroyed, scattered by emigration and exile, badly in need of funds. He urged party unity, discipline, and democracy by not recalling the Duma fraction, even if that meant abandoning the hope of direct action in the streets. He even agreed to maintain silence about Taratuta and the Schmidt inheritance.[30]

By autumn 1908 Bogdanov was the virtual leader of Bolshevism in exile. "The more I read your books and understand your thoughts," wrote Gorky, "the more revolutionary they appear." Gorky called Bogdanov "the greatest organizer of today's ideas." Kamenev was also supportive: "Even in 1905 I supported, foolishly or not, the revolutionary-proletarian character of the new philosophy in Marxism, understanding by 'new philosophy' that stream in it which you represent. I have said this in print and I will continue to stand my ground; even now I will always be ready to defend it in any way." Kamenev praised Bogdanov as the creator of a new philosophy and a "proletarian revolution." Bogdanov's empiriomonism, added Volsky (Valentinov), was real Marxist science, in contrast to Plekhanov's dogma; Bogdanov "strikes the hardest blow at militant individualism, showing the complete insubstantiality of the latter in the theory of consciousness." Shuliatikov too felt that Bogdanov had "opened a new era in the history of philosophy" with his collectivism. The individual should be replaced by the collective, in politics as well as in philosophy; "the centralization of organizational functions does not mean replacing many organizers with one."[31]

Bogdanov's collectivism provided a center around which the veterans of 1905 Bolshevism could rally. In thought, as in politics, the myth of the collective was to counterbalance the authority of the individual. As Lenin well knew, this alluded not only to bourgeois philosophy, but to Leninist politics. Bolshevism was threatening to become Bogdanovism.

Lenin and Plekhanov against Machism

George Plekhanov, the pope of Russian Marxism, led the attack on Bogdanov's collectivism in 1908, and Lenin was an eager imitator. As early as 1901 Lenin had declared himself a "definite opponent of both Hume's scepticism and Kant's idealism." Yet when Plekhanov attacked Mach and Avenarius at a party congress in 1905, Lenin treated him with sarcasm and levity.

Without being able to show that *Vpered* wants to "criticize" Marx, Plekhanov brings into earshot Mach and Avenarius. I am definitely puzzled about what relations these two writers (toward whom I have not the slightest sympathy) have to the question of social revolution. They have written about the individual and social organization of experience, or something of this sort, but truly have not thought much about the democratic dictatorship. Has Plekhanov learned that Parvus has become a supporter of Mach and Avenarius? (Laughter.) Or maybe Plekhanov has come to the point where he needs for a target Mach and Avenarius, not the village or the city.

For Lenin, the 1905 revolution meant that philosophy was far less important than militant politics. Bogdanov was a necessary Bolshevik ally, and Plekhanov a Menshevik enemy. In 1908 the situation was reversed. Bogdanov had become an enemy, and Plekhanov an ally, in a philosophical struggle to control Bolshevism.[32]

For many Russian Marxists, collectivism was threatening because of its scepticism toward all metaphysical truths and orthodoxies. Plekhanov as early as July 1905 pointed out the link between eighteenth-century scepticism and Bogdanov, noting that "the views of Mach and Avenarius represent only the latest variation on Hume's philosophy." Another essay dedicated to Plekhanov in 1906 attacked Bogdanov and Lunacharsky for creating "idealism under a Marxist flag" and went on to defend the "absolute reality of the external world." Collectivism was derided as a "complete muddle" (*putanitsa*).[33]

But collectivism was rooted in a broader contemporary trend in European thought, often characterized as "modernism." Modernism encompassed neo-Kantian idealism, religious symbolism, impressionism, intuitionism, and other points of view that seemed to threaten the absolute verities of nineteenth-century thought. The Catholic church was especially concerned with the modernist breakdown of old values. In September 1907 Pope Pius X issued his encyclical *Pascendi Gregis* attacking all modernism as theological heresy. Agnosticism leads to atheism, pronounced the Pope, even if disguised as fideism, a surrogate belief. Church teachings are not relatively, but absolutely, true. The modernists assert the primacy of individual experience, but "given this doctrine of experience united with that of symbolism, every religion, even that of paganism, must be held to be true." Scripture is the sacred word of God, not myth or text; the church is God's authority in the world, not an expression of collective experience. Modernism is nothing less than a "synthesis of all the heresies," and church authority must censor it out of existence.[34]

The revision of orthodoxy was thus as much a problem for the Church in 1908 as for the Marxists. Lenin proclaimed that the heresy laid down in Bogdanov's *Essays on Marxism* was "not Marxism"; it only sharpened the differences among the Bolsheviks and made a battle over philosophy "absolutely inevitable." Breaking off relations with Bogdanov in the spring of 1908, Lenin wrote an article entitled "Marxism and Revisionism" in which he made it plain that the enemy was not only philosophical idealism and "neo-Humeian, neo-Berkeleyan revisionism" but also political syndicalism. "Even that 'revisionism of the left,' which has appeared now in the Latin countries as 'revolutionary syndicalism,' is also attracted to Marxism, 'correcting' it; Labriola in Italy and Lagardelle in France label themselves in Marx's ranks, falsely interpreting what Marx really meant."[35] The key to attacking Bogdanov, however, was not to confront the syndicalist politics he shared with so many other Bolsheviks, but to criticize his philosophy.

Plekhanov led the attack on Bogdanov and Machism but was not supported by Karl Kautsky. In response to Plekhanov's complaint that "our German comrades are turning more and more away from Marxist materialism," Kautsky wrote that Machism was a "serious socialist point of view." "From what I know about Mach," wrote Kautsky, "he must be taken seriously." Thus daunted, Plekhanov launched his attack in the pages of Russian, not German, journals in the spring of 1908.[36]

In an article entitled "Basic Questions of Marxism," Plekhanov argued that Marxist materialism was an entire world view that should not be revised by "bourgeois ideologues," among whom he included Kant, Mach, Avenarius, and Dietzgen. Materialism was the correct world view, idealism the false one. "To be," wrote Plekhanov, "does not mean to exist in the mind. In this respect the philosophy of Feuerbach is much clearer than the philosophy of Joseph Dietzgen." Neither parliamentary reformists nor syndicalists understood Marxism, and any revision of Marxism resembled the very modernist heresies condemned so recently by Pius X. "Until now," wrote Plekhanov, "there were no attempts to 'supplement' Marx by a Thomas Aquinas. But there is nothing impossible about the fact that, despite the recent papal encyclical against the modernists, the Catholic world at one time pulled from its midst a thinker capable of this theoretical heroic act."[37]

Having equated revisionism with heresy, Plekhanov went on to attack Bogdanov directly in an article entitled "Militant Materialism." In it Plekhanov excommunicated Bogdanov as a lapsed comrade, an empiriomonist who, with Labriola and Lunacharsky, had tried to smuggle syndicalism into Russia "in the guise of a weapon 'suitable for orthodox Marxists.'" Mach stood in the tradition of English scepticism and agnosticism, a descendant of Hume and Bishop Berkeley, a tradition that could end only in idealism, not materialism. The world was no mere product of mind and experience; it existed outside the self.[38]

Further, Plekhanov polemicized, Bogdanov was really quite ignorant in matters of philosophy. Otherwise he would know that his idol Mach stood "on the same point of view as the eighteenth-century idealist Berkeley." Matter is not experience or idea, but thing-in-itself. "So, for example, you, Mr. Bogdanov, exist first 'as yourself' and second as perceived by, say, Mr. Lunacharsky, who considers you a deep thinker." Either a Marxist or a Machist, there was no middle ground for Plekhanov. "Machism," he concluded, "is only Berkeleyanism made over and embellished in the light of 'twentieth-century natural science' " and a contemporary variant of "subjective idealism."[39]

Plekhanov was thus the Menshevik point man in the attack on Bogdanov's philosophy and Bolshevism, apparently at the request of Paul Axelrod. According to Plekhanov, Axelrod "practically forced me to start a polemic with Bogdanov." Yet by December 1908 Plekhanov had drifted away from the Mensheviks to ally himself with a renegade Bolshevik, Lenin, who sought to use Plekhanov's philosophical attack on Bogdanov in order to destroy Bogdanov politically. The result was *Materialism and Empiriocriticism.*[40]

Materialism and Empiriocriticism

Between May 16 and June 10, 1908, Lenin resided at 21 Tavistock Street in London. For much of the time he worked in the British Museum, collecting notes for a future philosophical polemic against Bogdanov. He also pursued illegal work as usual, especially efforts to get help from the International Socialist Bureau in freeing those arrested for cashing Tiflis Ex notes. But his primary interest was literary. He pored through the works of Hume and Berkeley, Mach and Avenarius, and modern German philosophers, such as Wilhelm Wundt and Kuno Fischer. He devoured the pragmatism of William James, the energetics of Wilhelm Ostwald, the scientific essays of J. J. Thompson and J. B. Stallo.[41]

The first fruit of this activity was a polemical list of ten questions sent by Lenin to I. F. Dubrovinsky in Geneva. On May 28 Dubrovinsky confronted Bogdanov with the list at a public lecture: Does the lecturer acknowledge that the philosophy of Marxism is dialectical materialism? If he does not, why has he never analysed Engels's countless statements on this subject? Is the lecturer aware that Petzoldt in his latest book has classed a number of Mach's disciples among the idealists? Does the lecturer confirm the fact that Machism has nothing in common with Bolshevism? And so on. Lenin had escalated his conflict with Bogdanov from private disagreement to public warfare.[42]

Yet Lenin's isolation was such that it was not easy to find a publisher for his polemic. His dentist friend P. G. Dauge was a supporter of Dietzgen and Bogdanov and refused to publish Lenin's book. In July 1908 Lenin fumed that there was now a "schism with Bogdanov" over his philosophical views that was worse than that between Bolsheviks and Mensheviks. "I will leave the fraction as soon as the 'left' line and real 'boycottism' take over," he threatened. Lenin was ill now and in need of a publisher. He was reduced to asking his sisters in Moscow to find him one.[43]

"It is important that the book come out soon," Lenin wrote his sister Anna in August. "For me there are not only literary but also serious political circumstances connected with its publication." The problem was Bogdanov: "a complete break and war are now worse than with the Mensheviks." In September he sent Anna back to Moscow from Geneva with the request that she find a publisher as soon as possible. She approached the Zerno house of L. O. Krumbügel, a twenty-eight-year-old Social Revolutionary with a wealthy father. But Krumbügel thought the book would merit only a small edition, and wanted to think it over.[44]

By late October Lenin had completed his manuscript and again asked Anna Elizarova to get him a contract. He agreed to tone down his language to please the censor, using "fideism" instead of "priestism," for example, to mollify the church. She approached Skvortsov about using Gorky's Znanie house, but Gorky was busy publishing Bogdanov's works. She also tried Bonch-Bruevich, but he was in debt and could not promise any royalties. As of December 1, 1908, Lenin still could not find a publisher and was increasingly frustrated.[45]

Gorky was determined not to help Lenin. "With regard to publishing Lenin's book," he wrote K. P. Piatnitsky, "I am against it because I know the author. He is a clever fellow, a wonderful man, but he is a fighter who scoffs at gentlemanly conduct. Let Znanie edit his book and he will say: what fools, meaning Bogdanov, myself, Bazarov, Lunacharsky. The argument between Lenin and Plekhanov on one side and Bogdanov, Bazarov, and Co. on the other is very important and deep. The first two, differing on tactical questions, both believe in and advocate historical fatalism; the opposing side teaches philosophical activity. For me it is clear on whose side truth lies."[46]

In December 1908, Lenin moved from Geneva to Paris, and finally obtained a contract from Krumbügel and the Zerno house. Three thousand copies would be printed, and Lenin would receive royalties and fifty free copies. Anna signed the contract, and Lenin agreed to tone down his acerbic comments on Bazarov and Bogdanov. By February 1909 Lenin had received corrected galley proofs from Moscow and returned them. In the meantime polemics with Bogdanov had intensified, and Lenin was running short on funds.[47]

In March 1909 the censorship struck again in St. Petersburg. The Senate Criminal Cassation Division ordered a new edition of Marx's *Communist Manifesto* seized and destroyed, along with a new edition of Marx's letters to Kügelman with an introduction by Lenin. St. Petersburg officials even proposed that criminal proceedings be launched against Lenin and his sister, but admitted that "the names, surnames, occupations, and places of residence of these people are unknown." To

be safe, Lenin agreed to have the manuscript printed on the presses of
Russia's most reactionary publishing house, controlled by the powerful
A. S. Suvorin. Krumbügel had cleverly made this arrangement in the full
knowledge that books printed by Suvorin were not subject to normal
censorship review. Lenin's attack on Bogdanov was to be printed by
what was virtually an arm of the Russian government.[48]

Lenin still insisted that nothing should be toned down about
"Bogdanov, Lunacharsky, and Co.," who were "dishonorable Machists"
and "enemies of Marxism in philosophy." He continually demanded that
Anna hurry up the publication. It was "devilishly important" that the
book come out as soon as possible, he wrote Anna in early April 1909.
With the aid of Krumbügel and L. S. Peres, another Bolshevik, the final
corrections were negotiated and *Materialism and Empiriocriticism* appeared
in the middle of May in an edition of two thousand copies at a price of
two rubles, sixty kopeks, rather high-priced by standards of the day. At
that price, wrote Gorky, "who will read it?"[49]

Lenin was pleased with the book, which he found well edited but
expensive. The other Bolsheviks were not. Gorky found in it "the sound
of a hooligan" yelling "I am the best Marxist of all," and concluded that
Lenin was a publicist, not a philosopher, an "individualist" and a
"hopeless case." Gorky wrote Bogdanov that he, not Lenin, represented
true Bolshevism, adding that "as far as Lenin is concerned, you are right:
he thinks like a priest."[50]

Friedrich Adler was equally dismayed. "Lenin has written a large book
of 450 pages against Machism," he wrote his father, "in which he
carefully attacks me, but without really disturbing me at all. He is
capable only of petty arguments, since he does not really understand the
question. Still, the book is a remarkable achievement. In about a year he
has gone through the entire literature, of which he previously had no
idea, and then has been able to make criticisms."[51]

What was the content of Lenin's Aesopian polemic against Bolshevik
collectivism?

Orthodoxy against Science

Lenin's book was a ringing defense of orthodox Marxism, as articulated by Plekhanov, against Bolshevik collectivism, as articulated by
Bogdanov, Gorky, and Lunacharsky. Philosophically, it defended materialism against idealism; politically, it tried to link Bogdanov's philosophy with the Mensheviks, without mentioning the syndicalist politics
that actually linked Bogdanov with the Bolsheviks. Like Plekhanov,
Lenin attacked Bogdanov's empiriomonism; unlike Plekhanov, Lenin
did not attack syndicalism. But he did employ the tried and true
Aesopian techniques of legal Marxism.

Lenin admitted at the outset that Machism was merely a "synonym for 'empirio-critics,'" which in turn was "a muddle, a mixture of material-ism and idealism." His main target was Bogdanov, who had "abandoned the materialist standpoint" and "condemned himself to confusion and idealist aberrations." Machism, in turn, led into the swamp of fideism, the substitution of belief for reason. Philosophy was Aesopian politics, and Lenin noted that philosophers must be judged not by the labels they give themselves, but by "how they settle fundamental theoretical questions, by their associates, by what they are teaching and by what they have taught their disciples and followers." Bogdanov had simply created new names for the ideas of Hume, Berkeley, and Mach, and was guilty by association of any consequences.[52]

Lenin's political opponents thus appear in disguise throughout the book. Sorel is not a syndicalist, but a "notorious muddler." Viktor Chernov is not a Socialist Revolutionary, but a "principled literary opponent." Friedrich Adler is not an Austrian socialist, but a "German Machist would-be Marxist." Lunacharsky says "shameful things" using words with "special meanings." Lenin, understanding that special meaning, wanted cooperation "while there is still ground for a fight on comradely lines." Philosophy is a partisan struggle between materialism and idealism, an extension of the world of politics into the world of ideas in which there can be no neutrality.[53]

In this context, then, Machism was an "incredibly muddled, confused, and reactionary" philosophy based on scepticism that tried to refute materialism. Following Plekhanov, Lenin traced the thought of Mach and Bogdanov back to Hume and Berkeley. He decried the notion that matter might exist only in our sensations of the world. Machism was "a sheer plagiarism on Berkeley" that tried to eliminate the material world. Lenin's response was simple: "The existence of matter does not depend on sensation. Matter is primary. Sensation, thought, consciousness are the supreme product of matter organized in a particular way. Such are the views of materialism in general, and of Marx and Engels in particular."[54]

Lenin held to a simple copy theory of reality. The external world reflected by our mind "exists independently of our mind," he wrote. Objective truth also existed outside the mind. Mach and Bogdanov had fallen into idealism, agnosticism, and relativism. "If truth is only an organizing form of human experience," wrote Lenin, "then the teaching of, say, Catholicism is also true." Relativism and solipcism led to religion; materialism was the basis of science. The word *experience* was thus "only a shield for idealist systems."[55]

How could Mach and Bogdanov believe that such verities as space and time do not exist, that they are simply mental ways of organizing experience? This was muddled idealism, a flirtation with religion, "a hash, a potpourri of contradictory and disconnected epistemological propositions." Bogdanov's idea that the self was a mere complex of experiences was a "complex of absurdities, fit only for deducing the immortality of the soul, or the idea of God." Collectivism was a "reactionary muddle."[56]

To substitute the collective for the individual, wrote Lenin, was like "thinking that capitalism will vanish by replacing one capitalist by a joint stock company." The Machists were also distorting the ideas of Dietzgen, a materialist who was occasionally "muddled," but not an idealist. Scientists who argued that atoms did not exist, but were scientific hypotheses, were trying to replace materialism with idealism and agnosticism. Motion without matter was as unthinkable as a revolution without a proletariat.[57]

Knowing nothing about modern physics, Lenin depended on the defense of atomism by Ludwig Boltzmann, the expert in statistical mechanics who attacked both Mach and Ostwald for their arguments that energy, not matter, was the principle substance of the physical world. Bogdanov's reinterpretation of Mach was "only words, concealing an idealist philosophy." The choice was Bolshevik materialism or Menshevik idealism; any middle ground was "contemptible, conciliatory quackery." Lunacharsky's idea of god building, a surrogate socialist religion, was also based on a denial of objective reality, agnosticism, and subjectivism. "The shameful things to which Lunacharsky has stooped are not exceptional; they are the product of empirio-criticism, both Russian and German."[58]

Lenin's *Materialism and Empiriocriticism* was thus an attack on scientific relativism and philosophical sensationalism in the name of orthodox materialism. For the alert reader, it was also a political attack on Lenin's rival Bogdanov, and, to a lesser extent, on Bogdanov's supporters Lunacharsky and Gorky. In his review of Lenin's book, Bogdanov accused his rival of basing his views on religious authority, the "fetishes of power." The real criterion of truth, wrote Bogdanov, was not dogma but practice, not theory but experience. Absolute truth was an idealist fiction, a matter of faith, not scientific knowledge. It was Lenin (that is, his legal Marxist pseudonym V. Ilin) who supported idealism, clericalism, and priestism with his religious authority, not Bogdanov.[59]

Bogdanov denied that he was a mere imitator of Mach and Avenarius. He was interested in an ideology that could organize mass experience—not Catholicism, as Lenin implied, but Marxism. The usefulness of an idea was not to be judged by "whether a majority or minority accepts it", but by "whether it corresponds to collective labor's demand for progress." In other words, party policy should be decided by workers, not Bolsheviks or Mensheviks. Lenin did not understand Marx in the first place, and Lenin's polemical methods reminded Bogdanov of his childhood Sunday school courses in the Orthodox church. Bogdanov noted that the Bolshevik Lenin had written *What Is to Be Done?*, but "I do not know what Russian Marxist faction V. Ilin belongs to."[60]

Bogdanov concluded that Lenin was merely a student of Plekhanov, and a mistaken one. His argument was from scripture, not experience. He had no real philosophy and no unity of thought. He was "apparently a very young philosopher, at least I have not seen his name before in the scholarly literature." Lenin believed in a cult of the absolute; he wanted only to "sharpen and deepen the practical contradictions inside the left wing of Russian Marxism," namely, Bolshevism. Marxism must reject absolute orthodoxy of any kind, including that of Marxism itself. Party unity could only be achieved through collective action.[61]

Lenin's *Materialism and Empiriocriticism* thus served only to deepen the split between Lenin's authority and Bogdanov's collectivism. It was a political tract in the guise of a philosophical monograph; as such, it reflected a sharpening political quarrel within Bolshevism to which we must now turn.

The Bolshevik Center Schism: Paris against Geneva

Lenin's attack on Bogdanov's philosophy was part of a larger political struggle within the Bolshevik Center in 1909. The fifth conference of the RSDRP in Paris in January 1909 did little to unite the Bolsheviks, beyond condemning the "disorganizing opposition to central committee activity" by all fractions. The conference consisted of a tiny group of only sixteen voting delegates, which did not include Lenin, Bogdanov, or the police agent Ya. A. Zhitomirsky. But it did agree to condemn any attempt to liquidate underground activity, and to move its journal *Sotsial Demokrat* from Vilna to Paris.[62]

As soon as the conference dispersed, Bogdanov attacked Lenin and the editorial board of *Proletarii* for creating an "anti-boycott center" that supported parliamentary activity and a policy of schism inside the Bolshevik Center. At a meeting of the editorial board with Lenin absent, Bogdanov succeeded in passing a resolution that *Proletarii* would remain neutral in matters of philosophy. In late February 1909 Lenin responded with an attack on "the swamp of god building and god seeking" (Lunacharsky) and began breaking off relations with Bogdanov entirely. Lenin succeeded in getting the editorial board to reverse itself and reject an article by Lunacharsky, further widening the split within Bolshevism. "The atmosphere here is very difficult," wrote Lenin's sister Maria Ulianova from Paris, "and Volodina's [Lenin's] predictions about a schism are coming true, if they have not already. The war against A. A. [Bogdanov] and Nik-cha [Krasin] has begun."[63]

In the spring of 1909, European socialism was deeply divided over the question of parliamentary participation and mass action. Kautsky opposed either strategy in favor of preparations for the day when the socialists would seize power. The Dutch socialists voted to expel dissidents of a syndicalist inclination from their party. Mach's ideas were spreading through the writings of Friedrich Adler, who emphasized the importance of the experience of the general strike over Marxist theories; theories were not truths, but tools, and it was fruitless to waste time arguing about the meaning of Marx's ideas. Kautsky, the leader of SPD orthodoxy, was interested in Mach and Dietzgen's ideas; Plekhanov's attack on them was wrong, he felt, at a time when the party needed clarity and unity in preparing for revolution. The Russians, noted Kautsky, would be much better off if they stopped arguing about Machism and Dietzgenism and considered philosophical views a "private matter."[64]

But Lenin could not be so tolerant, because the other Bolsheviks were drifting away. The young historian M. N. Pokrovsky left Paris for Geneva to work with Bogdanov, and criticized Lenin for underestimating the possibilities of revolution. Lenin paraphrased Pokrovsky: "Of course recallism is stupid, of course it's syndicalism, but for moral considerations I, and probably Skvortsov too, shall be for Maximov [Bogdanov]." Even Krasin was drifting away from the Bolshevik Center.[65]

Another potential deserter in Lenin's mind was Stalin. "How do you like Bogdanov's new book?" Stalin wrote in the spring of 1909. "In my view, some individual blunders of Ilich [Lenin] are significantly and correctly noted in it. He also notes correctly that Ilich's materialism is in many ways different from Plekhanov's, which in spite of the demands of logic (in the interests of diplomacy?) Ilich tries to bury."[66]

Lenin, Zinoviev, and Taratuta resisted Bogdanov's attempt to convene a meeting of the Bolshevik Center in April because "certain members" had embarked on a "schismatic path." As a result Bogdanov's "Geneva circle of Bolsheviks" refused any longer to obey the Center, and began making contacts among other Bolshevik émigrés in various European cities. The "stinking squabble," as Lenin called it, continued. "The Geneva group," he charged, "announced its break with the Bolshevik Center and urged the Paris one to follow suit." He also charged that Lunacharsky's religion of socialism, his "god building," was now anathema, and "party condemnation is necessary and obligatory."[67]

In June 1909 things came to a head in Paris. Labor radicalism was on the wane in France as well at the time. A strike of postal workers had recently failed to achieve any real gains, and the CGT was split over the issue of syndicalism and parliamentary participation. Sorel was moving away from syndicalism toward the royalism and nationalism of CharlesMaurras and Action Francaise.[68] In this grim atmosphere the Bolshevik Center, disguised as usual as the editorial board of *Proletarii*, convened.

The Paris meeting on June 21 through June 30, 1909, included twelve representatives of what was left of Bolshevism: nine members of the Bolshevik Center and three representatives of Russian party branches— M. P. Tomsky (St. Petersburg), V. M. Shuliatikov (Moscow), and N. A. Skrypnik (Urals). With Krupskaya as secretary, Lenin managed to place on the agenda a number of resolutions condemning the "recallism" and "god building" of Bogdanov and his circle. Lenin's main object of attack was Bogdanov for his "destruction of organizational unity of the Bolshevik fraction"; the editorial board "disclaims any responsibility for all political measures taken by Comrade Bogdanov." After days of fighting and arguing, Bogdanov wrote with a combination of sarcasm and weariness that "the battle ended yesterday very propitiously for me—I have been expelled from the Bolshevik Center."[69]

Lenin was supported in varying degrees by Zinoviev, Kamenev, Tomsky, and Rykov. The conference agreed to reduce *Proletarii* to a monthly journal, and to enter negotiations with Trotsky to establish a new organ of the RSDRP central committee, *Pravda*. Bogdanov, Krasin, Pokrovsky, and Shantser fired off a pamphlet indicting Lenin and the remnants of the Bolshevik Center for illegally expelling them. Many Bolsheviks left for Gorky's home on Capri, where they established a workers' school and continued their debate with Lenin. "The Bolshevik Center," wrote Bogdanov in disgust, "has now become ideologically, materially, and organizationally the uncontrolled dictator of Bolshevik affairs." Again, Lenin and Bogdanov parted ways.[70]

The Paris Okhrana was well aware that Bolshevism was in crisis, and not entirely displeased. Bogdanov and Krasin, they reported, "having begun by criticizing Marx on philosophy, passed on to criticizing the Bolshevik Center, turning to recallism and ultimatism and finally, having seized a large part of the money stolen at Tiflis, began to agitate secretly against the Bolshevik Center in general and its individual members in particular." Lenin wanted to "compel Bogdanov's supporters either to separate completely or to stop agitating and submit to the majority, and to transfer to the Bolshevik Center the seized five-hundred-ruble notes and the school on the island of Capri." The Okhrana mistakenly thought that Bogdanov would submit to a Leninist majority created for that purpose, but he did not. Instead he left for Capri to form a new Bolshevik Center.[71]

By the summer of 1909 Lenin and the other Bolsheviks were deeply divided over questions of money, politics, and philosophy. Lenin had succeeded in expelling Bogdanov and his followers in name only. They, too, had claims on the legitimacy of Bolshevism. Lenin had written a classic polemic defending Marxist orthodoxy; his opponents continued to make the mistake of treating Bolshevism as useful collectivist myth rather than orthodox truth. In Lenin's philosophical crudity lay his political genius.

VIII

BOLSHEVISM WITHOUT LENIN

COLLECTIVISM AND THE
CAPRI SCHOOL

The higher the organizer raises himself above
the collective, the less he lives a life with his
subordinates, the easier and more often his
authority is based on purely personal, petty
individual motives—moods, caprices, etc.

—A. A. Bogdanov, *The Decline of
a Great Fetish* (1910)

He knew that what one calls a "person" was
after all merely an assembly of bits and
qualities and odours and so on; apart from
those bits and qualities, the person did not
exist, was merely an illusion, and vanished
into nothingness.

—ARTHUR KOESTLER, *The Age of Longing*

In the summer of 1909 Bolshevism disintegrated into two warring
factions. Lenin and Krupskaya remained in Paris and nominally presided
over the editorial board of *Proletarii* and the Bolshevik Center, from
which Bogdanov had been expelled. Bogdanov and many other Bolsheviks left Paris to escape Lenin and took refuge at Gorky's home on the
Isle of Capri. Here they established themselves as the true heirs of 1905
Bolshevism, a collective of collectivists, seeking a philosophy of proletarian culture to maintain Bolshevism in exile. In public, Lenin chastised
them as dissident heretics to the Marxist orthodoxy of himself and
Plekhanov. But he realized that he now had few supporters left, and that
Capri had become the center of a Bolshevism without Lenin.

Lenin and Plekhanov against Bolshevism

In July 1909 Lenin published in *Proletarii* the resolutions of the editorial
board meeting and accused Bogdanov of "breaking away from us" by

144

trying to organize a "workers' school" on Capri without Lenin, a "fraction breaking away from the Bolsheviks." Lenin's main ally was now Plekhanov, who announced his break with the Mensheviks in an open letter proclaiming that "only one way is possible—the strengthening and broadening of our illegal party organization and struggle for ideological influence over it." Whether or not Lenin's *Materialism and Empiriocriticism* had encouraged Plekhanov's attraction to Bolshevism, the two were now allies in a war on Machist heresy and syndicalist politics.[1]

Lenin was not idle that summer. He signed an agreement with the Kuklin Library in Geneva to move to Paris all 137 boxes of books and archives. He publicly protested the trip of Tsar Nicholas II to Europe and tried to get the ISB to do likewise. He became involved with A. M. Ignatiev in an abortive plot to kidnap the tsar from Peterhof, using the imperial convoy of Kuban Cossacks, then told Ignatiev to cease and desist in this violent adventure. He watched helplessly as the by-elections to the third Duma produced some victories for the "recallists" among the RSDRP. And he tried to negotiate with Trotsky in Vienna to join the editorial board of *Proletarii* and to have Trotsky's *Pravda* printed on its Paris presses.[2]

The negotiations with Trotsky fell through, and Lenin raged against the Capri School. What was this "band of riff-raff of Maksimov [Bogdanov] and Co." doing on Capri anyway? Was this "gang of adventurists" running some kind of brothel there? "A complete break and war" with Bogdanov's circle "are now stronger than with the Mensheviks," he protested. Bogdanov's syndicalist tactics of boycotting the Duma might have been appropriate in 1907, but certainly not in 1909. This was anarchism, Jesuitism, and deception. In October Lenin noted that even Viktor Taratuta had now declared himself "for Geneva," that is, a Bogdanov supporter; "I think that is wrong," Lenin wrote V. A. Karpinsky. "We will not go to Geneva."[3]

By the autumn of 1909 Leninism and Bolshevik collectivism were becoming increasingly distinct political philosophies. Party workers in St. Petersburg noted that this was, in part, a difference between émigrés and *praktiki* inside the country. *Proletarii* distinguished between "old" and "new" Bolshevism. Bogdanov charged that Lenin had now "passed over to a Menshevik point of view of parliamentarism." In fact, Lenin did share with the Mensheviks a great hostility to Bogdanov's collectivism. Martov called Lunacharsky's theory of a socialist religion "reactionary heresy" and a "complete break with the materialist basis of scientific socialism." L. O. Axelrod ("Ortodoks") charged that Bolshevism had become a kind of empiriocritical demagoguery, dogma and propaganda joined in revolutionary romanticism. But whereas Martov associated Bolshevism with Sorelian myth and syndicalist direct action, Lenin did not. He preferred to attack collectivist philosophy, which he abhorred, but not syndicalist politics, which he had for a time admired.[4]

Plekhanov, however, continued to make the connection between Bolshevism and syndicalism in a way that Lenin would not. The "religious sermons" of Bogdanov and Lunacharsky, he noted, were "not so foreign to politics." "Mr. Lunacharsky," he sniffed, "generally watches very attentively to see what the demand is. When there was a demand for syndicalism, he hastened to walk hand in hand through our literature with the well-known Italian syndicalist Arturo Labriola, whom he passed off as a Marxist on more than one occasion." Lunacharsky's god building was just another "modish game." Gorky and Lunacharsky had begun with the idea that God was a fiction, and now recognized humanity as a new God. This was un-Marxist. But the revolt against Marxist authority was also an inclination toward revolutionary syndicalism, "the illegitimate daughter of anarchism."[5]

The Organization of Collectivism

In 1908 Gorky praised Bogdanov as a great "organizer of ideas" that reflected the "collective experience" of the Russian proletariat. By January 1909 Gorky, Bogdanov, and Lunacharsky were planning a new collection of essays on the "philosophy of collectivism" which would, naturally, not include Lenin among its authors. Krasin, Pokrovsky, and Bazarov were all to be involved, if they were willing. What did they mean by collectivism?[6]

Collectivism and socialism stressed the well-being of society over the individual. Moreover, as Ludwig Feuerbach pointed out in *The Religion of Humanity*, socialism had a religious dimension; "God is man, man is God," he wrote, and through the "idea of the species" man could build for himself a kind of collective religion of humanity. Ernst Haeckel, the German Darwinist, also argued that the individual was only a "tiny grain of protoplasm in the perishable framework of organic nature"; in a monist universe, there was no division between mind and matter, science was only an approximation of truth, and man's immortality was not individual but cosmic. Nature, of which man was a biological part, was eternal.[7]

Many nineteenth-century European socialist thinkers connected the idea of the individual self with private property, and saw socialism as a substitute religion that would do away with bourgeois individualism. This was particularly true in England, where positivism—the faith in the unlimited power of science to control nature—led many to the ethical socialism of the Labor Churches and Fabianism. Winwood Reade, a freethinker, in his book *The Martyrdom of Man* (1872) argued that Christianity would have to be replaced by socialism in a manner that would give up the belief in the individual soul and its immortality. Sidney Webb wrote that "we must abandon the self-conceit of imagining that we are independent units and bend our proud minds, absorbed in their own cultivation, to this subjection to the higher end, the Common Weal." Annie Besant, the theosophist, also urged "generous self-sacrifice to the common good."[8]

Another English socialist, E. Belfort Bax, called for a new "religion of socialism, a sense of oneness with the social body" and a "readiness to sacrifice all, including life itself, for the cause." Bax's ideal individual was the "Russian nihilist or the Paris workman [who] in deliberately exposing himself to certain death, believing in no personal immortality," still sacrifices himself for the cause. The American socialist Edward Bellamy in his book *The Religion of Solidarity* (1874) argued that individuality was a prison from which man must escape into universal solidarity; individualism leads to fear of death, whereas self-sacrifice and social solidarity provides a kind of immortality.[9]

We have seen that many Bolsheviks sought to counter a Russian mood of symbolist decadence, individual mysticism, and general gloom with one of collective humanism, drawing upon the ideas of Joseph Dietzgen. The Moscow Bolsheviks were especially articulate. In 1908 Shuliatikov attacked the emerging Russian avant-garde's obsession with death as a consequence of bourgeois decline; more positively, V. M. Friche predicted a future "collectivist society" in which theater would give way to the cinema, providing the masses with "collective festivals" (often on film), including mass parades and choral concerts. Such festivals, argued Bazarov, would appeal not to the idea of individualism (a German import to Russia), but to a new proletarian consciousness.[10]

Gorky and Lunacharsky were the main Bolshevik proponents of a new collectivist religion. People have always created their gods, argued Gorky, and bourgeois society had created its individual gods and heroes to justify a world of private property. But this was cynicism. "Not 'I' but 'we'—here is the principle on which the personality should be emancipated. Then, finally, man will feel himself to be the incarnation of all wealth, of all the world's beauty, of all experience of humanity and spiritually the equal of all his brothers." An "integral personality" would be possible only in a world where the line between the hero and the crowd disappeared, through a "religion of humanity" based on mutual respect.[11]

In early 1908 Gorky wrote an essay entitled "The Destruction of the Personality," but Lenin refused to publish it in *Proletarii*. According to Gorky, "the collective does not seek immortality; it has it. The personality, maintaining its position as lord of the people, needs to learn for itself the thirst for eternal life." Individualism created individual and immortal gods. Bourgeois society was degenerating into hopeless cynicism, witnessed by an increase in mental illness and suicide. Contemporary Russian literature was full of themes of individual death. Hope lay in collective immortality. "There is no personal immortality, and we all inevitably disappear, in order to yield on earth to people stronger, more beautiful, more honest than we, people who will create a new, beautiful, clean life and, perhaps, by the miraculous power of their united wills, will defeat death."[12]

Lunacharsky, too, sought a religion of collectivism that would produce a victory over death. Citing Mach, he called for the immortality of creative, remembered acts, expressed through the ideology of the working class. "Man does not need God," he wrote. "Man himself is God. Man is a god for man. He does not need personal immortality, since his immortality is the life of the species and hope in eternal victory of life over dead matter." For the individual, real salvation from death would come through humanity as a collective; "here a real victory over death is possible."[13]

In 1907 Lunacharsky began writing a long, rambling tome entitled *Religion and Socialism*. Published in 1908 and 1911 in two volumes, the book articulated a "proletarian world view" that was indebted to Feuerbach and Dietzgen, as much as to Marx and Engels. Lunacharsky argued that scientific socialism was a religion of humanity and compared it with various other world religions. Like Comte, Lunacharsky worshipped the god of science and rationalism but also praised religion's "festive power." Like Kautsky, he saw Christ as a proletarian leader of the downtrodden masses of Galilee, an "ideology of the tormented poor of Jerusalem and the Jews in general." Early Christianity resembled revolutionary communism, an apocalyptic revolt of the propertyless classes against Roman authority. Collectivism for Lunacharsky meant a proletarian religion appealing to mass psychology through festival and myth. As to theory, Lunacharsky praised Bogdanov as "the only Marxist philosopher continuing the pure philosophical tradition of Marx."[14]

In the spring of 1909 Bogdanov and his supporters published their *Essays on the Philosophy of Collectivism*. In it they defined collectivism as "the world view of the proletarian class—the embryo of a universal ideology for a future society." Bogdanov described truth and reality in relative terms as that which reflects collective experience; his suggestion that $2 \times 2 = 4$ is only a convenient metaphor, not a true statement, presaged Orwell's subsequent example of $2 + 2 = 5$ as correct party logic in his novel *1984*. The future belonged to the scientific and technical intelligentsia as organizers of nature along the lines of a "collectivist conception of experience." Collectivism was the true philosophy of Marxism, based on proletariat, not party. "The working class as a social system does not exist unless the proletariat is organized into a party, syndicates, etc."—a living collective.[15]

Bogdanov's relativism and syndicalism were shared by Lunacharsky. Collectivism, he pointed out, often demands "the sacrifice of an individual." A future socialist society would provide numerous collective projects that would require individual sacrifice under a "plan." Whereas anarchism is an individualist utopia, syndicalism offers a form of collectivism where a "socialist, purely proletarian spirit predominates." What is needed is an "international confederation of workers' syndicates" to organize the proletariat and link the socialist parties of different nations. "The syndicate and the union of syndicates," concluded Lunacharsky, "right up to their international confederation, are both the consequence and the justification of the proletariat's collectivist inclinations."[16]

Bolshevik collectivism was a matter of philosophy and religion, but also of politics. Collectivism meant the Bolshevik collective, not Lenin's individual authority, and syndicalist unity with the trade unions, not party dictates. Yet collectivism was also authoritarian, not democratic, grounded in the authority of manipulated myth, if not party hierarchy. The other Bolsheviks were not democrats. Proletarian morality, as Stanislav Volsky pointed out, was a matter of sacrificing self to the "fighting proletariat." The individual is to be transformed into a conscious supporter of the collective. The bourgeois "I" will give way to the proletarian "we," expressed in "proletarian psychology, proletarian consciousness, and proletarian morality." Solidarity will become the "obligatory norm." The "new man" of socialism will be "free, bold, and young." Yet Volsky imagined a future "morality of an armed camp" in which enemies of the revolution would "probably perish, if not as physical beings, in any case as independent creative forces."[17]

Collectivism was a part of the Bolshevik answer to the neo-Kantian individualism expressed by the liberal intelligentsia in its 1909 volume of essays *Vekhi* (Signposts). As we have seen, this continued a debate begun in exile in Vologda at the turn of the century. But collectivism also provided a political focus for those Bolsheviks drawn to European syndicalism who sought to use the power of myth, more than authority, to build a new socialist society.

N. E. Vilonov and the Capri School

In January 1909 the Okhrana reported a new organization in Geneva, the "Fund for Directing Workers to Russia." Its purpose, they assumed, was to facilitate revolutionary activity by supplying money and passports for illegal travelers. They also noted that "recallism" was especially strong in Moscow, and that some connection between that area and Europe was emerging. They were correct.

N. E. Vilonov, at 26, had spent his early adulthood in the workers' cause. Active in Kiev labor circles since the turn of the century, he was a "Leninist before Lenin," a voracious reader who believed in party organization and peasant propaganda. Like Lenin, Vilonov owed a debt to Populism, Jacobinism, and the Social Revolutionary party. Unlike Lenin, he envisaged a real workers' party in which radical intellectuals would play a lesser role than workers themselves. Like Bogdanov, Vilonov held a utopian vision of a collectivist future. In the winter of 1908–1909, after a period of revolutionary activity in the Urals region, Vilonov emigrated to Europe and discovered Gorky and Bogdanov.[18]

In February 1909 Vilonov wrote his wife Maria that he and Gorky were planning to start a school for party workers on Capri, adding that "the theoreticians have agreed and the money will be found." In fact, Bogdanov had approved the plan and sent it to Lenin in Paris, asking that it be printed in *Proletarii*. Lenin was predictably furious. "If you have the money for setting up such a school," he told Bogdanov, "then give it to us, and we will set it up, but in Paris, not on Capri." Taratuta supported Lenin. Vilonov found the Paris idea to be "nonsense," because Capri was cheaper and "better conspiratorially."[19]

In March 1909 Gorky urged Bogdanov to break with Lenin and come to Capri. "The ideology of the party, its true ideology," he wrote, "is empiriomonism." Bogdanov should come to Capri to "complete his system" of philosophy. He should get away from people like Lenin, "individualists with the psychology of police agents." The way to resolve the crisis with Bolshevism was to establish a new "philosophy of collectivism" and a psychological and political reorganization of the party" under the leadership of Bogdanov, not Lenin. Bogdanov agreed.[20]

The idea of bringing Russian "students" to a "school" on Capri masked a project to "train organizers and propagandists" for future party work inside Russia. Party workers from Moscow and the Urals would be brought to Capri for several months in the summer and returned to Russia to "strengthen the intellectual energy of our party." The Stolypin regime had decimated the RSDRP now; many members were in jail or exile. Those still active had little knowledge or training in Marxist philosophy or party organization.[21]

Gorky hoped to rally the other Bolsheviks around Bogdanov. He wrote Pokrovsky in Finland, urging him to join them in publishing a "workers' encyclopedia" on Capri. Bogdanov was very upset at his impending "expulsion" from the fraction by Lenin; "I would advise you and A. A. [Bogdanov] and anyone else who is 'expelled' to remove yourselves immediately so that by autumn each can find his own location." Pokrovsky agreed that the present party crisis was a catastrophe and consented to talk with Bogdanov about coming to Capri. He added that in the struggle between Lenin and Bogdanov, "the victor will be the man who first sees reality."[22]

The Capri School was funded by Gorky's wealthy friends (including the opera singer Fedor Chaliapin) but not supported by the Moscow

RSDRP committee. Lenin wrote the committee warning them that the Capri School was connected with "god building," and true Bolsheviks should not associate themselves with "an enterprise whose Bolshevik and Marxist character is insecure." Bogdanov replied that *Proletarii* had ample opportunity to organize such a school, but had done nothing. He and "comrade Gorky" had served the party for many years. They would now organize their own Bolshevik group.[23]

In Moscow, arrangements were in the hands of Stanislav Volsky and Vilonov's wife. Party workers were recruited and given round-trip train tickets to Capri via Berlin and Naples. Volsky was arrested in May 1909 (but allowed to emigrate the following October), and Lunacharsky showed little enthusiasm for coming to Capri. Vilonov wrote his wife that he was sorry about Volsky's "illness" (arrest) and warned her to beware of Lenin's lies—"only one thing is accurate: his desire to break up the school." Bogdanov hoped to get students even from outside Moscow. But plans were still in jeopardy.[24]

In June 1909, as Lenin was reading Bogdanov out of the Bolshevik Center, the Capri School continued to take shape. Trotsky wanted Gorky to write an article on the project for *Pravda*, but warned that "it is impossible to make leaders in a laboratory." Vilonov left Capri for Moscow, and discovered the desperate need for literate party workers in industrial areas; some Moscow Bolsheviks agreed to support the school only if controlled by the Bolshevik Center. But that Center was now split, with Krasin and Bogdanov declaring their independence, and the thirteen students who left Moscow for Capri in July were thoroughly confused. Grigor Alexinsky wrote Vilonov that "I don't know who is a Leninist and who is not."[25]

In late July the students arrived in Vienna, where Trotsky gave them a tour of local art museums. Vilonov hoped to recruit Trotsky as a lecturer, although Trotsky was lukewarm about the idea. M. N. Liadov, a long-time party leader, announced in *Proletarii* his break with Lenin and the editorial board and his departure from the Bolshevik Center. By early August students arrived on Capri, where an organizational meeting was held to elect a governing council. On August 5 the "First Higher Social Democratic School for Workers" formally opened.[26]

The Capri School featured lectures by Bogdanov, Gorky, Lunacharsky, and others on a wide variety of topics. In his lectures on the trade unions, Lunacharsky spent some time discussing revolutionary syndicalism, much to the dismay of more orthodox Marxists. Usually students would study in the morning, attend lectures in the afternoon, break for dinner, and spend evenings learning about "practical work," presumably illegal activities. Sundays were for rest and recreation. Bogdanov became a guide in Marxist matters, and his wife a mother hen to the students. Gorky and Lunacharsky taught debating. Liadov gave a series of lectures on the history of the RSDRP; Pokrovsky lectured on the history of Russia. Syndicalism again found its way into the lectures of Alexinsky ("on syndicalism and finances"). The students wanted to hear Lenin, who, of course, refused to come to Capri. Instead, he suggested that the students move to Paris. The school council voted to do so if Lenin provided three thousand francs toward expenses; he did not.[27]

The Capri School was fraught with controversy from the moment it opened. Trotsky criticized it for sponsoring an idea of "true Bolshevism" that was "sectarian." Andreeva was increasingly protective of Gorky and hostile to Bogdanov and Lunacharsky. The "Sasha" letter demanding that the Bolsheviks return money to the Urals bank robbers created further division as a possible police provocation; the Okhrana was well aware of the school's activities, intercepting its mail and planting an agent (A. S. Romanov) among the students. Then there was Lenin.[28]

Lenin wrote a letter to the Capri School in the name of the Bolshevik Center in mid-August 1909 asking for "details" of school operations, hinting at financial aid, and suggesting that students might want to move to Paris. I. F. Dubrovinsky refused to lecture on Capri, saying that he was still "solid with the *Proletarii* editorial board", i.e., Lenin. Lenin wrote Tomsky that the school was just a brothel for "recallist nonsense." Finally, in September a group of students admitted that the Capri School was not really a party school at all, but a "private enterprise;" the council denied that it was "destroying the unity of the Bolshevik fraction" and agreed to move to Paris if Lenin would foot the bill.[29]

Lenin responded to Capri School students with a conciliatory letter inviting them to Paris. The Capri School was really the "new center of a new fraction," he noted, dubbing them "Bogdanovites." When Bogdanov learned that Vilonov and five students were planning to join Lenin, he became furious and expelled them from the school. They promptly left for Paris. "Organizational and political questions," observed Alexinsky, "now divide not so much Bolshevism from Menshevism, but left Bolsheviks (recallists, ultimatists) from rights (Lenin and the *Proletarii* editorial board)."[30]

By November 1909 Lenin had succeeded in splitting Bolshevism even further. "I don't know if you are a 'Vperedist' or a 'Leninist' or something else," Andreeva wrote Ladyzhnikov in Berlin, "but if you value A. M. [Gorky] come here as soon as you can. I warn you that I am now, in the words of Bogdanov, Lunacharsky, and Co., a 'vile old lady'; they even tried to declare me insane and I won't play any more games with them." Gorky was ill, and Lenin wrote him a soothing letter apologizing for thinking he belonged to Bogdanov's "new faction" when, of course, he did not. Gorky even invited Lenin to Capri. By December Bogdanov had resigned from the council, declaring his hostility to Lenin's "authoritarianism." The council voted 7–4, with one abstention, not to accept the resignation of "the most valuable leader of the school."[31]

But it was too late. Bogdanov left for Paris in December 1909, and he and Lunacharsky no longer had Gorky's support. The Paris Okhrana duly reported this break, and the collapse of the Capri School, to St. Petersburg. Bogdanov, in an open letter to the RSDRP, formally declared the formation of a new faction around a revived *Vpered*, the same name as the original Bolshevik journal of 1904. Lenin promptly attacked them as "anti-Marxists" hiding under the collectivist labels of "proletarian philosophy" and "proletarian culture." In a letter to Gorky, Lenin called Bogdanov's new group "nihilists" who had not yet learned that the words and methods of 1905 were no longer applicable. He also admitted that the schism between the collectivists and Lenin was "no less deep than that between Bolsheviks and Mensheviks."[32]

The Long Plenum

In the winter of 1909–1910 Bolshevism virtually disappeared as an organized fraction of the RSDRP. The "long plenum" of the RSDRP central committee, which convened in Paris from January 15 to February 5, 1910, was intended to unify the disparate party fractions: Bolsheviks, Mensheviks, Poles, Bundists, and Trotsky's Vienna circle. Instead the long plenum became a theater of mutual recrimination, leaving Lenin isolated and Bolshevism in receivership.

European socialism was still deeply divided on issues of reform and revolution. Marxist rhetoric no longer served to reconcile parliamentary participants and advocates of the syndicalist strike. In Holland majority socialists faced a revolt of the radicals around the journal *Tribune,* including future Comintern luminaries Henriette Roland-Holst, Hermann Gorter, and Anton Pannekoek. Expelled from the party, the Tribunists formed their own party, and petitioned the ISB for membership; Kautsky and Lenin supported them, but to no avail. Ironically, the Dutch left resembled collectivism more than Leninism, urging the use of the mass strike to raise proletarian consciousness.[33]

Similar issues divided Russian socialists gathered in Paris. Bogdanov and Shantser, representing the new *Vpered* fraction, succeeded in having it recognized as a party "editing group." Lenin promptly attacked them for opposing the "party line" with anti-Marxist views, and succeeded in having Dubrovinsky replace Bogdanov on the central committee. But Lenin's victory was short-lived. Noting the "sharp crisis" in the party and the "decline of mass struggle" and "flight of the intelligentsia from the party" inside Russia, the plenum voted to subsidize Trotsky's *Pravda,* to allow Bogdanov and his supporters to participate in the organization of a new party school, and to include *Vpered* in the "general system of party literary activity abroad."[34]

Most important, the plenum forced Lenin to dissolve his operations, including the Bolshevik Center and *Proletarii*. A "Declaration of the Bolsheviks" agreed to eliminate the center, to cease editing *Proletarii*, to transfer seventy-five thousand francs to the RSDRP central committee and another four hundred thousand francs to three SPD trustees, Franz Mehring, Karl Kautsky, and Klara Zetkin. These substantial sums, representing the loot from the Tiflis Ex and the Schmidt inheritance, would become the object of Lenin's incessant attention and litigation for the next several years. The fact that the RSDRP entered German receivership also helps explain Lenin's subsequent hatred for "the renegade Kautsky" who engineered the demise of Bolshevism.[35]

To make matters worse, Martov made public the end of Bolshevism, as well as its past indiscretions. In a pamphlet published shortly after the Paris plenum, Martov included a resolution condemning "certain comrades" for "destroying party discipline." Lenin was excluded from the RSDRP central committee, and a Russian Bureau was established to emancipate the RSDRP from a "foreign clique" of émigrés and to bring more *praktiki* into its operations. More distasteful, Martov told the story of the Lbov partisans and the Bolshevik double cross in the weapons deal. For the Mensheviks, the transfer of illegal Bolshevik funds to the trustees was a compromise; they wanted them to go to the central committee. But they applauded the dissolution of Bolshevism as an organized party fraction.[36]

Lenin wrote his sister Anna Elizarova that attempts to make peace with the Mensheviks had failed. "We have closed down the fraction's organ and will move more aggressively toward unification," he promised. But the division between Lenin and the other Bolsheviks was not so easily eliminated. The agreement with the trustees on money matters was signed with the Bolsheviks, but it was by no means clear whether that meant Lenin or Bogdanov.[37]

The Taratuta Affair

Bolshevik expropriations and other money matters were also the object of an RSDRP party court investigation of Viktor Taratuta in the spring of 1910. On February 2, 1910, the first of seven hearings was held in Paris to discuss charges that Taratuta was a police agent-provocateur, responsible for the arrest of Kamo and other participants in the Tiflis Ex. Martov and the Mensheviks were the main prosecutors. They excoriated the Bolshevik Center for its illegalities after 1907. The whole affair dragged on into 1911 before the court finally dismissed the accusations against Taratuta for lack of evidence. Taratuta declared his innocence, arguing that Bogdanov had started the rumors as part of his campaign against Lenin. Whatever the truth of the matter, in July 1910 a real Okhrana agent, Roman Malinovsky, filed his first report on RSDRP illegal activity inside Russia, leading to numerous arrests; yet he was soon to become a leading figure in the party itself, and a confidant of Lenin.[38]

The Taratuta affair indicated that the division between Lenin and the other Bolsheviks reached deep into the Russian underground. Stalin at first referred to this division as a "tempest in a teapot," and showed signs of supporting Bogdanov against Lenin. By December 1910 Stalin decided to cast his lot with Lenin. In a letter intercepted by the Paris Okhrana, Stalin wrote that Bogdanov and the *Vpered* group should either wake up or "stew in their own juice"; party unity was now a necessity, and "the line of the Lenin-Plekhanov bloc is the only correct one." Lenin was a "shrewd peasant" (*umnyi muzhik*) who could most effectively lead the Bolsheviks in the future.[39]

By January 1911 Stalin appears to have become a Leninist at last. "You have certainly heard about the 'tempest in a teapot,'" he wrote a party member in Moscow; "the Lenin-Plekhanov bloc, on the one hand, the Trotsky-Martov-Bogdanov bloc, on the other. The workers' attitude toward the first bloc, I know, is favorable." Under the misconception that Bogdanov was allied with the Mensheviks, Stalin agreed to support "Lenin & Co." But he also voiced the usual complaint of the *praktiki* that "émigré squabbling" was only helping to destroy the Bolshevik underground inside Russia.[40]

The Taratuta affair, like the Paris plenum, marked a defeat for Lenin. Despite his virtual alliance with the Mensheviks on matters of philosophy, he had completely lost control of his own fraction and its finances. To make matters worse, Bogdanov and his supporters were now laying claim to the mantle of Bolshevism themselves.

Vpered and "Left" Bolshevism

In December 1909 the remnants of the Capri School began to reorganize around Bogdanov and a new journal, *Vpered*. Bogdanov made clear that he was laying claim to the legacy of Bolshevism. Among Bogdanov's supporters were Lunacharsky, Gregor Alexinsky, F. I. Kalinin, Stanislav Volsky, Gorky, Pokrovsky, Liadov, Shantser, and several Capri School students. At Paris in January 1910 they achieved central committee recognition as a "literary group." This enabled them to "fight openly to revive the unity of Bolshevism."

Bogdanov still controlled some of the money from the Tiflis Ex, although how much is unclear. With it he proposed to set up a new party school under the RSDRP central committee that would include all the various fractions. But unity was highly unlikely. In March 1910 Alexinsky accused Lenin of "selling out and betraying Bolshevism" by handing over its money and its authority at the Paris plenum. Lenin replied that the *Vpered* group was "stupid" and wrote Vilonov, now on his deathbed in a Swiss sanatorium, that he was glad Vilonov had rejected Mach in favor of Marx and materialism. Lenin also sought to split Bogdanov's new circle by making amends to Gorky; Lenin wrote him that Bolshevism was in great danger of perishing, but promised that "we will resurrect the Bolshevik fraction again." How Lenin intended to do this was unclear.[41]

The *Vpered* group in May 1910 dispatched an open letter to "comrade Bolsheviks," presumably written by Bogdanov. The letter accused Lenin of "surrendering all Bolshevik positions, one after another," to the Menshevik-dominated RSDRP. This was "uncontrolled bossing by irresponsible persons" who were simply "ideological Mensheviks." Bolshevism was now completely cut off from events inside Russia and was in danger of dying out. It was necessary to "reconstruct the Bolshevik fraction on a new basis," namely, "the collective, not individual personalities." Thus did Bogdanov lay claim to Bolshevism and accuse Lenin of being a Menshevik.[42]

Despite his isolation (Dubrovinsky was arrested in June 1910), Lenin was able to maintain some support from a distance inside Russia. Letters reached him saying that *Materialism and Empiriocriticism* had helped put an end to "philosophical uncertainties" for party members. Lunacharsky wrote an entire pamphlet disclaiming Lenin's label of "god builder"; but people remembered the label better than they remembered Lunacharsky's disclaimer. Lunacharsky wrote openly that the RSDRP was "experiencing a deep crisis"; Lenin continued to proclaim his own orthodoxy.[43]

In another pamphlet the *Vpered* group reviewed the history of Bolshevism since 1905. The fraction was clearly threatened by schism; unity was needed. Yet this unity should be based on the assumption of continuing revolutionary possibilities; "all the conditions which led the proletariat along the road to revolution are still there, and even more strongly in effect." True Bolshevism was the most correct application of Marxism to Russian reality. The key to its success was proletarian consciousness, based on experience and articulated in ideology. The party was the vanguard of the proletariat and should lead the way to a "dictatorship of proletariat and peasantry." Organization should come from below, not above, through democratic centralism, where "leading collectives, starting with the factory and ending with the central committee, elect gatherings of organized workers." The illegal fighting organization of 1905 should not be liquidated, nor should illegal labor unions. Different opinions should be tolerated within the party, and the proletariat should become the "leader of the whole democracy."[44]

For Lenin, such talk of proletarian democracy by a dozen or so émigré workers and intellectuals was nonsense. Their "scientific socialism" merely covered up "empty thoughts." Talk of a proletarian democracy and proletarian culture was a disguise for "Machism and recallism." In fact, the first issue of *Vpered,* which appeared in July 1910 in Paris, billed itself as a "popular workers' journal," calling for labor solidarity and collective energy on the part of the proletariat. It also praised Italian syndicalists as "young and energetic fighters for the workers' cause" and, in an article entitled "How Not to Keep Accounts," attacked Lenin for giving up Bolshevik money to the German trustees. As Lenin correctly noted, behind the talk of proletarian culture lay the politics of syndicalism and the sordid tale of party funds.[45]

The *Vpered* circle continued to articulate the philosophy of collectivism in the name of Bolshevism. Collectivism was now redefined as "proletarian culture," a collectivist ideology that would create a class-based proletarian science, art, music, and literature. Bogdanov continued to argue that the "fetishism of private property" and the bourgeois self would give way to the "needs of the collective." Technology, party, and labor unions would create an "all-proletarian collectivism" that would include a "new conception of truth" for workers. Truth was relative, like any other "ideological form." It was only a tool in the "struggle with nature." "The meaning of truth," concluded Bogdanov, "is to change the world according to the needs and tasks of its collective subject."[46]

Collectivist relativism stood in sharp contrast to Lenin's conception of materialist absolute truth. Bazarov claimed that Lenin's materialism was only an inverted idealism, a superfluous and contradictory copy theory of reality that led to a philosophical "blind alley." The materialism of Lenin and Plekhanov had "very little in common with Marx's philosophy." M. N. Liadov argued that in 1905 the RSDRP had been a real collective of workers; now "all these Plekhanovs, Lenins, and Martovs" were merely squabbling émigrés out of touch with the "collective proletarian movement" inside Russia. Menshevism was "intelligentsia individualism"; Bolshevism was "proletarian *partiinost*'" (party spirit). "A proletarian movement," concluded Liadov, "can only be led by a conscious proletarian social democratic party; only the friendly collective creativity of conscious proletarians can recreate a proletarian party." [47]

Thus collectivism in theory was distinguished from both Leninism and Menshevism. The collectivists were organizing a school in Bologna, Italy, for workers to strengthen ties between émigré Bolsheviks and Russian *praktiki.* Theoretical differences again were sharpened by syndicalism and money.

The Bologna School

The Capri School never really disbanded. Its key members— Bogdanov, Lunacharsky, Liadov, Stanislav Volsky, and Alexinsky—

continued to maintain themselves as a circle of Bolsheviks around the journal *Vpered*. In June 1910 they also began to plan a new workers' school at Bologna, using funds stolen by Urals Bolsheviks from a bank in Miass in the summer of 1909. "The money was really transferred," recalled one participant, "not because the Urals people wanted to enter this school as students, but mainly because they wanted to organize a party-propaganda school abroad, to prepare party workers for Russia." F. I. Kalinin was put in charge of the new school, which consisted of a four-room apartment in Bologna occupied by the Bogdanovs and Lunacharskys.[48]

While Bologna claimed to be a party school, it had the support of neither the RSDRP central committee nor Lenin. The Okhrana had three agents in place, so that when students returned to Russia they were promptly arrested. The initial plan was for local RSDRP organizations inside Russia to choose students for a four-month term, and for instructors to be representative of the different RSDRP fractions. But when the school opened on November 21, 1910, it consisted of Bogdanov and his friends—Lunacharsky, Liadov, Volsky, Alexinsky, Gorky, Pokrovsky and seventeen students.[49]

The collectivists proved to be poor organizers. Pokrovsky and Vladimir Menzhinsky soon left because of Bogdanov's constant attacks on Lenin. Gorky declined to lecture, as did Karl Kautsky. Trotsky participated for a month, but proved to be arrogant, if brilliant, and "tried to dislodge our pupils from their extreme left viewpoint." Trotsky also objected to the syndicalism he discovered there. Mutual collective education, including practical work in propaganda, conspiracy, and agitation, soon degenerated into fractional infighting. And there was the usual (and justified) fear of police provocation.[50]

Syndicalism, like Bolshevism, was on the wane in 1910. Bologna was the site of a congress of Italian syndicalists in December, where Georges Sorel publicly announced his withdrawal from the movement because "syndicalism has not realized its expectations." Privately Sorel wrote a friend that "syndicalism is falling apart" and that he was "happy no longer to have any connection with the revolutionary movement." Sorel's drift to the right seemed to confirm Lenin's fear that syndicalism masked idealism and reaction. Lenin naturally refused to participate in the Bologna enterprise, but agreed to lecture to the students if they came to Paris.[51]

Like the Capri School, Bologna proved an abortive attempt to organize Bolshevism without Lenin. Bogdanov's attacks on Lenin became a "sad polemic," as Menzhinsky put it, and "new combinations with Trotsky have apparently produced little to cheer about." Karl Kautsky praised the school for its attempt to raise proletarian conscious-ness and solidarity. But he urged its participants not to limit themselves to illegal activities outside parliament; this could lead to the disorganization of the working class. The best example of this process was French syndicalism.[52]

The Bologna School was an intriguing experiment. It had the support of a socialist municipal government, and of Garibaldi University, of which it was a temporary department. As treasurer, Lunacharsky could do little about the final three-thousand-franc deficit except cover it with money from *Vpered*. In early 1911 the school disbanded and moved to Paris, home of Bogdanov's great nemesis, Lenin. To make matters worse, Lenin was repairing relations with Gorky, further splitting the collectivists into small circles incapable of reconstituting the Bolshevik movement they remembered.

Gorky against Bogdanov

The Capri School ended cordial relations between Gorky and the other collectivists. "Why are you nagging me all the time about 'Bolshevism?'" he wrote a friend in January 1910. "You are an attentive reader. Bolshevism is as dear to me, insofar as the monists run it, as socialism is dear and important to me, because it is the only way man can most rapidly arrive at a deep and complete consciousness of his personal human achievement. I don't see any other way." Gorky—the poet of the proletariat's "collective soul," as the future head of the Cheka, Felix Dzherzhinsky, called him—clearly imagined a Bolshevism closer to the Old Believers and Stenka Razin than to Marx. Nevertheless, within a few months Gorky was breaking off relations with Bogdanov and moving closer to Lenin. Why?[53]

For one thing, Andreeva was now thoroughly disgusted with Bogdanov and Lunacharsky. They were her "enemies," trying to have her committed to a psychiatric ward and break up her relationship with Gorky. The Bolshevik circle of 1905 was now destroyed. "What a fate for everyone," Andreeva complained. "S. T. [Morozov] shot himself, A. M. [Gorky] became an empiriocritic, and I . . . ? My God! Only A. M. has emancipated himself and removed all his chains." Gorky, Andreeva continued, had parted company with Bogdanov and his circle, "although in principle he still agrees with them, still the connection has been severed."[54]

In March 1910, Gorky wrote Bogdanov that they should no longer correspond. In contrast, Gorky invited Lenin to visit Capri, which he did during the first two weeks in July. This time, in contrast to April 1908, the visit was quite pleasant. Together with Gorky and Andreeva, Lenin enjoyed going to see movies at a nearby "Edison theater," toured the museums of Naples, and visited Pompei and Mount Vesuvius. Having dispensed with Bogdanov, Lenin and Gorky began to build a new relationship.[55]

Gorky and Lenin continued to correspond in 1910, and Lenin was naturally attracted by the great writer's financial resources. Gorky felt that Bogdanov, however interesting as a writer and a thinker, was personally unstable and rude. Gorky was tired of "playing politics." He now praised Lenin highly, seeing in him a better leader for Bolshevism. He donated five hundred francs to Lenin and Plekhanov for their new journal, *Rabochaia gazeta*. As for Bogdanov, Gorky wrote him in December 1910 that, much as he respected Bogdanov as a thinker and a revolutionary, he could no longer be "a private in your army."[56]

In January 1911, Lenin moved the entire "Library and Archive of the RSDRP" from Geneva to Paris, removing it from Bogdanov's control. Lenin and Krupskaya had packed up these materials in November 1905 for safekeeping. Much of the collection was then shipped to Russia; the rest was now in Lenin's hands. In January and March 1911 Gorky came to Paris to see Lenin, undoubtedly to provide support for Lenin's own school for party workers at Longjumeau outside Paris. Lenin told Gorky he wanted nothing more to do with "the rogue Trotsky," nor was unification with the Mensheviks possible. Certainly they should have nothing to do with Bogdanov and the Vperedists.[57]

Bolshevism without Lenin was no more successful than Leninism without the other Bolsheviks. Bolshevik collectivism always threatened to abandon Marxism for syndicalism; Leninist authoritarianism inclined towards Jacobin dictatorship and Menshevik parliamentarism. Perhaps the shrewdest observer of this dilemma was Lenin's ally George Plekhanov.

In August 1909 Plekhanov noted that the "schism in the camp of the Bolsheviks" was a good thing if it could facilitate RSDRP party unity. Lenin, a weak Marxist, faced a bewildering array of opponents— "mystics and empiriomonists, god builders and supermen"—whose theories inclined them toward "anarchosyndicalism, recallism, and other isms." Bogdanov was not really a Marxist at all, and Plekhanov hoped that Lenin and the Bolsheviks would surgically remove the cancer of syndicalism. If the Mensheviks agreed not to liquidate the illegal underground party structure, then perhaps unity was possible between Lenin's Bolshevism and Plekhanov's Menshevism.[58]

Plekhanov realized that this unification was unlikely. "The success of the liquidators in the Menshevik camp is directly proportional to the mistakes of the sectarians from the Bolshevik camp," he complained. Bogdanov's collectivism was foggy philosophy and utopianism; Lenin was a throwback to Populist Jacobinism, a Blanquist, close to the Social Revolutionaries. "Whatever my differences with the Bolsheviks," he wrote, "we have in common a party point of view. In saying this, I have in mind the Leninist crowd of Bolsheviks and not Maximov's [Bogdanov's] crowd, which represents the anarcho-syndicalists and not the social democrats." Plekhanov admitted that Lenin had made many mistakes; but Lenin was correct to reject both the liquidation of the underground party by the Mensheviks and the reactionary idealist philosophy of the collectivists.[59]

Plekhanov thus attacked syndicalism in politics and Machist idealism in philosophy. Syndicalism was utopian socialism and anarchist "putschism"; Machism and empiriomonism were un-Marxist and idealist. Lenin attacked the philosophy, but not the politics, of the other Bolsheviks, for it was philosophy, and not politics, that linked those Bolsheviks with certain Mensheviks. From the Social Revolutionary point of view, Lenin had helped create Bolshevism, but had now become a Menshevik, in alliance with Plekhanov. Of course Lenin did not admit this. "A proof by opposites: to Lenin's left are the recallists; recallists are anarchists; therefore Lenin is a Bolshevik."[60]

In what state, then, was Bolshevism by early 1911? Bogdanov and Lunacharsky had gone their own way with the *Vpered* circle of collectivists, relativists in philosophy and syndicalists in politics. What he called the "bitter experience of 1908 to 1911" convinced Lenin that unification with the Mensheviks was impossible. Lenin declared that a state of war existed, but with whom? Politically, both the RSDRP and the Bolshevik fraction had disintegrated into a bewildering collection of individuals and circles scattered across Europe and Russia. Bolshevism seemed not to exist. Yet there was a good reason to maintain the useful fiction of Bolshevism. For the German socialist trustees controlled substantial sums of money to be returned on that happy day when the fissiparous Russians could reunite. Until then, it would remain the object of continuous coveting and intrigue, and the master of the intriguers was Lenin.

IX

LENIN WITHOUT BOLSHEVISM

RUSSIAN POLITICS AND GERMAN MONEY

> For my part, I must say that this business—
> snatching part of the money from them—
> doesn't please me one bit. I know very well
> that the Party needs the money. . . . To me
> the whole business stinks, with your
> permission, of robbery and extortion.
> —Rosa Luxemburg, March 1911

In 1911 and 1912 Lenin and the other Bolsheviks continued to disagree over questions of both politics and money. The long plenum had produced an agreement whereby the Bolsheviks turned over the bulk of their treasury to the SPD trustees. But who were the Bolsheviks? And who was their leader? Bogdanov or Lenin? Bolshevism was a radical sect born out of the revolutionary experience of 1905, trying to survive in exile. Money was essential to their survival.

Shortly after the long plenum, Lenin drafted a letter to the three trustees (Zetkin, Kautsky, and Mehring) arguing that the RSDRP funds under their control really belonged to the Bolsheviks, not the Mensheviks. The Mensheviks, claimed Lenin, "absolutely did not take any part in the central work of the party" after the spring of 1908, and even tried to "break it up." As for the Bolsheviks, Riazanov pointed out a year later, in February 1911, that "the Bolsheviks have split into two fractions: 1) Leninists—the earlier Bolshevism without Machism, Expropriations, and anti-parliamentarism, and 2) pure Bolsheviks, 'Vperedists,' with Bogdanov, Lunacharsky, and Liadov." By the end of 1911, Lenin had broken with Plekhanov and the Polish socialists within the RSDRP and found himself further isolated. Yet in 1912 Lenin was able to take over Bolshevism without the other Bolsheviks, many of whom began to abandon politics altogether. How did it happen?[1]

Bologna against Longjumeau

During the winter of 1910–1911, Lenin and Plekhanov proposed to the students at the Bologna School that they come to Paris for a better education in Marxist theory. But relations between the school and the "school committee" of the RSDRP in Paris remained strained; recriminations and ultimata failed to resolve issues of politics or money. In March 1911 Lunacharsky had to borrow funds from *Vpered* to cover the deficit in Bologna. The *Vpered* circle was beginning to disintegrate; Shantser died in Russia, and Pokrovsky departed for historical scholarship. Talk of a coming "proletarian culture" could not disguise the fact that the collectivist group, like the Leninist circle, was in disarray. Even Bogdanov began drifting away from politics.[2]

In May 1911 F. I. Kalinin noted that "the Leninists have organized a school." The site this time was Longjumeau, a suburb of Paris, and the school was modeled on Capri and Bologna. Eighteen students (RSDRP party workers) attended classes from June to August 1911, and of the 147 lectures they heard, Lenin gave 56. Zinoviev, Kamenev, Riazanov, and Lunacharsky also contributed, although Gorky, Plekhanov, and the Mensheviks declined. Kalinin noted that "the Leninists remain isolated from all tendencies," and that Bogdanov had drifted away from *Vpered*.[3]

As the organization of Longjumeau School indicated, Lenin still had considerable sums of money under his control, despite the long plenum. Kalinin claimed that Lenin had subsidized Tyshko and the Poles with six thousand francs, and that Lenin still had in his possession eighty thousand more, half of which he hoped to use in the upcoming Duma campaign. As the RSDRP began planning a party conference that summer, Lenin would clearly be a factor. Plekhanov saw a conference as futile now, and predicted the "final breakup of our party." The RSDRP in 1911 had become a collection of émigré intriguers, cut off from Russia, arguing over money, and calling each other names. At Longjumeau, as one student pointed out, Lenin had behaved like a "blinded, medieval, fanatical cardinal, who burns in the name of Christ all heretics, even when they are not heretics." Lenin had to learn to coexist with "syndicalists like Volsky and Lunacharsky" who supported the "Italian movement." But would he?[4]

The Bologna School convened again in the summer of 1911, giving lectures and training party workers for illegal work in the Urals region. Lunacharsky wrote Kautsky and the trustees that summer to ask for money, claiming that Lenin was responsible for the party schism. But Kautsky claimed neutrality and denied that Lenin still had funds under his control. Talk of a unity conference of the RSDRP sounded more and more unreal. The party had become, wrote Rosa Luxemburg, a "handful of fighting cocks" who "scream for the ears and souls of the German trustees," and little more.

Nevertheless, plans went forward for a party conference. In September 1911 the RSDRP central committee urged all fractions to "fight for an all-party conference against the schism, against two conferences and two parties." The *Vpered* circle felt cheered by reports that inside Russia citizens were eagerly reading their literature, and that a branch had been established in Baltimore, Maryland, of all places. Kalinin even claimed that in Kiev and other cities "they are introducing resolutions against Lenin's activities."[5]

The picture was not bright. D. Z. Manuilsky hoped that the Paris *Vpered* circle might ally with Plekhanov and receive some funds from the trustees; he charged that the "Leninist type of bandits" were now "completely isolated from the party and have no money." He noted that Bogdanov had not yet returned the money belonging to *Vpered*, and that the group had split into two factions, one in flight from politics, the other continuing to dream about proletarian culture and syndicalism. Kamenev criticized Lunacharsky for wanting "not only to build a god, but to build a party," but the possibility of rebuilding Bolshevism as an organization seemed remote. Bolshevism had degenerated from a struggle over philosophy to a struggle for money.[6]

Lenin and the Trustees

From its inception the RSDRP was a little brother of the Socialist Party of Germany (SPD), which provided political and economic support, and thus expected to have a voice in party orthodoxy and finances. In 1908 the SPD held a secret tribunal to consider the case of Parvus, who owed money to Gorky and the Bolsheviks. In 1910, as Lenin put it, the Bolsheviks had been "dissolved as a fraction" and their funds surrendered to three SPD trustees, who could dole it out only for legal enterprises— publishing a journal, rather than robbing a bank, for example.[7]

In March 1911, Klara Zetkin complained that she had still not actually received any money from Lenin, who visited her that month in Stuttgart. An SPD ultimatum to Lenin produced no results. "Reliable people report," Axelrod helpfully wrote Kautsky, "that Lenin and Co. still have hidden away at least one hundred thousand rubles of the party for their cliquish purposes, which will probably enable him to pursue his plans without party funds." By July 1911, Lenin had turned over considerable sums to the trustees. They had agreed to let him have thirty thousand francs to hold a party conference. The Mensheviks were outraged.[8]

Lenin cleverly argued that he had held the money until then "not as a representative of the Bolsheviks, but as a member of the [RSDRP] central committee." When he tried to give Kautsky money in February 1911, he refused to accept it. On July 7, 1911, the National Bank of Paris, at Lenin's written request, transferred the money (or some of it) to the trustees. Leo Jogisches wrote Kautsky that Lenin wanted only to "use the chaos in the party to get the money for his own fraction and to deal a death blow to the party as a whole before any plenum can meet."[9]

The trustees were thoroughly confused. Kautsky wondered why Lenin did not want a party conference to settle the matter. How else could the trustees find an "authority outside the central committee with whom the trustees can deal"? If anything, the trustees inclined toward Lenin. Kautsky saw no alternative. Zetkin criticized Martov's brochure published after the long plenum, and said she supported the "tactical firmness of the Bolsheviks, and especially you [Lenin] personally." Accused by the Mensheviks of making decisions in Lenin's favor, the trustees denied interfering in the "organizational conflict of our Russian comrades" but maintained that they would "decide into whose hands the party funds trusted to us should go."[10]

At the Jena congress of the SPD (September 1911), Axelrod did his best to convince the trustees that funds should be transferred to the Mensheviks. Trotsky made similar efforts. But both were denied by Kautsky, who increasingly sided with Lenin, as did Zetkin and Rosa Luxemburg. Zetkin praised Lenin as a "very worthy man" who had "given up all the money in his possession," and promised to "decide this business in favor of the Bolsheviks. My personal opinion is that formal and *de facto* justice is on their side." In fact, all three trustees were increasingly tired of arguing with the Russians. In the autumn of 1911 they all resigned: Mehring on October 2, Kautsky on October 18, and Zetkin on November 16.[11]

The frustrated Lenin now decided to take them to court. His purpose was to recover what amounted to half of the funds acquired from the Schmidt inheritance and other sources; he had already kept control of half himself. His supporters were G. L. Shklovsky, a Bolshevik living in Bern, Switzerland, and two leading Swiss socialists, Karl Zgraggen and Karl Moor. Zgraggen, like Lenin, was a lawyer. (In 1917 he would help transport Russian revolutionaries back to St. Petersburg by sealed train.) In addition, Lenin retained two more lawyers: George Ducos de la Haille, a militant Paris socialist and Dreyfusard, and Emile L. D. Vinck, another socialist from Brussels. Lenin began compiling a bibliography of all works on courts of arbitration and contracts in order to support his case.[12]

In late October 1911 Lenin wrote Zetkin, the last remaining trustee, that the retirement of the other two trustees made the contract with the Bolsheviks null and void. She had no right to make decisions, threatened Lenin, and must "return the money to the one from whom you received it, i.e., me." If he received no reply, said Lenin, he would take legal action. In November Zetkin resigned, despite (or because of) Lenin's ultimatum that she come to a "peaceful settlement" or face "open warfare." She also tried to get Taratuta to turn over additional money from the Schmidt inheritance that was not under Lenin's control.[13]

Immediately after the retirement of the trustees, Kautsky and Zetkin wrote Lenin a letter in which they noted that the right to the trust fund was an open question. Only an agreement between the central committee of the RSDRP and the Bolsheviks could resolve it, since they were the parties to the 1910 contract, or treaty, signed at Paris. Civil court proceedings, said Zetkin, might justify Lenin's claim. But she also threatened to bring the entire matter before the Second International and make it public. Lenin, of course, maintained his "exclusive right to the monies held by Zetkin."[14]

"If the fate of the party until now has been decided in Paris," wrote Sergo Ordzhonikidze in late 1911, "now it is decided in Berlin." The RSDRP was in receivership to the SPD. The Mensheviks, the central committee, and the Foreign Bureau were all running out of money. Ordzhonikidze, on Lenin's instructions, demanded that Zetkin give him ten thousand francs to convene a new party conference. To hold Bolshevik funds was illegal, Lenin reminded Zetkin. The Okhrana reported that Zetkin held some eighty thousand francs remaining from the Schmidt inheritance, but that Zetkin would not return the money to Lenin until the RSDRP achieved reunification. In December 1911 that seemed most unlikely.[15]

The Prague Conference

In January 1912 Lenin managed to convene a conference of his supporters in Prague that has gone down in history as the Prague conference of the RSDRP. In fact, it consisted of twelve Leninists and two Mensheviks. They promptly elected a new RSDRP central committee composed of one Menshevik, Lenin, and four Leninists: Ordzhonikidze, Zinoviev, S. S. Spandarian, and F. I. Goloshchekin. The other member was a loyal Leninist and an agent of the Okhrana, R. V. Malinovsky. Within a year of the conference Lenin was arbitrarily to "coopt" six more supporters, including Stalin. In addition, the editorial board of the RSDRP central organ, *Sotsial-demokrat,* was composed of Lenin, Kamenev, and Zinoviev. The conference resolutions were all authored by Lenin, including one that terminated a subsidy to Trotsky's Vienna *Pravda.* The Prague conference was not a victory for Bolshevism, but for Lenin.[16]

Having declared themselves the RSDRP, Lenin, Zinoviev, and Kamenev signed a statement that they were the "Bolshevik representatives with whom the central committee concluded its agreement at the plenum of January 1910." They, not the Bolshevik collectivists, were the rightful claimants of the "property of the Bolsheviks." They argued that the transfer of funds to the central committee had been "conditional"; the Mensheviks had violated the agreement, and the trustees had resigned.

The money held by Klara Zetkin thus belonged to the RSDRP, which now meant that it belonged to the Leninists.[17]

The other Bolsheviks—Bogdanov, Krasin, and Kamo, who escaped from jail in Tiflis and arrived in Brussels in December 1911—also claimed money acquired from the Tiflis Ex of 1907. At a stormy meeting in Paris, Kamo argued that Lenin, Krasin, and Bogdanov had no right to the fruits of expropriation. He also accused Taratuta of being a provocateur. Bogdanov claimed that the *Vpered* group had never withheld funds from the Bolshevik Center, charging that "certain members" (Lenin?) had tried to burn notes from the Tiflis Ex. Whatever the truth of the matter, Krasin now left Berlin to head the Siemens and Schukert office in Moscow, and Kamo returned to Tiflis to begin planning more bank robberies. On September 24, 1912, Kamo robbed the Tiflis post office and was promptly arrested. The Bolshevism of 1905 virtually expired.[18]

Having achieved a victory at Prague, Lenin went to Berlin in February 1912 to see Kautsky and demanded the money held by the trustees. Failing in this, Lenin began legal proceedings. He wrote Zgraggen that the 1910 agreement was now "no longer in force." He proclaimed that until 1910 "I held the money," which had been given to him by Elizabeth Schmidt, whose brother Lenin characterized as "a Bolshevik who died in jail." A meeting of other RSDRP fractions in Paris in late February disagreed. Lenin's "fractional activity," they charged, had "finally antagonized every national organization and party tendency except the Leninist." Lenin's seizure of power at Prague would be brought before the ISB. He had split the party and usurped control. His resolutions were mere "biased information of schismatics."[19]

Isolated from the party he claimed to dominate, Lenin turned to Gorky. "We have finally succeeded," Lenin wrote him, "despite the liquidator rabble, in resurrecting the party and its central committee. I hope you are as happy as we are at this." In March 1912 Gorky visited Lenin in Paris, complaining that he no longer had any money. Lenin told Gorky that the party now had a "healthy treasury." The two men continued to correspond over the following months as Gorky turned away from Bogdanov to Lenin as the most likely leader of a revolution in Russia.[20]

The Prague conference in the eyes of the *Vpered* circle was illegitimate, a meeting of the "Leninist fraction" without any support inside Russia. On the eve of elections to the fourth Duma, Lenin had launched a "fratricidal war" when what was needed was unity and cooperation. But that was precisely the point. At Prague Lenin had achieved in name what he had not achieved in fact, legitimate control of the RSDRP. Lenin now claimed the mantle of Russian Marxism as well as of Bolshevism.[21]

Lenin against Bolshevism

In May 1912 Lenin wrote his lawyer, de la Haille, explaining the background of the trustees, whose court of arbitration, he argued, no longer existed. Lenin urged a return to the *status quo* of January 1910. "Zetkin should return the money to Lenin, from whom she received it," he claimed. He also enclosed a letter from Elizabeth Schmidt, who had executed her brother's will giving his inheritance to "the political fraction headed by Lenin." Lenin promised to pay de la Haille five thousand francs if he could get Zetkin to return the money by August 1. "I myself was a lawyer," mused Lenin. "I studied French law and German law, regulating arbitration court relations. I have no doubt that Zetkin is completely wrong."[22]

In the meantime the SPD promised to provide the RSDRP twenty-five thousand marks toward the coming Duma elections, but only if the party was reunited. The *Vpered* circle was running out of "donations" provided by the Miass expropriation and demanded money from Bogdanov. The Mensheviks wanted another court of arbitration to obtain some of the fifty thousand marks still held by Zetkin. Trotsky and Lenin were conducting their own campaigns to obtain the money. Bogdanov's calls for "collectivism" in financial matters fell on deaf ears. Kautsky and the Mensheviks wanted to expel Lenin from the ISB and were dissuaded only by thoughts of the unfavorable publicity that would result.[23]

With nothing to lose, Lenin openly pursued his attack on syndicalism and on the other Bolsheviks. Under the pseudonym "I," Lenin wrote an article for Trotsky's *Pravda* arguing that syndicalism was a "nonsocialist extreme" fashionable in Italy. "The syndicalists incline to anarchism, succumb to revolutionary phrasemongering, destroy discipline in the workers' struggle, reject the use of a parliamentary tribune by the socialists, or defend withdrawal from it." At the same time, Lenin claimed that all money held by the trustees rightfully belonged to the "Lenin group" of Bolsheviks, and not to the "small individual group" around *Vpered* whose inclinations were more syndicalist than socialist.[24]

Trotsky made one final attempt to unify the RSDRP, but the Vienna conference (August 1912) of thirty-three party members failed to unite the anti-Leninists. Trotsky hoped to unify the party and strengthen its ties with Russia; he also opposed the "dictatorship" of the German trustees over party funds, and unsuccessfully tried to obtain them for himself. But Trotsky was hardly the leader around whom the dissident blocs and fractions of the RSDRP could unite. The party now existed in name only.[25]

The RSDRP ended the year 1912 deeply divided. Axelrod unsuccessfully tried to get Kautsky to support the "non-Leninist direction" in the

Duma elections without success. Huysmans complained that the ISB had received no party dues from the Russians since 1908. De la Haille was making no progress toward acquiring funds for Lenin, and Lenin's August 1 deadline had long passed. One of the Duma delegates elected by Bolshevik supporters in October 1912 was Malinovsky, a police agent. And Lenin complained that inside Russia he had "no publishing connections at all."[26]

In January 1913 Lenin wrote Gorky a long letter venting his frustrations. Rumors abounded that the *Vpered* circle wanted to return to the Bolshevik fold. Well and good, said Lenin, but cautioned: "Do remember the last 'goodbyes' with Bogdanov, Lunacharsky, and Bazarov on Capri in the spring of 1908. You recall I said that we must separate for two or three years, and M. F. [Andreevna] as chairman protested furiously, calling me to order, and so on." Now five years had gone by, and the Bolsheviks were still in disarray. Lenin was unsure whether or not Bogdanov and his friends were "capable of learning from the difficult experience of 1908–1911 at all." For as Lenin correctly surmised, the *Vpered* circle was also in a state of decline.[27]

The End of *Vpered*

> Tomorrow I expect to take a trip to the planet Mars, and if so, will immediately commence to organize the Mars canal workers into the IWW, and will sing the good old songs so loud that the learned stargazers on earth will once and for all get positive proofs that the planet Mars is really inhabited.
>
> —JOE HILL, the day before his execution, 1915

Mars, the red planet, was the setting for Bogdanov's utopian socialism in *Red Star* (1907). In 1911 Bogdanov wrote a second Martian utopia entitled *Engineer Menni* which again imagined a socialist society, massive canal construction, and a planned economy. A Plan of Great Works transformed the entire planet, nationalizing the land from the peasantry, and collectivizing all individuals into a "single rational organism of humanity." New institutions included a Council of Syndicates, workers' schools, a Workers' Encyclopedia, and a "universal organizational science." Bogdanov thus expressed syndicalist ideas disguised as science fiction. Lenin found the novel to be only "Machist idealism." Gorky found it "not so bad, for the legal press," but maintained his distance from the *Vpered* circle.[28]

The latter claimed branches in all major European cities and inside

Russia. But *Vpered* was mainly a collection of Russian socialist émigrés who were neither Mensheviks nor Leninists. Revolution was on the wane all across Russia, and Gorky noted a wave of suicides among the youth; socialism had broken up into sectarian splinter groups. In November 1912 Bogdanov, Lunacharsky, Bazarov, and Alexinsky all agreed to write for a new RSDRP journal in St. Petersburg entitled *Pravda*. Gorky and Lenin were also involved, Lenin supporting the collectivists despite his distaste for the writings of Bogdanov and Lunacharsky. Once again, attempts at cooperation proved fruitless.

In February 1913 Lenin moved to Cracow (a city in Austrian Poland) and promptly began protesting against Bogdanov's participation in *Pravda*. "Under the guise of Marxism," Lenin complained, Bogdanov wanted to "conduct an anti-Marxist, idealist philosophy (Machism)." Bogdanov's ideas were a scandal, "archstupidity," said Lenin. "You can't make anything out of this mush," he added. "I read his *Engineer Menni*. The same Machism: idealism, so vague that neither a worker nor a stupid editor at *Pravda* could understand it. No, this Machist is hopeless, as is Lunacharsky."[29]

Bogdanov's massive tome on a *General Organizational Science* which appeared in 1913 and articulated his world view of "tectology" was no more pleasing to Lenin, who complained that "cooperation with Bogdanov is impossible." The *Pravda* circle in St. Petersburg was making deep inroads into the local metalworkers' union, largely with the aid of police agent Malinovsky. Many members of the union's board were Bolsheviks; but they were not Leninists.[30]

"Nothing new with us," wrote Krupskaya in April 1913. "The Plekhanovites are eagerly 'allying' themselves with the Bolsheviks, and the *Vpered* group is about to self-destruct." Lunacharsky was imagining a future proletarian culture; Bogdanov was writing articles on the Taylor System of time-and-motion study in factories. Under the Aesopian title "From a Dictionary of Foreign Words," Bogdanov also wrote in *Pravda* about Bolshevik tactics and strategy. Like the syndicalists, he argued that "a partial strike even when prolonged sometimes simply wastes energy, when a general strike would quickly attain success." Properly educated by "energy, together with experience," workers could someday gradually take over the state. Bogdanov denied that he was a recallist, or that he had any connection with the *Vpered* group. Lenin wrote *Pravda* that Bogdanov's views were anti-Marxist heresy.[31]

Lunacharsky left the *Vpered* group in June 1913, leaving it in control of a few supporters of Lenin and Plekhanov. Lenin claimed to be a centrist, wrote Bogdanov, but he was continually "correcting his role in the Bolshevik split." Lenin charged that Bogdanov was a liar who supported "empiriomonism and other nasty things that disgrace a proletarian party." *Pravda* refused to print Lenin's letters and articles. By July 1913 the journal was closed by the censor, Bogdanov had left its editorial board, and Lenin was more concerned with paying for Krupskaya's surgery in Switzerland.[32]

By the end of 1913 the old Bolshevik circle was virtually nonexistent. Bogdanov and his wife had left for Moscow and given up émigré politics entirely. Lunacharsky was expelled from Germany in February 1914 as an "undesirable foreigner" because of his inflammatory speeches to Russian students in Berlin. The *Vpered* group had disintegrated. Lenin wrote Gorky urging him to emancipate himself from all god building and god seeking, different forms of "self deception" and "contemplating one's navel" that differed "no more than a yellow devil is different from a blue devil." Gorky remained on Capri, tired of émigré politics and philosophical name-calling.[33]

Lenin's closest companion was the Okhrana agent Roman Malinovsky, with whom he traveled through Europe in January 1914. By this time Malinovsky was on a retainer of one hundred rubles a month from the police, to whom he reported on a regular basis. In May 1914 Malinovsky was revealed to be a police spy. He promptly resigned from the RSDRP Duma delegation and left for Poland to visit Lenin. Aside from Krupskaya and Malinovsky, Lenin was now quite alone.[34]

The German Legacy

Lenin continued to pursue the funds held by the SPD with little success. Sceptical lawyers demanded documentary proof that Lenin had any right to the money. Lenin bombarded them with promises of fees and strident claims. He persuaded other Bolsheviks to write August Bebel to ask for help. But Bebel died in the summer of 1913, and de la Haille and Zgraggen were having doubts of their own. De la Haille wrote Zetkin that Lenin claimed to have a mandate from a Bolshevik fraction that was "nonexistent" and noted that Lenin was "not qualified to reclaim the funds on deposit." In addition, Lenin complained that he was running out of money. [35]

For a time it looked like Kautsky might be able to bring Lenin together with the trustees at the Jena congress of the SPD but he could not. Zetkin said that no conference was needed, since the exact terms were spelled out in a contract between the "Lenin group" and the RSDRP central committee. She told Axelrod that "the deposit in question is not the private property of comrade Lenin and his fraction, but the collective property of the RSDRP." Such financial collectivism hardly impressed Lenin, who instructed Karl Zgraggen to sue the trustees in court. The Mensheviks and other party fractions were no more successful than Lenin.[36]

Lenin continued to keep the party divided because he hoped to claim the disputed party funds for himself. He feared that the ISB might succeed in reunifying the party where the SPD had failed. "Our business is not progressing well," Lenin wrote de la Haille in February 1914; the SPD wanted to create a new court of arbitration ("a completely stupid proposal")—perhaps a lawsuit would scare them into returning the money. Instead, the ISB and the SPD were now seriously considering drumming Lenin out of the European socialist movement.[37]

By March 1914 the Mensheviks and the SPD were suggesting an ISB conference at which the matter of the German money would be settled once and for all. When the conference convened in Brussels in July, no fewer than 28 delegates claiming to represent 10 separate RSDRP fractions showed up. Zinoviev, Kamenev, and Litvinov all refused to attend, so Lenin sent as his proxy his close friend Inessa Armand. Lenin furiously wrote that "they only want to scold me" and instructed Armand to demonstrate that "only we are the party." There was talk of expelling Lenin and the Bolsheviks from the Second International. Vandervelde and Kautsky wished to put the matter before the impending August conference of the International; Plekhanov charged Lenin with stealing party funds. The ISB unanimously condemned Lenin's "disorganizing role" in the RSDRP and was seriously considering his expulsion, when outside events intervened: Europe went to war.[38]

On the eve of World War I, Lenin and the Bolsheviks were a tiny and divided fraction of an equally divided socialist party. They had neither unity nor money. Their leadership was divided between European émigrés and exiles in Siberia. Yet on the eve of war there was also great labor unrest inside Russia; strikes were increasing in number and violence and "the syndicalist leaders enjoy a high reputation," as one socialist put it.[39] Lenin was in virtual isolation politically, but therein lay precisely the advantage of flexibility in responding to a violent world where mass collectivism craved individual authority.

War and Revolution

With the outbreak of World War I, Lenin and the other Bolshevik émigrés in Germany and Austria-Hungary headed for neutral Switzerland. Viktor Adler succeeded in getting Lenin released from Austria by persuading the police that he was, indeed, an enemy of the Russian government. The war saved Lenin from probable expulsion from the Second International at its August 1914 Paris conference, which was canceled. Charles Rappaport, a French socialist, noted that Lenin was an "incomparable organizer" of "iron will" who "sees in capital punishment the only means of assuring the existence of the social democratic party." Lenin was a "Social Democratic Tsar, who regards himself as a super-Marxist, but who is, in reality, nothing but an adventurer of the highest order." Yet Lenin was now the least of the worries of European socialist parties, whose support was melting away in the face of nationalism and patriotic worker support for governments. The great general strike expected to follow the outbreak of war never materialized.[40]

In Swiss exile Lenin remained isolated from his own fraction. The *Vpered* circle reconstituted itself in Geneva, joined by Lunacharsky who arrived from Paris. The Second International was virtually defunct, and there was talk of creating a third. Lenin found greater support for his idea that the war should be transformed into a civil war and a social revolution. When his old comrade Parvus arrived in Zurich in May 1915, complete with cigars, blondes, and champagne breakfasts, Lenin found a new source of potential support. But the Mensheviks, Social Revolutionaries, and Trotsky were also moving to Switzerland, which became a microcosm of Russian émigré politics by the summer of 1915. The *Vpered* group called for a Third International to replace the Second, and sharply attacked Plekhanov's defense of the Russian government as the lesser evil. "We want only that the proletariat consider itself a great power, with its own policy of war and peace—peace between nations, and war between classes."[41]

The Zimmerwald conference of September 1915 brought together in a Swiss village near Bern representatives of all the RSDRP fractions (including Lenin, Trotsky, Martov, and Axelrod) except for the *Vpered* circle. Lenin proposed to use five thousand francs from the money held by the SPD "incorrectly and illegally" in order to help organize the internationalists among the socialists. But Zetkin was unwilling to release any of the funds, which still remained under her control at a Stuttgart bank at the end of 1915.[42]

In February 1916 Lenin moved from Bern to Zurich and began writing a new book under contract with Gorky and Pokrovsky. Gorky planned a series of works under the Aesopian title "Europe before and during the War" which would pass the military censorship in different countries and be socialist in content. Lenin had completed the manuscript and sent it on to Pokrovsky in Paris, proposing that he publish it under the usual pseudonym, presumably V. Ilin. The original idea was that Lenin would write an introductory volume to the series, which would include volumes by Lunacharsky (on Italy), Zinoviev (on Austria-Hungary), Pokrovsky (on France), and so forth. The result was Lenin's *Imperialism*.[43]

Lenin encountered a second level of censorship. The publisher, the Parus house, wanted to shorten *Imperialism* by deleting Lenin's attacks on Kautsky. The manuscript arrived in St. Petersburg belatedly (the first copy had been intercepted and read by the French military censor), and Lenin refused to cut it. The editors of the firm, after all, were Mensheviks; even Pokrovsky criticized the book as "Plekhanovite." But Lenin had no choice; the title remained the Aesopian "Contemporary

Capitalism" and the passages on Kautsky were cut, to be resurrected as
The Renegade Kautsky after the 1917 revolution. Again, Lenin faced a
"vile bloc" of Machists and Mensheviks who refused to publish his
writings or to provide any money.[44]

In December 1916, Lenin received his royalties, but was unhappy with
his book. "My fate," he added, "is one military campaign after
another—against political stupidity, banality, opportunism, etc. This
since 1893." But he thanked Pokrovsky for saving his brochure from
further editing by Gorky and his friends.[45]

When news of the Russian Revolution reached Switzerland in March
1917, the Bolsheviks began to regroup. Lunacharsky left for Zurich to
see Lenin, and found him still gloomy about revolutionary possibilities.
He advised Lenin not to accept the offer of transportation to Russia by
German train because it would give Lenin's enemies a "cheap and
convenient weapon against him." Lenin refused the advice, embarking
on his famous trip to the Finland Station.[46]

In 1917 Lenin and the other Bolsheviks were able to work together
toward a successful seizure of power in a moment of spontaneity and
mass unrest which no other political party was prepared to manipulate.
As in 1905, syndicalism remained a central element in Bolshevik
thinking, even in Lenin's. Bogdanov reemerged from self-imposed
isolation to produce revolutionary pamphlets calling for proletarian
struggle and an end to World War I. Lunacharsky became active in the
Petrograd Soviet and worked together with anarchists and syndicalists in
forming worker committees. Even Lenin saw that the distinction
between Bolshevism and syndicalism was at this point academic. In *State
and Revolution*, written in August 1917, he called for the "expropriation
of the capitalists, the conversion of all citizens into workers and
employees of one huge 'syndicate'—the whole state—and the complete
subordination of the whole of the work of this syndicate to the really
democratic state of the Soviets of Workers' and Peasants' Deputies." [47]

In 1917, after years of waiting and struggle, Lenin had triumphed over
Bolshevism. While the tension remained, between individual authority
and collectivist myth, it was a creative tension, facilitating both party
organization and mass propaganda. Lenin was a public proponent of
"workers' control" in 1917. When accused of being a syndicalist, he
protested that "this argument was an example of the stupid schoolboy
method of applying Marxism without studying it, just learning it by
rote." Syndicalism, he added, "either repudiates the revolutionary
dictatorship of the proletariat, or else relegates it, as it does political
power in general, to a back seat. We, however, put it in the forefront."[48]
In 1917, Lenin continued to realize that the most effective syndicalist and
collectivist myth was one articulated as orthodox Marxist truth.

X

A CHILDHOOD DISEASE
COMMUNISM OVER SYNDICALISM

> The Russian version means the supremacy of the political over the industrial groups. The Syndicalist version means the supremacy of the economic organizations over the political organizations. And the whole thing (putting it plainly) means that the two ideas cannot exist side by side. One or the other must go.
>
> THE INDUSTRIAL WORKER
> January 1922

> Bolshevism was but the Russian name for the IWW.
>
> THE REVOLUTIONARY AGE
> April 1918

In March 1918 the Bolshevik fraction of the Russian Social Democratic Workers' Party declared itself the Russian Communist Party (Bolsheviks) [RKP(b)]. Leninism had come to power in Russia in the name of Bolshevism, but not social democracy. The Mensheviks were merely tolerated, the left Social Revolutionaries temporary participants in a coalition government. An authoritarian political party ruled in the guise of workers' councils, and a duly elected Constituent Assembly was dispersed at gunpoint. By the end of March 1918 the new Bolshevik rulers had been compelled to sign a punitive peace with the Central Powers at Brest Litovsk, taking Russia out of the war.

Throughout his life Lenin saw the shadow of syndicalism, or what he called "left Bolshevism," lurking beside him. The Bolshevik movement from 1904 to 1912 had been spawned by syndicalist enthusiasms for direct action, the general strike, and worker participation in the revolutionary struggle through both party and labor unions. Lenin constantly fought the drift toward a more spontaneous, less authoritarian mass movement based on collectivist myth, supporting instead a rigidly structured socialist party. But both authority and myth, as we have seen,

175

were essential components in Bolshevism, the first emphasized by Lenin and the second by Bogdanov.

There were two moments in Lenin's life when collectivist spontaneity threatened to overtake authoritarian organization. The first was the 1905 revolution and its aftermath, especially the period 1907–1910, when the other Bolsheviks led by Bogdanov developed a theory of collectivism and direct action that eschewed participation in trade unions or parliamentary elections in favor of continued revolutionary activity. By labeling the other Bolsheviks Machists, recallists, boycottists, and god builders, Lenin successfully portrayed Bolshevism as a group of disparate heresies, rather than a dominant force within his own fraction.

The second moment occurred after 1917, when a variety of political organizations sprang up and articulated the ideas of workers' control of industry, proletarian culture, and syndicalism. Bogdanov's Proletkult movement, organized in the summer of 1917, attracted hundreds of thousands of participants across the country. The subsequent Workers' Opposition and Workers' Truth groups represented an ongoing syndicalist challenge to Leninist authority within the Bolshevik party. Thus Lenin faced, both before and after the revolution, the difficult task of controlling a volatile and violent revolutionary movement that he himself had helped set in motion, and at both moments he faced a common rival: syndicalism.[1]

Lenin against Left Communism

As early as 1892 Karl Kautsky noted that Marxism as a revolutionary movement had to control its less orthodox and more adventurist elements, especially romantic revolutionary intellectuals and radical workers. Kautsky characterized such elements as primitive, utopian, and yet a necessary "childhood disease which threatens every young socialist movement." During the years before 1914, German social democrats generally felt that they were the wise parents of recalcitrant Russian socialist children. August Bebel noted the "childishness" of the RSDRP at the Stuttgart congress in 1907, and even told Maxim Litvinov to his face that "you are children." At the same congress Lunacharsky compared syndicalism to a "childhood disease" (detskaia bolezn') that any workers' movement must experience and then outgrow.[2]

The characterization of syndicalism as a childhood disease persisted in Russia after 1917. In May 1918 Lenin referred to Nikolai Bukharin and the "left" communists who opposed signing the Brest Litovsk treaty as people experiencing "left adolescence" (levoe rebiachestvo) and playing into imperialist hands because of their "childish helplessness" (detskaia bespomoshchnost'). The idea of an "infantile disorder" (the common English translation used in Lenin's 1920 pamphlet) suggests a Freudian psychological malfunction that will be a permanent and lifelong part of the patient's psyche, an irrational behavior pattern that one might call childish. But the idea of a "childhood disease" suggests measles more than neuroses, an inevitable but passing and relatively harmless contagion through which all children must go but which then does not recur in adult life. In 1920 Lenin characterized "left communism" as a "very young trend" and promised that "the disease can be easily cured, and we need to work to cure it with maximum energy; this disease will pass without any danger, and afterwards the organism will become even stronger." Whatever "left communism" meant after 1917, it was related to a childhood disease before 1914 which Bolshevism had experienced and successfully outgrown.[3]

In 1909 Lenin had countered the syndicalist threat within Bolshevism by breaking with his own fraction and writing *Materialism and Empiriocriticism*, an Aesopian indictment of Bogdanov and the other Bolsheviks who sought to maintain Bolshevism without Lenin. In 1920 Lenin again sought to deal with syndicalism in his well-known pamphlet *Left-wing Communism: An Infantile Disorder*. In both cases Lenin was concerned that some Bolsheviks sought to transform Marxism into useful myth, rather than party orthodoxy, in order to mobilize workers to action. In 1920 Lenin feared that his Communist rivals inside and outside Soviet Russia wished to transform the new Communist International, or Comintern, into a radical revolutionary organization that would be self-destructive for communist parties and harmful to more pragmatic trade and diplomatic ties of Russia with the capitalist world. But what Lenin called "left Bolshevism" after 1905 and "left-wing communism" after 1917 were not minority factions, but major groupings that threatened Lenin's control of his own organization: the Bolshevik Center in 1909 and the Comintern in 1920.

The Syndicalist Wave

European and American syndicalists greeted the Russian Revolution as if it were their own. In 1919 Sorel praised Lenin as "the greatest theoretician that socialism has had since Marx." The IWW greeted its fraternal comrades in Russia as if one big union had come to power. Yet syndicalist spontaneity soon ran into difficulties in association with the new Comintern, an organization international and revolutionary in form, but Russian and authoritarian in content.[4]

The founding congress of the Comintern, held in Moscow in April 1919, was sparsely attended. Few European or American comrades could get through the blockade maintained by the Allied Powers against a Soviet Russia involved in a bloody civil war. The congress resolutions were vaguely syndicalist in tone, however, praising revolutionary activities such as "mass action" and relegating "bourgeois parliamentarism" to a subordinate value as a strategy. "A coalition is necessary," wrote Bukharin, "with those elements of the revolutionary workers' movement who, though they did not previously belong to the Socialist Party, now, on the whole, take up the standpoint of the proletarian dictatorship in the form of the Soviet system, e.g., some of the sections among the Syndicalists."[5]

This promise of a coalition with former syndicalists helped bring many left-wing European socialists into the Comintern, especially in Holland. Pannekoek, Gorter, and Roland-Holst all became key figures in the early Comintern. For a time some thought a true international socialist organization might be centered in Amsterdam, not Moscow. In his report to the first Comintern congress, the Dutch socialist S. J. Rutgers admitted that "spiritually we stood close to the syndicalist elements of the Dutch Labor movement, and when the world war broke out our party with one anarchist group and in conjunction with the syndicalists formed a revolutionary committee." The Dutch left, like the IWW, had a syndicalist heritage that would make affiliation with a Comintern increasingly difficult.[6]

Lenin was well aware that anarchism and syndicalism were still powerful mass movements inside Soviet Russia. In a meeting with the grand old man of Russian anarchism, Prince Peter Kropotkin, in May 1919, Lenin told him that syndicalism was a movement harmful to the revolution. Yet he realized the need for foreign support from former syndicalists. Lenin wrote the English socialist Sylvia Pankhurst that the Comintern should not alienate "those among the workers who, while advocating Sovietism, refuse to participate in the parliamentary struggle." Antiparliamentarism was a mistake due to a lack of revolutionary experience. In October 1919, he wrote German, French, and Italian communists a letter repeating this sentiment, noting that not to participate in parliamentary elections would be "an undoubted mistake" and "an even greater offense against the ideas of Marxism and its practical policy (a strong, centralized, political party) and a leap towards the ideas and practice of syndicalism." Again, Lenin presented his own views as Marxist orthodoxy, and his rivals' views as mistakes or worse. But many still disagreed with him.[7]

By early 1920 Lenin was deeply concerned with anarchism and syndicalism in Russia and abroad. Anarchist groups had been especially active that winter in Moscow, and had even bombed party headquarters. The guerrilla forces of Nestor Makhno were flying the black flag of anarchism in the Ukraine, fighting off White and Red armies alike. In January 1920 two American anarchist leaders, Alexander Berkman and Emma Goldman, were deported to Russia. In March Lenin plied them with questions about the labor movement, the socialist parties, and the IWW in America. Sorel dedicated the fourth edition of his *Reflections on*

Violence to Lenin. Kropotkin told Lenin that "the syndicalist movement will emerge as the great force in the course of the next fifty years, leading to the creation of the communist stateless society." At the ninth RKP(b) party congress in late March, Lenin noted that party membership stood only at six hundred thousand, while the trade unions claimed three million members. *Pravda* denounced trade union autonomy as "syndicalist contraband." In May 1920 the Moscow printers went on strike. Enthusiasm for trade unions, rather than the party, also emerged in Bukharin's *The Economics of the Transition Period* and a new edition of Bogdanov's *Short Course in Economic Science*, both of which Lenin read and annotated with concern. Thus, in Soviet Russia in 1920 labor unrest was epidemic and trade unions were as widespread as any other infectious disease.[8]

In this setting Lenin began to write his second Aesopian indictment of syndicalism, *Left-Wing Communism: A Childhood Disease*. This time the censor was not the imperial police, but his own party, over which he still could not claim control.

Left-Wing Communism: A Childhood Disease

> Oh! How I understand Lenin.
> —Georges Sorel

> A schism is better than a muddle.
> —Lenin

Lenin's famous 1920 pamphlet is generally interpreted as a piece of tactical political advice directed at emerging foreign communist parties that makes two points: first, that the Russian Bolshevik experience in creating a successful revolution should serve as the model for foreign communist parties, whose countries must inevitably go through a similar experience; second, that all communist parties must give up uncompromising opposition to bourgeois society, especially its trade unions and its parliaments, and engage in legal political activity, joining labor unions and running candidates for elected public office.[9]

Prepared for distribution at the second Comintern congress in the summer of 1920, the pamphlet has been viewed as an outline of tactics and strategy for the Comintern and foreign communist parties in the years to come. But in 1920 the Comintern was a frail reed, bent by the winds of revolution in the aftermath of World War I, its future unknown. Lenin was still recalling the seductive appeal of syndicalism that had enticed his own movement since 1905. *Left-Wing Communism* was directed as much against the known historical experience of Russian Bolshevism as against the future unknown deviations of Western Com-

Lenin at the time of the Second Congress of the Comintern and the writing of Left-Wing Communism: A Infantile Disorder, *Moscow, July 1920. From* Vospominaniia V. I. Lenina *(Moscow, 1979), supplement.*

munism. It reminded Russian leaders of past mistakes, and promised good Russian behavior to Western politicians, both in the oblique Aesopian language customary in Lenin's writings.

Why did Lenin choose to describe left Bolshevism in terms of childhood diseases? As we have seen, syndicalism was traditionally criticized as childish or infantile by European Marxists. But in addition, Lenin celebrated his fiftieth birthday on April 22, 1920, and his secretary, E. D. Stasova, gave him a birthday cartoon. Drawn by the artist Karrik in 1900 on the occasion of a jubilee for the Populist thinker N. K. Mikhailovsky, the cartoon showed various Russian Marxists of the day as small children lined up to greet the great man. Stasova editorialized in her note to Lenin that in 1900 the Russian social democrats were still in their infancy, but in 1920 had come to maturity largely through Lenin's efforts.[10]

Left-Wing Communism is dated April 27, 1920. This date probably marked the beginning, rather than the end, of Lenin's writing of the book. No preliminary drafts or notes of the book have been found, only a ninety-three-page handwritten manuscript and a typed version with

editorial corrections. In addition, there is no evidence in Soviet chronol-
ogies of Lenin's extremely busy life that he was actually working on the
book before April 27, and there is considerable evidence of work
between then and July 19. The effects of the Allied blockade were still
being felt, so that getting people or information into the country was
time consuming and often dangerous. Yet Lenin's pamphlet is full of
references to West European communist publications from January
through mid-April 1920. Written in great haste, his pamphlet was
directed not only at the representatives of foreign communist parties
about to gather in Moscow for the second Comintern congress, but at
the left wing of his own party and the leaders of Western governments—
audiences that Lenin appreciated only in April.[11]

In late March or early April 1920, Lenin received the first eight
volumes of the Comintern journal, *Communist International*. These were
bound and distributed to delegates to the ninth RKP(b) party congress in
Moscow. They made it very clear that the Comintern, especially its
Dutch, German, and American members, were drifting toward syndicalism. The first issue of April 1919 featured the resolution of Bukharin
calling for mass action and criticizing participation in parliamentary
elections. Other issues contained articles by Dutch socialists making clear
their cooperation with syndicalists and anarchists. By April 1920 Lenin
was aware that the syndicalist wave might inundate the Comintern.[12]

Syndicalism was, in fact, on the rise again. In October 1919, S. J.
Rutgers was sent to Europe to establish Comintern branches in Berlin,
Vienna, and Amsterdam. But the West European Bureau in Amsterdam
held its own conference in early February 1920, with representatives
from America and Great Britain, and began to issue its own bulletin as
"the provisional Bureau in Amsterdam of the Communist International." The bureau resolved to turn industrial unions to more radical
paths, and "came close to adopting the line of the West European
syndicalists, who renounced political activity in its entirety." For the
next three months, Amsterdam, as much as Moscow, could lay claim to
being the active center of the Comintern. In addition, a disparate but
substantial number of German syndicalist organizations came together in
February 1920 in Hannover as the Allgemeine Arbeiter-Union
Deutschlands (AAUD), modeling itself after the IWW.[13]

Syndicalism threatened Lenin at home as well as abroad. In January
1920 Zinoviev, as head of the Comintern, wrote an appeal to the IWW
arguing that "the Communists and the IWW are in accord. The capitalist
State must be attacked by DIRECT ACTION," and urging that the
IWW cooperate with the CPUSA in a relationship of "brotherhood." On
March 25, in the wake of the abortive right-wing Kapp Putsch in Berlin,
Zinoviev urged the KPD (Communist Party of Germany) to "arm
yourselves! Form workers' councils! Assemble your Red Army!" In fact,
the failure of the KPD to offer significant resistance to the Kapp Putsch

led on April 4, 1920, to the formation of a schismatic Communist Workers' Party of Germany (KAPD), an antiparliamentary and quasi-syndicalist organization of whose existence Lenin was unaware until after April 23, when he was able to get a copy of the new party's journal, *Kommunistische Arbeiter Zeitung*.[14]

In the meantime Lenin had been reading the American socialist leader Daniel De Leon's *Industrial Unionism,* a pamphlet that argued the primacy of the party over the trade unions. Lenin was undoubtedly aware that this "Red Pope of Revolution" had been purged from the IWW in 1908, precisely the time when Lenin had nearly lost control of Bolshevism because of syndicalist enthusiasms in his own movement. In 1920 Lenin again faced losing control of the Comintern to the same kind of enthusiasms.[15]

In early May 1920 Lenin began a furious effort to get his hurriedly written pamphlet published and translated before the second Comintern congress met in July. Meanwhile, a two-man KAPD delegation arrived in Moscow after a perilous voyage in a fishing boat to Murmansk, and found Lenin immediately hostile to their antiparliamentary ideas. They were shown portions of the still unfinished manuscript. On May 5 the completed manuscript arrived at the Petrograd Section of the State Publishing House, and the next day was sent to the printer. Lenin immediately wanted to know how long the printing would take and requested two preprints. He also asked Zinoviev to "hold off printing until the text is corrected."[16]

Even as his book was in press, Lenin continued his research. These included articles from Italian communist newspapers and journals and the latest issue of *Communist International*. On May 12 Lenin dashed off a supplement to his book, using the new materials acquired through the Comintern's Petrograd headquarters. He may even have been under pressure to do so. In the main text Lenin wrote that "in 1908 the 'left' Bolsheviks were expelled from our Party for stubbornly refusing to understand the necessity of participating in a most reactionary 'parliament' " and that boycotting the Duma had been a "serious mistake." But in the supplement Lenin wrote that "in 1907–1908 the 'left' Bolsheviks at certain times and places agitated among the masses more successfully than we did," the "we" of Leninism presumably being distinguished from the "they" of left Bolshevism.[17]

Lenin had difficulty publishing *Materialism and Empiriocriticism* in 1909 with either Menshevik or Bolshevik houses. In 1920 he found that Zinoviev was not especially happy with printing *Left-Wing Communism* for the Comintern. In May 1920 Zinoviev dutifully criticized German syndicalism for encouraging the growth of "bourgeois labor unions." He agreed with Lenin that the new KAPD was "dragging the movement backwards from revolutionary Marxism to confused, obscure syndicalism." But Zinoviev did admit that "revolutionary syndicalism and the tactics of the IWW are a step forward" from other trade unions. He promised that the second Comintern congress would "put an end to all syndicalist prejudices on the role of the Communist Party" and would "separate the Communist wheat from the syndicalist weeds."[18]

This sounded like Lenin in 1907: Bolshevism must learn from syndicalism in order to destroy it. Zinoviev was slow in getting Lenin's book out, and Lenin complained about the delay. By June 12 the Russian edition had been printed, and by June 18 Lenin was able to send out autographed copies. Lenin did not have complete control over the publication of his own book, which was carried out not in Moscow, but in Petrograd, by the leaders (Zinoviev, L. Karakhan, M. Borodin) of the very organization Lenin was attacking for its syndicalism, the Comintern.[19]

Lenin made further changes in his book after the Russian edition and before the appearance of French, German, and English translations that summer. Again, he did not have a free hand. He depended on A. M. Heller, an American communist, for gathering from the Italian press "citations against Turati and other reformists" that would "prove their deviation from discipline and decisiveness." He had to respond to the protest of the Dutch communist D. J. Wijnkoop that he, Lenin, was saddling the entire Dutch party with the sins of the *Tribune* group and their syndicalism. In response, Lenin replaced the words "Dutch Tribunists" with "certain members of the Dutch Communist Party" and printed Wijnkoop's letter at the end of the English edition. As late as July 17, 1920, Lenin complained to Kamenev, Borodin, and Radek that the proposed English edition did not faithfully reflect the Russian original, and asked them to make changes in the galleys of all foreign editions. Finally, the English edition appeared on the eve of the congress on July 19 as *The Infantile Sickness of the 'Leftism' in Communism.*[20]

The Second Comintern Congress

By the time the second Comintern congress convened in July 1920, Lenin's antisyndicalist views were well known. In an interview with Jacob Friis, a Norwegian member of the Comintern executive, Lenin remarked that "antiparliamentarism is one of the childhood diseases of communism against which I have often had to fight." Lenin cited his opposition to Bukharin and Radek in 1918. A few days later he attacked an antiparliamentary article by George Lukacs in the Vienna journal *Kommunismus* as "very leftist and very bad." Lenin also persuaded the Comintern executive committee that it should denounce KAPD policies as a "capitulation before the views of syndicalism and industrialism which are reactionary." The committee obligingly resolved that syndicalism was "a step forward only in comparison with the old, musty counter-revolutionary ideology of the Second International," but a step backwards from Communism.[21]

Trotsky also argued that the party must maintain its control over the labor unions. He told the Comintern congress that the French Communist Party, for example, should "entirely absorb the revolutionary wing of the present Socialist Party, and the revolutionary section of French Syndicalism." The PCF should dominate the trade unions, because "a bona fide revolutionary syndicalist, like a bona fide revolutionary socialist, must become united in a Communist Party."[22]

Zinoviev, in contrast, was still more favorably inclined toward syndicalism than either Lenin or Trotsky. "The Russian Bolsheviks defined their attitudes toward revolutionary syndicalism already fifteen years ago [1905]," he wrote, "when revolutionary syndicalism was finishing its honeymoon." Bolshevism had tried to "separate the grain from the chaff and find the wholesome seed in the irresistible protest of the working masses against opportunism, expressing itself in sympathy with revolutionary syndicalism. We must follow the same line now."

Despite its "vagueness and muddle," concluded Zinoviev, syndicalism was "healthy." While the Comintern should struggle against "all syndicalist misconceptions, confusions and prejudices," it should also ally with the syndicalists because they were "as much enemies of the bourgeois order as we are." As late as August 1920 it would appear that Zinoviev did not share Lenin's violent antipathy to syndicalism or "left-wing communism," a fact which may have helped delay the publication of Lenin's pamphlet.[23]

Foreign syndicalists were still enthusiastic about Soviet Russia. Charles Ashley, an IWW spokesman, urged affiliation with the Comintern because it would lead the "class conscious efforts of the workers to achieve power," including the Shop Stewards in England and syndicalists in France. Other Wobblies also felt that the organization should join the Comintern. By the end of 1920 the romance was wearing off. Some IWW members returned from Russia to report that Russian nationalism and party authority were more dominant than internationalism and workers' control. The real childhood disease, wrote one, was now "Radekalism," the emergence of a new ruling class in Soviet Russia.[24]

Both the text and context of Lenin's *Left-Wing Communism* suggest that his underlying concern in 1920 was the syndicalist experience of Russian Bolshevism, as much as the control of European communism. Since 1905, Lenin had viewed syndicalism as a spontaneous and violent mood of labor unrest from which Marxists could learn much, but to which they should not lose control. The mood of syndicalism—one big union, the general strike, direct action, economic confrontation, workers' control—was essential in making a revolution. But in 1920 it was a liability for a besieged party clinging to power against enemies at home and abroad in the midst of a bloody civil war. What Lenin called "left-wing communism" in 1920 was an inheritance of the syndicalism of 1905. Once again, Lenin could not speak openly about a movement from which Bolshevism and the Comintern both continued to draw sustenance.[25]

Proletkult and the End of Collectivism

The Bolshevik Revolution brought many of Lenin's errant flock back to the fold. Many were veterans of the underground experience of 1905 and former supporters of Bogdanov. But in the early days of the revolution Lenin's power was tenuous and he badly needed support wherever he could find it. Thus Krasin quickly assumed a major role in the Commissariat of Foreign Trade, Lunacharsky became the first commissar for public enlightenment, and Bogdanov created his own Proletkult movement. These men were independent personalities who continued to play a role less submissive than Lenin might have desired.

In October 1920 a reunion of sorts occurred at M. S. Olminsky's apartment in Moscow. In attendance were Lenin, Gorky, Bogdanov, Andreeva, Kamo, and A. M. Ignatiev. The topic was ostensibly literary publication, but the makeup of the group suggests that matters of money may have also been discussed. For these were veterans of the Tiflis Ex and other underground adventures. Kamo, the urbane bandit, was about to get married, with Gorky as his best man. (In July 1922 Kamo died as violently as he had lived, run over on his bicycle by an automobile.) Ignatiev was inventing machine guns for aircraft. In March 1918 Martov openly attacked Bolshevik expropriations before the revolution; his Menshevik newspaper was promptly closed down, and Stalin denounced him for slandering the party. But for thousands of new party members, these embarrasing matters seemed increasingly out of date, and there were more pressing problems to be solved in a world of famine, social collapse, and civil war.[26]

Bogdanov continued to pursue the collectivist dream outside of the party. In 1917 he was an active member of the Petrograd Soviet, urging it to prepare workers for the coming revolution. He was a proponent of mass mobilization through slogans ("short and simple, so the masses can assimilate them"), but urged support for the provisional government in July, arguing that the soviets did not want to take power. In August 1917 he formed his own national organization, Proletkult, which sponsored art, literature, theater, and cinema across the country by and for workers.[27]

The Proletarian Culture movement was a mass movement that was not under party control. As such, its days were numbered. But from 1917 to 1920 it played a major role in creating a collectivist revolutionary culture and in rallying support for the new regime. Proletkult theaters were everywhere, even with the Red Army at the front, and spawned a generation of innovative directors, including Vsevolod Meyerhold and Sergei Eisenstein. Bogdanov still envisaged a universal science—the "organized experience of humanity"—that would produce a collectivist world view. He called for a Workers' University and a Workers' Encyclopedia. The individualism and authoritarianism of Christianity must give way to the collectivism of proletarian culture. "Christ, if he existed, was undoubtedly a proletarian," proclaimed Bogdanov.[28]

Bogdanov continued to work for a collectivist culture, but his relativism was to prove his undoing. Leninism in power was authoritarian and orthodox in its party interpretation of Marxism. Bogdanov argued that truth was still relative, a "tool for living," neither absolute nor eternal. Together with Bazarov, Bogdanov edited a book on Einstein's theory of relativity. The sense of building a future grounded on myth pervaded Bogdanov's writings, undermining by definition any ideology he might have created. Lenin created myth in the name of orthodox truth; Bogdanov created culture in the name of scepticism. In the end he died a victim of his own lifelong search for immortality, experimenting on himself with a new technique for blood transfusion.[29]

Proletkult had its origins in the years after 1905, and represented an echo of the collectivist and syndicalist tradition we have examined. It was a vision based on the proletariat, not the party, and was therefore intolerable to Lenin. Like syndicalism, it ended as an ephemeral movement and mood, leaving no permanent institutional legacy except its ideas and its culture, unacceptable in a world of socialist realism and party lines.

Kronstadt and the End of Syndicalism

In the years after 1917, syndicalism persisted in a variety of circles and factions that espoused the general idea of workers' control of factories in the new society. The Workers' Opposition movement of 1920 was roundly criticized for its syndicalist ideas, and helped precipitate a great debate in the winter of 1920–1921. This debate was made even more significant with the outbreak of armed violence by workers and peasants, soldiers and sailors, against the Bolshevik regime in the name of workers' control and soviet power—the Kronstadt naval base uprising of March 1921.[30]

Lenin was particularly disturbed at the popularity of the Workers' Opposition, led by Alexander Shliapnikov, for minimizing the role of the state. In January 1921 Lenin accused Bukharin of "a clean break with communism and a transition to syndicalism" for his apparent support of Shliapnikov's views. "Syndicalism," observed Lenin, "hands over to the mass of non-party workers who are compartmentalized in the industries, the management of their industries, thereby making the party superfluous." Syndicalism and party control were clearly inconsistent.[31]

"Marxists have been combatting syndicalism all over the world," Lenin told a congress of miners in Moscow. True revolutionary syndicalists were siding with Soviet Russia. But it would be quite improper for Russian workers to "rush into the arms of syndicalism" and learn "syndicalist nonsense" from groups like the Workers' Opposition. Bukharin and Shliapnikov represented a "syndicalist deviation" from party orthodoxy. The "syndicalist malaise," warned Lenin, "must and will be cured."[32]

To Lenin's outrage and embarrassment, the Kronstadt uprising coincided with the meeting of the tenth party congress in Moscow in March 1921. Clearly syndicalism had gone too far. Lenin fired off a draft resolution on "The Syndicalist and Anarchist Deviation in Our Party" which was adopted by the congress. He argued that it was necessary to "purge the party" of such deviations and to ban all factions. The Workers' Opposition wanted to set up an All-Russian Congress of Producers; this would mean that the trade unions would elect a national government of a sort. This was "bourgeois counter-revolution," fumed Lenin. Syndicalism and anarchism could no longer be tolerated. They were "incompatible with membership in the RKP(b)."[33]

The tenth party congress marked the end of syndicalism as a significant component of Bolshevism. After 1921 syndicalist ideas were heresies. A deviation, said Lenin, could still be rectified by an "exchange of opinion"; what could not be tolerated was the "propaganda of ideas" by a faction outside the party. Like Proletkult, syndicalism came to an end in 1921 as a collectivist contribution to the Russian Revolution and Bolshevik power. In 1905 collectivism had been essential; now it was superfluous and even dangerous. The party, not workers and intellectuals, was the dominant collective, and in its name all individualism—including that of the collectivists—was suspect.[34]

XI

CONCLUSION
LENIN OVER BOLSHEVISM

> This will be the century of authority, a
> century of Right, a century of Fascism. For
> if the nineteenth century was a century of
> individualism (liberalism always signifying
> individualism), it may be expected that this
> will be the century of collectivism, and hence
> the century of the state.
>
> —BENITO MUSSOLINI
>
> There is little question of avoiding
> collectivism. The only question is whether it
> is to be founded on willing cooperation or
> the machine gun.
>
> —GEORGE ORWELL, *1984*

We live in a century of collectivism, as Mussolini observed, in which the
state has all too often triumphed over the individual. Yet we must keep
in mind Orwell's observation as well; collectivism is both altruism and
authority, a force for good or evil in the world. Collectivism may
enhance the public welfare or lead to genocide. But it is an undeniable
part of our twentieth-century world.

The story of the Russian Revolution is, in part, the story of the
triumph of Lenin over the collectivist aspects of Bolshevism. Both
Lenin's authority and Bogdanov's proletarian myth were crucial to the
emergence of the Soviet political system after 1917. The dominance of a
single leader legitimized by revolution and the "dictatorship of the
proletariat" was the logical outcome of a Jacobin tradition extending
back to the French Revolution. The dehumanization of the individual as
a bourgeois fiction no longer needed in a socialist society, and the
elevation of the collective to immortal glory, was also a necessary
prelude to Soviet self-sacrifice. By 1930, Leninist authority had given
way to the Stalinist cult of personality, and Bogdanov's collectivism to
proletarian culture, collectivization, party loyalty, and Soviet patriotism.

Authoritarianism and collectivism were symbiotic, as well as distinct.
The deification of a single political leader had as its corollary the
submission and self-sacrifice of millions of individual members of

188

society. Throughout Russian history political autocracy went hand in hand with the collective submissiveness of the Russian Orthodox church, the naive monarchism of the peasant, and the martyrdom of the radical intelligentsia. Russian traditions of individual liberty and rights were never strong. Among the Bolsheviks they were further weakened by the discovery of European relativism as expounded by Mach and others. Bolshevism came of age at the precise time when European individualism was under attack from many sides.

European relativism and collectivism helped provide Bolshevism with two fundamental ideas: first, that truth was merely what proved useful and had no absolute measure of validity; second, that the individual was a fiction, less useful than the collective. Even when Lenin attacked the other Bolsheviks for their discovery of myth and the collective, he felt their appeal. His public defense of Marxist orthodoxy against modernist heresy was itself constantly changing and shifting with the political issues of the day. What Lenin understood best, however, was that relativist myth is most effective when disguised as orthodox truth. Lenin's political personality was formed in the Manichean tradition of Russian Orthodoxy, with the certainty of true faith; Bogdanov's emerged from the European modernist rebellion against absolute truth and individual autonomy. Both contributed to Bolshevism.

After the 1917 revolution, Lenin and Leninism became the objects of new cults, fostered in part by the other Bolsheviks. Bonch-Bruevich, Krasin, Lunacharsky, Bogdanov, and Stalin all helped deify Lenin, in life and after death. In so doing they helped justify the view that any individual may be sacrificed to the immortal collective, now the Leninist party. Already in 1920 the writer Evgenii Zamiatin in his novel *We* showed that unbridled collectivism could easily lead to the absolute authority of the individual "well doer" over the collective and submissive masses, the transformation of Easter into the Day of Unanimity, and the acceptance of death as the ultimate dissolution of self in the universe.[1]

Many Bolsheviks refused to accept this drift toward authoritarianism, and attempted to keep their syndicalist ideas alive in a variety of short-lived splinter groups claiming to derive their legitimacy from workers, not the party. The dream of workers' control persisted into the mid-1920s among those for whom the initials N.E.P. stood for "New Exploitation of the Proletariat." But the major figures of prerevolutionary collectivism made their peace with the new regime. The ruler cult of Lenin was heartily endorsed by Lunacharsky, who supervised the building of the mausoleum in Red Square; Krasin, who designed the sarcophagus and refrigeration unit; and Stalin, who supported the entire endeavor in the Politburo. But in the end the Lenin cult was not a collectivist substitute for religion, but a "party effort to fuse religious and political ritual to mobilize the population."[2]

Many of the other Bolsheviks had also vanished from the scene by the time Stalinism emerged in the 1930s. The legendary Kamo was killed in 1922; years later Stalin had the monument on his grave in Tiflis removed and his sister arrested. Krasin died in 1926 after a distinguished postrevolutionary career in diplomacy and foreign trade. Bogdanov perished in 1928 while conducting a blood transfusion experiment on himself, perhaps a suicide. And Lunacharsky died a broken man in France in 1933 after watching Stalin begin the process of cultural transformation, destruction, and export of art objects that characterized the First Five Year Plan. And although Lunacharsky had urged that Krasin be memorialized "in the immortal Leninist spirit, in the immortal spirit of the immortal proletariat," the collectivists vanished from history.[3]

In the 1940s and 1950s the concept of totalitarianism sufficed to explain Soviet history in a manner satisfactory to most Western observers. The nightmare of a particular generation faced with the evils of Stalinism and National Socialism became the analytic framework for another generation of scholars in the West. More recently we have seen that Bolshevism, Leninism, and Stalinism are distinct, if related, phenomena, whose ideological labels often covered up significant diversity, originality, confusion, and rivalry. We can no longer equate Bolshevism with Lenin, nor Leninism with Stalinism. As one observer has written, "Lenin's Bolshevism was a composite of disparate and even conflicting elements evolved over a long period of years and in response to changing circumstances," whereas Stalinism represented a "fringe phenomenon of Bolshevism" that triumphed in the 1930s and 1940s under the banner of excessive Russian nationalism and police authority.[4]

Collectivism was in the air after 1900, and Bolshevism reflected its appeal. "The individual," wrote the sociologist Ludwig Gumplowicz in 1902, "is not prior to his group, rather the group is prior to the individual. We are born in a group and we die in it—the group preceded us and will survive us."[5] Creative collectivity, the collective unconscious, and collectivism all marked the shift from a century of individualism and liberalism to one of totalitarian movements and states, purges, true believers, and genocide in the name of a collective ideal. Once the individual was denied the right to exist in theory, he could be destroyed in fact, his only crime that he existed in the first place and did not belong to the right group. In the brave new world of totalitarianism, executioners and victims became locked in a bureaucratic and ideological embrace from which there was often no escape except death. It was a collectivism of the machine gun, not willing cooperation.

The persistence of syndicalism within Bolshevism also suggests a common root of fascism and Stalinism as variants of totalitarianism. As A. J. Gregor has observed, "Mussolini's development was surprisingly similar to that followed by Lenin after 1900," although Mussolini's proletarian syndicalism became virulent nationalism by 1914. Both men developed Marxist movements adapted to their national environments under the influence of syndicalism. The collective, whether class or nation, provided the useful myth for mesmerizing and mobilizing the inchoate urban and rural masses of two developing nations. Bogdanov and the other Bolsheviks admitted the strategy of socialism as surrogate religion; Lenin did not. Lenin drew upon syndicalism only after disguising it as Marxist orthodoxy and defeating his Bolshevik rivals who espoused syndicalist views.[6]

Here we have seen that Leninist authority and Bolshevik collectivism were different sides of the same coin, and that Stalinism owed as much to the myth-making syndicalism and anti-individualism of Stalin's youth as to the dictatorial authority of Lenin. Stalin himself was a Leninist by convenience more than conviction, frequently at odds with Lenin and politically drawn to the ethic of direct action, expropriation, and self-sacrifice. One of the first to use the term "Leninism," Stalin was never an obedient Leninist. But he ultimately achieved the power to eliminate those who might remember that fact.

It would be wrong to blame Lenin and the other Bolsheviks for the final and terrible excesses of Stalinism. But together they created preconditions of individual authority, collectivist myth, and relativism which were essential to Stalinism. The deification of one man, the sacrifice of millions of individuals, and the elimination of truth as a measure of reality were all consistent with the complicated debates between Lenin and the other Bolsheviks which form the subject of this book. Lenin ultimately triumphed over the other Bolsheviks, in life as in death. But Leninism and Stalinism combined elements of both individual authority and collectivist self-sacrifice that continue to be essential to the Soviet experience as we know it in the twentieth century.

NOTES

Introduction

1. Historically the tendency to equate Leninism and Bolshevism dates from the 1917 revolution. The official Soviet view is that Lenin was an infallibly correct leader from whom the other Bolsheviks deviated on matters of politics and philosophy. A detailed study of the entire Lenin cult and its implications for historical writing is Nina Tumarkin, *Lenin Lives!* (Cambridge: Harvard University Press, 1983).

As early as 1939 the Trotskyist Boris Souvarine wrote that "without Lenin there would have been no Bolshevism. Not that his section had never attracted eminent men, but the Bogdanovs and Krasins were in turn to detach themselves from it as Trotsky and Plekhanov had done in the past, leaving Lenin with comrades incapable of meeting an unforeseen situation unaided." See Boris Souvarine, *Stalin*, trans. C. L. R. James (New York: Alliance, 1939), 77.

The view that Leninism and Bolshevism were virtually identical has persisted in Western historiography as well. For example, Leonard Schapiro in *The Communist Party of the Soviet Union* (New York: Random House, 1960), 58, describes the Bolshevism of 1904 as a "one-man party" with Lenin at the head of a "disciplined network of followers." More recently the German historian Dietrich Grille noted that "the concentration of attention on the person of Lenin has made all other leaders of Russian social democracy appear as insignificant party details." See Dietrich Grille, *Lenins Rivale: Bogdanow und Seine Philosophie* (Cologne: Verlag Wissenschaft und Politik, 1966), 25.

2. From 1903 on, the Mensheviks assumed that Lenin had significantly more control over the other Bolsheviks than was the case. Paul Axelrod in 1904 portrayed Bolshevism as a dictatorial one-man party of Lenin's with "Jacobin" characteristics, and the portrait has survived in works such as Fedor Dan's *The Origins of Bolshevism* (New York: Harper and Row, 1964), which devotes no attention to other Bolsheviks, including Bogdanov, Lunacharsky, Bonch-Bruevich, and Krasin. Dan also omits the 1906–1914 period when intra-Bolshevik divisions were deepest.

3. The Russian tradition of collectivism has been analyzed by George Kline, an American scholar, in "Changing Attitudes toward Individuals," in C. E. Black, ed., *The Transformation of Russian Society* (Cambridge: Harvard University Press, 1960), 606–624; "Theoretische Ethik im russischen Fruhmarxismus," *Forschungen zur Osteuropaischen Geschichte* 9 (1963): 269–279; "Nietzschean Marxism in Russia," *Boston College Studies in Philosophy*, vol. 2 (1968); and his monograph *Religious and Antireligious Thought in Russia* (Chicago and London: University of Chicago Press, 1968), especially pp. 103–126. Kline tends to overrate the influence of Nietzsche on the other Bolsheviks, and to underestimate the role of politics and European thought in shaping Bolshevik collectivism. For a treatment of Bogdanov's thought as a "blend of Marxism and Neopositivism," see Alexander Vucinich, *Social Thought in Tsarist Russia: The Quest for a General Science of Society, 1861–1917* (Chicago and London: University of Chicago Press, 1976), 206–230.

4. The most comprehensive history of the Jacobin and authoritarian-conspiratorial roots of Bolshevism is by Astrid von Borcke, *Die Ursprung des Bolschewismus: Die Jakobinische Tradition in Russland und die Theorie der Revolutionaren Diktatur* (Munich: Berchmans Verlag, 1977).

For an early attempt to comment on Lenin's opposition to the syndicalist movement, see Solomon Schwarz, *Lenine et le mouvement syndical* (Paris, n.d.), which traces Lenin's critical writings on the trade unions but contains little on the 1907–1910 period. Lenin's writings have been collected as *Anarchism and Anarcho-Syndicalism* (New York: International Publishers, 1972).

John Keep's *The Rise of Social Democracy in Russia* (Oxford: Clarendon Press, 1963) makes only passing mention of syndicalism (pp. 61, 63, 178, 279). Robert V. Daniels in *The Conscience of the Revolution: Communist Opposition in Soviet Russia* (Cambridge: Harvard University Press, 1960) notes the "dualistic character of the communist movement" (p. 5) with its divisions between "left" and "right" Bolshevism (p. 13) but contains very little on the influence of syndicalism on Bolshevism during 1905–1917; his recognition of the "utopian anarchism" of Lenin's pamphlet *State and Revolution* (p. 52) and the "syndicalist legacy of 1917 Bolshevism" (p. 119) is not developed in any systematic or detailed fashion.

For more recent investigations into the relationship between Bolshevism and syndicalism, see A. Tamborra, *Esuli Russi in Italia dal 1905 al 1917* (Rome and Bari: Laterza, 1977), chapter 17, and Robert C. Williams, "Collective Immortality: The Syndicalist Origins of Proletarian Culture, 1904–1910," *Slavic Review* 39, no. 3 (September 1980): 389–402.

It has also been pointed out that after 1917 the Bolsheviks "took over" the revolutionary thrust of anarchism and syndicalism and redirected them through the Comintern. See W. Kendall, "Comintern—60 Years After: Reflections on the Anniversary," *Survey* 24, no. 1 (Winter 1979): 145–156.

5. On god building, see Jutta Scherrer, "La crise de l'intelligentsia Marxiste avant 1914: A. V. Lunacarskij et le bogostroitel'stvo," *Revue des études slaves* 51, nos. 1–2 (1978): 207–215; idem., "'Ein gelber und ein blauer Teufel': Zur Entstehung der Begriffe 'bogostroitel'stvo' und 'bogoiskatel'stvo,'" *Forschungen zur osteuropaischen Geschichte* 25 (1978): 319–330; and Kendall E. Bailes, "Sur la 'theorie des Valeurs' de A. V. Lunacarskij," *Cahiers du monde russe et sovietique* 8, no. 2 (April–June 1967): 223–443.

In the Soviet view god building is a petty bourgeois reactionary philosophical tendency before 1914 that was anti-Marxist; see Institut Filosofii, Akademiia Nauk, eds., *Filosofskaia Entsiklopediia* (Moscow, 1960), 1:179. According to one Soviet scholar, "Lenin's criticism helped Gorky and then Lunacharsky recognize the falsehood of their 'god building' views and to overcome their ideological errors." See N. A. Trifonov, in A. V. Lunacharsky, *O Gor'kom* (Moscow: Khudozhestvennaia literatura, 1975), 8.

As an example of the confusion of Western scholars over the meaning of god building, see Adam Ulam, *The Bolsheviks* (New York, 1965), 273, where he describes it only as a "muddled philosophy" in which "the proletariat was to have a secular religion of its own," and "sophomoric mumblings" akin to the very different god-seeking movement. A more serious comment is Jutta Scherrer, "Die Petersburger Religios-Philosophischen Vereinigungen," *Forschungen zur osteuropaischen Geschichte* 9 (1963): 309–317, which clarifies the distinction between god building and god seeking, but does not relate philosophy to the struggle over politics and money in the Bolshevik underground.

The Soviet dissident historian Roy Medvedev has argued more recently that god building later provided the basis for Stalinism. Stalin, "by encouraging the cult of his own personality," was "putting into effect some ideas of very early opportunists, such as the 'god builders,' who sought to make a god of the collective power of humanity, who preached a new 'socialist' religion 'without a god.'" See Roy Medvedev, *Let History Judge* (New York: Knopf, 1972), 151.

6. Traditionally Bogdanov's collectivism has been considered a minor heresy to Lenin's orthodoxy and dominance of Bolshevism. Merle Fainsod, in his classic *How Russia Is Ruled*, 2d ed. (Cambridge: Harvard University Press, 1963), 46, referred only to "the philosophical heresies, the neo-Kantian Machism of Bogdanov and the God-Creator religionism of Lunacharsky and Gorky" which "challenged" Lenin's "control of the party faction." Another Lenin biographer, Louis Fischer, wrote that "the whole Marx-Mach, Lenin-Bogdanov controversy reflected the pathological state of a small party led by a combative talent intolerant of opposition and frustrated because his organization, cut off from home base, was melting away from lack of accomplishment"; *The Life of Lenin* (New York, 1964), 67. These views ironically derived from Lenin's own portrait of Bogdanov and the other Bolsheviks as a deviant minority.

More recently scholars have begun to recognize that Bogdanov was an influential thinker and a major leader of Bolshevism before 1914, a rival of Lenin in both politics and philosophy who threatened to take over the faction around 1909. The philosophical dispute was outlined by Kendall E. Bailes in his "Philosophy and Politics in Russian Social Democracy: Bogdanov, Lunacharsky and the Crisis of Bolshevism, 1908–1909" (Master's thesis, Columbia University, 1966). The first full biography of Bogdanov appeared in 1966: Dietrich Grille, *Lenins Rivale: Bogdanow und seine Philosophie* (Cologne, 1966).

By the 1970s scholars recognized that Lenin had distorted Bogdanov's views, that Bogdanov in his novels *Red Star* and *Engineer Menni* was a precursor of Soviet science fiction, that Bogdanov's philosophies of "tectology" and "empiriomonism" were forerunners of Western systems science. The utopian dream of a "proletarian culture" with its collectivist world view was recognized as an important part of Bolshevism. As the historian Peter Scheibert noted, "there remains in a Leninist Russia always something latently Bogdanovian"; "Lenin, Bogdanov, and the Concept of Proletarian Culture," in B. W. Eissenstat, ed., *Lenin and Leninism: State, Law, and Society* (Toronto and London: D. C. Heath, 1971), 43–57. The French historian Georges Haupt also pointed out that around 1907 "the leadership of the Bolshevik splinter group slipped from Lenin's hands and passed provisionally to the left-wing 'Bolshevik' Bogdanov" and that Lenin's famous tome *Materialism and Empiriocriticism* (1909) "was not so much a matter of eliminating a philosophical heresy, as is now widely believed, but rather, the stake in the battle of theory was the direction or leadership of the Bolshevik splinter"; see G. Haupt and J.-J. Marie, *Makers of the Russian Revolution*, trans. C. I. P. Ferdinand (Ithaca, N.Y.: Cornell University Press, 1974), 291.

More recently scholars have accepted the notion that there was "diversity in early Bolshevism" and that the *Vpered* circle of Bogdanov and Lunacharsky "was as legitimate an offspring of the Bolshevism of 1903 as was the fraction of Lenin." See Zenovia A. Sochor, "Was Bogdanov Russia's Answer to Gramsci?" *Studies in Soviet Thought* 22 (1981): 59–81, and John Biggart, "Anti-Leninist Bolshevism: The *Forward* Group of the RSDRP," *Canadian Slavonic Papers* 23, no. 2 (June 1981): 134–153. It has been argued that "Bogdanov was a major ideological force within the Bolshevik movement and in a sense he even became a kind of co-leader with Lenin in the Party, at least from 1904 to 1907"; see Leland Fetzer, ed. and trans., *Pre-Revolutionary Russian Science Fiction: An Anthology* (Ann Arbor, Michigan: Ardis, 1982), 1. None of these studies, however, has stressed the relationship between the philosophy of collectivism and the politics of syndicalism.

7. For some time scholars have recognized that the division within Bolshevism after 1905 involved a struggle for party funds. Leonard Schapiro noted that the Lenin-Bogdanov dispute "had little connection with the nature of sense perceptions. It is more probable that one of the main subjects of dispute was the question of the further disposal of the proceeds of the Tiflis robbery [of June 1907], which Bogdanov and Krasin wanted to use for an attempt to rescue Kamo from prison. But none of this aspect of the quarrel was made public. The dispute was throughout presented as one on issues of ideology." Schapiro, *Communist Party*, 110. Kendall Bailes, on the other hand, argued that "expropriations and the money obtained from them played only a subordinate part in the split, becoming an issue only after Bogdanov had ceased to work with Lenin in June of 1908"; he concluded that "questions of philosophy were the primary cause of the break." Bailes, "Philosophy and Politics," 27, 139. In fact, both "god building" in philosophy and the financial expropriations were related to the politics of syndicalism after 1905.

1. The Word: Lenin, Bonch-Bruevich, and the Art of Secret Writing

1. L. Trotsky, *The Young Lenin*, trans. M. Eastman (New York: Doubleday, 1972), 6.

2. D. Kahn, *The Codebreakers* (New York: Signet, 1973), provides the best general survey of the history of codes and ciphers.

3. M. A. Rose, *Reading the Young Marx and Engels: Poetry, Parody, and the Censor* (London: Croom Helm, 1978), 148, 153.

4. B. Wolfe, *Three Who Made a Revolution* (New York: Delta, 1978), 36.

5. V. I. Semevsky, *M. V. Butashevich-Petrashevskii i Petrashevtsy* (Moscow, 1922), 58–83.

6. V. Voinov, [A. V. Lunacharsky], "Petrashevskii-Butashevich," in *Russkii Biograficheskii Slovar'* (St. Petersburg, 1902), 13:634–636.

7. Institut Marksizma-Leninizma, eds., *K. Marks, F. Engel's i Revoliutsionnaia Rossiia* (Moscow: Politizdat, 1967), 244–245.

8. E. I. Pokusaev, ed., *N. G. Chernyshevskii: Stat'i, Issledovaniia i Materialy* (Saratov, 1965), vol. 4, especially B. I. Lazerson, "Ezopovskaia rech' v publitsistike Chernyshevskogo," 61–82. On the origins of Aesopian language in nineteenth-century Russia, see I. P. Foote, ed., *M. E. Saltykov-Shchedrin: Selected Satirical Writings* (Oxford: Clarendon Press, 1977), 17.

9. N. V. Valentinov, *Encounters with Lenin* (New York: Oxford University Press, 1968), 70.

10. L. Haimson, *The Russian Marxists and the Origins of Bolshevism* (Boston: Beacon Press, 1955), 54–55; R. Pipes, *Social Democracy and the St. Petersburg Labor Movement, 1885–1897* (Cambridge: Harvard University Press, 1963), 74. Plekhanov's book was published under a pseudonym (N. Beltov), passed by the censor prior to publication, and sold out all three thousand copies within three weeks. An awakened censorship then forbade a second printing of what they correctly perceived to be a revolutionary tract in the guise of a philosophical tome. See R. Kindersley, *The First Russian Revisionists: A Study of "Legal Marxism" in Russia* (Oxford: Clarendon Press, 1962), 74–76.

11. Wolfe, *Three Who Made a Revolution*, 221. On Bolshevik code words, see also D. J. Dallin, *Soviet Espionage* (New Haven and London: Yale University Press, 1955), 1. Also N. Krupskaya, *Memories of Lenin*, trans. R. E. Verney (London: Martin Lawrence, 1930), 1:77.

12. Kahn, *The Codebreakers*, 343.

13. Ibid., 344.

14. P. Kropotkin, *Memoirs of a Revolutionist* (New York: Anchor, 1962), 243.

15. A. Koestler, *Darkness at Noon* (New York: Macmillan, 1941), 24.

16. A. T. Vassilyev, *The Ochrana: The Russian Secret Police* (Philadelphia and London: Lippincott, 1930), 92–95.

17. Krupskaya, *Memories* 1:11.

18. R. McNeal, *Bride of the Revolution: Krupskaya and Lenin* (Ann Arbor: University of Michigan Press, 1972), 21–26. Also V. S. Drizdo et al., eds., *Vospominaniia o Lenine* (Moscow: Izdatel'stvo politicheskoi literatury, 1979), 1:68–69.

19. Reminiscences of A. Ulianova-Elizarova (1931) in V. I. Lenin, *Polnoe sobranie sochinenii* (Moscow: Izd. pol. lit., 1967), 55:xxxv–xxxvi (hereafter Lenin, *PSS*).

20. *Vospominaniia o Lenine* 1:69–70.

21. M. Futrell, *Northern Underground* (London: Faber and Faber, 1963), 109. Lenin, *PSS* 46:47. Also, Lenin's letter of October 26, 1900, to A. A. Yakubova, in Lenin, *PSS*, 46:53–57.

22. *Perepiska V. I. Lenina i rukhovodimykh im uchrezhdenii RSDRP s partiinymi organizatsiiami, 1903–1905 g.g.*, 3 vols. (Moscow, 1974–1977), 1:290, 317, 372–373, 377 (hereafter *Perepiska RSDRP*).

23. Vladimir Petrovich Makhnovets (1872–1921), also known in party circles as Akimov, used the pseudonym "V. Bakharev" to publish *O shifrakh* (Geneva, 1902). A product of Marxist circles in St. Petersburg in the 1890s, Akimov escaped to Geneva in 1898, and supported *Rabochee delo* against *Iskra* and the Bund and Martov against Lenin in 1903. Lenin labeled him an "economist." See J. Frankel, *Vladimir Akimov on the Dilemmas of Russian Marxism 1893–1903* (Cambridge: Cambridge University Press, 1969), 74–98.

24. Lenin, *PSS* 6:15–22.

25. Krupskaia to E. D. Stasova, January 24, 1903; cited in *Perepiska RSDRP* 1:72.

26. Tver committee of the RSDRP to Lenin, July 24, 1903; *Perepiska RSDRP* 3:438.

27. A. Bundovets, [P. I. Rozental] *Shifrovannoe pis'mo* (Geneva, 1904), 10.

28. L. D. Fotieva, *Iz zhizni V. I. Lenina* (Moscow, 1967), 8–9.

29. Lenin, *PSS* 46:406–407; N. E. Burenin to Krupskaya, May 23, 1905, *Partiia v revoliutsii 1905 goda* (Moscow: Marks-Engel's Institut, 1934), 211–212; Edgar Wolberg to Lenin, November 27, 1909, box XVII, folder 19; Okhrana Archive, Hoover Institution, Stanford, California.

30. The Censorship Statute of 1865 is reproduced in Charles Ruud, *Fighting Words: Imperial Censorship and the Russian Press, 1804–1906* (Toronto: University of Toronto Press, 1982), 237–252.

31. M. Ioffe, *Izdatel'skaia deiatel'nost' bol'shevikov v 1905–1907 gg.* (Moscow: Kniga, 1971), 210. O. D. Golobeva, "Izdatel'skoe delo v Rossii v period pervoi russkoi revoliutsii (1905–1907 gg.)," *Kniga* 4 (1972): 116–117.

32. As an example of the listing of confiscated books, see *Sistematicheskii ukazatel' literatury za 1911 god* (Moscow, 1912).

33. Ioffe, *Izdatel'skaia deiatel'nost' bol'shevikov v 1905–1907 gg.*, 166–167, 221–223. *Perepiska RSDRP* 1:172–173.

34. Engels to Paul Lafargue, December 30, 1871; Engels to C. Terzaghi, January 1872; in V. I. Lenin, *Anarchism and Anarcho-Syndicalism* (New York: International Publishers, 1972), 58, 68, 79.

35. Jack J. Roth, *The Cult of Violence: Sorel and the Sorelians* (Berkeley: University of California Press, 1980), 15–17, 21, 45–61, 79.

36. The best source of information on V. A. Posse is his memoir *Moi zhiznennyi put': do revoliutsionnyi period (1864–1917 gg.)* (Moscow-Leningrad: Zemlia i Fabrika, 1929). Paul Avrich, *The Russian Anarchists* (New York:

Norton, 1978), 139, notes that by 1917 Posse had been "propagating syndicalist doctrines" for over a decade.

37. *Zhizn'*, no. 1 (April 1902): 3.

38. Hubert Lagardelle, "Proletariat i armiia," ibid., 353–400.

39. *Zhizn'*, no. 6 (September–December 1902): 184.

40. Gorky to K. P. Piatnitsky, January 20–24, 1902; Maksim Gorky, *Sobranie sochinenii* (Moscow: Gos. izd. khudozh. lit-ry, 1949–1955), 28:224.

41. Posse, *Moi zhiznennyi put'*, 286.

42. Ibid., 323–324; Lenin, *PSS* 46:248–249.

43. V. A. Posse, *Teoriia i praktika proletarskago sotsializma* (Geneva, 1905), 49, 419.

44. Lenin, *PSS*, 46:260–261.

45. V. D. Bonch-Bruevich, *Vospominaniia* (Moscow, 1968), 102.

46. *Zhizn'*, no. 3 (June 1902): 159–160.

47. *Zhizn'*, no. 5 (August 1902): 198; see also Bonch-Bruevich's articles on Russian sectarians in the same journal, no. 1 (April 1902): 293–334, no. 2 (May 1902): 280–307, no. 3 (June 1902): 294–307.

48. Lenin, *PSS* 46:243–244, 268.

49. Lenin, *PSS*, 7:310. Also, P. N. Lepeshinsky, *Na povorote* (Moscow, 1955), 222.

50. *Razsvet: sotsial-demokraticheskii listok dlia sektantov*, no. 1 (January 1904): 3, 6.

51. Ibid., no. 3 (March 1904): 73–74.

52. V. D. Bonch-Bruevich, *Izbrannye sochineniia* (Moscow, 1961), 2:307–322, on the Geneva party library; see also A. S. Kudriatsov, ed., *Lenin v Zheneve* (Moscow, 1967).

53. Lenin, *PSS* 5:441.

54. Lenin, *PSS*, 46:382.

55. Bonch-Bruevich, *Vospominaniia*, 55, 111–112.

56. N. Tumarkin, "Religion, Bolshevism, and the Origins of the Lenin Cult," *Russian Review* 40, no. 1 (January 1981): 39–40.

57. *Fond dokumentov V. I. Lenina* (Moscow, 1970), 35–38, 42.

2. Matter into Energy: Vanguard Party and Workers' Collective

1. Valentinov, *Encounters*, 215, 218.

2. Lenin, *PSS* 8:241–242n.

3. Ibid. 4:553. See also K. Shtreb, *Lenin v Germanii* (Moscow: Gos. izd. pol. lit., 1959), 17–18. Z. Zeman and W. Scharlau, *Merchant of Revolution: The Life of Alexander Israel Helphand (Parvus), 1867–1924* (London, 1965), 52–58.

4. Lenin, *PSS* 4:2–13; Lenin's article "S chego nachat?" from *Iskra*, no. 4 (May 13–15, 26–28, 1901).

5. K. Kautsky, "Die Revision des Programms der Sozialdemokratie in Osterreich," *Neue Zeit* 20, no. 1 (1901–1902): 79.

6. Lenin, *PSS* 6:1–192 passim.

7. S. F. Vinogradov et al., *Lenin i Moskovskie Bol'sheviki* (Moscow: Moskovskii rabochii, 1969), 55–57.

8. G. A. Alexinsky, "Vospominaniia," box 230, folder 3, p. 114, Nicolaevsky Collection, Hoover Institution, Stanford, California.

9. Lenin, *PSS* 55:71–73, 76. Lenin wrote A. N. Potresov on June 27, 1899, that Bogdanov was a good "monist" (Marxist) who "does not ignore Kantianism, he rejects it"; *PSS* 46:31.

10. Krupskaya to Bogdanov, October 2, 1901, in M. S. Volin et al., eds., *Perepiska V. I. Lenina: redaktsii gazety "Iskra" s sotsial-demokraticheskimi*

organizatsiiami v Rossii, 1900–1903 gg. Sbornik dokumentov, 3 vols. (Moscow: Mysl', 1969–70), 1:255. Hereafter *Perepiska V. I. Lenina.*

11. Lenin, *PSS* 46:175. Also Krupskaya's letter to Bogdanov in *Perepiska V. I. Lenina* 1:545; 2:41–42, 89, 260.

12. L. Trotsky, *My Life* (New York: Scribner's, 1930), 144.

13. Valentinov, *Encounters*, 152–168.

14. I. Dubinsky-Mukhadze, *Shaumian* (Moscow: Molodaia gvardiia, 1965), 140.

15. On Bogdanov see especially the biography by Dietrich Grille, *Lenins Rivale: Bogdanow und seine Philosophie* (Cologne, 1966). The comparison with Gramsci is made in Z. A. Sochor, "Was Bogdanov Russia's Answer to Gramsci?" *Studies in Soviet Thought* 22, no. 1 (February 1981): 59–81.

16. James D. White, "Bogdanov in Tula," *Studies in Soviet Thought* 22, no. 1 (February 1981), 33–58.

17. A. Mendel, *Dilemmas of Progress in Russia: Legal Marxism and Legal Populism* (Cambridge: Harvard University Press, 1961), 136, 198–199, 284–285, 288–289.

18. I. P. Kochno, "Vologodskaia ssylka Lunacharskogo," in *Literaturnoe nasledstvo* (Moscow: Nauka, 1980), 82:606; *Perepiska V. I. Lenina* 1:444–446.

19. *Perepiska V. I. Lenina* 1:484–486, 520; 2:55, 80, 84.

20. Ibid. 2:231, 355.

21. Valentinov, *Encounters*, 235; A. V. Lunacharsky, *Revolutionary Silhouettes*, trans. M. Glenny (New York: Hill and Wang, 1968), 37.

22. See Bogdanov's pamphlets published under the pseudonym Riadovoi: *Iz-za chego voina chemu ona uchit?* (Geneva, 1904), 12; *Liberaly i sotsialisty* (Geneva, 1904), 12, 28; *Liberal'nye programmy* (Geneva, 1904), 5.

23. Bogdanov, *O Sotsializme* (Geneva, 1904), 15–17. Bogdanov's earlier writings include: *Osnovye elementy istoricheskago vzgliada na prirodu* (St. Petersburg, 1899); *Poznanie s istoricheskoi tochki vzreniia* (St. Petersburg, 1901); *Iz psikhologii obshchestva* (St. Petersburg, 1904). Among Marxists Bogdanov was probably best known for his survey of economics, *Kratkii kurs ekonomicheskoi nauki* (Moscow, 1897).

24. Bogdanov, *Kratkii kurs*, 9th ed. (Moscow, 1906), 279.

25. Bogdanov, *Iz psikhologii obshchestva*, 2d ed. (St. Petersburg, 1906), 5, 271.

26. Bogdanov, "Sobiranie cheloveka," *Pravda*, no. 4 (1904), in his collected essays *Novyi Mir* (Moscow: S. Dorovatsky i A. Charushnikov, 1905), 12, 21, 37.

27. Bogdanov, "Normy i tseli zhizni," *Obrazovanie*, no. 7 (1905), and "Prokliatye voprosy filosofii," *Pravda*, no. 12 (1904), reprinted in Bogdanov, *Novyi mir*, 55–169.

28. *Ocherki realisticheskago mirovozzreniia: sbornik statei po filosofii obshchestven-noi nauki i zhizni* (St. Petersburg: S. Dorovatsky i A. Charushnikov, 1904). In this volume see especially S. Suvorov, "Osnovy filosofii zhizni," 3–112, and A. V. Lunacharsky, "Osnovy positivnoi estetiki," 113–183.

29. V. Bazarov, "Avtoritarnaia metafizika i avtonomnaia lichnost'," in ibid., 183–278. See also in the same volume Bogdanov's "Obmen i tekhnika," 279–344.

30. A. V. Lunacharsky, "Tragizm i belaia magiia," *Obrazovanie*, no. 9 (September 1902); citation from his *Etiudy kriticheskie i polemicheskie* (Moscow, 1905), 199. Also his "Idealist i positivist, kak psikhologicheskie tipy," *Pravda*, no. 1 (January 1904); citation from *Etiudy kriticheskie i polemicheskie*, 278.

31. V. Bazarov, "Iz istorii prosvetitel'stva," *Pravda*, no. 6 (June 1904), 105–126, and no. 7 (July 1904), 113–127. Also A. V. Lunacharsky, "Zhizn' i literatura," *Pravda*, no. 11 (November 1904), 263, 269. Bogdanov, Lunacharsky,

Bazarov, and M. N. Pokrovsky were all frequent contributors to *Pravda* in 1904 and 1905.

32. Lenin's pamphlets were usually published in two or three thousand copies by Kuklin's printing house in Geneva in 1904 and 1905, while the pamphlets by Bogdanov and Lunacharsky usually ran three to five thousand copies. See A. F. Kostin, *Boevoi organ revoliutsii: k 70-letiu gazety 'Vpered'* (Moscow: Mysl', 1975), 218–219.

33. Valentinov, *Encounters*, 111–151.

34. Ibid., 205–208; Lenin, *PSS* 47:141.

35. Valentinov, *Encounters*, 179, 183.

36. Ibid., 183–184.

37. The most complete biography of Ernst Mach is J. T. Blackmore, *Ernst Mach: His Work, Life, and Influence* (Berkeley: University of California Press, 1972). The best treatment of Mach's thought is J. Bradley, *Mach's Philosophy of Science* (London: Athlone, 1971). On Mach's influence, see also D. S. Luft, *Robert Musil and the Crisis of European Culture 1880–1942* (Berkeley: University of California Press, 1980), and G. Holton, *Thematic Origins of Scientific Thought: Kepler to Einstein* (Cambridge: Cambridge University Press, 1973), and L. S. Feuer, *Einstein and the Generations of Science* (New York: Basic Books, 1974), and L. Kolakowski, *Main Currents of Marxism*, trans. P. S. Falk (Oxford: Oxford University Press, 1981), vol. 2, *The Golden Age*, 413–466.

38. W. Ostwald, "The Modern Theory of Energetics," *The Monist* 17, no. 4 (October 1907): 481–550; J. G. Hibben, "The Theory of Energetics and Its Philosophical Bearings," *The Monist* 13, no. 3 (April 1903): 321–330.

39. W. Ostwald, *Individuality and Immortality* (Boston and New York: Houghton-Mifflin, 1906), 34, 72.

40. Holton, *Thematic Origins of Scientific Thought*, 224. See also H. Kleinpeter, "On the Monism of Professor Mach," *The Monist* 16, no. 2 (April 1906): 161–168; P. Carus, "Professor Mach's Philosophy," *The Monist* 16, no. 3 (July 1906): 331–356.

41. E. Mach, *Analysis of Sensations* (1886; reprint, Chicago and London: Open Court, 1914), 4, 24–25, 37.

42. Ibid., 360, 363.

43. T. Bottomore and P. Goode, eds., *Austro-Marxism* (Oxford: Clarendon Press, 1978), 11; R. Florence, *Fritz* (New York: Dial, 1971), 35–40. See also Adler's subsequent analysis of Mach's philosophy, *Uberwindung des mechanischen Materialismus* (Vienna: Brand, 1918).

44. Feuer, *Einstein* 37–38.

45. L. Schapiro, *The Communist Party of the Soviet Union* (New York: Random House, 1960), 61.

46. A. Ulam, *The Bolsheviks* (New York: Collier, 1965), 202. See also Valentinov, *Encounters*, 83–85.

47. P. G. Dauge, "Moi vospominaniia o Lenine," *Vospominaniia o V. I. Lenine* (Moscow: Izd. pol. lit., 1979), 2:134–135.

48. Bogdanov wrote Krupskaya on May 28, 1904, that he had met Trotsky and that "I don't like him very much." See *RSDRP Perepiska* 2:302.

49. M. N. Liadov wrote the editorial board of *Iskra* on June 29, 1904, that Riadovoi "has been in the ranks of social democracy for over ten years" but that "Lenin does not consider it his right to reveal his identity." *RSDRP Perepiska* 2:367.

50. On the Amsterdam congress of the Second International, see James Joll, *The Second International 1889–1914* (New York: Harper and Row, 1966), 100–165. The story of the August 1904 discussions of Bogdanov and Lenin are in Krupskaya, *Memories* 2:107, and Valentinov, *Encounters*, 234–235.

51. S. M. Schwarz, *The Russian Revolution of 1905* (Chicago and London: University of Chicago Press, 1967), 260; M. N. Liadov, *Iz zhizni partii v 1903–1907 godakh: vospominaniia* (Moscow: Gos. izd-vo pol. lit-ry., 1956), 61–63.

52. Liadov, *Iz zhizni partii v 1903–1907 godakh*, 64–66.

53. *Literaturnoe nasledstvo* (Moscow: Nauka, 1980), 89:498; Lenin, *PSS* 46:396–397.

54. Lenin, *PSS* 46:404–406.

55. M. Panin, *Kustarnichestvo i partiinaia organizatsiia* (Geneva: Tipografiia partii, 1904), 25.

56. J. Stalin (Kutais) to M. N. Davitashvili (Leipzig), c. October 13, 1904, *RSDRP Perepiska* 3:52–54.

57. Valentinov, *Encounters*, 22; C. Weill, "A Propos du Terme 'Bolschevisme,'" *Cahiers du monde russe et sovietique* 16, nos. 3–4 (July–December 1975): 353–363.

3. Self-Sacrifice: Gorky's New Money and Moscow's Old Believers

1. Peter Lösche, *Die Bolschewiki im Urteil der deutschen Sozialdemokraten 1903–1920* (Berlin: Colloquium Verlag, 1967), 27–34; Botho Brachmann, *Russische Sozialdemokraten in Berlin 1895–1914* (Berlin, 1962), 39–44.

2. Abraham Ascher, *Paul Axelrod and the Development of Menshevism* (Cambridge: Harvard University Press, 1972), 196–199, 208–209, 217–218.

3. D. I. Antoniuk et al., eds., *Perepiska V. I. Lenina i rukovodimykh im uchrezhdenii RSDRP s partiinymi organizatsiiami, 1905–1907 gg.* (Moscow: Mysl', 1979), vol. 1, part i, pp. 71–72 (hereafter *Perepiska V. I. Lenina 1905–1907*).

4. B. A. Aizin et al., *Lenin v bor'be za revoliutsionnyi Internatsional* (Moscow: Nauka, 1970), 84; Axelrod to Kautsky, January 7, February 10, and February 17, 1905, file 16, box 2, folder 41, Nicolaevsky Collection; Brachmann, *Russische Sozialdemokraten in Berlin*, 55–56; Ascher, *Axelrod*, 224–225; Lenin to Essen February 3, 1905, *Perepiska V. I. Lenina 1905–1907*, vol. 1, part i, p. 131; Lösche, *Die Bolschewiki in Urteil der deutschen Sozialdemokraten*, 43.

5. Krupskaya, *Memories* 1:112, 115, 120–121; *Perepiska V. I. Lenina 1905–1907*, vol. 1, part i, pp. 90, 98, 293.

6. Lenin to Bogdanov and S. I. Gusev, February 11, 1905, *PSS* 9:244–248; L. Schapiro, *Communist Party*, 59; M. Ioffe, *Izdatel'skaya deiatel'nost'*, 50.

7. Axelrod to Kautsky, April 10, 1905, file 16, box 2, folder 41, Nicolaevsky Collection; M. N. Liadov and S. N. Pozner, eds., *Leonid Borisovich Krasin ("Nikitich"): gody podpol'ya, sbornik vospominanii, stat'i i dokumentov* (Moscow, 1928), 352–353 (hereafter Liadov and Pozner, *Krasin*).

8. Bebel to Axelrod, late May 1905, *Lenin v bor'be*, p. 82 n. 48.

9. Lenin to V. V. Gurevich-Kozhevnikova, November 6, 1902, in B. A. Bialik et al., *V. I. Lenin i A. M. Gor'kii* (Moscow: Nauka, 1969), 227; Vinogradov, *Lenin i Moskovskie Bol'sheviki*, 58.

10. Lenin to Bogdanov, in Lenin, *PSS* 34: 230; also *Leninskii sbornik* 15: 233, 266.

11. Krupskaya to Bogdanov, December 15, 1904; Gorky (1957) 344–345; *Leninskii sbornik*, 15: 274; Bogdanov to Lenin, December 23, 1904, in Gorky, 349; Gorky, *Letopis'* 1: 497, 501–502.

12. Lenin to Bogdanov, January 10, 1905, *Proletarskaia revoliutsiia*, no. 3 (1925): 30.

13. Lenin to Litvinov, January 29, 1905, *Proletarskaia revoliutsiia*, no. 2 (1925): 85.

14. J. Edie, J. Scanlon, and M. Zeldin, eds., *Russian Philosophy* (Chicago: Quadrangle, 1965), 1: 309.

15. Ibid., 153 (Lavrov), 256 (Dostoevsky); M. Confino, ed., *Daughter of a Revolutionary: Natalie Herzen and the Bakunin-Nechaev Circle* (Lasalle, Illinois: Library Press, 1974), 164.

16. George Plekhanov, "Notes to Engels' *Ludwig Feuerbach* (1892)," in Edie, Scanlon, and Zeldin, *Russian Philosophy* 3:381.

17. See J. Bergman, "The Political Thought of Vera Zasulich," *Slavic Review* 38, no. 2 (June 1979): 243–258.

18. Walter Sablinsky, *The Road to Bloody Sunday: Father Gapon and the St. Petersburg Massacre of 1905* (Princeton: Princeton University Press, 1976), 44–45.

19. M. F. Andreeva, *Perepiska, vospominaniia, stat'i, dokumenty* (Moscow: Iskusstvo, 1968), 590, 592; L. B. Krasin, *Dela davno minuvshikh dnei: vospominaniia* (Moscow, 1934), 94, 104.

20. Gorky, *Sobranie sochinenii* 28:320; Andreeva, *Perepiska*, 80, 420; Liadov and Pozner, *Krasin*, 71–72.

21. Gorky, *Sobranie sochinenii* 28:349; Paris Okhrana, report no. 6, January 24, 1905, file XVIIa, folder 2, Okhrana Archives.

22. M. Gorky, *M. Gor'kii v epokhu revoliutsii 1905–1907 godov: Materialy, vospominaniia, issledovaniia* (Moscow: Nauka, 1957), 297. Hereafter Gorky (1957).

23. Sablinsky, *Bloody Sunday*, 189–190.

24. Zeman and Scharlau, *Parvus*, 69–70; Gorky (1957), 69–71, 347–348.

25. Ioffe article in *V. I. KPSS* 2 (1966): 71.

26. *Arkhiv Gor'kogo* (Moscow, 1954), 7:131–132, 292–294; Gorky, *Sobranie sochinenii* 28:401; *V. I. Lenin i A. M. Gor'kii: pis'ma, vospominaniia, dokumenty* (Moscow: Izd. Akademiia Nauk SSSR, 1958), 205, 411.

27. Ioffe, in *V. I. KPSS* 2 (1966): 73, 75; Zeman and Scharlau, *Parvus*, 83.

28. Gorky, *Sobranie sochinenii* 23:345–367.

29. Gorky, *Mother* (New York: Collier, 1962), 144.

30. On Savva Morozov, see Gorky (1957), 12–36.

31. *Arkhiv Gor'kogo* 4: 172; see also the portrait of Morozov in V. Nemirowitch-Dantchenko, *My Life in the Russian Theater*, trans. J. Cournos (Boston: Little-Brown, 1936), 130–134, and V. T. Bill, "The Morozovs," *Russian Review* 14, no. 1 (January 1955): 109–116.

32. Liadov and Pozner, *Krasin*, 142.

33. B. Mogilevsky, *Nikitich* (Moscow, 1963), 58.

34. Andreeva, *Perepiska*, 676.

35. Liadov and Pozner, *Krasin*, 358.

36. E. N. Andrikanis, *Khoziain "chertova gnezda"* (Moscow, 1960), 28, 32–53.

37. Ibid., 40, 47. Also Gorky, *Letopis'*, 1:552–553.

38. Liubov Krasin, *Leonid Krasin* (London: Sheffington, 1929), 27. See also B. G. Kremnev, *Krasin* (Moscow, 1968).

39. Gorky, *Sobranie sochinenii* 17:54.

40. Kremnev, *Krasin*, 113.

41. Ibid., 128. Also S. M. Pozner, *Pervaia boevaia organizatsiia bol'shevikov, 1905–1907 gg.* (Moscow, 1934), 48, 51, 54, 80.

42. Liadov and Pozner, *Krasin*, 214–216.

43. On Lunacharsky, see R. C. Williams, *Artists in Revolution: Portraits of the Russian Avant-Garde 1905–1925* (Bloomington: Indiana University Press, 1976), 23–58. On his later years as commissar of public enlightenment in Soviet Russia, see Sheila Fitzpatrick, *The Commissariat of Enlightenment: Soviet Organization of the Arts under Lunacharsky* (Cambridge: Cambridge University Press, 1970).

44. Lunacharsky's speech of June 22, 1918, in *Communist International*, no. 3 (July 1, 1919): 353–354.

45. Karl Kautsky, *Der Ursprung des Christentums: ein historische Untersuchung* (Stuttgart: Dietz, 1908), 307–308.

46. R. M. Chadbourne, *Ernst Renan* (New York, 1968), 50–51. Dennis Boak, *Jules Romains* (New York: Twayne, 1974), 26.

47. *Literaturnoe nasledstvo* 80:522–524.

48. Liadov, *Iz zhizni partii*, 72. A. V. Lunacharsky, "Kak Peterburgskie rabochie k tsariu khodili," published in Geneva in April 1905, in *Literaturnoe nasledstvo* 80:546–558; also Lunacharsky, "Vozrozhdenie pravoslavnoi tserkvi," *Vpered*, no. 16 (April 30, 1905), in ibid., 558–560.

49. Lunacharsky, "Tverdyi kurs," *Vpered*, no. 5 (February 7, 1905), in *Literaturnoe nasledstvo* 80:536.

4. Experience: Leonid Krasin and the Revolution of 1905

1. Esther Kingston-Mann, "Lenin and the Challenge of Peasant Militance: From Bloody Sunday, 1905, to the Dissolution of the First Duma," *Russian Review* 38, no. 4 (October 1979): 434–455.

2. *Partiia v revoliutsiia*, 186–187, 216.

3. Liadov and Pozner, *Krasin*, 368–370. Lenin, *PSS* 47:35–36, 38, 47.

4. Lenin, *PSS* 47:39–40, 51–52. *Partiia v revoliutsii*, 194–195.

5. Ascher, *Axelrod*, 229. Zeman and Scharlau, *Parvus*, 58–59. Lenin, *PSS* 47:56–57.

6. Elwood, *Resolutions and Decisions* 1:54–65.

7. I. Kuznetsov and A. Shumakov, *Bol'shevistskaia pechat' Moskvy* (Moscow: Rabochii, 1968), 42. S. Vinogradov, *Ego zvali Marat* (Moscow: Moskovskii rabochii, 1967), 79, 121.

8. M. N. Pokrovsky, *Izbrannye proizvedeniia* (Moscow, 1966), 1:8. I. Stepanov, *Ot revoliutsii do revoliutsii* (Moscow and Leningrad, 1925), 110. Ioffe, *1905–1907*, 100. The Moscow literary-lecture group consisted mainly of doctors, lawyers, teachers, and university professors:

M. G. Lunts	V. L. Shantser
M. N. Pokrovsky	S. I. Chernomordik
I. I. Skvortsov (Stepanov)	M. F. Vladimirsky
N. A. Rozhkov	M. N. Liadov
P. Ya. Gurov	V. M. Shuliatikov
K. N. Levin	P. G. Dauge
V. Ya. Kanel	D. I. Kursky
I. G. Naumov	N. L. Meshcheriakov
S. Ya. Tseitlin	V. A. Obukh
V. M. Friche	S. I. Mintskevich
R. S. Zemliachka	M. A. Sil'vin-Tagansky

9. Vladimir Maksimovich Friche (1870–1929) was a prolific literary critic. His studies include *Osnovnye motivy zapadno-evropeiskogo modernizma* (1909), *Torzhestvo pola i gibel' tsivilizatsiia* (1910), *Poeziia koshmarov i uzhasa* (1912), *Ocherk razvitiia zapadnykh literatur* (1908), *Leonid Andreev* (1909), *Khudozhestvennaia literatura i kapitalizma* (1906), and *Ot Chernyshevskogo k "Vekham"* (1910).

10. V. M. Shuliatikov, *Izbrannye literaturno-kriticheskie stat'i* (Moscow and Leningrad, 1929), 13. See also his other essays: *Novaia stsena i novaia drama* (1908), *Neoaristokraticheskaia aristokratiia* (1909), *Opravdanie kapitalizma v zapadno-evropeiskoi filosofii (ot Dekarta do Makha)* (1908). See also the collection of essays by the Moscow literary group, *Tekuschii moment: sbornik* (Moscow, 1905).

11. Ioffe, *1905–1907*, 98–99. Golubeva, "Izdatel'skoe delo," 126–127. G. E. Ryklin, *Pero i serdtse bol'shevika (o I. I. Skvortsove-Stepanove)* (Moscow, 1968), 13.

12. Vinogradov, *Shantser*, 120–121. G. Alexinsky, "Vospominaniia," box 230, folder 3, pp. 40–41, Nicolaevsky Collection, Hoover Institution. Stepanov, *Ot revoliutsii*, 11.

13. A. Ya. Zaitsev *Bol'shevistskaia pechat' v dooktiabr'skii period: sbornik statei* (Moscow: Izdatel'stvo MU, 1959), 54. Bonch-Bruevich, *Izbrannye sochineniia* 2:357.

14. *Partiia v revoliutsii*, 150–151, 155–156. Gorky (1957), 344.

15. *Partiia v revoliutsii*, 156–157. Gorky (1957), 51. Kuznetsov and Shumakov, *Pechat'* 50–58.

16. *Partiia v revoliutsii*, 171–173.

17. Bogdanov's September 12 letter is cited in Zaitsev, *Bol'shevistskaia pechat'*, 54. *Partiia v revoliutsii*, 177–178.

18. Kremnev, *Krasin*, 121–122. Krasin, *Vospominaniia*, 38.

19. Futrell, *Northern Underground*, 66–84.

20. Ibid., 80–81. S. S. Elizarov et al., eds., *Maksim Gor'kii v epokhu revoliutsii 1905–1907*, 63–65.

21. Gorky (1957), 63–64.

22. L. Engelstein, *Moscow, 1905: Working Class Organization and Political Conflict* (Stanford, 1982), 15, 69.

23. Vinogradov, *Marat*, 123. Alexinsky, "Vospominaniia," 21.

24. Figures on the Moscow central committee expenditures for 1905 are taken from M. N. Pokrovsky, ed., *1905* (Moscow and Leningrad, 1926), passim. Elizarov, *Gork'ii*, 65–66. Vinogradov, *Lenin i moskovskie bol'sheviki*, 119.

25. Engelstein, *Moscow, 1905*, 84, 93, 153, 220, 235. V. Nevsky, ed., *Dekabr' 1905 goda na Krasnoi Presne* (Moscow and Leningrad, 1924), 81–82.

26. Andrikanis, *Khoziain*, 83–84.

27. Ibid., 86–89.

28. Vinogradov, *Marat*, 154.

29. Krupskaya, *Memories* 1:153, 155. Liadov and Pozner, *Krasin*, 186.

30. Elwood, *Resolutions and Decisions* 1:100–102.

31. Kremnev, *Krasin*, 130.

32. Krupskaya, *Memories* 1:155. Valentinov, *Encounters*, 235–236.

33. "Tsenzura," *Bol'shaia sovetskaia entsiklopediia* (Moscow, 1934) 60:472, 472. Ioffe, *1905–1907*, 162–163.

34. H. J. Tobias, *The Jewish Bund in Russia from Its Origins to 1905* (Stanford: Stanford University Press, 1972), 130, 241.

35. Andreeva, *Perepiska*, 610. Gorky, *Letopis'* 1:591. Futrell, *Northern Underground*, 58–59.

36. Andreeva, *Perepiska*, 426–427. *Arkhiv Gor'kogo* (Moscow: Nauka, 1976), 14:200–201.

37. M. Gorky, *V Amerike: ocherki* (Stuttgart, 1906), 74.

38. Andreeva, *Perepiska*, 133.

39. *Arkhiv Gor'kogo* 4:197–198. Andreeva, *Perepiska*, 134. Liadov and Pozner, *Krasin*, 256.

40. *Arkhiv Gor'kogo* 4:202–203. B. Mogilevsky, *Prizvanie inzhenera Krasina* (Moscow, 1970), 64–65.

41. Andreeva, *Perepiska*, 140, 420.

42. *Arkhiv Gor'kogo* 7:148. Berlin Okhrana report of December 6, 1906, box 324, file XVIIa, folder 2, Okhrana Archive.

43. Gorky, *Sobranie sochinenii* 23:400–405. Gorky's article, "Delo Nikolaia Shmita," appeared in the Paris monthly *Krasnoe Znamia*, no. 6 (1906) and simultaneously in the London *Times*. Also *Gorky v epokhu*, 60–61. *Arkhiv Gor'kogo* 7:149–150.

44. *Arkhiv Gor'kogo* 7:155. Gorky, *Letopis'* 1:650. Paris Okhrana, report no. 190, May 26, 1907, file XVIIa, folder 2, Okhrana Archive.

45. N. N. *O proletarskoi etike* (Moscow, 1906) was an anonymous pamphlet edited by N. A. Rozhkov. The ideas and style suggest that the author was Bogdanov, or perhaps Krasin. See especially pp. 11, 17, 25, 32, 49, 53–54.

5. Myth: Lunacharsky, Syndicalism, and Collective Immortality

1. David Lane, *The Roots of Russian Communism* (Assen: Van Gorcum, 1969), 3, 41, 44. John Keep, *The Rise of Social Democracy*, 288–289.

2. Ia. A. Berzin-Ziemelis, "Pervye vstrechi s Leninym," in M. F. Biron and A. K. Mishke, eds., *Lenin v vospominaniiakh revoliutsionnerov Latvii* (Riga, 1969), 36–37. Lenin, *PSS* 15:391.

3. A. Balabanoff, *Impressions of Lenin* (Ann Arbor: University of Michigan Press, 1964), 17–25. A. P. Dudden, *Joseph Fels and the Single Tax Movement* (Philadelphia, 1971), 126–137. A. Balabanoff, *My Life as a Rebel* (New York, 1938), pp. 71–75.

4. H. Pelling, *The Origins of the Labor Party 1880–1900* (London: St. Martin's, 1954) provides good background on the 1907 London congress setting.

5. David Shub, *Lenin* (New York: Doubleday, 1948), 122. Elwood, *Resolutions and Decisions* 1:115.

6. F. D. Kretov, *Bor'ba V. I. Lenina za sokhranenie i ukreplenie RSDRP v gody Stolypinskoi reaktsii* (Moscow: Mysl', 1969), 77.

7. Ibid., 11, 17.

8. Ibid., 17–18, 75–77. W. E. Walling, "Evolution of Socialism in Russia," *International Socialist Review* 8, no. 1 (July 1907): 42–46.

9. V. Lenin and L. Kamenev, *O boikote tretei dumy* (Moscow, 1907), 7.

10. *Leninskii sbornik* 25:11.

11. Lenin to Lunacharsky, November 11, 1907, in *Literaturnoe nasledstvo* (Moscow, 1971), 80:33–34. *Proletarii*, no. 22 (February 19/March 4, 1908): 8; no. 23 (February 27/March 11, 1908): 7–8; and no. 36 (October 30, 1908): 6.

12. J. Estey, *Revolutionary Syndicalism* (London: King, 1913) is still a good general study; see also Rudolf Rocker, *Anarcho-Syndicalism* (London: Secker and Warburg, 1938). On the relationship between syndicalism and modernist thought, see E. E. Jacobiti, "Labriola, Croce, and Italian Marxism (1895–1910)," *Journal of the History of Ideas* 36, no. 2 (April–June 1975): 297–318, and the older but insightful essay by J. W. Scott, *Syndicalism and Philosophical Realism* (London: A. and C. Black, 1919).

13. G. Sorel, *Reflections on Violence* (London: Collier-Macmillan, 1961), 64, 124–125.

14. Frank E. Manuel and Fritzie P. Manuel, *Utopian Thought in the Western World* (Cambridge: Harvard University Press, 1979), 748, 750.

15. I. L. Horowitz, *Radicalism and the Revolt against Reason* (New York: Humanities Press, 1961), 252–254; J. J. Roth, *The Cult of Violence: Sorel and the Sorelians* (Berkeley, Los Angeles, and London: University of California Press, 1980), 37–38.

16. J. Joll, *The Second International 1889–1914* (New York: Harper and Row, 1966), 203–204.

17. Paul Mazgai, *The Action Française and Revolutionary Syndicalism* (Chapel Hill: University of North Carolina Press, 1979), 76–95.

18. Roth, *Sorel*, 40–42; Mazgai, *Action Française*, 115–117. Lagardelle's letter to Meerheim is cited in Akademiia Nauk, SSSR, Institut istorii, *Istoriia vtorogo internatsionala* (Moscow, 1966), 2:246.

19. B. Holton, *British Syndicalism 1900–1914: Myths and Realities* (London:

Pluto, 1976), passim. On syndicalism in Japan, see Hyman Kublin, *Asian Revolutionary: The Life of Sen Katayama* (Princeton: Princeton University Press, 1964), 194–208.

20. Roth, *Sorel*, 28–29, 32; David Roberts, *The Syndicalist Tradition and Italian Fascism* (Chapel Hill: University of North Carolina Press, 1979), 54, 73–79.

21. Roberts, *Syndicalist Tradition*, 57–85.

22. Ibid., 85. Roth, *Sorel*, 74–75. Arturo Labriola, "From Parliaments to Labor Unions," *International Socialist Review* 7, no. 11 (May 1907); 667–677.

23. A. J. Gregor, *Young Mussolini and the Intellectual Origins of Fascism* (Berkeley, Los Angeles, and London: University of California Press, 1979), 37–49, 51–73. Also Ernst Nolte, *Three Faces of Fascism*, trans. L. Vennewitz (New York, Chicago, and San Francisco: Holt, Rinehart, Winston, 1966), 154–155, 164.

24. P. Renshaw, *The Wobblies* (New York: Doubleday, 1967), 64–66. M. Dubovsky, *We Shall Be All: A History of the I.W.W.* (New York: Quadrangle, 1969), 78.

25. P. Foner, *History of the Labor Movement in the United States* (New York: International Publishers, 1965), vol. 4, *The I.W.W., 1905–1917*, 36, 52, 69. Gorky's story "The Masters of Life" appears in *Mother Earth* 1, no. 11 (January 1907): 48–60.

26. Dubovsky, *We Shall Be All*, 138–140.

27. Paul Avrich, *The Russian Anarchists* (New York: Norton, 1978), 76–78, 85–86.

28. Ibid., 93–94, 102–106, 111. Peter Kropotkin, *Russkaia revoliutsiia i anarkhizm* (London, 1907), 7, 12, 74, 85.

29. P. Strel'sky, *Samoorganizatsiia rabochago klassa* (St. Petersburg, 1906), 90. Viktor Chernov, *Filosofskie i sotsiologicheskie etiudy* (Moscow, 1907), 364–379, and *Teoretiki romanskogo sindikalizma* (Moscow, 1908), introduction, 189.

30. D. I. Novomirskii, *Iz programmy sindikal'nago anarkhizma* (Odessa: Golos i trud, 1907), 17, 20, 24, 26, 36, 44, 60, 97.

31. V. Bazarov (V. I. Rudnev), *Anarkhicheskii kommunizm i marksizm* (St. Petersburg, 1906), 155, 160.

32. V. Sorel, *Razmyshleniia o nasilii*, trans. V. Fritche (St. Petersburg: Pol'za, 1907), 56–57. See also Sorel's *Sotsial'nye ocherki sovremennoi ekonomii: degeneratsiia kapitalizma i degeneratsiia sotsializma*, trans. G. Kirdetsov (St. Petersburg: Dorovatovsky i Charushnikov, 1907), introduction, v.

33. P. Strel'sky, *Novaia sekta v riadakh sotsialistov* (Moscow, 1908), 22–23, 33. Also by the same author, "Predposylki 'revoliutsionnyi sindikalizma,'" *Obrazovanie* 23, no. 13 (May 1907): 6–26. Other essays on syndicalism include V. A. Posse and A. Nedrov, *Rabochii vopros* (St. Petersburg, 1906), and L. Kozlovsky, *Ocherki sindikalizma v Frantsii* (Moscow, 1907). From the anarchist point of view, see M. Korn (M. Izdina), *Revoliutsionnyi sindikalizm i anarkhizm* (Geneva: Khleb i volia, 1907). Struve's comment on Sorel is cited in Richard Pipes, *Struve: Liberal on the Right, 1905–1944* (Cambridge: Harvard University Press, 1980), 106.

An official Soviet comment was that "in 1908 the French syndicalist Georges Sorel's book *Social Essays on Contemporary Economics* was published in translation in Russia, where it said that Marxism was based on hypotheses, contradicted by observation and belief, and the teaching that capitalism would collapse was only a 'myth' which in real life 'might happen, but will never actually take place,'" from *Istoriia SSSR* (Moscow, 1966), 2:270–271.

34. *Dnevnik sotsial-demokrata*, no. 2 (August 1905): 11, 21.

35. G. Plekhanov, "Pis'ma o taktike i bestaktnosti," *Golos truda*, no. 12 (March–April 1906); reproduced in Plekhanov, *Sobranie sochinenii* 15: 112–122.

Also his "Gde zhe pravaia storona i gde 'ortodoksiia'?" *Kur'er*, no. 20 (June 8, 1906), in *Sobranie sochinenii* 15:146, 153.

36. Plekhanov, *Sobranie sochinenii* 15:391, 411–412. *Sovremennyi mir*, no. 1 (January 1907): 260–265. M. Iovchuk and I. Kurbatova, *Plekhanov* (Moscow: Molodaia gvardiia, 1976), 251–252.

37. G. Plekhanov, *Materialismus Militans* (Moscow: Progress, 1973), 12, an essay published in 1907. G. Plekhanov, "Arturo Labriola," *Sovremennyi mir*, nos. 11–12 (December 1907), in Plekhanov's *Sobranie sochinenii* 16: 8, 22.

38. Arturo Labriola, "L'onesta polemica contro G. Plekhanoff e per il sindicalismo," *Pagine Libere* 2, no. 6 (March 15, 1908): 326. Plekhanov's April 1908 review of Enrico Leone's book on syndicalism, in *Sobranie sochinenii* 16:81, 126. Other reviews of books by Olivetti, Chernov, and Paul Louis by Plekhanov in 1908 are contained in *Sobranie sochinenii* 16:127–146.

39. Joseph Dietzgen, *Some of the Philosophical Essays on Socialism and Science, Religion and Ethics, Critique-of-Reason and the World at Large* (Chicago: Charles Kerr, 1906), 90–154.

40. Ibid., 90–91, 115, 134, 141, 150, 233.

41. Ibid., 282–283, 302, 305.

42. C. Huygens, "Dietzgens Philosophie," *Neue Zeit* 21 (1902): 197–207. Pannekoek edited Dietzgen's *Das Wesen der Menschlichen Kopfarbeit* (Stuttgart, 1903) and cited Dietzgen's work in his *Religion und Sozialismus* (Bremen, 1906), 6, 28. See also Pannekoek's essay "Socialism and Religion," *International Socialist Review* 7, no. 9 (March 1907): 551, 555.

43. D. A. Shannon, *The Socialist Party of America: A History* (New York: Macmillan, 1955), 18–19, 66.

44. N. Rumiantseva, *F. A. Sorge* (Moscow, 1966), 173. Karl Kautsky, *Ethik und Materialistische Geschichts-Auffassung* (Stuttgart, 1906), introduction, v.

45. Pannekoek, "Socialism and Religion." Also his article "The Social Democratic Party School in Berlin," *International Socialist Review* 8, no. 6 (December 1907): 323, and M. Hitch, "Dietzgenism," in the same journal, 8, no. 5 (November 1907): 295, 298.

46. T. C. Hall, "The Element of Faith in Marxism," *International Socialist Review* 8, no. 7 (January 1908): 392, and "Socialism and Religion," ibid., 9, no. 1 (July 1908): 41. Arturo Labriola, "From Parliaments to Labor Unions," ibid. 7, no. 2 (May 1907): 671. Friedrich Adler, "The Discovery of the World Elements," ibid. 8, no. 10 (April 1908): 577–588.

47. *Vospominaniia o Lenine* 2:137.

48. P. Dauge, *Iosif Ditsgen* (Moscow, 1934), 124–125. Ioffe, *1905–1907*, 215. Lenin, *PSS* 15:391. Joseph Dietzgen, *Erkenntnis und Wahrheit* (1888) in the edition of his son, Eugen Dietzgen (Stuttgart, 1908), 394, 416, 419.

49. Iosif Ditsgen, *Zavoevaniia (Akvizit) filosofii i pis'ma o logike: spetsial'no demokraticheskaia proletarskaia logika* (St. Petersburg, 1906). Ernst Untermann, *Antonio Labriola i Iosif Ditsgen* (St. Petersburg, 1907). Reviewed by Plekhanov in *Sovremennyi mir*, no. 7 (1907); see Plekhanov, *Sobranie sochinenii* (Moscow-Leningrad, 1928), 18:274–292.

50. Lenin, *PSS* 47:143, and 55:255, 397. I. Gelfond, "Filosofiia Ditsgena i sovremennyi pozitivizm," in *Ocherki po filosofii Marksizma: filosofskii sbornik* (St. Petersburg, 1908), 243–290; also Lunacharsky's remarks, ibid., 155, 159.

51. Franz Mehring, *Gesammelte Werke* (Berlin, 1961), 13:212–213. Karl Kautsky, "Ein Brief uber Marx und Mach," *Der Kampf* 2 (1908–1909): 451–452, dated March 26, 1909. Henriette Roland-Holst, *Joseph Dietzgens Philosophie in ihrer Bedeutung für das Proletariat* (Munich: Verlag fur die Proletariat, 1910), 6–7, 28, 35, 59, 76. Hermann Gorter, *Der Historische Materialismus*, trans. A. Pannekoek (Stuttgart, 1909), 128.

52. Ernst Untermann, *Die logischen Mängel des engeren Marxismus: Georg*

Plekhanow et alii gegen Josef Dietzgen (Munich: Verlag der Dietzgenischen Philosophie, 1910), 15, 31, 561, 569. V. I. Lenin, "K dvadtsatipiati letiiu smerti Iosifa Ditsgena," in *PSS* 23:117–120, published in *Pravda* on May 5–18, 1913. Ortodox (L. Akselrod), in *Nasha Zaria*, no. 9 (September 1913): 1–9. Adolf Hepner, *Josef Dietzgens Philosophische Lehren* (Stuttgart, 1916), 16. M. Klein, E. Lange, and F. Richter, eds., *Zur Geschichte der Marxistisch-Leninistischen Philosophie in Deutschland* (Berlin, 1969), 2:445–464.

53. Vladimir Soloviev, *Sobranie sochinenii* (St. Petersburg, n.d.), 10:190.

54. J. Woodward, *Leonid Andreyev: A Study* (Oxford: Oxford University Press, 1969), 138. Fedorov's ideas are collected as N. F. Fedorov, *Filosofiia obshchago dela: stat'i, mysli, i pis'ma Nikolaia Fedorovicha Fedorova* (Verny, 1906; Moscow, 1913). Boris Savinkov wrote under the name Ropshin, *The Pale Horse* (New York: Knopf, 1919), 96, 137.

55. A. I. Izgoev in *Vekhi* (Moscow, 1909), 118–119.

56. Enrico Ferri, *Socialism and Modern Science*, trans. R. R. LaMonde (1894; reprint, Chicago: Kerr, 1909), 68, 72. Gustav Bjorklund, *Death and Resurrection from the Point of View of the Cell Theory* (London: Open Court, 1910), 34, 91, 123–124. F. A. Le Dantec, *The Nature and Origin of Life, in the Light of New Knowledge* (New York: Barnes, 1906), 248–250. M. Guyau, *The Non-Religion of the Future* (New York: Holt, 1897), 532–533.

57. A. Kollontai, "Problema nravstvennosti s pozitivnoi tochki zreniia," *Obrazovanie* 14, no. 10 (October 1905): 96, and the same author, "Etika i sotsial-demokratiia," *Obrazovanie* 15, no. 2 (February 1906): 24–27. N. A. Rozhkov, *Osnovy nauchnoi filosofii* (St. Petersburg, 1911), 131–132.

58. A. V. (Voinov) Lunacharsky, "Massovaia politicheskaia stachka," *Proletarii*, no. 1 (May 14–27, 1905): 3–4. Ibid., no. 4 (June 4–17, 1905): 1, 4. Also *Literaturnoe nasledstvo* 80:5–7, 26.

59. Gorky, *Letopis'* 1:633. *Arkhiv Gor'kogo*, (Moscow: Nauka, 1976), 14:22. Gorky's letter to Grigorii Alexinsky, dated 1907, box 3, Alexinsky Archive.

60. V. Desnitskii, *A. M. Gor'kii* (Moscow, 1959), 196–197. *Arkhiv Gor'kogo* 4:221. *Literaturnoe nasledstvo* (Moscow, 1970), 82:555. An official Soviet version is that "in an afterward to Labriola's book, Lunacharsky approached syndicalist dogmas uncritically and allowed them to remain, departing from Marxist teachings"; see *Istoriia KPSS* (Moscow, 1966), 2:253.

61. *Literaturnoe nasledstvo* 80:619–626.

62. Lunacharsky, *Vospominaniia i vpechatleniia*, 47.

63. *Arkhiv Gor'kogo* 4:210–216, and 14:19.

64. A. V. Lunacharsky, "Vopros o vzaimootnoshenii partii i professional'nykh soiuzov na Shtuttgartskom Mezhdunarodnom Kongresse," typescript dated Geneva, 1907, in the Alexinsky Archive, pp. 50, 54–56, 63, 66, 75, 80, 87. The edited version appeared as "Novye puti," *Raduga*, no. 3 (November 1907): 45–78. Lunacharsky's remarks also appeared in "Nekotorye prognozy," *Raduga*, no. 3 (November 1907): 76–78.

65. Lenin's reply appeared in *Raduga*, no. 3, as well, and was later published in *Leninskii sbornik*, (Moscow, 1933), 25:112–121.

66. *Arkhiv Gor'kogo* 14:16–19, 28–30.

67. G. Haupt, *Socialism and the Great War: The Collapse of the Socialist International* (Oxford: Oxford University Press, 1972), 20–23.

68. I. M. Krivoguz, *Vtoroi internatsional 1889–1914* (Moscow, 1964), 300. *Daniel De Leon: The Man and His Work, A Symposium* (New York: Socialist Labor Party, 1920), 59–61, 130. Lenin, *PSS* 47:300. Balabanoff, *My Life as a Rebel*, 82, 85.

69. Lenin, *Khronika* 2:345. Paris Okhrana, report no. 381, September 13, 1907, box XXVb, folder 1, Okhrana Archive.

70. Okhrana report, ibid.

71. Lenin, *Khronika* 2:335–340.
72. Ibid., 359–364. Lenin, *PSS* 55:240–241, 501.
73. G. V. Kniazeva, *Bor'ba bol'shevikov za sochetanie nelegal'noi i ilegal'noi partiinoi raboty v gody reaktsii (1907–1910 gg.)* (Leningrad, 1964), 58–59. F. D. Kretov, *Bor'ba V. I. Lenina za sokhranenie i ukreplenie RSDRP v gody Stolypinskoi reaktsii* (Moscow: Mysl', 1969), 23. Lenin, *Khronika* 2:370.
74. Brachmann, *Russische Sozialdemokraten*, 75–77.

6. Expropriation: Stalin and the Georgians as Bank Robbers

1. Krupskaya, *Memories* 1:162.
2. Lenin, *PSS* 47:120–121. *Literaturnoe nasledstvo* 80:36. Lenin, *Sochineniia* (Moscow, 1935), 28:508–509, 512–513.
3. A. Rubakin, *Rubakin* (Moscow, 1967), 61. A. Senn, *The Russian Revolutionaries in Switzerland 1914–1917* (Madison: University of Wisconsin Press, 1971), 6–7.
4. Kretov, *Bor'ba*, 60. Lenin, *Khronika* 2:397.
5. Krupskaya, *Memories* 1:172–173. Lenin, *Sochineniia* 28:518–519, 523–524, 529–531.
6. Avrich, *Russian Anarchism*, 38–40.
7. A. Maskulia, *Mikha Tskhakaia* (Moscow, 1968), 69, 77–78.
8. Lenin, *PSS* 46:518 n. 298. *Perepiska V. I. Lenina 1905–1907*, vol. 1, no. 1, pp. 51, 154–157. Krupskaya, *Memories* 1:123, 125.
9. R. C. Elwood, *Resolutions and Decisions of the Communist Party of the Soviet Union* (Toronto: University of Toronto Press, 1974), vol. 1, *The Russian Social Democratic Labor Party 1898–October 1917*, 100, 115 (hereafter Elwood, *Resolutions*).
10. Lenin, *PSS* 47:112–113. S. Volsky, "Revoliutsionnyi sindikalizm," *Raduga*, no. 1 (June 1907), pp. 38–79. Lenin, *PSS* 47:152–154.
11. Lenin, *Sochineniia* 28:535–539.
12. Ibid., 508, 541.
13. *Arkhiv Gor'kogo* 7:173; 14:33–34; 4:225–226.
14. B. A. Bialik et al., eds., *V. I. Lenin i A. M. Gor'kii* (Moscow: Nauka, 1958), 206–207. Gorky, *Letopis'* 2:10, 15. *Arkhiv Gor'kogo* 4:230; 7:177.
15. Lenin, *Sochineniia* (1935), 28:533. *Arkhiv Gor'kogo* 4:235–237. N. B. Malinovskaya to G. Alexinsky, April 2, 1908, box 2, Alexinsky Collection. *Arkhiv Gor'kogo* 7:181 and 14:207–208.
16. Lenin, *PSS* 15:437. Krupskaya, *Memories* 1:184.
17. *Arkhiv Gor'kogo* 14:39–41; 7:182–183.
18. *Arkhiv Gor'kogo* 4:259, 261. Gorky and Andreeva to Alexinsky, 1908, n.d., and Gorky to Alexinsky, 1908, n.d., box 3, Alexinsky Collection. S. Livshits, "Kapriiskaia partiinaia shkola (1909 g.)," *Proletarskaia revoliutsiia*, no. 6 (1924): 36.
19. *Arkhiv Gor'kogo* 4:260–266. Gorky to Alexinsky, Summer 1908, box 3, Alexinsky Collection.
20. V. Prokofiev, *Dubrovinskii* (Moscow, 1969), 193–195. Lenin, *PSS* 14:3–4.
21. Lenin, *Sochineniia* (1935), 28:514–515, 534. C. Huysmans, *Correspondance entre Lénine et Camille Huysmans 1905–1914* (Paris and The Hague: Mouton 1963), 47–48, 50.
22. Huysmans, *Correspondance*, 52–53, 56, 62–63. Lenin, *Sochineniia* (1935), 28:548.
23. K. Ostroukhova, "Gruppa 'Vpered' (1909–1917 gg.)," *Proletarskaia revoliutsiia*, no. 6 (1924): 15. Kniazeva, *Bor'ba*, 52–53.

24. Avrich, *Russian Anarchism*, 47.

25. A. Talanov, *Bessmennyi chasovoi (tov. Kamo)* (Moscow, 1968), 27. S. M. Pozner, ed., *Boevaia gruppa pri TsK RSDRP(b) (1905–1907 gg.)* (Moscow and Leningrad, 1927), 71. B. Brachmann, *Russische Sozialdemokraten*, 152.

26. Wolfe, *Three Who Made a Revolution*, 389–390. B. Mogilevsky, *Nikitich* (Moscow, 1963), 68–69.

27. Paris Okhrana, report no. 270, August 30, 1906, box XIIc(2), folder 12B, Okhrana Archive. V. Alekseev, "Demskaia ekspropriatsiia," in *1905* (Ufa, 1925), 161. Report of Paris Okhrana dated December 7, 1906, box XXb, folder 2, Okhrana Archive.

28. B. Kremnev, *Krasin*, 151. Liadov and Pozner, *Krasin*, 45, 385. Testimony of Georgy Chicherin, April 28, 1910, in box 4, Alexinsky Collection. Futrell, *Northern Underground*, 63–64. Brachmann, *Russische Sozialdemokraten*, 152. Maskulia, *Mikha Tskhakaia*, 105–107.

29. Okhrana, report no. 394, September 11, 1907, box XXVc, folder 1; and report no. 402, September 27, 1907, Box XXVc, folder 1, Okhrana Archive. Liadov and Pozner, *Krasin*, 45. S. M. Pozner, *Boevaia gruppa*, 252.

30. Report to the Paris Okhrana from the Swiss Department of Justice and Police, January 21, 1908, box XXb, folder 1; Report of the Russian Consul, Stockholm, January 24, 1908, box XXB, folder 1, Okhrana Archive.

31. Karl Baedeker, *Russia: A Handbook for Travellers* (New York: Scribner's, 1914), 465–471.

32. D. Shub, *Lenin* (New York: Doubleday, 1948), 123. L. Trotsky, *Stalin*, 104. B. Souvarine, *Stalin,* trans. C. Jones (New York: Alliance, 1939), 92, 95.

33. Paris Okhrana, report no. 280, July 8, 1907, box XXVc, folder 2; and report no. 420, October 12, 1907, box XXVIIc, folder 1, Okhrana Archive. Also report no. 451, October 13, 1907, box XXVc, folder 1. Brachmann, *Russische Sozialdemokraten*, 74.

34. Paris Okhrana, report no. 490, November 13, 1907, box XXb, folder 2; also the report on Kamo dated November 14, 1907, box XXVIIc, folder 1, Okhrana Archive.

35. Okhrana file on Zhitomirsky as a "deep cover" agent, box IIIf, Okhrana Archive.

36. L. Shaumian, *Kamo* (Moscow: Politizdat, 1959), 97. Bavarian police report II 9693I, January 27, 1908, box XXVe, folder 2, Okhrana Archive. N. Burenin, *Pamiatnye gody: vospominaniia* (Leningrad: Lenizdat, 1961), 259–260. Liadov and Pozner, *Krasin*, 247. Shaumian, *Kamo*, 123.

37. Lenin, *PSS* 47; 148–150, 318. *Golos sotsial-demokrata*, no. 3 (March 1908): 18. Huysmans, *Correspondance*, 54.

38. Paris Okhrana, report no. 527, December 12, 1907, on the Schmidt inheritance, box XXVb, folder 2, and report no. 538, December 16, 1907, box XIc(4), folder 1, Okhrana Archive.

39. Volsky, "Kak Lenin zhil v emigratsii," box 164, file 1, folder 2(3), p. 70, Nicolaevsky Collection, Hoover Institution. On the Taratuta Affair, see "Delo Viktora," box 7, Alexinsky Collection. O. Piatnitsky, *Izbrannye vospominaniia i stat'i* (Moscow, 1969), 105–106.

40. Volsky, "Kak Lenin," 69–72.

41. G. Alexinsky, "Vospominaniia," box 230, file 3, p. 96, Nicolaevsky Collection, Hoover Institution. Vol'sky, "Kak Lenin," 71.

42. N. Andrikanis, *Khoziain*, 89. Georgy Chicherin testimony, April 28, 1910, box 4, Alexinsky Collection. Gorky, *Sobranie sochinenii* (1955), 29:27. Paris Okhrana, report no. 529, December 12, 1907; box XXVc, folder 2, Okhrana Archive.

43. Paris Okhrana report dated May 29, 1908; box XVIIm, folder 5, Okhrana Archive. L. Kamenev, *Dve partii* (n.p., 1911), 143–144.

44. Andrikanis, *Khoziain*, 223–224. Paris Okhrana, report no. 204, June 13, 1908; box XXVb, folder 2, Okhrana Archive. See also Krasin's letter to Gorky and Andreeva, October 24, 1908, in Andreeva, *Perepiska*, 168.

45. *Leninskii sbornik* (1975), 38:32–35. Lenin, *PSS* 47:283–284. Burenin, *Pamiatnye gody*, 250–272.

46. I. F. Detushev, *Velikye nezabyvaemye dni* (Moscow, 1970), 224–236. Burenin, *Pamiatnye gody*, 262–270. Liadov and Pozner, *Krasin*, 247. Krupskaya, *Memories* 186.

47. Paris Okhrana, report no. 375, July 16, 1909; box XVIb(6)(a), Okhrana Archive. Lenin, *PSS* 47:216–217. *Leninskii sbornik* (1975), 38:32–35. Volsky, "Kak Lenin," passim.

48. Paris Okhrana, report no. 1373, December 3, 1915, box XXVc, Okhrana Archive.

49. L. Shaumian, *Izbrannye sochineniia* (Moscow, 1957), 1:267–268. V. Dubinsky-Mukhadze, *Shaumian* (Moscow, 1965), 156.

50. R. Tucker, *Stalin*, 105. S. Alliluyev, *The Alliluyev Memoirs*, trans. D. Tutaev (New York: Putnam, 1967), 132. Stalin, *Works* 2:47–80, 82, 90–94.

51. Dubinsky-Mukhadze, *Shaumian*, 139–140. L. Shaumian, *Izbrannye sochineniia* 1:285–288, letter of Shaumian to Tskhakaya, early November 1908. B. Morozov et al., *Iz istorii bor'by V. I. Leniny za ukreplenie partii* (Moscow, 1964) 181.

52. E. Smith, *Young Stalin*, 225. S. Beridze, *Mikha Tskhakaia* (Tiflis, 1965), 57–58. Stalin, *Works* 2:150–162, 169–173. M. S. Iskenderova et al., *Ocherki istorii kommunisticheskoi partii Azerbaidzhana* (Baku, 1963), 129.

53. Dubinsky-Mukhadze, *Shaumian*, 156, in a letter of Stalin to M. Toroshelidze dated spring 1909.

54. Kretov, *Bor'ba*, 141.

55. Lenin, *PSS*, 47:283–284.

56. K. E. Moring, *Die Sozialdemokratische Partei in Bremen 1890–1914* (Hannover, 1968), 106–117.

57. *KPSS v resoliutsiakh* (1970), 1:241–247. Schapiro, *Communist Party*, 108.

58. G. Alexinsky, "Chto zhe dal'she?" *Proletarii*, no. 34 (September 7, 1908), pp. 2–4. Kretov, *Bor'ba*, 79. Prokofiev, *Dubrovinskii*, 195. Lenin, *PSS* 28:550.

59. Shaumian, *Izbrannye sochineniia* 2:285–287, letter from Shaumian to Tskhakaia, early November 1908.

60. Krupskaya, *Memories*, 191. Liadov and Pozner, *Krasin*, 166–167.

61. Grille, *Lenins Rivale*, 32. Kremnev, *Krasin*, 162. Paris Okhrana, report no. 127089, April 5, 1909, box XVIIa, folder 1a; also report no. 208, April 27, 1909, box XXVc, folder 1, Okhrana Archive.

62. F. P. Bystrykh, *Bol'shevistskie organizatsii Urala v revoliutsii 1905–1907 godov* (Sverdlovsk, 1959), 322. The "Sasha letter" is dated July 1907 and may be found in box 11, Alexinsky Collection.

63. "Sasha Letter," box 11, Alexinsky Collection. Paris Okhrana, report no. 133, April 20, 1908, box XXVc, folder 1, Okhrana Archive. Avrich, *Russian Anarchism*, 69. Kretov, *Bor'ba*, 118–119. Paris Okhrana, report no. 441, November 26, 1908; box XXVc, folder 1, Okhrana Archive.

64. *Proletarii*, no. 45 (May 26, 1909): 1–4.

65. Kamenev, *Dve partii*, 144–145. Also, box 11, Alexinsky Collection. *Leninskii sbornik* (1933), 25:42–43. Paris Okhrana intercepted letter from a Social Revolutionary in Paris to a Mrs. Golubeva in Kiev, December 14, 1909, box XXIVj, folder 1, Okhrana Archive.

7. Mind over Matter: Orthodoxy against Science

1. Ioffe, *Izdatel'skaya deiatel'nost'*, 213.

2. Lenin, *Khronika* 2:306–310, 319, 331, 334, 342.

3. Ibid., 341, 346. Lenin, *PSS* 6:467 n. 1. Golubeva, "Izdatel'skoe delo," 126.

4. Lenin, *Khronika* 2:396, 408. V. Lenin, *Podgotovitel'nye materialy k knige "Razvitie kapitalizma v Rossii"* (Moscow: Izd. pol. lit., 1970), 633. *Zagranichnaia gazeta*, no. 2 (March 23, 1908): 7.

5. G. Alexinsky, "Vospominaniia," 199, 284–289.

6. For a succinct elaboration of Bogdanov's world view, see A. Vucinich, *Science in Russian Culture* (Stanford: Stanford University Press, 1970), 446–454.

7. A. Bogdanov, *Empiriomonism* (St. Petersburg, 1906), 3:iv–v, 101.

8. N. Eurich, *Science in Utopia* (Cambridge: Harvard University Press, 1967), 244. I. F. Clarke, *The Pattern of Expectation 1644–2001* (New York: Basic, 1979), passim.

9. Grille, *Lenins Rivale*, 162. Liadov and Pozner, *Krasin*, 139–140.

10. A. Bogdanov, *Krasnaia zvezda (utopiia)* (1907; reprint, Moscow, 1918), 10, 37.

11. Ibid., 38, 44, 47, 74.

12. Ibid., 83, 93, 95.

13. Ibid., 161–162.

14. Liadov and Pozner, *Krasin*, 140.

15. Blackmore, *Mach*, 237–238.

16. Ibid., 239.

17. N. V. Volsky to Ernst Mach, November 6, 1907, box 2, Boris Souvarine Collection, Hoover Institution. Published in *Le Contrat Social* 4, no. 3 (May–June 1961): 171–177.

18. Ernst Mach to N. V. Volsky, December 1, 1907, box 2, Volsky Papers, Hoover Institution.

19. Bogdanov's article appeared in *Neue Zeit* 26 (1907–1908): 695–700.

20. A. Bogdanov, "K kharakteristike filosofii proletarii," *Raduga*, no. 4 (February 1908): 88–112.

21. *Ocherki po filosofii Marksizma: filosofskii sbornik*, (St. Petersburg, 1908), 10–11, 14, 66, 69, 71, 91.

22. Ibid., 125, 148, 157, 159.

23. Ibid., 159.

24. Ibid., 160.

25. Ibid., 215–242; Bogdanov's article is entitled "Strana idolov i filosofiiamarksizma."

26. A. Bogdanov, *Prikliucheniia odnoi filosofskoi shkoly* (St. Petersburg, 1908), 21, 33, 35, 38, 66.

27. Gorky to E. P. Peshkova, February 1908; J. Scherrer and G. Haupt, "Gor'kij, Bogdanov, Lenin. Neue Quellen zur ideologischen Krise in der Bolschewistischen Fraktion (1908–1910)," *Cahiers du monde russe et sovietique* 19, no. 3 (July–September 1978): 324. See also V. Shuliatikov, *Iz teorii i praktiki klassovoi bor'by* (Moscow, 1907), 46, 79. E. Gorodetsky and Yu. Sharapov, *Ya. M. Sverdlov* (Sverdlovsk, 1973), 58–59. Gorky to Bogdanov, March 24, 1908, in Haupt and Scherrer, "Gor'kij, Bogdanov, Lenin," 323.

28. F. Adler, "Die Entdeckung der Weltelemente: zur Ernst Machs 70 Geburtstag," *Der Kampf* 1, no. 5 (February 1908): 231–240, translated by Ernst Untermann for the *International Socialist Review* 8, no. 10 (April 1908): 579–588. *Zagranichnaia gazeta*, no. 3 (March 30, 1908), p. 5, and no. 4 (April 13, 1908), pp. 3–5.

212 Notes for pages 132–139

29. *Golos sotsial-demokrata*, nos. 4–5 (April 1908): 3–12.

30. Kamenev to Bogdanov, May 26, 1908, *Pod znamenem Marksizma*, nos. 9–10 (1932): 203. Andreeva, *Perepiska*, 167. *Proletarii*, no. 31 (June 17, 1908): 2–3. Bogdanov to the editorial board of *Proletarii*, June 27, 1908, in *Leninskii sbornik* (1933), 25:35.

31. Gorky to Bogdanov, fall 1908, in Haupt and Scherrer, "Gor'kij, Bogdanov, Lenin," 327. Kamenev to Bogdanov, November 28, 1908, cited in V. Ignatiev et al., *Iz istorii bor'by Leninskoi partii protiv opportunizma* (Moscow, 1966), 194. Kretov, *Bor'ba*, 116. N. Valentinov, *Filosofskie postroeniia Marksizma* (Moscow, 1908), 155, 251. V. Shuliatikov, *Opravdanie kapitalizma v zapadno-evropeiskoi filosofii (ot Dekarta do E. Makha)* (Moscow, 1908), 7, 13.

32. *Vospominaniia Lenina* 2:63. Lenin, *PSS* 10:134.

33. G. Plekhanov, *Izbrannye filosofskie proizvedeniia* (Moscow, 1957), 3:71. N. Rakhmetov [O. Blium], *K filosofii Marksizma: dve stat'i o russkikh empiriokritikakh* (Geneva, 1906), 11, 36.

34. A. Lilley, *The Programme of Modernism*, trans. G. Tyrrell (New York and London: Putnam, 1908), 149–245, a translation of Pope Pius X's encyclical "Pascendi Gregis." See especially pp. 168, 184, 204, 214. See also B. Reardon, *Roman Catholic Modernism* (Stanford: Stanford University Press, 1970).

35. Lenin, "Marksizm i revizionizm," (1908) in *PSS* 17:25. *Leninskii sbornik* (1924), 1:90–96.

36. Plekhanov, *Izbrannye filosofskie proizvedeniia* (Moscow, 1957) 6:272, 722n.

37. G. Plekhanov, *Osnovye voprosy Marksizma* (St. Petersburg, 1908), 125, 143.

38. G. Plekhanov, "Materialismus militans: otvet g. Bogdanovu," in Plekhanov, *Izbrannye filosofskie proizvedeniia* 3:202–301. Originally published in *Golos sotsial-demokrata*, nos. 6–7 (May–June 1908): nos. 8–9 (June–July 1908); and in Plekhanov's *Ot oborony k napadeniiu* (St. Petersburg, 1910), 208–9, 224.

39. Plekhanov, "Materialismus militans," 231, 235, 261.

40. Plekhanov to Axelrod and Martynov, October 5, 1908, in his *Sochineniia* 19:vi, n. 1.

41. Lenin, *Khronika* 2:410–416.

42. Lenin, *Sochineniia* (1935), 28:546. Lenin, *PSS* 55:252.

43. Lenin, *PSS* 55:250–251. I. Dubinsky-Mukhadze, *Kavkazskie druz'ia Ilicha* (Tiflis, 1974), 105.

44. *Perepiska sem'i Ulianovykh 1883–1917* (Moscow: Izd. pol. lit., 1969), 176–179.

45. Lenin, *PSS* 55:255–261. *Perepiska Ulianovykh*, 184–186. *Voprosy istorii KPSS* 5 (1969): 46.

46. Bialik, *Lenin i Gor'kii* (1958), 43.

47. Lenin, *PSS* 55:262–268.

48. "Tsenzura," in *Bol'shaia sovetskaia entsiklopediia* (Moscow, 1934), 60:472. Lenin, *Perepiska Ulianovykh*, 194–195.

49. Lenin, *PSS* 55:280, 282, 289. Lenin, *Perepiska Ulianovykh*, pp. 199–201. *Voprosy istorii KPSS*, no. 5 (1969): 44. *Arkhiv Gor'kogo* 7:194.

50. Lenin, *PSS* 55:291. J. Scherrer, "Ein gelber und ein blauer Teufel. Zur Entstehung der Begriffe 'bogostroitel'stvo' und 'bogoiskatel'stvo'," *Forschungen zur osteuropaischen Geschichte* 25 (1978): 327–328.

51. R. Florence, *Fritz: The Story of a Political Assassin* (New York: Dial Press, 1971), 43.

52. Lenin, "Materialism and Empiriocriticism," in *Collected Works* (Moscow, 1972), 14:22, 66, 186, 218.

53. Ibid., 98, 292, 345.

54. Lenin, *Materialism and Empiriocriticism* (London, 1948), 10, 36, 48.

55. Ibid., 115, 122, 150.

56. Ibid., 220–221, 232, 234.

57. Ibid., 234, 252–253, 264, 273.

58. Ibid., 342, 353.

59. A. Bogdanov, *Vera i nauka (o knige V. Il'ina)* (Moscow, 1910), 146, 152, 159.

60. Ibid., 183, 186, 189, 191, 194.

61. Ibid., 211, 221, 222.

62. *KPSS v resoliutsiakh* (Moscow, 1954), 1:205. Kretov, *Bor'ba,* 23–24, 100.

63. P. V. Barchugov, *Soveshchanie rasshirennoi redaktsii "Proletariia"* (Moscow: Gospolizdat, 1961), 36. Kniazeva, *Bor'ba*, 137. Lenin, "Ne po doroge," *Proletarii*, no. 42 (February 25, 1909), pp. 6–7. Lenin, *Perepiska Ulianovykh*, 191–192.

64. *International Review of Social History* 3 (1967): 438. F. Adler, "Wozu brauchen wir Theorien?" *Der Kampf* (March 1909): 256–263. Kautsky to Axelrod, March 20, 1909, Axelrod Archive, International Institute for Social History, Amsterdam.

65. M. Pokrovsky, *Izbrannye proizvedeniia* (Moscow, 1966), 1:14–15.

66. Stalin to M. Toroshelidze, spring 1909, cited in Dubinsky-Mukhadze, *Shaumian*, 156.

67. Lenin, *PSS* 47:180, 284–285. Kniazeva, *Bor'ba*, 125–126. Lenin, *PSS* 17:415–426.

68. P. Mazgai, *The Action Française and Revolutionary Syndicalism* (Chapel Hill: University of North Carolina Press, 1979), 110–115.

69. Prokofiev, *Dubrovinskii*, 202. Kniazeva, *Bor'ba*, 129–138. *KPSS v rezoliutsiakh* (Moscow, 1954), 1:219–229. Bogdanov letter of June 26, 1909, box 1, Alexinsky Collection.

70. Kretov, *Bor'ba*, 135–136. Kniazeva, *Bor'ba*, 141–142. Kremnev, *Krasin*, 163.

71. Paris Okhrana, report no. 336, June 26, 1909, box XVIb, folder 6a, Okhrana Archive.

8. Bolshevism without Lenin: Collectivism and the Capri School

1. *Proletarii*, (June 16 and June 24, 1909). Plekhanov, *Sochineniia* 19:vii. *Perepiska Ulianovykh*, 205–206.

2. *Fond dokumentov V. I. Lenina* (Moscow: Izd. pol. lit., 1970), 50, on the Kuklin Library. Lenin, *PSS* 47:286–287, and 19:52–57. Burenin told the story of the attempt to kidnap Nicholas II in Burenin, *Pamiatnye gody*, 266–270. Kniazeva, *Bor'ba*, 139. *Leninskii sbornik* (1933), 25:35–36.

3. *Leninskii sbornik* (1933), 15:38–41. Lenin, "O fraktsii storonnikov otzovizma i bogostroitel'stva," *Proletarii*, nos. 47–48 (September 24, 1909). Lenin to Karpinsky, October 1909, *Leninskii sbornik* 13:173.

4. "Beseda s peterburgskimi bol'shevikami," *Proletarii*, no. 49 (October 16, 1909): 5–7. The comments of Martov and Ortodoks-Axelrod appeared in the Menshevik collection of essays *Na rubezhe* (St. Petersburg, 1909), 9–10, 35–36, 262.

5. G. Plekhanov, "O tak nazyvaemykh religioznykh iskaniiakh v Rossii," in his *Izbrannye filosofskie proizvedeniia* 3:326–437, especially pp. 329, 371, 380, 383, 385, 392, 394, 434.

6. Scherrer and Haupt, "Gor'kij, Bogdanov, Lenin," 327. *Arkhiv Gor'kogo* 7:185–186.

7. L. Feuerbach, *The Essence of Christianity* (New York: Harper and Row, 1957), 172, 184. E. Haeckel, *The Riddle of the Universe* (London, 1913), 12, 156, 245.

8. Winwood Reade, *The Martyrdom of Man* (1872; reprint, London: Pemberton, 1968), 437. W. Wolfe, *From Radicalism to Socialism: Men and Ideas in the Formation of Fabian Socialist Doctrine 1881–1889* (New Haven: Yale University Press, 1975), 236, 272, 276.

9. E. Bax, *The Ethic of Socialism* (1889; reprint, London, 1907), 18, 21–22. E. Bellamy, *The Religion of Solidarity* (1874; reprint, Yellow Springs, Ohio: Antioch Bookplate Co., 1940), 31–32, 41.

10. *Krizis teatra: sbornik statei* (Moscow, 1908), 172, 179, 185. V. Bazarov, "Lichnost' i liubov v svete novago religioznago soznaniia," in *Literaturnyi raspad* (St. Petersburg, 1908), 1:229–230.

11. M. Gorky, "O tsinizme," in *Stat'i 1905–1916 gg.* (Petrograd, 1918), 71, 74–75.

12. M. Gorky, "Razrushenie lichnosti," in *Ocherki filosofii kollektivizma: sbornik pervyi* (St. Petersburg: Znanie, 1909), 357, 396.

13. *Literaturnyi raspad* 1:155, 172, 230. Ibid., 2:87–88, 118.

14. A. Lunacharsky, *Religiia i sotsializm*, 2 vols. (St. Petersburg, 1908 and 1911), 1:26, 45, 227, 371, 385.

15. *Ocherki filosofii kollektivizma*, 5, 23, 29, 54, 127, 133.

16. Ibid., 240, 254, 307–308, 323, 326.

17. S. Volsky, *Filosofiia bor'by: opyt postroeniia etiki Marksizma* (Moscow: Slovo, 1909), 10, 86, 123, 248, 287, 300, 310.

18. Paris Okhrana, report dated January 16, 1909, box XXVb, folder 1; also report no. 6 dated the same day, box XVIIa, folder 2, Okhrana Archive. N. Volsky, "Vilonov—Leninets ran'she Lenina," box 164, file 1, folder 3a, Nicolaevsky Collection. St. Volsky, *Encounters*, 119. See also Gorky's account of Vilonov in Gorky, *Sobranie sochinenii* (Moscow, 1952), 17:82–91.

19. Volsky to David Shub, June 26, 1946, David Shub Papers, Yale University. Lifshits, "Kapriiskaia shkola,", 41–42.

20. Gorky to Bogdanov, March 1909, in Scherrer and Haupt, "Gor'kij, Bogdanov, Lenin," 324.

21. Arkhiv Gor'kogo 7:190–191.

22. Ibid. 14:126, 128.

23. Lifshits, "Kapriiskaia shkola," 44, 43. Bogdanov to the editorial board of *Proletarii*, April 11, 1909, box 1, Alexinsky Collection.

24. Lifshits, "Kapriiskaia shkola," 43–46. *Arkhiv Gor'kogo* 7:192–193, and 14:48–49. Bogdanov to the Capri School, June 1, 1909, box 1, Alexinsky Collection.

25. Trotsky to Gorky, June 9 and 20, 1909, box 2, Alexinsky Collection. Lifshits, "Kapriiskaia shkola," 46–48. The Capri School students were as follows:

I. I. Pankratov	V. E. Liushvin
N. U. Ustinov	A. S. Romanov
K. A. Alferov	F. I. Kalinin
V. B. Kosarev	F. I. Siatkovsky
I. G. Batyshev	N. N. Kozyrev
M. I. Lobanov	M. Ia. Yakovlev
I. I. Babintsev	A. M. Lukhman

Source: Kretov, *Bor'ba*, 142.

26. Lifshits, "Kapriiskaia shkola," 50–53, 64. Kretov, *Bor'ba*, 142. Kniazeva, *Bor'ba*, 141.

27. Lifshits, "Kapriiskaia shkola," 55–57, 64. V. Kosarev, "Partiinaia shkola na ostrove Kapri," in *25 Let RKP(b) 1898–1923* (Moscow, 1923), 152–162. Okhrana intercept of a Capri School student, Starover, dated August 10, 1909,

box XXIVj, folder 1, Okhrana Archive. On the Capri School, see also box 4, Alexinsky Collection.

28. Trotsky to Capri School, August 6, 1909, and S. Semkovsky to the School, August 31, 1909, box 2, Alexinsky Collection. Andreeva, *Perepiska*, 618. Letters of V. A. Stoliarov (August 10, 1909) and V. Arbatsky (September 12, 1909), boxes XIVi and XIVj, folder 1, Okhrana Archive.

29. Lifshits, "Kapriiskaia shkola," 55–57. *Leninskii sbornik* (1933), 25:37, 43–44. I. F. Dubrovinsky to the Capri School, September 3, 1909, box 1, Alexinsky Collection.

30. *Leninskii sbornik* (1933), 25:45–47. Lifshits, "Kapriiskaia shkola," 64–69. Sofia Shavdia to V. K. Shavdia, intercepted letter, October 22, 1909, box XVIIb, folder 1, Okhrana Archive.

31. Andreeva, *Perepiska*, 171–172. Bialik, *Lenin i Gor'kii*, 44–46. Bogdanov to the Capri School council, December 8, 1909, box 1, and the council's reply, box 6, Alexinsky Collection.

32. Lifshits, "Kapriiskaia shkola," 71. Lenin, *PSS* 19:190–191. Bialik, *Lenin i Gor'kii*, 47–48. Paris Okhrana, report no. 623, December 4, 1909, box XIV, folder 2, and report no. 656, December 17, 1909, box XVIIa, folder 2, Okhrana Archive.

33. Kretov, *Bor'ba*, 157–158. *Lenin v bor'be*, 158–160. A. Pannekoek, *Die taktischen Differenzen in der Arbeiterbewegung* (Hamburg, 1909), 26, 104, 121. H. Gorter, *Sociaal-Demokratie en Rivisionisme* (Amsterdam, 1909), 27.

34. *Leninskii sbornik* (1933), 25:54–55.

35. *KPSS v rezoliutsiakh* (1970), 288–299. Kretov, *Bor'ba*, 169.

36. L. Martov, *Spasiteli ili uprazniteli* (Paris, 1910), 22, 32–33. Volsky, "Kak Lenin zhil", 77.

37. Lenin, *PSS* 55:306. *Leninskii sbornik* (1975), 38:57.

38. "Delo Viktora," box 7, Alexinsky Collection. Martov, 16-page brief to the party court dated June 1910, box 17, file 1, folder 13, Nicolaevsky Collection. L. Kamenev, *Dve partii*, appendixes 15 and 17. R. C. Elwood, *Roman Malinovsky: A Life without a Cause* (Newtonville, Mass: Oriental Research Partners, 1977), 33.

39. Stalin to Vel'tman, Paris, Okhrana intercept, December 31, 1910, box XVIIu, folder 1, Okhrana Archive.

40. Stalin to V. S. Bobrovsky, Moscow, January 24, 1911, Okhrana intercept, box XVIIu, folder 1, Okhrana Archive. K. Ostroukhova, "Gruppa 'Vpered' (1909–1917 gg.)," *Proletarskaia revoliutsiia*, no. 6 (1924): 198.

41. Volsky, "Kak Lenin zhil," 42. Bogdanov to the RSDRP central committee, January 27, 1910, box 1, Alexinsky Collection. N. Nelidov and P. Barchugov, *Leninskaia shkola v Lonzhiumo* (Moscow, 1967), 22, 26. Lenin, *Sochineniia* (1935), 18:554, 559–560. Lenin to Vilonov, March 27, 1910, *Leninskii sbornik* 13:174–175. Bialik, *Lenin i Gor'kii* (1958), 51–53. Paris Okhrana, report no. 220, March 24, 1910, box XVIIa, folder 1a, Okhrana Archive.

42. Ostroukhova, "Gruppa 'Vpered,'" 202. Kretov, *Bor'ba*, 176.

43. Lunacharsky in "Proletarskoe znamia," nos. 2–3 (May–June 1910), 4. V. Anisimov to Lenin, May 8, 1910, Okhrana intercept, box XVIIa, folder 1a, Okhrana Archive. Grille, *Lenins Rivale*, 37. Ostroukhova, "Gruppa 'Vpered,'" 205.

44. A. Bogdanov, *Sovremennoe polozhenie i zadachi partii: platforma, vyrabotannaia gruppoi bol'shevikov* (Paris: Izd. gruppa Vpered, 1911), 2–3, 7, 13, 15–17, 28, 32.

45. Lenin, *PSS* 16:177–204. Ostroukhova, "Gruppa 'Vpered,'" 202. *Vpered*, no. 1 (July 1910): 9, 34, 38, 60–62; also no. 2 (August 1910): 72–82.

46. A. Bogdanov, *Padenie velikago fetishizma (sovremennyi krizis ideologii)*

(Moscow: Dorovatovsky and Charushnikov, 1910), 41, 100, 109, 126–127.

47. V. Bazarov, *Na dva fronta* (St. Petersburg: Prometii, 1910), xxii, xxvi, xxix, 98, 198. M. Liadov, *Po povodu partiinago krizisa: chastnoe zaiavlenie* (Paris: Vpered, 1911), 10–16.

48. S. Lifshits, "Partiinaia shkola v Bolon'e (1910–1911 gg.)," *Proletarskaia revoliutsiia*, 6 (1924): 109–144. Volsky, "Kak Lenin zhil," 51. Paris Okhrana, report no. 111, December 15, 1910, box XXIVj, folder 2, Okhrana Archive.

49. *Otchet vtoroi vysshei sotsial-demokraticheskoi propagandistsko-agitatorskoi shkoly dlia rabochikh Noiabr 1910–Mart' 1911 g.* (Paris, 1911), 8–9.

50. Gorky, *Sobranie sochinenii* 29:142. A. V. Lunacharsky, *Revolutionary Silhouettes* (New York: Hill and Wang, 1967), 63. *Otchet*, 11–12. Bogdanov to Mark Andreevich, November 12, 1910, box 1, Alexinsky Collection.

51. Roth, *Sorel*, 44. *Le Mouvement Socialiste* (March 1911), 184–185. Roberts, *Syndicalism*, 83. *Otchet*, 16–17, 25–26.

52. T. Gladkov and M. Smirnov, *Menzhinskii* (Moscow, 1969), 124–125. *Otchet*, 14–16.

53. Gorky, *Sobranie sochinenii* 29:104.

54. Andreeva, *Perepiska*, 173, 176.

55. Gorky to Bogdanov, March 20, 1910, in N. Trifonov, "A. V. Lunacharskii i M. Gor'kii," in K. D. Muratova, ed., *M. Gor'kii i ego sovremenniki* (Leningrad: Nauka, 1968), 145.

56. Bialik, *Lenin i Gor'kii* (1958), 54–57. *Arkhiv Gor'kogo* 14:335–336. Gorky, *Sobranie sochinenii*, 61–62, 65–66.

57. *Fond dokumentov V. I. Lenina* (Moscow, 1970), 37–38. Bialik, *Lenin i Gorkii* (1958), 61–66.

58. Plekhanov in *Dnevnik sotsial-demokrata* 9 (August 1909): 16–17.

59. Ibid. 10 (February 1910): 4, 35, 40, and 12 (June 1910): 29.

60. Plekhanov, *Izbrannye filosofskye proizvedeniia*, third letter in his "Materialismus Militans" series, 3:263, 300. Plekhanov, *Anarkhizm i sotsializm*, 3d ed. (Berlin, 1911), in his *Sochineniia* 16:192–196. On the Socialist Revolutionary view see "Krizis Bol'shevizma," in *Znamia truda*, 23–24 (December 1909), reprinted with Lenin's annotations in *Leninskii sbornik* (1933), 25:193–202.

9. Lenin without Bolshevism: Russian Politics and German Money

1. The most complete account of Bolshevik finances before 1914 may be found in Dietrich Geyer, ed., *Kautskys Russisches Dossier: Deutsche Sozialdemokraten als Treuhänder des russischen Parteivermögens 1910–1915* (Frankfurt and N.Y.: Campus Verlag, 1981). Geyer also distinguishes (p. 7) between Bolsheviks and Leninists. Lenin to the trustees, February–March 1910, *Leninskii sbornik* (1933), 25:55–58. Volsky to Alexinsky, 1911, box 2, Alexinsky Collection. D. Gol'dendakh to Kautsky, February 17, 1911, in Geyer, *Kautskys Russisches Dossier*, 291.

2. *Otchet*, 26–31. *Vpered*, 2 (February 1911): 69. Also 3 (May 1911): 78. F. I. Kalinin to Alexinsky, May 16, 1911, box 1, Alexinsky Collection.

3. Nelidov and Barchugov, *Leninskaia shkola*, 52, 56, 63–64. Kalinin to Alexinsky, July 4 and 7, 1911, box 1, Alexinsky Collection, Ya. Master (Strauyan) to Alexinsky, July 13, 1911, box 2, Alexinsky Collection.

4. Kalinin to Alexinsky, June 28, 1911, box 1, Alexinsky Collection. *Listok zagranichnago Biuro Tsentral'nogo komiteta*, no. 1 (September 8, 1911), pp. 3–4. Longjumeau student to the *Vpered* group, August 1911, box 6, Alexinsky

Collection. Ostroukhova, "Gruppa 'Vpered,' " 207–210 (Kautsky-Lunacharsky letters). R. Luxemburg, *Briefe an Karl und Luise Kautsky* (Berlin, 1923), 162–163.

5. *Listok*, 3–4; RSDRP central committee to *Vpered*, September 8, 1911. Paris Okhrana, report dated August 4, 1911, box XXIVj, folder 1, Okhrana Archive. Kalinin to Alexinsky, October 1911, box 1, Alexinsky Collection.

6. Kalinin to Bogdanov, December 3, 1911, box 1, and Manuilsky to Alexinsky, late 1911, box 2, Alexinsky Collection. L. Kamenev, *Mezhdu dvumia revoliutsiami* (Moscow, 1923), 267–279.

7. Zeman and Scharlau, *Parvus*, 124. Lenin to M. G. Filia, January 19, 1911, *Leninskii sbornik* 38:38.

8. S. Bronner, ed., *The Letters of Rosa Luxemburg* (Boulder, Colorado: Westview, 1978), 141–142. Lenin to Zinoviev, June 1911, *Leninskii sbornik* 38:39–41. Axelrod to Kautsky, June 5, 1911, box 16, file 2, folder 41, Nicolaevsky Collection. Lenin to Kautsky, June 6, 1911, *Leninskii sbornik* 38:41–42. *Leninskii sbornik* 38:97 n. 3.

9. Lenin to Zgraggen, February 26, 1911, *Leninskii sbornik* 38:54. Lenin to Zetkin, July 5, 1911, *Leninskii sbornik* 38:43. Leo Jogisches to Kautsky, July 10, 1911, fond G4 (Russenfond), International Institute for Social History, Amsterdam, cited in J. Nettl, *Rosa Luxemburg* (London: Oxford, 1966), 2:580. Luxemburg to Luise Kautsky, July 1911, Luxemburg, *Briefe*, 159–160.

10. Geyer, *Kautskys Russisches Dossier*, 321–322. Zetkin to Lenin, July 14, 1911, *Leninskii sbornik* 38:117 n. 1. *Listok*, 7. Ascher, *Paul Axelrod*, 287.

11. Zetkin to Kautsky, October 10, 1911, *Leninskii sbornik* 38:40–41.

12. L. Haas, *C. V. Moor* (Zurich: Bensiger Verlag, 1970), 87–89, 94, 96–97, 125–126.

13. Lenin to Zetkin, October 30, 1911, *Leninskii sbornik* 38:46; Lenin to Zetkin, November 16, 1911, ibid., 48–49; Zetkin to Taratuta, November 16, 1911, ibid., 56.

14. *Leninskii sbornik* 38:50 n. 5, referring to letter from Kautsky and Zetkin to Lenin, November 18, 1911.

15. Ordzhonikidze letter to "comrades in Russia," November 1911, cited in Volsky, "Kak Lenin zhil," 79. Ordzhonikidze to Zetkin, November 22, 1911, *Leninskii sbornik* 38:51. Lenin, *PSS* 21:34–36. Okhrana, report no. 1597, December 13, 1911, box XVIIa, folder 2, Okhrana Archive.

16. Elwood, *Resolutions and Decisions* 1:146–150. Elwood, *Malinovsky*, 26–27, 34.

17. *Leninskii sbornik* 38:52. *KPSS v rezoliutsiakh*, 343.

18. Kamo affidavit on expropriations, November 5, 1911, box 4, Alexinsky Collection. Shaumian, *Kamo*, 178. Okhrana, report no. 1722, January 13, 1912, box XXVIIc, folder 1, Okhrana Archive. Bogdanov to Ian Strauian (Master), January 8, 1912, box 1, Alexinsky Collection. Mogilevsky, *Nikitich*, 78.

19. Schapiro, *Communist Party*, 129. Brachmann, *Russische Sozialdemokraten*, 94–95. Lenin to Zgraggen, February 26, 1912, *Leninskii sbornik* 38:53–55. Elwood, *Resolutions and Decisions* 1:158.

20. Lenin to Gorky, February 1912, Bialik, *Lenin i Gor'kii* (1958), 69. Lenin to Gorky, September 15, 1911, ibid., 67–68.

21. *Vpered* circular to the RSDRP, 1912, box 5, Alexinsky Collection.

22. Lenin's letters to de la Haille of May and June 10, 1912, *Leninskii sbornik* 38:57–65.

23. Bogdanov to the *Vpered* group, June 25, 1912, box 1; M. Merkel to *Vpered*, June 2 and July 5, 1912, box 2; varia from June 1912, box 4; *Golos Sotsial-demokrata* to Zetkin, June 21, 1912, box 5, Alexinsky Collection. Also intercepted letter from a Menshevik, June 21, 1912, box XVIIa, folder 1B, Okhrana Archive.

24. Lenin, *PSS* 21:407–409. Lenin's July 23, 1912, summary of the Schmidt inheritance case, in *Leninskii sbornik* 38:66–71.

25. Trotsky to *Vpered*, February 26, 1911 and July 26, 1912, box 2; Trotsky to Alexinsky, May 13, 1912, box 5, Alexinsky Collection. Elwood, *Resolutions and Decisions* 1:159–167.

26. Lenin to Haille, September 23, 1912 and Lenin to Kamenev, December 26, 1912, *Leninskii sbornik* 38:74–77. Lenin to M. A. Ulianova, December 21, 1912, Lenin, *PSS* 55:330–331. Axelrod to Kautsky, September 6, 1912, box 16, file 2, folder 41, Nicolaevsky Collection. Huysmans to Lenin, September 10, 1912, Huysmans, *Correspondance*, 117. Elwood, *Malinovska*, 28–31.

27. Lenin to Gorky, early January 1913, Bialik, *Lenin i Gor'kii*.

28. Grille, *Lenins Rivale*, 166–167. Gorky to Alexinsky, 1912, n.d., box 3, Alexinsky Collection. A. Bogdanov, *Inzhener Menni: fantasticheskii roman*, 3d ed. (Petrograd, 1918), 29, 43, 115. Bialik, *Lenin i Gor'kii*, 81–82, 87–88.

29. *Vpered* materials for February 1912, box 8, Alexinsky Colelction. Lenin to Gorky, February 1913, Bialik, *Lenin i Gor'kii*, 94. Lenin to *Pravda*, February 14, 1913, box XVIIIa, folder 3, Okhrana Archive.

30. G. Swain, "Bolsheviks and Metal Workers on the Eve of the First World War," *Journal of Modern History* 16, no. 2 (April 1981): 273–292. Lenin to N. G. Poletaev, February 25, 1913, box XVIIa, folder 3, Okhrana Archive.

31. *Pravda*, no. 87 (April 27, 1913): 5; no. 97 (May 11, 1913): 2; no. 102 (May 18, 1913): 3. Part of Bogdanov's series on a "dictionary of foreign words," where he used an old Russian Aesopian tradition of dictionary definitions of political terminology. Lenin to *Pravda*, late May 1913, *Leninskii sbornik* 25:334–335. Krupskaya to M. N. Kovaleva, April 2, 1913, box XVIIa, folder 3, Okhrana Archive.

32. Kalinin to *Vpered*, June 2, 1913, box 1, Alexinsky Collection. Ostroukhova, "Gruppa 'Vpered,'" 213. Grille, *Lenins Rivale*, 168. Lenin, *PSS* 23:246–247. *Leninskii sbornik* 25:336–340.

33. Bialik, *Lenin i Gor'kii* 105–112. *Vpered* circular of January 18, 1914, in *Literaturnoe nasledstvo* 80:631. Brachmann, *Russische Sozialdemokraten*, 116. *Archiv Gor'kogo* 19:359–360.

34. Elwood, *Malinovsky*, 32–33, 52–57.

35. Lenin correspondence on the trustees, 1913, *Leninskii sbornik* 38:82–84, 94–97, 103–106, 108–109. Haille to Zetkin, August 22, 1913, box 16, file 3, folder 52, Nicolaevsky Collection.

36. Lenin to G. L. Shklovsky, September 1913, *Leninskii sbornik* 38:111–114. Heinemann to Zetkin, November 26, 1913, box 2, Alexinsky Collection. Chicherin to *Vpered*, December 8, 1913, box 1, Alexinsky Collection. Zetkin to Haille (September 13, 1913) and to Axelrod (September 13 and November 11, 1913), S. Semkovsky to Zetkin, October 21, 1913, box 16, file 3, folder 52, Nicolaevsky Collection.

37. Lenin correspondence with de la Haille and Shklovsky, winter 1913–1914, *Leninskii sbornik* 38:126–138.

38. Lenin, *PSS* 25:460 and 48:352. R. Elwood, "Lenin and the Brussels 'Unity' Conference of July 1912," *Russian Review* 39, no. 1 (January 1980): 32–49. Shub, *Lenin*, 154–155. Schapiro, *Communist Party*, 138. Alexinsky, "Vospominaniia," 205. RSDRP letter to Huysmans, March 31, 1914, box 16, file 3, folder 66, Nicolaevsky Collection.

39. A. N. Chkhenkeli to S. Semkovsky, July 7, 1914, box 2, folder 119, Okhrana Archive.

40. Shub, *Lenin*, 153–154.

41. Senn, *Switzerland*, 44, 76–80. Zeman and Scharlau, *Parvus*, 157–158, 162. *Vpered*, no. 1 (August 25, 1915): 1–3.

42. Senn, *Switzerland*, 89–102, 108–109, 119–120. Lenin to the International Socialist Commission, September 1915, *Leninskii sbornik* 38:169–170. Haas, *Moor*, 128.

43. Lenin, *PSS* 27:520–521 n. 123; 49:245, 256–259; 55:517 n. 342.

44. Lenin, *PSS* 49:245–259, 285, 299–302; 55:517 n. 342. Bialik, *Lenin i Gor'kii* (1958), 188–189.

45. Lenin, *PSS* 49:340–344, 351.

46. Lunacharsky's correspondence of spring 1917 in *Literaturnoe nasledstvo* 80:636–642.

47. A. Bogdanov, *1-oe Maia: mezhdunarodnyi prazdnik truda* (Petrograd, 1917), 9–13. A. Rabinowitch, *Prelude to Revolution: The Petrograd Bolsheviks and the July 1917 Uprising* (Bloomington: Indiana University Press, 1968), 66, 83. Lenin, *Gosudarstvo i revoliutsiia*, in *PSS* 33:80, 97.

48. Lenin, "Derzhat li Bol'sheviki gosudarstvennyi vlast'?" (1917), in *PSS* 34:306.

10. A Childhood Disease: Communism over Syndicalism

1. On syndicalism and Bolshevism after 1917 see especially V. I. Lenin, "Detskaia bolezn' "levizny" v kommunisme," *PSS* 41:1–104; H. M. Bock, *Syndikalismus und Linkskommunismus von 1918–1923* (Meisenheim am Glan: Verlag Anton Hain, 1969); T. Draper, *The Roots of American Communism* (New York: Viking, 1957); J. W. Hulse, *The Forming of the Communist International* (Stanford: Stanford University Press, 1964); F. Borkenau, *World Communism* (Ann Arbor: University of Michigan Press, 1962); B. Lazitch and M. Drachkovitch, *Lenin and the Comintern* (Stanford: Hoover Institution Press, 1972); N. G. Sevriugina and N. N. Surovtseva, "Iz istorii sozdaniia V. I. Leninym knigi 'Detskaia bolezn' "levizny" v kommunizme," *Voprosy istorii KPSS*, no. 3 (1960), 9–24.

2. Karl Kautsky, *The Class Struggle (The Erfurt Program) (1892)*, trans. W. E. Bohn (New York: Norton, 1971), 198. Ulam, *The Bolsheviks*, 266–267. Lunacharsky's letter to his wife is dated August 20, 1907, and may be found in *Literaturnoe nasledstvo* 80:623–625.

3. Lenin, *PSS* 36:283–314; 41:13, 39–49. Bock, *Syndikalismus*, 189.

4. Sorel, *Reflections on Violence*, 279.

5. "Resolutions of the First Congress of the Communist International," *Communist International*, no. 1 (April 1919): 52.

6. *Communist International*, no. 4 (August 1919): 120. *Solidarity*, September 17, 1919. *Industrial Worker*, October 30, 1920, p. 1.

7. V. D. Bonch-Bruevich, *Izbrannye sochineniia* (Moscow, 1963), 3:404. *Communist International*, no. 5 (September 1919): 51–52. Ibid., no. 6 (October 1919): 895–900.

8. P. Avrich, *The Russian Anarchists* (New York: Norton, 1978), 226–227. Lenin, *PSS* 41:621. Jack Roth, *The Cult of Violence*, 151. S. Cohen, *Bukharin and the Bolshevik Revolution* (New York: Vintage, 1975), 87–106. R. V. Daniels, *Conscience of the Revolution* (New York: Simon and Schuster, 1969), 126. R. Drinnon, *Rebel in Paradise: A Biography of Emma Goldman* (Chicago: University of Chicago Press, 1961), 234–235.

9. Lenin, *PSS* 41:13, 39–49.

10. Ibid. 40:325, 408.

11. Sevriugina and Surovtseva, "Iz istorii," 16.

12. N. Bukharin and M. Albert, "Resolutions of the First Congress of the Communist International," *Communist International*, no. 1 (April 1919): 52. Rutgers' comment appeared in the same journal in no. 4 (August 1919): 120.

13. Hulse, *Forming*, 156. Draper, *Roots*, 232–236. Bock, *Syndikalismus*, 188ff.

14. G. Zinoviev, "An Appeal of the Executive Committee of the Third International at Moscow," *The One Big Union Monthly* 2, no. 9 (September 1920): 26–30. Hulse, *Forming*, 162. Lazitch and Drachkovitch, *Lenin*, 250–252.

15. M. Dubovsky, *We Shall Be All: A History of the IWW* (New York: Quadrangle, 1969), 135–141.

16. Bock, *Syndikalismus*, 253–254. Sevriugina and Surovtseva, "Iz istorii," 21–22.

17. *Leninskii sbornik* 37:203. Lenin, *PSS* 41:17–18, 94.

18. G. Zinoviev, "Pressing Questions of the International Labor Movement," *Communist International*, nos. 11–12 (June–July 1920): 2112–2134.

19. *Leninskii sbornik* 35:122–123; 37:215; Lenin, *PSS* 41:621, 626, 629.

20. Sevriugina and Surovtseva, "Iz istorii," 20. Lenin, *PSS* 41:104, 643, and 51:217–218, 242.

21. The Friis interview, published in *Die Rote Fahne* on June 5, 1920, is in *Leninskii sbornik* 37:212–213. The executive committee thesis appeared in *Communist International*, nos. 11–12 (June–July 1920): 2140.

22. Trotsky's comments appeared in Ibid., 2212, and no. 13 (August 1920): 58.

23. G. Zinoviev, "What the Communist International Has Been up to Now and What It Must Become," *Communist International*, nos. 11–12 (June–July 1920): 2247–2262 and no. 13 (August 1920): 45–46.

24. Charles Ashleigh, "Third International," *Solidarity*, August 21, 1920, p. 2. G. Andreytchine, "Where Are We Going?," *The One Big Union Monthly* 2, no. 10 (October 1920): 25–27. M. Kaminev, "Radek-alismus Children Sicken of Communism," *The One Big Union Monthly* 2, no. 12 (December 1920): 24–28.

25. In *Left-Wing Communism*, as in *Materialism and Empiriocriticism*, Lenin makes few direct references to syndicalism. He did briefly note the need for a struggle against "a certain section of the Industrial Workers of the World and anarcho-syndicalist trends" in America, and against "former syndicalists" in France. Lenin, *PSS* 41:75–76.

26. A. M. Gorky, *Letopis' zhizni i tvorchestvo A. M. Gor'kogo*, (Moscow, 1959), 3:178, 193, 195. A. Antonov-Ovseenko, *The Time of Stalin* (New York: Harper and Row, 1981), 5.

27. A. Bogdanov, *Uroki pervykh shagov revoliutsii* (Moscow, 1917), 14.

28. A. Bogdanov, *Nauka i rabochii klass* (Moscow, 1918), 4, 15. Also his *Elementy proletarskoi kultury i razvitii rabochego klassa* (Moscow, 1920), 12, 50.

29. A. Bogdanov, *Filosofiia zhivogo opyta: populiarnye ocherki* (Moscow, 1920), 15–16. See also Bogdanov et al., *Teoriia otnositel'nosti Einshteina i ee filosofskoe tolkovaniia* (Moscow: Mir, 1923).

30. R. V. Daniels, *Conscience of the Revolution*, 119–171.

31. V. I. Lenin, "The Party Crisis," *Pravda*, no. 13 (January 21, 1921), in *PSS* 42:234–244.

32. Lenin, *PSS* 42:245–255, speech to the Second All-Russian Congress of Miners, January 23, 1921.

Also his January 25 article "Once Again on the Trade Unions and the Current Situation and the Mistakes of Trotsky and Bukharin," *PSS* 42:264–304.

33. Lenin, *PSS* 43:93–97.

34. Lenin, "Report on Party Unity and the Anarcho-Syndicalist Deviation," *Pravda*, no. 68 (March 30, 1921), in *PSS* 43:98–106.

11. Conclusion: Lenin over Bolshevism

1. Evgenii Zamiatin, *We*, trans. G. Zilboorg (New York: Dutton, 1924), 127, 173.

2. Tumarkin, *Lenin Lives!* p. 197. P. Avrich, "Bolshevik Opposition to Lenin: G. T. Miasnikov and the Workers' Group," *Russian Review* 43 (1984): 1–29.

3. Roy Medvedev, *Let History Judge*, 202. B. Mogilevsky, *Nikitich*, 110.

4. Robert Tucker, "Stalinism versus Bolshevism: A Reconsideration," Kennan Institute for Advanced Russian Studies, Woodrow Wilson International Center for Scholars, Occasional Paper no. 169 (Washington, D.C., 1982), pp. 9, 16, 19. On the concept of totalitarianism, see A. Gleason, "'Totalitarianism' in *1984*," *Russian Review* 43, no. 2 (April 1984): 145–159.

5. L. Gumplowicz, *Die sociologische Staatsidee* (Innsbruck: Wagner'schen Universitats, 1902), 211.

6. A. J. Gregor, *Contemporary Radical Ideologies: Totalitarian Thought in the Twentieth Century* (New York: Random House, 1967), 129.

SELECTED BIBLIOGRAPHY

Archives

Alexinsky Collection, Columbia University, New York. Contains extensive files of RSDRP party correspondence from 1905 to 1917 related to the *Vpered* circle, the Capri School, and the Bolshevik underground.

Nicolaevsky Collection, Hoover Institution, Palo Alto, California. Correspondence and other materials collected by Boris Nicolaevsky, a Menshevik historian.

Okhrana Archive, Hoover Institution, Palo Alto, California. Records of the Paris branch of the Imperial Russian political police, including reports on revolutionaries at home and abroad.

Primary Sources

Adler, Friedrich. "Der 'Machismus' und die materialistische Geschichtsauffassung." *Die Neue Zeit*, Vol. 1, no. 19 (February 4, 1910): 671–682.

_____. *Ernst Machs Uberwindung des mechanischen Materialismus.* Vienna: Brand, 1918.

Adler, Max. "Mach und Marx. Ein Beitrag zur Kritik des modernen Positivismus." *Archiv für Sozialwissenschaft und Sozialpolitik* 33 (1911): 348–400.

Akselrod, L. [Ortodoks]. *Filosofskie ocherki:otvet filosofskim kritikam istoricheskago materializma.* St. Petersburg, 1906.

_____. *Etiudy i vospominaniia.* Leningrad, 1925.

Andreeva, Maria Fedorovna. *Perepiska, vospominaniia, stat'i, dokumenty.* Moscow: Iskusstvo, 1968.

Andrikanis, E. N. *Khoziain 'chertova gnezda'.* Moscow, 1960.

Antoniuk, D. I., et al., eds. *Perepiska V. I. Lenina i rukovodimykh im uchrezhdenii RSDRP s partiinymi organizatsiiami 1905–1907 gg.* 5 vols. Moscow: Mysl', 1979.

Bakharov, V. [V. P. Makhnovets]. *O shifrakh.* Geneva, 1902.

Balabanoff, A. *Impressions of Lenin.* Ann Arbor: University of Michigan Press, 1964.

_____. *My Life as a Rebel.* Bloomington: Indiana University Press, 1973.

Bazarov, V. A. [Rudnev]. *Anarkhicheskii kommunizm i marksizm.* St. Petersburg, 1906.

_____. *Iz istorii noveishei russkoi literatury.* Moscow, 1910.

_____. *Na dva fronta.* St. Petersburg, 1910.

Bebel, August. *Khristianstvo i sotsializm.* Geneva, 1905.

Bialik, B. A., et al., eds. *V. I. Lenin i A. M. Gor'kii.* 3d ed. Moscow: Nauka, 1969. (1st ed., 1958.)

Bogdanov, A. A. [Malinovsky]. *Kratkii kurs ekonomicheskoi nauki.* Moscow, 1897.

_____. *Osnovnye elementy istoricheskago vzgliada na prirode.* St. Petersburg, 1899.

_____. *Poznanie s istoricheskoi tochki vzreniia.* St. Petersburg, 1901.

_____. *Iz psikhologii obshchestva.* St. Petersburg, 1904.

———. *Iz-za chego voina i chemu on uchit?*. Geneva, 1904.

———. *Liberaly i sotsialisty*. Geneva, 1904.

———. *Liberal'nye programmy*. Geneva, 1904.

———. *O sotsializme*. Geneva, 1904.

———. *Revoliutsiia i filosofiia*. St. Petersburg: Obrazovania, 1905.

———. *Novyi mir (stat'i 1904–1905)*. Moscow, 1905.

———. *Empiriomonizm*. 3 vols. St. Petersburg, 1904–1907.

———. *Prikliucheniia odnoi filosofskoi shkoly*. St. Petersburg, 1908.

———. *Krasnaia zvezda*. St. Petersburg, 1908. Translated as *Red Star: The First Bolshevik Utopia*, ed. Loren Graham and Richard Stites; trans. Charles Rougle. Bloomington: Indiana University Press, 1984.

———. *K tovarischcham bol'shevikam*. Paris, 1910.

———. *Padenie velikogo fetishizma*. Moscow, 1910.

———. *Vera i nauka*. Moscow, 1910.

———. *Kul'turnye zadachi nashego vremeni*. St. Petersburg, 1911.

———. *Sovremennoe polozhenie i zadachi partii*. Paris, 1911.

———. *Inzhener Menni*. Moscow, 1913. Translated in *Red Star: The First Bolshevik Utopia*, ed. Loren Graham and Richard Stites; trans. Charles Rougle. Bloomington: Indiana University Press, 1984.

Bonch-Bruevich, V. D. *Materialy k istorii i izucheniiu russkago sektanstva i raskol*. St. Petersburg, 1908.

———. *Iz mira sektantov: sbornik statei*. Moscow, 1922.

———. *Bol'shevistskie izdatel'skie dela v 1905–1907 g.g.: moi vospominaniia*. Leningrad, 1933.

———. *Vospominaniia*. Moscow: Khudozhestvennaia literatura, 1968.

Burenin, N. *Pamiatnye gody: vospominaniia*. Leningrad: Lenizdat, 1961.

Chernov, V. M. *Monisticheskaia tochka zreniia v psikhologii i sotsiologii*. Moscow, 1906.

———. *Filosofskie i sotsiologicheskie etiudy*. Moscow, 1907.

———. *Teoretiki romanskogo sindikalizma*. Moscow, 1908.

Dauge, P. *Filosofiia i taktika. Otdel'nyi ottisk predisloviia k 'Melkim filosofskim stat'iam I. Ditsgena'*. Moscow, 1907.

Elizarov, S. S., et al., eds. *M. Gor'kii v epokhu revoliutsii 1905–1907 godov: Materialy, vospominaniia, issledovaniia*. Moscow: Akademiia Nauk, 1957.

Elwood, R. C. *Resolutions and Decisions of the Communist Party of the Soviet Union*. Vol. 1, *The Russian Social Democratic Labor Party 1898–October 1917*. Toronto: University of Toronto Press, 1974.

Fond dokumentov V. I. Lenina. Moscow, 1970.

Fotieva, L. *Iz zhizni V. I. Lenina*. Moscow, 1970.

Gorky, M. *Sobranie sochinenii*. Moscow: Gos. izdat. khudozhestvennoi literatury, 1949–1955.

———. *V. Amerike: ocherki*. Stuttgart, 1906.

Guesde, Jules. *Kollektivizm*. Geneva, 1903.

Huysmans, Camille. *Correspondance entre Lenine et Camille Huysmans 1905–1914*. Ed. Georges Haupt. Paris and The Hague: Mouton, 1963.

Institut Marksizma-Leninizma pri TsK KPSS. *Vladimir Il'ich Lenin: Biograficheskaia khronika*. Moscow, 1971.

Iz istorii noveishei russkoi literatury. Moscow: Zveno, 1910.

Kautsky, Karl. "Die Revision des Programms der Sozialdemokratie in Oesterreich." *Die Neue Zeit* 1, no. 3 (1901–1902).

———. *Der Ursprung des Christentums: ein historische Untersuchung*. Stuttgart: Dietz Verlag, 1906.

KPSS v rezoliutsiiakh. Moscow, 1970.

224 Selected Bibliography

Krasin, L. B. *Dela davno minuvshikh dnei: vospominaniia*. 3d ed. Moscow, 1934.
Krizis teatra: sbornik statei. Moscow: Problemy iskusstv, 1908.
Krupskaya, N. *Memories of Lenin*. Trans. R. E. Verney, 1930. 2 volumes.
London: Martin Lawrence, 1930.
Lenin, V. I. *Pol'noe sobranie sochinenii*. 55 vols. Moscow: Izd. pol. lit., 1967–.
———. *Anarchism and Anarcho-syndicalism*. New York: International Publishers, 1972.
Lepeshinsky, P. N. *Na povorote*. Moscow, 1955.
Liadov, M. N. *Iz zhizni partii v 1903–1907 godakh: vospominaniia*. Moscow: Gos. izd-vo pol. lit.-ry, 1956.
Liadov, M. N., and Pozner, S. M., eds. *L. B. Krasin ("Nikitich"): gody podpol'ia, sbornik vospominanii, stat'i i dokumentov*. Moscow, 1928.
Literaturnoe nasledstvo, Vol. 80 (1971). "V. I. Lenin i A. V. Lunacharskii: Perepiska, doklady, dokumenty."
Literaturnyi raspad. Vol. 2. St. Petersburg, 1909.
Lunacharsky, A. V. *Kak peterburgskie rabochie k tsariu khodili*. Geneva, 1905.
———. *Etiudy kriticheskie i polemicheskie*. Moscow, 1905.
———. *Revolutionary Silhouettes*. New York: Hill and Wang, 1967.
Mach, E. *Analysis of Sensations*. 1886 Reprint. Chicago and London: Open Court, 1914.
Mehring, Franz. "Kant, Dietzgen, Mach und der Historische Materialismus." *Neue Zeit* 28, no. 1 (1910).
N. N. *O proletar'skoi etike*. Moscow, 1906.
Novomirsky, D. I. *Iz programmy sindikal'nago anarkhizma* Odessa: Golos i trud, 1907.
Ocherki po filosofii Marksizma: filosofskii sbornik. St. Petersburg, 1908.
Ocherki realisticheskago mirovozreniia: sbornik stat'ei po filosofii obshchestvennoi nauke i zhizni. St. Petersburg: Dorovatsky and Charushnikov, 1904.
Otchet vtoroi vysshei sotsial'demokraticheskoi propagandistsko-agitatorskoi shkoly dlia rabochikh. Noiabr 1910–Mart' 1911 g. Paris: Izd. Gruppy 'Vpered', 1911.
Partiia bol'shevikov v period reaktsii, 1907–1910 g.g. Moscow, 1961.
Partiia v revoliutsii 1905 goda. Moscow: Marx-Engels Institute, 1934.
Perepiska sem'i Ulianovykh, 1883–1917 Moscow: Izd. pol. lit., 1969.
Perepiska V. I. Lenina i redaktsii gazety "Iskra" s sotsialdemokraticheskimi organizatsiiami v Rossii, 1900–1903 gg. 3 vols. Moscow: Institut Marksizma-Leninizma pri TsK KPSS, 1969.
Perepiska V. I. Lenina i rukovodimykh im uchrezhdenii RSDRP s partiinymi organizatsiiami, 1903–1905 g.g. 3 vols. Moscow: Institut Marksizma-Leninizma pri TsK KPSS, 1974–1977.
Plekhanov, G. P. *Izbrannye filosofskie proizvedeniia*. 3 vols. Moscow, 1957.
———. *Materialismus militans*. Moscow: Progress, 1973.
Pokrovsky, M. N., ed. *1905*. Moscow and Leningrad, 1926.
Posse, V. A. *Moi zhiznennyi put': dorevoliutsionnyi period (1864–1917 g.g.)*. Moscow and Leningrad: Zemlia i fabrika, 1929.
Rezoliutsiia, priniataia na sobranii ideinago kruzhka bol'shevikov v Zheneve, 1909–ix–29. Geneva, 1909.
Rudnev, V. V. *Anarkhicheskii kommunizm i marksizm*. St. Petersburg, 1906.
Semashko, N. A. *Prozhitoe i perezhitoe*. Moscow: Gos. izd. pol. lit., 1960.
Shuliatikov, V. M. *Professional'noe dvizhenie i kapitalisticheskaia burzhuaziia*. Moscow: Rabochii, 1907.
———. *Opravdanie kapitalizma v zapadnoevropeiskoi filosofii. Ot Dekarta do E. Makha*. Moscow, 1908.

_____. *Iz teorii i praktiki klassovoi bor'by*. Moscow: Dorovatsky and Charushnikov, 1908.

_____. *Izbrannye literaturno-kriticheskie stat'i*. Moscow, 1929.

Sorel, Georges. *Les preoccupations metaphysiques des physiciens modernes*. Paris, 1907.

_____. Razmyshleniia o nasilii. St. Petersburg: Pol'za, 1907.

_____. *Sotsial'nye ocherki sovremennoi ekonomii: degeneratsiia kapitalizma i degeneratsiia sotsializma*. St. Petersburg, 1907.

_____. *Reflections on Violence*. New York: Collier, 1961.

Stepanov, I. *Ot revoliutsii do revoliutsii*. Moscow and Leningrad, 1925.

Strel'sky, P. *Novaia sekta v riadakh sotsialistov*. Moscow, 1907.

Trifonov, N. A. "A. V. Lunacharskii i M. Gor'kii." In *M. Gor'kii i ego sovremenniki*, ed. K. D. Muratova, 110–157, Leningrad: Nauka, 1968.

Trotsky, L. *My Life*. New York: Scribner's, 1930.

Volsky, S. [A. V. Sokolov]. *Filosofiia bor'by: opyt postroeniia etiki Marksizma*. St. Petersburg, 1909.

Vospominaniia V. I. Lenina. 5 vols. Moscow: Izd. pol. lit., 1979.

Yushkevich, P. *Teoriia i praktika sindikalizma*. Moscow, 1906.

Secondary Sources

Aizin, B. A., et al. *Lenin v bor'be za revoliutsionnyi Internatsional*. Moscow: Nauka, 1970.

Ascher, Abraham. *Paul Axelrod and the Development of Menshevism*. Cambridge: Harvard University Press, 1972.

Avrich, Paul. *The Russian Anarchists*. New York: Norton, 1978.

Bailes, Kendall. "Sur le 'Théorie des Valeurs' de A. V. Lunacharskij." *Cahiers du monde russe et sovietique* 8, no. 2 (April–June 1967): 223–443.

Balmuth, Daniel. *Censorship in Russia 1865–1905*. Washington, D.C.: University Press of America, 1979.

Barchugov, P. V. *Soveshchanie rasshirennoi redaktsii 'Proletariia'*. Moscow: Gospolizdat, 1961.

Berezhnoi, A. F. *Tsarskaia tsenzura i bor'ba bol'shevikov za svobodu pechati (1895–1914)*. Leningrad: Izd. Leningrad. U., 1967.

_____. *Lenin—sozdatel' pechati novogo tipa (1893–1914 gg.)*. Leningrad: Izd. Leningrad. U., 1971.

_____. *Lenin i zhurnalistika. Seminarii*. Leningrad: Izd. Leningrad. U., 1973.

Besançon, A. *The Rise of the Gulag: Intellectual Origins of Leninism*. Trans. Sarah Matthews. New York: Continuum, 1981.

Blackmore, John. *Ernst Mach: His Work, Life, and Influence*. Berkeley: University of California Press, 1972.

Bonnell, V. *Roots of Rebellion: Workers' Politics and Organizations in St. Petersburg and Moscow, 1900–1914*. Berkeley: University of California Press, 1983.

Borcke, Astrid von. *Die Ursprung des Bolschewismus: Die Jakobinische Tradition in Russland und die Theorie der Revolutionare Diktatur*. Munich: Berchmanns Verlag, 1977.

Bradley, J. *Mach's Philosophy of Science*. London: Athlone, 1971.

Cohen, Stephen. *Bukharin and the Bolshevik Revolution: A Political Biography 1888–1938*. New York: Alfred A. Knopf, 1971.

_____. *Rethinking the Soviet Experience: Politics and History Since 1917*. New York: Oxford University Press, 1985.

Dan, F. *The Origins of Bolshevism*. New York: Harper and Row, 1964.

Daniels, R. V. *The Conscience of the Revolution: Communist Opposition in Soviet Russia*. Cambridge: Harvard University Press, 1960.

Deich, G. M. "Iz istorii pervogo izdaniia raboty V. I. Lenina 'Materializm i empiriokrititsizm'." *Voprosy istorii KPSS*, no. 5 (May 1969): 37–48.

Diersch, Manfred. *Empiriokritizismus und impressionismus: Uber Beziehungen zwischen Philosophie, Aesthetik, und Literatur im 1900 in Wien*. Berlin: Rutten und Loening, 1973.

Dubinsky-Mukhadze, I. *Shaumian*. Moscow: Molodaia gvardiia, 1965.

Dubovsky, M. *We Shall Be All: A History of the Industrial Workers of the World*. New York: Quadrangle, 1969.

Elwood, R. C. *Roman Malinovsky: A Life without a Cause*. Newtonville, Mass.: Oriental Research Partners, 1977.

Fischer, L. *The Life of Lenin*. New York, 1964.

Fitzpatrick, S. *The Commissariat of Enlightenment: Soviet Organization of the Arts under Lunacharsky*. Cambridge: Cambridge University Press, 1970.

Florence, Ronald. *Fritz: The Story of a Political Assassin* New York: Dial, 1971.

Foner, Philip. *History of the Labor Movement in the United States. Vol. 4; The Industrial Workers of the World, 1905–1917*. New York: International Publishers, 1965.

Futrell, Michael. *Northern Underground*. London: Faber and Faber, 1963.

Golubeva, O. D. "Izdatel'skoe delo v Rossii v period pervoi russkoi revoliutsii (1905–1907 gg.)." *Kniga*, no. 4 (1972): 115–141.

Grille, D. *Lenins Rivale: Bogdanow und seine Philosophie*. Cologne: Verlag Wissenschaft und Politik, 1966.

Gurov, P. Ia. *Bol'shevistskaia pechat' nakanune i v period pervoi russkoi revoliutsii, 1905–1907 gg*. Moscow, 1957.

Haimson, L. *The Russian Marxists and the Origins of Bolshevism*. Boston: Beacon Press, 1955.

Haupt, Georges. "Lenine, les Bolcheviks et la II-e Internationale." *Cahiers du monde russe et sovietique* 7, no. 3 (July–September 1966): 378–407.

Imnaishvili, R. S. *Kamo*. Tiflis, 1968.

Ioffe, A. M. "Partiinyi otdel izdatel'stva 'Znanie.'" *Voprosy istorii KPSS* 2 (1966): 69–76.

———. *Izdatel'skaia deiatel'nost' bol'shevikov v 1905–1907 gg*. Moscow: Kniga, 1971.

Iskanderov, M. S., et al. *Ocherki istorii kommunisticheskoi partii Azerbaidzhana*. Baku, 1963.

Kahn, David. *The Codebreakers*. New York: Signet, 1973.

Kindersley, R. *The First Russian Revolutionaries: A Study of Legal Marxism*. Oxford: Clarendon Press, 1962.

Kline, G. *Religious and Antireligious Thought in Russia*. Chicago: University of Chicago Press, 1968.

Kniazeva, G. V. *Bor'ba bol'shevikov za sochetanie nelegal'noi i legal'noi partiinoi raboty v gody reaktsii (1907–1910 gg.)*. Leningrad, 1964.

Kolakowski, L. *Main Currents of Marxism*. 3 vols. Oxford: Oxford University Press, 1978.

Kostin, F. *Boevoi organ revoliutsii: k 70-letiiu gazety 'Vpered'*. Moscow: Mysl', 1975.

Kretov, F. D. *Bor'ba V. I. Lenina za sokhranenie i ukreplenie RSDRP v gody Stolypinskoi reaktsii*. Moscow: Mysl', 1969.

Kuznetsov, I., and Shumakov, A. *Bol'shevistskaia pechat' Moskvy*. Moscow: Rabochii, 1968.

Lane, David. *The Roots of Russian Communism*. Assen, Netherlands: Van Gorcum, 1969.

Lifshits, S. "Kapriiskaia partiinaia shkola (1909 g.)," *Proletar'skaia revoliutsiia*, no. 6 (1924): 33–73.

Losche, P. *Der Bolschewismus im Urteil der deutschen Sozialdemokratie 1903–1920*. Berlin: Colloquium Verlag, 1967.

Maskulia, A. V. *Mikha Tskhakaia*. Moscow, 1968.

Mazgaj, Paul. *The Action Francaise and Revolutionary Syndicalism*. Chapel Hill: University of North Carolina Press, 1979.

Medvedev, Roy. *Let History Judge*. New York: Knopf, 1972.

Mogilevsky, B. *Prizvanie inzhenera Krasina*. Moscow, 1970.

Morozov, B. M., et al., eds. *Iz istorii bor'by V. I. Lenina za ukreplenie partii*. Moscow, 1964.

Morozova, V. P. "Izdatel'stvo sotsial-demokraticheskoi partiinoi literatury V. Bonch-Bruevicha i N. Lenina (Avg.-Dek. 1904)." *Voprosy istorii KPSS*, no. 4 (1962): 93–102.

Novich, I. *M. Gor'kii v epokhu pervoi russkoi revoliutsii*. Moscow: Khudozhestvennaia literatura, 1955.

Ostroukhova, K. "Gruppa 'Vpered' (1909–1917 gg.)." *Proletar'skaia revoliutsiia*, no. 6 (1924).

Pipes, Richard. *Social Democracy and the St. Petersburg Labor Movement 1885–1897*. Cambridge: Harvard University Press, 1963.

Pozner, S. M. *Boevaia gruppa pri TsK RSDRP (b) 1905–1907 gg*. Moscow, 1927.

———. *Pervaia boevaia organizatsiia bol'shevikov, 1905–1907 gg*. Moscow, 1934.

Reisberg, A. *Lenins Beziehungen zur deutschen Arbeiterbewegung*. Berlin: Dietz Verlag, 1970.

Rigberg, B. "The Tsarist Press Law, 1894–1905." *Jahrbucher fur Geschichte Osteuropas* 13 (1965): 331–343.

———. "The Efficacy of Tsarist Censorship Operations, 1894–1917," *Jahrbucher fur Geschichte Osteuropas* 14 (1966): 327–346.

———. "Tsarist Censorship Performance, 1894–1905." *Jahrbucher fur Geschichte Osteuropas* 17 (1969): 59–76.

Roberts, David. *The Syndicalist Tradition and Italian Fascism*. Chapel Hill: University of North Carolina Press, 1979.

Rose, M. A. *Reading the Young Marx and Engels: Poetry, Parody, and the Censor*. London: Croom-Helm, 1978.

Rosenthal, I. S. "Iz istorii rasprostraneniia knigi V. I. Lenina 'Materializm i empiriokrititsizm.'" *Voprosy istorii KPSS*, no. 7 (1979): 93–102.

Roth, Jack. *The Cult of Violence: Sorel and the Sorelians*. Berkeley: University of California Press, 1980.

Ruud, Charles. *Fighting Words: Imperial Censorship and the Russian Press, 1804–1906*. Toronto: University of Toronto Press, 1982.

Sablinsky, W. *The Road to Bloody Sunday: Father Gapon and the St. Petersburg Massacre of 1905*. Princeton: Princeton University Press, 1976.

Savitskaia, R. M. "Iz istorii napisaniia i izdaniia knigi V. I. Lenina 'Materializm i empiriokrititsizm'." *Uchenye zapiski Moskovskogo bibliotekhnogo instituta*. 6 (1960).

Schapiro, Leonard. *The Communist Party of the Soviet Union*. New York: Random House, 1960.

Scherrer, Jutta. "La crise de l'intelligentsiia Marxiste avant 1914: A. V. Lunacarskij et le bogostroitel'stvo." *Revue des études slaves* 51, nos. 1–2 (1978): 207–215.

_____. "'Ein gelber und ein blauer Teufel': Zur Entstehung der Begriffe 'bogostroitel'stvo' und 'bogoiskatel'stvo." *Forschungen zur osteuropaischen Geschichte* 25 (1978): 315–329.

_____. "Pour une théologie de la révolution: Merejkowski et le symbolisme russe." *Archives de sciences sociales des religions*, no. 45/1 (January–March 1978): 27–50.

Schurer, Heinz. "Anton Pannekoek and the Origins of Leninism." *Slavonic and East European Review* 41, no. 97 (June 1963): 327–344.

Schwarz, Solomon. *The Russian Revolution of 1905*. Chicago: University of Chicago Press, 1967.

_____. *Lénine et le mouvement syndical*. Paris, n.d.

Sevriugina, N. G., and Surovtseva, N. N. "Iz istorii sozdaniia V. I. Leninym knigi 'Detskaia bolezn' "levizny" v kommunizme.'" *Voprosy istorii KPSS*, no. 3 (1960): 9–24.

Shaumian, L. *Kamo*. Moscow, 1958.

Shub, David. *Lenin*. New York: Doubleday, 1948.

Sirianni, C. *Workers' Control and Socialist Democracy: The Soviet Experience*. London: Verso, 1982.

Strauss, Leo. *Persecution and the Art of Writing*. Glencoe, Illinois: Free Press, 1952.

Tamborra, A. *Esuli Russi in Italia del 1905 al 1917*. Rome and Bari: Laterza, 1977.

Theen, Rolf. *Lenin: Genesis and Development of a Revolutionary*. Princeton: Princeton University Press, 1973.

Titov, A. I. *Kak V. I. Lenin gotovil svoi trudy*. Moscow: Politizdat, 1969.

Tumarkin, N. *Lenin Lives! The Lenin Cult in Soviet Russia*. Cambridge: Harvard University Press, 1983.

Ulam, Adam. *The Bolsheviks*. New York: Collier, 1965.

Valentinov, N. V. *Encounters with Lenin*. New York: Oxford, 1968.

Vinogradov, S. *Ego zvali Marat*. Moscow: Moskovskii rabochii, 1967.

Vucinich, A. *Social Thought in Tsarist Russia: The Quest for a Science of Society, 1861–1917*. Chicago: University of Chicago Press, 1976.

Wildman, Alan. *The Making of a Workers' Revolution: Russian Social Democracy, 1891–1903*. Chicago: University of Chicago Press, 1967.

Williams, Robert C. *Culture in Exile: Russian Emigres in Germany, 1881–1941*. Ithaca, N.Y.: Cornell University Press, 1972.

_____. *Artists in Revolution: Portraits of the Russian Avant-Garde, 1905–1925*. Bloomington: Indiana University Press, 1977.

_____. "Collective Immortality: The Syndicalist Origins of Proletarian Culture, 1904–1910." *Slavic Review* 39, no. 3 (September 1980): 389–402.

Wolfe, Bertram. *Three Who Made a Revolution*. New York: Delta, 1978.

Zeman, Z. A. B., and Scharlau, W. *Merchant of Revolution: The Life of Alexander Israel Helphand (Parvus), 1867–1924*. London, 1965.

INDEX

Adler, Friedrich, 42, 44–45, 96, 138, 142
Adler, Viktor, 172
Aesopian language, 2–3, 5, 8–10, 15, 21, 25, 29–30, 138, 218 n.31. *See also* censorship; cryptography
Akimov, Vladimir, 14, 196 n.23
Alexinsky, G.A., 33, 73, 151, 152, 155, 157–58, 170
anarchism, 19–20, 86, 89–91, 107, 112, 113, 178
Andreev, Leonid, 98
Andreeva, Maria, 33, 55, 60, 62, 63, 73, 77–78, 152, 159, 185
Andrikanis, N.A., 117–19
Armand, Inessa, 172
Ashley, Charles, 184
Atabekian, Alexander, 107
Avenarius, Richard, 41. *See also* Mach
Aexlrod, L.O., 145
Axelrod, Paul, 31, 40–41, 50, 51, 77, 104, 106, 136, 164–65, 168–69, 171

Bailes, Kendall, 195 n.7
Bakunin, Michael, 19, 54
bank robbery. *See* expropriation; Tiflis State Bank
Bauman, N.E., 33, 55, 73
Bax, E.Belfort, 147
Bazarov (V.A. Rudnev), 35–36, 39–40, 91, 130, 147, 157, 170
Bebel, August, 50, 51, 67, 171, 176
Belinsky, Vissarion, 53
Bellamy, Edward, 147
Berdyaev, Nikolai, 33, 36, 38–39, 64
Berkeley, Bishop George, 43
Berkman, Alexander, 178
Bernstein, Eduard, 7, 20
Besant, Annie, 147
Bloody Sunday, 49, 51, 53, 54, 60, 62, 66, 68, 73. *See also* Russian Revolution of 1905
Bogdanov, A.A.: as Bolshevik leader, 34–35, 40, 45–48, 49–53, 64, 66, 69–70, 73–74, 76, 78, 92, 106, 119, 121–22, 126, 132–34, 141–43, 144–45, 150–51, 153, 155–56, 158, 163, 167, 169–71, 174, 194 n.6; collectivism, 2–3, 35, 38–39, 43, 45, 63, 79–80, 97, 129–31, 133–34, 140–41, 145–46, 148, 156, 176, 185–86, 188–89; and Gorky, 78–79, 106, 108–11, 133, 138, 144, 150–53, 159–60, 167–69; and Lenin, 2–3, 33–34, 36–37,
46, 47–48, 51–53, 69–70, 76, 106, 108–10, 122, 125–27, 129, 133–43, 144–45, 150–53, 158, 170, 194–95 nn.6–7, 197 n.9; philosophy of science, 30, 41–42, 45, 127, 129–32, 135–36, 139–40, 148, 186; revisions of Marx, 1, 29, 82, 126–28, 130–32, 134–36, 148; after Revolution of 1917, 185–86, 190; socialist philosophy, 37–38; writings, 36–39, 73, 82, 97, 109, 127–30, 132, 144, 148, 169, 170, 179
Bologna, Italy, 157–59, 162–63
Bolshelviks and Bolshevism: arms and militarism, 62, 70–72, 112–13, 124, 154; collectivism, 35, 53, 79–80, 97, 126–27, 129, 133–34, 138, 145–49, 157, 189; finances, 3, 47–48, 49, 52–53, 55, 56–57, 59–61, 63, 77–79, 83, 101, 103–4, 106–7, 110, 112–19, 121, 123–24, 154–55, 157, 158, 162, 164–67, 195 n.7; and Leninism, 1–4, 48, 127, 132–33, 143, 145, 160, 166–67, 192 nn.1–2; and Mensheviks, 5, 6, 46, 48, 50–51, 66, 67, 70, 103, 106, 130; myth and authority, 1–4, 6–7, 19, 28, 30–31, 64, 94, 96–97, 138–39, 141, 189, 191; origin and composition of party, 1, 5, 26, 45–48, 81, 83, 153–54; parliamentarianism, 70, 73, 75–76, 77, 82–84, 103–4, 112, 120, 122, 141–42, 145, 169, 182; political division, 47–48, 49–50, 65, 66, 69–70, 73, 75–76, 84–85, 106–7, 108–11, 119–24, 125–26, 130, 132–37, 139–43, 144, 150–55, 160–61, 162, 164, 167–69, 171, 194–95 nn.6–7; publishing, 18–19, 23, 25–27, 48, 57, 69–70, 101, 108 (*see also* specific journals); revolutionary theories, 2, 3–4, 19–20, 149; and Revolution of 1905, 49–50, 60–61, 64–65, 66, 73–75, 76, 77, 79–90, 176; in Soviet official history, 2, 35, 69, 192 n.1, 193 n.5, 205 n.33, 207 n.60; syndicalism, 23–24, 84–85, 92–93, 100–2, 104, 108, 135, 148–49, 151–52, 158, 174, 193 n.4. *See also* Communist International; Russian Social Democratic Workers' Party; Russian Communist Party
Boltzmann, Ludwig, 140
Bonch-Bruevich, V.D., 3, 21, 23–28, 40, 46, 47, 57, 69, 189
Braun, Adolf, 31

Bronstein, L.D. *See* Trotsky
Brusnec, M.I., 61
Buddhism, 44–45
Bund, 15, 77, 81
Bukharin, Nikolai, 176, 178, 179, 181,
    186–87
Burenin, N.E., 16, 72, 77

Capri, 109–11, 144, 150–53, 157
censorship, 5–6, 8–11, 16–19, 21, 24–25,
    76, 126, 137, 173, 195 n.10
Chaliapin, Fedor, 110
Chernov, Victor, 90
Chernyshevsky, N.G., 7, 10, 14–15
Christianity, 21–22, 23, 25–27, 53–54, 58,
    63–64, 94, 134–35, 148
ciphers. *See* cryptography
Classon, R.E., 61
codes, prison, 8, 11–12. *See also*
    cryptography
collectivism: Bolshevik supporters,
    99–102, 133, 147–49; definition, 3,
    38–39, 146; Lenin's opinion of, 99, 133,
    145–46; after Revolution of 1917,
    185–86, 188–90; and religion, 39,
    99–100, 146–49; and science, 43, 45,
    91–92, 99, 129, 146, 186. *See also*
    syndicalism
Communist International (Comintern),
    103, 177–79, 181–84, 193 n.4
Communist Workers' Party of Germany,
    181–82
cryptography, 5–16, 51
Curie, Marie, 42

Dan, Fedor, 84, 192 n.2
Daniels, Robert V., 193 n.4
Darwinism, 99
Dauge, P.G., 33, 46, 68, 96–97, 136
Deborin, A.M., 132
De la Haille, George Ducos, 165, 168,
    169, 171
De Leon, Daniel, 89, 103, 182
Dietzgen, Joseph, 93–98, 99, 130
Dostoevsky, Fyodor, 54
Dubrovinsky, I.F., 111, 136, 152, 153,
    156
Duma, 73, 75, 78, 82, 83, 84, 91, 103–4,
    112, 145, 168, 169

Economism, 7, 32
Einstein, Albert, 29, 41–43, 44
Elizarova, Anna, 13–14, 32–33, 137, 154
emigres, Russian, 7, 22, 23, 26, 32, 37,
    51, 105–7, 132, 145, 154, 173
empirocriticism. *See* science, philosophy
    of
Engels, Friedrich, 19–20
Essen, A.M., 50

expropriation, 75, 82, 83, 104, 106–8,
    112–16, 122–23, 154, 158, 168

Fainsod, Merle, 194 n.6
Fedorov, N.F., 98
Fels, Joseph, 82, 112
Feuerbach, Ludwig, 146
Fischer, Louis, 194 n.6
Fotieva, L.A., 15
France, 85–87, 142, 159
Friche, V.A., 40, 68, 91, 147

Gapon, Father Georgi, 51, 54–56, 64–65,
    71–72, 99
Geneva, 105–6
Germany. *See* Communist Workers' Party
    of Germany; Socialist Party of Germany
god building. *See* religion
Goldman, Emma, 178
Goloshchekin, F.I., 166
Gorky, Maxim: and Bogdanov, 78–79,
    106, 108–11, 132, 133, 138, 144,
    150–53, 159–60, 167–69; Capri school,
    143, 144–45, 150–53, 155, 159;
    collectivism, 3, 79–80, 100–1, 109,
    146–48; financial contributions, 3, 26,
    33, 52–53, 55–57, 70, 76–79, 89, 110,
    160; and Lenin, 47, 52, 56, 77, 101,
    105, 106, 108, 109–11, 137–38, 147,
    156, 159–60, 167, 169, 171, 173–74;
    philosophy, 23, 56, 57–58, 66, 159;
    political activities, 55–56, 59, 60–61, 73,
    78–79; writings, 21, 54–55, 56–57, 70,
    101, 173
Gorter, Hermann, 97, 153, 178
Gramsci, Antonio, 35
Gregor, A.J., 190
Grille, Dietrich, 192 n.1
Gumplowicz, Ludwig, 190

Haeckel, Ernst, 21, 146
Haupt, Georges, 194 n.6
Haywood, Bill, 89, 103
Heller, A.M., 183
Helphand, Alexander. *See* Parvus
Holland, 153, 178, 181, 183
Huysmans, Camille, 112, 169

Ignatiev, A.M., 118–19, 145, 185
individualism, 36, 38–40, 43–45, 58,
    131–32, 146–47, 149, 187, 188–90
Industrial Workers of the World (IWW),
    88–89, 95, 174, 181–82, 184
International Socialist Bureau (ISB), 67,
    70, 103, 109, 111–12, 136, 145, 153,
    168–69, 171–72
Italy, 87–88, 158
Izgoev, A.I., 98–99

Iskra, 5, 6, 21, 23–26, 31–33, 37, 46, 48, 50, 52, 55, 59, 107

Jews. *See* Bund
Jogisches, Leo, 164

Kalinin, F.I., 158, 163, 164
Kalmykova, A.M., 21
Kamenev, L.B., 133, 163, 164, 166, 172
Kamo, 34–35, 75, 82, 113, 114–16, 167, 185, 190
Kant, Emmanuel, 36
KAPD. *See* Communist Workers' Party of Germany
Karpinsky, V.A., 145
Kautsky, Karl, 1, 32, 35–36, 50, 51, 63–64, 67, 95, 97, 135, 141–42, 154, 158–59, 163, 164–66, 167, 168–69, 171, 172, 173–74, 176
Kerr, Charles, 95
Kline, George, 192 n.3
Koestler, Arthur, 12, 144
Kollontai, Alexandra, 99
Kommissarzhevskaya, Vera, 62
Krasin, L.B., 1, 26, 34, 49–52, 55, 59, 60–63, 66, 70–72, 75, 77–79, 107, 113–14, 115, 119, 120, 123, 129, 167, 189–90
Kronstadt uprising, 186–87
Kropotkin, Peter, 12, 112, 178, 179
Krumbugel, L.O., 137–38
Krupskaya, N.K., 8, 9, 12–16, 28, 33, 46, 47, 51, 52, 67, 73, 103, 105, 111, 126, 170–71
Krzhizhanovsky, Yurii, 55
Kuklin, G.A., 21–22, 23–24, 26, 28, 40

Labriola, Arturo, 87, 92–93, 96, 100, 102
Ladyzhnikov, I.P., 26, 57, 110
Lagardelle, Hubert, 22, 86–87, 100
Lavrov, Peter, 53–54
Lbov, 123–24
Le Dantec, Felix, 99
Lenin, V.I.: authoritarianism, 2, 29, 30–32, 34, 37, 40–41, 64–65, 82, 127, 175–76, 184; and Bogdanov, 2–3, 33–34, 36–37, 46, 47–48, 51–53, 69–70, 76, 106, 108–10, 122, 125–27, 129, 133–43, 144–45, 150–53, 158, 170, 194–95 nn.6–7, 197 n.9; as Bolshevik leader, 28, 37, 40, 45–48, 50–51, 62, 67, 70, 73, 75–76, 82–85, 102–3, 112, 119, 122–23, 141–43, 144–45, 150–56, 160–61, 162–63, 166–68, 172, 173–74, 192 n.2; censorship, 8, 10, 18, 76, 126, 137, 173; and collectivism, 138–41, 145, 186, 189; cryptographer, 11–16; cult of, 4, 28, 63, 188–89, 192 n.1; exile, 6–7, 18, 33, 51, 66, 101, 103, 105–7, 126,

156, 172–73; finances, 22, 23–24, 49, 52, 70, 101, 111–12, 122–23, 154, 157, 163–69, 171–72, 185; and Gorky, 47, 52, 56, 77, 101, 105, 106, 108, 109–11, 137–38, 147, 156, 159–60, 167, 169, 171, 173–74; Leninism, 1, 48, 127, 132–33, 143, 145, 166–67, 191, 192 n.1; materialism and science, 3, 29–30, 41–42, 45, 96–97, 111, 125, 133–36, 138–40, 157; publishing ventures, 23, 25–26, 31, 34, 37, 40, 46, 52–53, 76, 105, 173–74, 199 n.32; revolutionary theory, 2, 6–7, 14–15, 19, 66–67, 75–76, 81–82, 84, 92; as Soviet leader, 176–79, 181, 185, 187–191; and Stalin, 119–21, 142, 155; and syndicalism, 22, 23, 81–82, 84, 92, 101–2, 125, 135, 168, 174–76, 178–83, 180, 182–83, 186–87, 191, 220 n.25; writing style, 5, 8, 10, 15, 18, 28, 64, 126, 180
—writings: *After Twelve Years*, 126; *Development of Capitalism in Russia, The*, 6, 10–11, 126; *Imperialism*, 16, 173–74; *Left-Wing Communism*, 4, 177, 179–83, 184, 220 n.25; *Materialism and Empirocriticism*, 15, 30, 121, 122–23, 125, 136–41, 145, 156, 177, 182, 194 n.6; *One Step Forward, Two Steps Back*, 31, 40–41; *Renegade Kautsky, The*, 174; *State and Revolution*, 23, 174; *Two Tactics of Social Democracy in the Democratic Revolution*, 66; *What Is to Be Done?*, 6, 14–15, 32, 34, 48, 126, 140
Leone, Enrico, 87
Lepeshinsky, P.N., 46
Liadov, M.N., 33, 46, 55, 64, 151, 157–58
Litvinov, Maxim, 72, 112–13, 115–16, 172
Lunacharsky, A.V., 10, 36, 39–40, 46, 63–65, 82, 84, 97, 99–102, 105, 109–11, 130–32, 141, 146–49, 151–53, 157–59, 163, 170–71, 174, 176, 189–90
Luxemburg, Rosa, 4, 102, 105, 162, 163, 165

Mach, Ernst, and Machism, 29–30, 34, 39–45, 91–92, 96–97, 120, 127, 129–32, 135–36, 139–40
Makhno, Nestor, 178
Makhnovets, V.P. *See* Akimov
Maliantovich, P.N., 78
Malinovsky, A.A. *See* Bogdanov
Malinovsky, R.V., 166, 169, 171
Mandelshtam. *See* Liadov
Manuilsky, D.Z., 164
Marat. *See* Shantser
Marchlewski, Julian, 56
Martens, Ludwig, 113
Martov, Yu. O., 106, 145, 154, 185
Marx, Karl, 8, 10, 125–26

Marxism, 7, 19, 29, 38, 41, 44, 85, 127,
    134–36. *See also* specific Marxist parties,
    theories, and movements.
Medvedev, Roy, 193–94 n.5
Mehring, Franz, 154, 165
Mensheviks and Menshevism, 5, 6, 25,
    31, 34, 37, 40–41, 46–47, 48, 50–51, 52,
    66, 67, 70, 73, 75, 77, 81, 84, 91,
    103–4, 106–7, 112, 115, 119, 122, 130,
    132–33, 134, 136, 138, 154–55, 156,
    157, 160–61, 162, 165, 166, 168, 172,
    175, 192 n.2
Menzhinsky, Vladimir, 158
Miagkov, E.D., 69, 76
Mikhailov, M.A., 117
modernism, 134–35, 189
Monatte, Pierre, 86
Moor, Karl, 165
Morozov, S.T., 58–63, 77–79
Mussolini, Benito, 88, 188, 190–91
myth. *See* religion

Novomirsky, D.I., 90–91

October Manifesto, 17, 73, 75
Okhrana, 32, 50, 55, 62, 78, 79, 103, 111,
    113, 114–16, 123, 126, 143, 149, 152,
    153, 154–55, 158, 166, 171
Old Believers, 21–22, 24–25, 48, 49, 53,
    58
Olminsky, M.S., 185
Ordzhonikidze, Sergo, 166
Orwell, George, 188
Ostwald, Wilhelm, 42–43

Pannekoek, Anton, 95, 122, 153, 178
Parvus (Alexander Helphand), 31, 56–57,
    173
Pascal, Blaise, 7
physics, 6, 29–30, 41–44, 59, 132, 140. *See
    also* science
Piatnitsky, K.P., 26, 78
Plekhanov, G.V., 1, 10, 21, 23, 31, 41,
    54, 70, 77, 91–93, 96–97, 102, 103, 106,
    131, 133–36, 145–46, 160–61, 163, 172,
    195 n.10
Pocket Dictionary of Foreign Words, 10
Pokrovsky, M.N., 33, 68, 142, 150, 158,
    163, 173–74
Posse, V.A., 19, 21–24, 25
Pravda, 37, 39–40, 45, 143, 153, 170
Proletarian Culture (Proletkult), 176,
    185–86
Proletarii, 67, 69–70, 83, 103, 105–6, 109,
    119, 121, 141, 142–43, 144, 145, 151,
    154
Proudhon, Pierre, 19

Rabochii, 69–70

Rappaport, Charles, 172
Reade, Winwood, 146–47
religion and myth, socialist, 3, 6, 19, 20,
    29–30, 35–36, 39, 45, 57–58, 63–65,
    84–86, 91, 93–100, 111, 131, 146–49,
    177, 189, 193–94 n.5. *See also*
    Christianity; Old Believers
Renan, Ernst, 64
Riazanov, David, 163
Roentgen, Wilhelm, 42
Roland-Holst, Henriette, 97, 153, 178
Romains, Jules, 64
Rozhkov, N.A., 33, 68, 99
RSDRP. *See* Russian Social Democratic
    Workers' Party
Rudnev, V.A. *See* Bazarov
Russian Communist Party (RKP), 175,
    179, 181, 187
Russian Ministry of the Interior, 17
Russian Orthodox Church, 17, 189
Russian Populism, 6–7, 10–11, 24, 32, 54
Russian Revolution of 1905, 17, 29, 48,
    49, 50–51, 53, 54, 60, 62, 64–65, 66–68,
    71–76, 81, 89, 98, 176
Russian Revolution of 1917, 174–78, 181,
    185, 188
Russian Social Democratic Workers' Party
    (RSDRP): central committee, 26, 46,
    51, 57, 61–62, 69, 77, 117, 122, 153–54,
    158, 163, 164, 166; communication,
    14–16, 51; Fifth Congress (London),
    81–83, 92, 111–12; finances, 50–52, 55,
    56–57, 59–62, 67–70, 73, 77, 79, 83,
    112, 117, 154, 162, 164–66, 168,
    171–72, 173; Kursk committee, 9;
    library, 25–26, 28, 145, 160; Long
    Plenum, 153–55, 162; Moscow
    committee, 32–33, 46, 52, 60, 62–63,
    68–69, 73, 74, 83, 117, 150–51;
    organization, 5, 6, 31, 67, 81, 82, 83,
    141, 150, 153, 160–61, 164, 166–67,
    172; Paris conference, 141; Prague
    conference, 166–67; publishing, 25–26,
    31, 46–47, 57, 67–70, 73, 170 (*see also*
    specific journals); St. Petersburg
    committee, 83; Second Congress
    (Brussels and London), 25, 34, 46;
    Fourth Congress (Stockholm), 75–76,
    108; Third Congress (London), 51, 60,
    62, 67–68, 107–8; Tver committee, 15,
    16, 58; Zimmerwald conference, 173.
    See also Bolsheviks; Mensheviks
Russo-Japanese War, 25, 37, 46, 71–72
Rutgers, S.J., 178, 181
Rutherford, Ernest, 42

Saltykov-Shchedrin, M.E., 5
Savelev, I.I., 35
Savinkov, Boris, 98

Schapiro, Leonard, 192 n.1, 195 n.7
Scheibert, Peter, 194
Scherrer, Jutta, 193 n.5
Schmidt, Ekaterina, 60, 74, 117–19
Schmidt, Elizabeth, 117–19, 167, 168
Schmidt, N.P., 60–61, 68, 73–75, 78–79, 107; inheritance, 75, 117–19, 154, 165–68
science fiction, 38, 109, 126, 128–29, 169, 194 n.6
science, philosophy of, 6, 21, 29–30, 36, 39–45, 93, 95, 127–29, 131–33, 138–40. See also Mach
Second International, 47, 101–3, 166, 172–73
self-sacrifice, 3–4, 30–31, 53–54, 56, 58, 61, 63, 81, 86, 147, 148–49, 188, 191
Shantser, V.L., 33, 68, 69, 73, 74, 163
Shaumian, Stepan, 121–22
Shklovsky, G.L., 165
Shliapnikov, Alexander, 186–87
Shuliatikov, V.M., 40, 68, 132, 133, 147
Skvortsov, I.I., 33, 35–36, 68
Socialist Party of Germany (SPD), 50, 51, 67, 103, 122, 142, 154, 162, 164–66, 168, 171–72
Social Revolutionary party, 55, 66, 68, 69, 90, 112, 113, 115, 175
Sokolov, A.V. See Volsky, Stanislav
Soloviev, Vladimir, 98
Sorel, Georges, 19, 20–21, 85–87, 91, 131, 158, 177, 178–79, 205 n.33
Souvarine, Boris, 192 n.1
Spandarian, S.S., 166
Stalin, Joseph, 4, 48, 75, 107, 119–21, 142, 155, 166, 189–91, 193–94 n.5
Stasova, E.D., 180
Stepanov. See Skvortsov
Stolypin, P.A., 18, 82, 83, 103
Strelsky, P., 90
strikes: in Europe, 7, 23, 86–87; general, 2, 20, 22–23, 38, 66, 72–73, 75, 81, 84, 85, 87, 89–91, 99, 102; in Russia, 17, 25, 58, 62, 66, 72–73, 74–75, 81, 83, 100, 120, 172, 179; in the United States, 88–89. See also syndicalism
Struve, P.B., 10, 21, 91
Suvorov, S., 39
syndicalism: and Bolsheviks, 23–24, 38, 84–85, 92–93, 100–2, 104, 108, 135, 148–49, 151–52, 158, 174, 177, 184, 193 n.4; in Europe, 20–23, 81, 85–88, 102, 141–42, 158–59, 177–78, 181; Lenin's opinion of, 22, 81, 84, 92, 101–2, 168, 174–76, 178–83; after Revolution, 176–79, 181–87, 189–90, 205 n.33, 207

n.60; in Russia, 89–91. See also collectivism; strikes

Taratuta, V.K., 117–19, 122, 145, 154–55, 165, 167
Ter-Petrosyan, S.A. See Kamo
Third International. See Communist International
Thompson, J.J., 42
Tiflis State Bank robbery, 103–4, 106–7, 109, 114–16, 123, 154–55, 167
Tkachev, P.N., 7
Tolstoyism, 13, 21, 24
totalitarianism, 190–91
Trotsky, Leon, 4, 34, 46, 57, 143, 145, 151, 153, 158, 168, 184
Tsiurupa, A.D., 55
Tskhakaya, M.G., 107, 113, 119–22

Ulyanov, Alexander, 6, 7, 28
Ulyanov, V.I. See Lenin
Ulyanova, Anna. See Elizarova
United States, 76–79, 88–89, 95, 103, 178
Untermann, Ernst, 95, 97

Valentinov. See Volsky, N.V.
Vilonov, N.E., 149–51, 152, 156
Vinck, Emile, 165
Vologda province, 32–34, 36–37, 39
Volsky, N.V., 34, 41, 46, 130, 133
Volsky, Stanislav, 33, 67, 68, 73, 74, 83, 108, 149, 151, 157–58
Vorovsky, V.V., 33
Vpered, 26, 48, 51–53, 55, 64–65, 67, 69, 153, 155–59, 163, 164, 169–71, 173, 194 n.6

Walling, William, 83–84
Webb, Sidney, 147
Wijnkoop, D.J., 183
Witte, Sergei, 73
Wolfe, Bertram, 10
Workers' Opposition movement, 186–87
World War I, 172–74, 175

Zamiatin, Evgenii, 189
Zasulich, Vera, 10, 54
Zetkin, Klara, 154, 164–68, 171, 173
Zgraggen, Karl, 165, 171
Zhitomirsky, Ya.A., 116
Zhizn', 21–25
Zilliacus, Konni, 71–72
Zinoviev, G.E., 163, 166, 172, 181, 182–83, 184

Robert C. Williams is Professor of History, Dean of the Faculty, and Vice President for Academic Affairs at Davidson College in Davidson, North Carolina. He received his Ph.D. in History from Harvard University and has taught at Williams College and Washington University in St. Louis. He is the author of six books and numerous articles in modern Russian history and the history of nuclear energy, and the recipient of fellowship awards from the American Council of Learned Societies, the American Philosophical Society, and the George F. Kennan Institute for Advanced Russian Studies. He has also served as a Phi Beta Kappa Associates lecturer and on the editorial board of the *Slavic Review*.